SELECTED CHRISTIAN HEBRAISTS

The Christian Hebraists singled out here – Andrew of St Victor, William Fulke, Gregory Martin, Richard Simon and Alexander Geddes – contributed in different ways to the reception of the Hebrew Bible in the Christian Church. All were strongly influenced by Origen and Jerome, who supplied a foundation on which subsequent study of the Hebrew Bible in the Christian Church rests.

The concern of these studies is with how the exercise of critical methods can be reconciled with the assumption that the Hebrew Bible is a Christian book. With *Andrew of St Victor* this concern is expressed as a robust, human and historical interest. *William Fulke*, influenced by Renaissance linguistic science, asserted that the quality of a translation from Hebrew into English is determined entirely by scholarly competence and integrity. *Gregory Martin* accepted the idea of an English translation with the greatest reluctance; he even rejected Fulke's demand for a return to the 'original' languages of Hebrew and Greek, and translated from the Latin Vulgate.

Much greater critical inroads were made by *Richard Simon* and *Alexander Geddes*. Simon made out a case for the autonomy and comprehensiveness of the critical exegesis of the Hebrew Bible. Geddes's objective was to employ his critical reconstruction of the Bible in order to reformulate Christianity so that God might be worshipped in a temple of reason.

McKane thus reviews the shifts in the Church's understanding of the nature and authority of its scriptures, particularly the Old Testament, and shows how the beginnings of the critical scholarship of modern times is connected with, and has grown out of, that change in understanding.

SELECTED CHRISTIAN HEBRAISTS

WILLIAM McKANE

St Mary's College, St Andrews

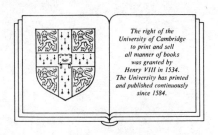

The right of the
University of Cambridge
to print and sell
all manner of books
was granted by
Henry VIII in 1534.
The University has printed
and published continuously
since 1584.

CAMBRIDGE UNIVERSITY PRESS

CAMBRIDGE

NEW YORK   NEW ROCHELLE   MELBOURNE   SYDNEY

Published by the Press Syndicate of the University of Cambridge
The Pitt Building, Trumpington Street, Cambridge CB2 1RP
32 East 57th Street, New York, NY 10022, USA
10 Stamford Road, Oakleigh, Melbourne 3166, Australia

First published 1989

Printed in Great Britain at the University Press, Cambridge

British Library cataloguing in publication data

McKane, William, *1921* –
Selected Christian Hebraists.
1. Bible. Hebrew. Interpretation,
ca 1150–ca 1700
I. Title
220.4′4′09

Library of Congress cataloguing in publication data

McKane, William.
Selected Christian Hebraists.
Bibliography.
Includes index.
1. Hebraists, Christian.   2. Old Testament scholars.
I. Title.
PJ4533.M35   1988   221′.092′2   88–9550

ISBN 0 521 35507 9

WG

TO MY WIFE
AGNES MATHIE HOWIE

CONTENTS

PREFACE

This book arose out of public lectures which were offered in St Mary's College, St Andrews as 'The St Mary's College Lectures' in the Candlemas Term during the years 1982-5. Their character was influenced by the circumstance that Archibald Hay, who was associated with the College shortly after its foundation in 1538 (or 1539), urged that it should be a Trilingual College after the model of the Collège de France which was founded in 1530. The emphasis on Hebrew and Greek can be seen after the Reformation in the provisions of Andrew Melville's 'New Foundation' (*Nova Erectio*) of 1579. The subject *Selected Christian Hebraists* was perceived as one which would give scope for the exercise of trilingual scholarship.

I am most grateful to my colleague, Dr. R. B. Salters, for the help which he has given me with the reading of the proofs of this book.

ABBREVIATIONS

BDB	Brown F., Driver S. R., Briggs C. A., *A Hebrew and English Lexicon of the Old Testament* (Oxford, 1907, 1966).
BSOAS	*Bulletin of the School of Oriental and African Studies*
CHB	*Cambridge History of the Bible*
DNB	*Dictionary of National Biography*
ET	*Expository Times*
GK	Gesenius W., Kautzsch E., *Gesenius' Hebrew Grammar*, English translation revised by Cowley A. E. (Oxford, 1910).
JBL	*Journal of Biblical Literature*
JTS	*Journal of Theological Studies*
KB²	Koehler L., Baumgartner W., *Lexicon in Veteris Testamenti Libros*, 2nd edition (Leiden, 1958).
KB³	*Hebräisches und Aramäisches Lexikon zum Alten Testament*, 3rd edition (Leiden, 1967, 1974, 1983).
KJV	King James Version
NEB	New English Bible
NTS	*New Testament Studies*
PG	*Patrologiae Graecae*
PL	*Patrologiae Latinae*
RSV	Revised Standard Version
SVT	*Supplements to Vetus Testamentum*
ZThK	*Zeitschrift für Theologie und Kirche*

INTRODUCTION

The first chapter of the book addresses fundamental questions about the Church's first Bible (the Septuagint) and asks why it should have been Greek, given the Palestinian beginnings of Christianity. It considers the extent to which Greek was spoken in Palestine and, in particular, the evidences of the presence of Greek-speaking Jewish Christians in the Jerusalem milieu at the beginnings of Palestinian Christianity. It envisages a selective use of a Greek Bible, as well as the Hebrew Bible and its Aramaic translations, in order to construct a primitive Christian theology in a Jerusalem context, and supposes that a high value would have been placed on the Greek expression of this theology when the Christian Church broke through the limits of Palestinian Christianity into the Gentile world. The adoption of the Septuagint as the Bible of the Church would then be a natural development. In the final part of the first section of this chapter the distance which was created between the Church and the plain sense of the Hebrew Bible is considered in exegetical terms.

In the second part of the chapter there is a consideration of the contribution of Origen to the study of the Church's Bible, through his work as a textual critic, exemplified in his Hexapla. Here the Hebrew Bible makes its entrance, and through the use which he makes of his synopsis in six columns, Origen, in an indirect way, becomes the first Christian translator of the Hebrew Bible into Greek. How much Hebrew he knew, if any, is a matter of debate, but it is clear that his objective in the fifth column of his Hexapla was to modify the Septuagint so as to produce a literal Greek translation of the Hebrew, in which every element of the Hebrew text would have a corresponding element in the Greek translation. The format of the Psalm fragments of the Hexapla, edited by Cardinal Mercati, establishes Origen's intention of setting out a one–one correspondence between the Hebrew and the three Greek translations (Aquila, Symmachus and Theodotion) which appear in the Hexapla. Two of these (Aquila and Theodotion) are certainly of Jewish origin.

As a translator Origen is not to be ranked highly, because his work is joinery, founded on other Greek translations and not his own turning of the Hebrew Bible into Greek. If his objective was to achieve a one–one correspondence between the reformed Septuagint and the text of the extant Hebrew Bible, two ways in which this could have been done are discernible: (a) He knew enough Hebrew to exercise control over the operation, though he was helped by the literal translations of Hebrew into Greek which he had before him. (b) He was so deficient in Hebrew that he had to rely entirely on these translations. In the latter case he was unable to ascertain that he had achieved his end: he had to rest on the assumption that the translations in question had aimed at a one–one correspondence between Hebrew and Greek, and that he could rely on them to enable him to modify the text of the Septuagint with a view to obtaining a similar result. Thus Origen is a translator of the Hebrew Bible into Greek only in the sense that he added to and subtracted from the text of the Septuagint in order to make it quantitatively identical with the text of the Hebrew Bible. The additions were not translated by him directly from Hebrew, but were lifted from the other Greek translations, principally Theodotion.

The third part of the first chapter is devoted to Jerome, the first Christian Hebraist, and, in particular, to his occupation with the Septuagint and the Hebrew Bible. The 'selected Christian Hebraists', apart from Andrew of St Victor, look back in important respects to Origen, but it is Jerome who stands out especially as the founder of their biblical scholarship, even where they have ceased to bow to his authority and are striking out in new directions on their own account.

The phrase *Hebraica veritas* 'the truth of the Hebrew' is an expression of Jerome's devotion to the study of the Hebrew Bible. It is more precisely an indication of a continuation of Origen's basic concern in the Hexapla and is founded on the same assumption that Origen had made, namely, that the text of the Hebrew Bible which was extant in their times had obtained at all times. The description of the Hebrew Bible as *Hebraica veritas* supposes that the text of the Hebrew Bible had enjoyed a massive stability and had been immune from variation and change. Were that so, the relation between the Hebrew Bible and the Septuagint would be beautifully simplified, but to the detriment of the Septuagint. If the Septuagint is largely a faithful translation of a Hebrew text quantitatively different from the text which was extant in the times of Origen and Jerome, Origen's operations in the fifth column of his Hexapla are misconceived and Jerome's *Hebraica veritas* loses its simplicity and charm. Hence in addition to considerations bearing on the peace of the Church which Augustine laid on the conscience of Jerome, there are intellectual flaws in the idea of *Hebraica veritas*.

To say this is not to assert that it would be practical wisdom for a translator to do other than accept the text of the Hebrew Bible established in his time as the basis of a translation, and, in this regard, Jerome has been imitated by a host of successors. With Jerome and his great enterprise in the Vulgate we are launched into Hebrew scholarship in the context of the Christian Church. That the resources of Jewish learning were brought to bear on the translation of the Hebrew Bible into Latin through Jerome's tutors and assistants is not an entirely novel factor, in so far as the Church's first Bible, the Septuagint, had been translated by Jews and for Jews. The novelty consists in the circumstance that a Christian scholar in the context of the Church enlisted the help of Jewish Hebraists in order to achieve an accurate Latin translation. Moreover, Jerome is the fountain-head of a great stream of discussion about the criteria which have to be met and the effects which have to be secured by a translator of the Hebrew Bible. The minute scrutiny and nice criticism of his work by generations of scholars absorbed with problems of translation in different areas – grammar, lexicography, style, choice of language – are testimonies to the thoughtfulness of his Vulgate.

On a number of counts Andrew of St Victor is a less obvious candidate for inclusion in this book than the other 'selected Christian Hebraists'. Andrew has been described as a 'twelfth century Hebraist', but reasons will be offered why his knowledge of Hebrew should not be exaggerated and why the conclusion that it was scanty does not seem unjust. Moreover, it is unlikely that he had any Greek, and so the area of study between the Hebrew Bible and the Septuagint lies beyond his linguistic range. Nor was he concerned with the Old Latin, the version which preceded Jerome's Vulgate in the Western Church and which had been translated from the Septuagint. In all these respects problems which are before the minds of Origen and Jerome are outside his field of vision. Jerome is, nevertheless, the foundation of his Old Testament scholarship, but it is the product of Jerome's Hebrew scholarship, the Vulgate, which cements Andrew's relation with Jerome. The Hebrew Bible from which the Vulgate was translated does not, for the most part, enter into this relation.

It might then appear that his qualifications are slim and that, in particular, the study of the Hebrew Bible in the context of the Christian Church is not furthered through him. In short, it is Andrew's Old Testament exegesis which makes him worthy of notice. There are features of it which make him exceptional in a mediaeval Christian context. The liveliness of his interest in Jewish exegesis gives him access to the Hebrew Bible and mediates its 'literal' or plain sense to him. It would be wrong to suppose that Andrew's field of interest as an Old Testament exegete, his concentration on the literal sense and his neglect of Christian interpretations of Old Testament texts, were entirely determined by the information which he received from Jews, probably through conversations conducted in French. Clearly this was of great value to him, but the cast of his own mind was the decisive factor and what he gathered from Jews enabled him to undertake with more assurance an enquiry to which he was already committed.

In the interests of the literal sense and against Christian interpretations of the Old Testament Andrew does not hesitate to disagree with Jerome, but he pursues the kind of Old Testament exegesis which engages his interest without general polemical intentions. He is happy to cultivate his own plot and concerned to maintain it, but he does not disavow the higher senses of the Old Testament which were discerned by mediaeval Christian exegetes and he is not moved by an iconoclastic zeal against them. He does not have a head for their theological heights; he is happy to concede the higher ground to other scholars and to work at the level of historical particularities. His interest in the literal sense is not simply a narrow grammatical precision, but rather an engaging human interest in the world of the Old Testament, its times, places, circumstances and people. Andrew is, of course, a Catholic and not a humanist in a restrictive sense, but it is his contentment to explore the human possibilities of an ancient society and to resign an interest in the higher Christian senses of Old Testament texts which convey an impression of modernity. This should not be exaggerated and certainly it should not be supposed that Andrew's attitude to the Old Testament was, to a significant degree, an anticipation of the historical–critical approach of modern Old Testament scholarship. There is a decisive respect in which this is not so: he does not make the assumption that the particular historical circumstances which he discerns as a background to prophetic utterances will necessarily indicate the period in which the prophet in question was active. He feels no intellectual difficulty in interpreting Isa. xl–lv in the historical context of the approaching end of the Babylonian exile, and, at the same time, ascribing these chapters to Isaiah of Jerusalem. He delights in finding a well-defined and sufficiently full historical setting for his exegesis, but he is not intellectually embarrassed by the assumption that Isaiah of Jerusalem projected into the remote future such a detailed prediction of how it would unfold.

Andrew's place among the selected Hebraists is assured because he dwells on the human level of the Old Testament and helps to uncover a problem concerning the Church's attitude to the Old Testament which was there from the beginning but only gradually emerged from concealment. The Church had adopted the Septuagint as a Christian Bible and it was inevitable that a Christian significance should be attached to its contents. The Hebrew Bible when it came into the possession of the Church was similarly regarded as a source of Christian truth. Such an attitude to the Hebrew Bible was always difficult and sometimes impossible to reconcile with a just treatment of its historical and human dimensions, because Christological exegesis, operating in a vacuum and acquiring the advantage of timeless truth, disengages the Old Testament from its historical moorings and dehumanizes it. Moreover, such exegesis is difficult to reconcile with the fact that the Hebrew Bible belonged to Israel and to the Jews before it belonged to the Church and that thereafter it belonged to both the Synagogue and the Church. The chapters which follow are largely engaged with these matters and, especially, with the differing boundaries which were fixed by Christian scholars for the interpretation of the Old Testament by means of humanist scholarship.

The anticipations of modernity in Andrew of St Victor are such that they have facilitated the asking of exegetical questions which are hardly in the sights of William Fulke and Gregory Martin in the second half of the sixteenth century in England, though Fulke has more awareness of them than Martin. His plea for greater economy in the application of Christian interpretations to Old Testament texts has the effect of directing more attention to the literal or plain sense of the Old Testament, the area on which Andrew had concentrated his scrutiny. But the extent of the common ground which has been disclosed is modest, for Fulke's motivation differs from that of Andrew:

he has a theological earnestness which contrasts with Andrew's contentment with the human scene of the Old Testament. When he urges that the Christological interpretation of the Old Testament has gone too far and counters Martin's exegesis in particular cases, he uses the tools of humanist scholarship and fashions his arguments in agreement with what he regards as biblical science. The point which he finally makes against Martin is, however, a theological one, namely, that the sense at which he has arrived, and not the Christological sense advanced by Martin, is the one intended by the Holy Ghost.

Both Fulke and Martin have better foundations for the study of the Hebrew Bible than Andrew of St Victor and their right to be included with the selected Hebraists does not require an elaborate demonstration. Both had competence in Hebrew, Greek and Latin and were familiar with patristic literature; both were engaged with the problems of Bible translation, Fulke as a defender of English translations made from the Hebrew Bible and the Greek New Testament, and Martin as one who was engaged with the translation of the Vulgate into English. But whereas Fulke embraces translation as a means of renewal and as a revolutionary agent within the Church, Martin accepts its necessity with a deep reluctance. The better course is to avoid vernacular translations and to abide with the Vulgate, but the Catholic Church in England is in a missionary situation and the instrument of an English translation of the Vulgate is needed to convert the land from its general apostasy and to win it back to the true Faith. Fulke confronts Martin's post-Tridentine conservatism with an account of the adventurousness of European Catholic scholars in pre-Tridentine times, when they followed unhindered an enthusiasm awakened by the Renaissance for the first springs of biblical scholarship, expressed in the preparation of critical texts, the compilation of dictionaries and synopses of the original texts and the ancient versions of the Bible (the Polyglots). The fruit of such scholarship was translation, and these translations were done from the Hebrew Bible and the Greek New Testament into Latin and other languages. It is in the spirit of such scholarly enterprises that Fulke defends vigorously new translations of the Bible into English.

When the matter is so stated the future seems to lie with Fulke rather than Martin, but it should not be supposed that Martin's attitude is singularly archaic in a post-Tridentine context. It was to some extent shared by so daring a thinker as Richard Simon in the seventeenth century, and the key to it is the perception that any dislocation or diminution of the authority of the Vulgate should not be entertained. Hence in adjudicating between the scholarship of Fulke, an Anglican leaning towards Puritanism, and Martin, an English Catholic who went into exile for his Faith, the differences in their churchmanship should be carefully weighed. The view that Catholic tradition is irreversible, held by Martin, has to be contrasted with the freedom which Fulke feels to accept what he deems good and to reject what he regards as bad. The tradition of the Roman Catholic Church is then good only in parts and the Bible is invoked by Fulke as a judge.

In all these circumstances it is Fulke rather than Martin on whom attention
should be focused, if the subject is the Hebrew Bible in the Christian Church.
He had enjoyed a scientific education and had published scientific works. He
was concerned to lay the foundations of a biblical science and to define the
area within which results should depend entirely on competence in the
methods of a humanist scholarship. Hardly any anticipations of a historical –
critical exegesis of the Bible are to be discerned, except that Fulke is aware
of differences in vocabulary and style in biblical books which have to be
correlated with the idiosyncrasies of individual authors. It is this which leads
him to conclude that Paul is not the author of the Epistle to the Hebrews.
Otherwise, his biblical science more or less reaches its terminus with the
achievement of an English translation and is strongly expressed in relation
to the English translations of the Bible criticized by Martin. His answer to
Martin in short is that bad translation is caused by bad scholarship and that
the remedy is a scientific one – better scholarship. When his rigour extends
to the field of Old Testament exegesis, the justification of the intrusion has,
as we have seen, a theological character. The Bible competently translated
is an approximation to the mind of the Holy Ghost and a curtailment of the
Christian interpretation of Old Testament texts is also agreeable to the mind
of that Spirit. The promotion of the plain sense of the Old Testament in these
instances may also be regarded as an adumbration of a historical – critical
attitude, but the nature of the attached theological justification is a warning
not to make too much of it. It is evident that there is no weakening of Fulke's
conviction that the goal of Old Testament exegesis is the eliciting of Christian
truth.

The division of labour between biblical science and Christian theology
which Fulke applies to the Hebrew Bible is the one which obtained in Calvin's
Academy at Geneva, and, in a wider biblical context, the same assumptions
are at work in Zwingli's submissions at the first Zurich disputation of 1523.
The arrangements at Geneva are set out in a document first published in
1559 (*Leges Academiae genevensis*).[1] The Professor of Hebrew at Geneva was
required not only to teach the language, but also to read books of the Hebrew
Bible with a view to imparting grammatical and linguistic knowledge. Calvin
was one of two Professors of Theology, and although he uses his knowledge
of Hebrew in his Old Testament commentaries, his exegesis is directed
towards theology rather than philology. It would not be seriously wrong to
conclude that the Professor of Hebrew operated within the limits of a biblical
science which was thought to comprise grammar, lexicography and translation, although Calvin, as an Old Testament commentator, furnishes his own
Latin translation. Nevertheless, we can discern the laying of a foundation by
the application of humanist scholarship and then a limit which is set to its
operation, where a biblical theology assumes responsibility for the Christian
interpretation of the Old Testament.

Zwingli assumes a similar function and scope for a humanist biblical
scholarship. Its goal is to provide as perfect an access as possible to the plain

sense of the Bible, expressed characteristically by translation. What is then provided is an approximation to the infallible word of God whose further interpretation can be entrusted to 'Christian hearts', that is, to those who are illumined by the Holy Spirit and discern the mind of that Spirit as it is declared in the Bible.[2]

Richard Simon is a critic of both Origen and Jerome and, in so far as he submits the assumptions of Origen's Hexapla and Jerome's concept of *Hebraica veritas* to a severe scrutiny, he also administers a cold douche to Reformed scholars like William Fulke who supposed that an embracing of the Hebrew Bible was unambiguously a return to the fountainhead of revealed truth. He is perhaps the most consummate scholar of the selected Hebraists, more subtle in his textual criticism than the others, knowledgeable in many departments of Hebrew scholarship, himself a stylist and aesthetically demanding in the criticisms which he makes of translations of the Hebrew Bible from Jerome up to his own times. His contribution to the study of the Hebrew Bible in the Christian Church, and the manner in which he gathers to himself the issues which it raises, will be best elicited by a concentration on his textual criticism at one pole and his theological argument at the other.

He takes up the cause of the Septuagint against what he regards as the misconceived objective of Origen in the fifth column of his Hexapla to achieve a Greek text quantitatively identical with the text of the Hebrew Bible which was extant in his time. His defence of the Septuagint is made on text-critical and not theological grounds: he rejects the view which had won credence in the Church at an early date that the Alexandrian translators of the Hebrew Bible into Greek had been inspired. His perception is that the Hebrew text which was before these translators differed from the Hebrew text extant in the times of Origen and Jerome. When Origen equalizes the Septuagint with the text of the Hebrew Bible as it then was, he is erasing evidence which bears on the history of the text of the Hebrew Bible. He is making the same assumption as is contained in Jerome's *Hebraica veritas*, but a more profound appreciation of the facts reveals that the text of the Hebrew Bible had been subject to change and that the text from which the 'ancient' Septuagint was translated had as much right to the title *Hebraica veritas* as the one which was extant in the time of Origen and Jerome. The 'ancient' Septuagint is a witness to that text and it should be treasured as such rather than subordinated to the false simplification of *Hebraica veritas*. Moreover, so-called secondary versions, regarded as inferior because they were translated from the Septuagint and not from the 'original' Hebrew, should be reassessed. The Old Latin, a translation from the Septuagint which was superseded by Jerome's Vulgate, has an independent value in·so far as it gives access indirectly to a Hebrew text different from the one which Jerome employed when he created the Vulgate.

It is evident that with the delivery of this criticism Simon is expressing certain doubts about the wisdom of the replacing of the Old Latin by Jerome's Vulgate in the Western Church, but, more particularly, he is encountering and unmasking the deceptive clarity of the Reformed demand for a return to the 'original' Hebrew. This was thought to have a sound text-critical foundation, but it is beneath this foundation that Simon has tunnelled. Fulke was not much engaged with the thought of recovering a pure Hebrew text, but a text-critical enterprise of this kind on a large scale, allied to a belief in the Hebrew Bible as the infallible word of God, can be seen in the work of Benjamin Kennicott in the eighteenth century. Fulke does not discern any serious difficulty here, because he assumed that the Hebrew text which was used by those producing new English translations was the 'original' word of God and that a return had been made to the first pure fountain. Hence the problems which were uncovered by Simon were hidden from his view.

Simon also contradicts Fulke by his dictum that the Hebrew Bible is theologically obscure. This emphasis on theological obscurity is not only directed against the assumption of Fulke that the Hebrew Bible translated into English is theologically transparent. It is also a stance through which Simon aims to achieve maximum critical freedom for himself, while representing that he does not infringe Catholic orthodoxy. If the Hebrew Bible is theologically obscure, it is not to be used as a supreme authority in relation to Christian truth in the manner Protestants suppose. In so far as the drive to produce translations of the Hebrew Bible into vernacular languages derives from this expectation, the goal which is pursued by the Protestants is the light of a false dawn.

But Simon is also engaged in a battle for survival as a critical scholar who holds that the entire field of Old Testament exegesis is accessible to his non-theological scholarship, and that it is the proper business of Church dogmatics and not of exegesis to express the Christian truth of the Hebrew Bible. According to this view such truth is not revealed in the Hebrew Bible itself, but has to be supplied by means of an interpretation authenticated by the Catholic Church. Consistent with this Simon does not regard patristic exegesis as exegesis in a strict sense and displays no interest in the Christological interpretation of Old Testament texts, even where he has before him verses with which a Christian content had been associated in the Church through a long history of exegesis.

With Simon a point has been reached where a method critical in character and using the tools of a humanist scholarship claims the entire domain of the Hebrew Bible. Yet he urges that no violence is done to Christian theology: there is no denial that the Bible is the word of God. It is simply that this claim lies beyond the concerns of the critical biblical scholar. It is neither denied nor affirmed by him and it is the business of the Church, not of the critic, to affirm and establish it. This resolution of the relation between the human and the divine in the Hebrew Bible, between plain sense and Christian interpretation, between scripture and tradition, was unacceptable to Catholic orthodoxy.

Alexander Geddes was an eighteenth-century Scottish Catholic who was educated in Paris and whose biblical scholarship rested on the same intellectual foundations as those of Richard Simon. Like Simon he was a trilingual scholar and was familiar with the ancient versions and the patristic literature. His scholarship was characteristically expressed in the translation of the Hebrew Bible into English, and so his concern with translation was not only theoretical or general but descended to the detail of the practical difficulties which a translator encounters when he practises his art. His correspondence with Robert Lowth, then Bishop of London, embraces both matters of theory and practice. He questions the wisdom of Lowth's contention that the metrical structure of Hebrew poetry is so integral to its exegesis that an attempt should be made to represent it in an English translation, and expresses his own view that it should be surrendered in favour of an elevated English prose. He weighs up the merits and deficiencies of the King James Version and invites Lowth to consider how a new English translation of the Hebrew Bible ought to be related to it. But he also seeks reinforcement for his own judgement in connection with the many small decisions which a translator has to make and he tells Lowth that a 'Yes' or 'No' answer to his queries will suffice.

When Geddes left Fochabers to take up residence in London, he had already begun another kind of journey which would remove him from the context of the Roman Catholic Church and bring his activity as a priest to an end. In London his environment was scholarly and literary rather than ecclesiastical, and his published work brought his conflict with the Church to a head. Such ecclesiastical connections as he had were with Church of England scholars, but these were only incidentally ecclesiastical and were essentially scholarly. From this point of view Geddes does not fit perfectly into the mould of a study of the Hebrew Bible in the Christian Church, because his London context was not the Church. He valued highly his intellectual communion with Anglican scholars and benefitted greatly from it at a time when he must have felt the pain of his isolation, but he pursued his work on the Hebrew Bible as a private scholar supported by a patron, and even as a scholar he had a sharper appetite than most Hebraists for literary recognition and acclaim.

His connections with Benjamin Kennicott in the early days of his residence in London show that he regarded the provision of a critical text of the Hebrew Bible as a necessary foundation for his enterprise as a translator. He shares the text-critical assumptions and expectations associated with Kennicott's great collation of mediaeval Hebrew manuscripts and he supposes that a consequence of this collation will be the availability of a purer Hebrew text than had obtained until then. Part of his resolve as a translator of the Hebrew Bible is to benefit from the advance in text-critical science which he supposes to have been made by Kennicott, and to bring Kennicott's 'variations' to bear on the received Hebrew text, wherever in his judgement they improve it.

Geddes describes the compass of the critical exegesis of the Hebrew Bible along lines similar to those drawn by Simon, but this was not an idiosyncrasy in the context of eighteenth-century Old Testament scholarship and such a division of labour between the critical exegete and the biblical theologian is, for example, assumed by Lowth. The contribution of Geddes is perhaps best elucidated through a comparison with Simon. Both were Catholics and both, on the basis of similar educations, approached the Hebrew Bible with good linguistic equipment and a depth of historical perspective. Both pursued scholarly objectives which brought them into conflict with ecclesiastical authority, but here the comparison begins to falter. Simon's biblical scholarship is much more influenced by his Catholic formation than is that of Geddes: his objective is to win critical freedom for himself and to establish at the same time that, in asserting it, he does not abandon the household of faith. Simon represents that the exercise of his biblical scholarship does not make him less than a good Catholic, and his genuine concern to demonstrate that this is so should not perhaps be doubted. Simon, far from being ambitious to create a new theology, mounts an argument which hinges on the non-theological character of his scholarship. In this respect, though the comparison is not profound, he can be likened to Andrew of St Victor who was also content to leave theology to the theologians.

Geddes is a different person: he rebels against Catholic orthodoxy and he appears in a new environment – in a condition of exile from which he never returns. It is difficult to detect any residual Roman Catholicism informing his scholarship and if he has any ecclesiastical context in his London period it is supplied by the Church of England. Unlike Simon his biblical learning is directed towards the creation of a new Christianity which conforms to his interpretation of the Bible, is more rationalist than orthodox Trinitarian formulations and leans towards Unitarianism. It is this brand of religious seriousness, a passion to rationalize Christianity, which is the special mark of Geddes. The critical study of the Hebrew Bible does not co-exist easily with powerful theological preoccupations, and it lies in the nature of their scholarly interests and the mental habits which these encourage that Hebraists do not usually set themselves up as great theological innovators. What stands out in the story of Geddes is that his dedication to critical Old Testament learning is yoked to a greater ambition and a larger concern, and that his ultimate aim is to convert his critical gains into a new version of Christianity. While he was pursuing this goal, there are signs that within himself a state of embitterment threatened to prevail and that the sweetness of his reason was soured. The intemperance of his language then contrasts strongly with the coolness and care of his earlier critical utterances.

1

THE FOUNDATIONS

The Church's first Greek Bible

There is some value in being strict about terminology in so far as narrow inexactness may give rise to a wider confusion. The term 'Septuagint' refers to a particular Greek translation of the first five books of the Hebrew Bible, the Pentateuch or Torah. According to the Letter of Aristeas[1] this enterprise was undertaken at Alexandria in the third century B.C. by a Ptolemaic king, Philadelphos, in order that the Jewish law might be represented in his royal library. To this end, so the account runs, he secured seventy-two translators from Palestine, six from each of the twelve tribes of Israel, and the work was done on the island of Pharos which was connected to Alexandria by a causeway.

The elaboration of this narrative by the Alexandrian Jew, Philo,[2] who died in A.D. 40, introduced miraculous elements: all the translators worked independently, but arrived at an identical result. Hence they were inspired and the translation which they produced was free from all error. When Christian scholars[3] appropriated this elaborated account of the origin of the Septuagint, they applied it not to the Torah but to the entire Greek Bible which had been embraced by the Christian Church, and this is what the Septuagint has come to mean in Christian use. As such, it contains all the books which comprise the Hebrew Bible, as well as those which are commonly called the Apocrypha.[4]

It has been supposed that the date assigned for the translation of the Torah into Greek in the Letter of Aristeas is about right, though Kahle[5] has argued that the Letter should be interpreted as propaganda for an authorized Greek version of the Torah which was done in Alexandria towards the end of the second century B.C. The intention of the Letter, according to Kahle, was to represent that this was a first translation of the Torah into Greek and that is why it is ante-dated by one hundred and fifty years. In any case we can conclude that the translation of the Torah into Greek was made by Alexandrian Jews to meet the needs of Greek-speaking Jews in Alexandria and elsewhere, rather than under the patronage of a Ptolemaic king, as the Letter of Aristeas represents.[6] We should also suppose that the other books of the Hebrew Bible were subsequently translated into Greek in the same Jewish setting.

This brings us to the question of the 'Alexandrian Canon', a Jewish canon of the Greek Bible, whose existence has been vigorously denied by A.C. Sundberg.[7] Writing the prologue to a Greek translation of his grandfather's work (Wisdom of Ben Sira / Ecclesiasticus), and discussing the difficulties of translating his grandfather's Hebrew into Greek, the translator refers to 'the Law and the Prophets and the remainder of the books'.[8] The prologue was written in Alexandria in the closing decades of the second century B.C.[9] and has been taken as evidence that at the time of writing all or most of the books which make up the Hebrew Bible in its three divisions of Law, Prophets and Writings had been translated into Greek. Sundberg has interpreted the loose expression, 'the remainder of the books', over against the precise mention of the Law and the Prophets, as a reference to a collection of books, some translated from Hebrew into Greek and some written originally in Greek, not at that time subject to any canonical definition or limitation. He holds that not until the Synod of Jamnia in A.D. 90 were the contents of what became 'The Writings' in the Hebrew Bible defined, and that there never was a Jewish Greek Bible which imposed a canonical definition on 'the remainder of the books'. In other words, there never was a Jewish Alexandrian canon.[10]

The Jews had lost interest in the Greek translation of the Hebrew Bible which originated and was developed in Alexandria and had produced new translations into Greek in the second century A.D. on the basis of a Hebrew text which had become authoritative in Palestine. Thereby they obtained Greek translations in accord with the detailed exegetical techniques which had been applied to the Hebrew text, especially to the Torah.[11] The only canon which the Jews ever had is the one represented by the Hebrew Bible, and the Christian Church, which appropriated the Alexandrian Greek translation done by Jews, eventually made a selection of 'the remainder of the books' and created a Christian Greek Bible more extensive in its third part than the Hebrew Bible.

Whether or not Sundberg's argument is regarded as conclusive,[12] it has the merit of reminding us that the Greek Bible which is loosely called the Septuagint is almost entirely dependent on the Christian Church for its survival. The manuscripts in which it is preserved are of Christian provenance and only a few Jewish fragments of it are extant. This leads on to a consideration of the Greekness of the primary documents of the Church on which Burkitt said:

From the alien religion out of which Christianity had sprung the Church had inherited her sacred books in a Greek translation, and the writings of Christians that after a time were added on to the Canon of Scripture as a New Volume – these writings were composed in Greek also. In a word, the Church grew up on Greek soil.[13]

But we have to set against this another quotation from the same author:

We all know that this is not the whole truth. The Church may have grown up on Greek soil, but Christianity itself is not Greek in origin. The very earliest stage of all, that stage which it is most important for all of us to know and understand, is not Greek but Semitic.[14]

If the Greek New Testament is regarded as, for the most part, outside the range of our interest, and attention is focused on the Church's first Greek Bible and the quotations from it which appear in the New Testament, questions rise in the mind. If the origins of Christianity are Palestinian and Semitic, at what stage did the early Christian Church adopt its Greek Bible? Should we suppose that a Jewish Greek Bible was already used in a Jerusalem context by some Jewish Christians who were Greek-speaking? The second question raises a doubt whether Palestinian Jewish Christianity is necessarily to be equated with Semitic Christianity, if the intention of the equation is to represent that Hebrew and Aramaic were the languages used and that Greek was not used. Nevertheless, it would be reasonable to suppose that the languages which predominated among Jewish Christians in a Jerusalem setting would be Hebrew and Aramaic and that the Bible which they principally used would be the Hebrew Bible and its Aramaic Targums.

Despite his reference to 'the alien religion out of which Christianity had sprung', Burkitt holds[15] that the employment of passages from the Hebrew Bible to elucidate the claims which the Church made for Jesus reaches back to primitive Palestinian Christianity. According to Burkitt, it was to such a compilation of confirmations of Christian claims that Papias referred when he said that Matthew composed the Logia.[16] Burkitt draws a distinction between Matthew, the Publican, who selected testimonies from the Hebrew Bible and compiled them, and the author of the Gospel, and suggests that it was the use of these testimonies which gave rise to the title 'The Gospel according to Matthew'. 'To collect and apply the oracles of the Old Testament in the light of the New Dispensation was the first literary task of the Christian Church.' Burkitt's remark that after the fall of Jerusalem in A.D. 70 the surviving Palestinian Christians 'seem to have mingled themselves with the Greek-speaking urban population'[17] is offered as an explanation of why the 'Semitic' Palestinian Christian community petered out. In any case, if quotations from the Hebrew Bible, whether in Hebrew or an Aramaic translation, served the ends of Palestinian Jewish Christians, and if these have survived in the New Testament, this has to be set against the gulf which Burkitt places between Palestinian and Greek Christianity.

If Aramaic in particular is considered, there are the instances of Aramaic said to have been spoken by Jesus,[18] and there is the scholarship which has explained features of the Greek of the Gospels and the Acts in connection with the original Aramaic from which it was translated.[19] A quotation from Ps. xxii 2, attributed to Jesus and spoken from the cross, is given in Aramaic and must be regarded as an important pointer that the earliest Jewish Christians used an Aramaic translation of the Hebrew Bible.[20] Another example bearing on this is Deut. xxx 12–13 (Rom. x 6–7). The Christian application of the passage is built on an Aramaic paraphrase in the Jerusalem Targum[21] which introduces the prophet Moses at Deut. xxx 12 and the prophet Jonah at Deut. xxx 13: 'Would that we had one like to the prophet Moses who would ascend to heaven and bring it [the Law] down to us!'

(verse 12). 'Would that we had one like the prophet Jonah who would descend to the depths of the Great Sea [the Mediterranean] and bring it [the Law] up for us!' (verse 13). The references in the Jerusalem Targum are to the giving of the Law to Moses on Mount Sinai and to Jonah's descent into the deep in the belly of the great fish. Paul sets to work on this Aramaic paraphrase and both the ascent into heaven and the descent into the deep are related to Christ. The second of these developments involves the transformation of the Great Sea (the Mediterranean) into the abyss (ἄβυσσος) or pit of death ('to bring up Christ from the dead'). The first is founded on a correspondence perceived between the bringing down of the Law from Mount Sinai by Moses and the coming down of Christ to earth ('to bring Christ down'). Hence Jonah is related to the resurrection of Christ here as elsewhere (Mt. xii 39f.). It is the particular Aramaic paraphrase of the Jerusalem Targum which generates Paul's Christian interpretation.[22]

The same set of problems comes to the surface in connection with Dodd's argument[23] that coherently organized quotations from the Hebrew Bible formed a sub-structure of Christian theology from the earliest days of the Church,[24] and that we should suppose the originator of this creative use of the Hebrew Bible to have been Jesus himself. Dodd rejects the hypothesis of Rendell Harris[25] that a 'Book of Testimonies' was one of the earliest literary products of the Church, but in two chapters of his book[26] he conducts detailed arguments which attend closely to the Greek text of quotations from the Hebrew Bible in the New Testament as compared with the Greek text of these passages in the Septuagint or other Jewish Greek versions of the Hebrew Bible. The aim of these arguments is to show that the quotations in the New Testament have a pattern and constitute a sub-structure of Christian theology, that this state of affairs obtained within the first twenty years of the life of the Church, and that its beginnings should probably be traced to the founder of Christianity.[27]

What strikes one about this procedure is that the Greek documents by means of which the argument is developed (the books of the New Testament) do not reach back to the earliest period of Palestinian Christianity. The form of the argument must be that although the integration of quotations from the Septuagint or other Greek versions of the Hebrew Bible into a Greek New Testament represents a later stage, these quotations are best understood as the deposit of an exegetical practice which originated with Palestinian Christianity. Since the investigation is carried out in this framework, there are questions which Dodd does not ask. In what language did Jesus utter passages from the Hebrew Bible if he originated this exegetical practice? What language or languages were used by the earliest Jewish Christians when they employed these quotations in a Jerusalem setting?

In connection with these questions something has been said about Hebrew and Aramaic and the position of Greek must now be considered. Attention should be given to fragments of a Greek translation of the Hebrew Bible which are of Palestinian origin and come from a Jewish milieu.[28] The most

important of these finds consists of extensive fragments of the Twelve
Prophets on a leather scroll published by Barthélemy.[29] The question
about the right terminology to use for Greek translations of the Hebrew
Bible in general, and for this translation in particular, need not engage
us too seriously. For the most part, the apparatus and procedures of textual
criticism have been applied to the Septuagint, as can be seen in the Göttingen
edition,[30] and these are the assumptions which are adopted by Barthélemy
who describes the fragments of the Twelve Prophets as a Palestinian recension of the ancient Septuagint.[31] Kahle, on the other hand, has urged that
text-critical methods cannot be applied to a translation of Hebrew into
Greek. Where there are textual differences between Greek manuscripts
of the Septuagint, all that can be said is that these are variant translations
or Targums of the Hebrew Bible. If an 'authorized' translation emerges,
it does so subsequent to the period of these variant Targums, perhaps
through the selection of one of them, so that the search for an original
Greek text is misdirected.[32] Kahle's interpretation of the Letter of Aristeas
is in accord with this, since he supposes that it refers to an 'authorized'
translation of the Torah which was made at the end of the second century B.C.
after a period of earlier Greek translations of the Torah in an Alexandrian
milieu.[33]

In describing the Palestinian Greek Targum represented by the leather
scroll of the Twelve Prophets Kahle remarks: 'Sometimes texts of a better
standard were produced owing to a better understanding of the Hebrew; at
other times we find an adaptation to another Hebrew text.'[34] Hence Kahle
acknowledges that different Greek translations arise not only from different
styles of translation or varying degrees of competence, but also from different
Hebrew *Vorlagen*. These are called 'revisions' by Tov,[35] where there is a
continuous reference to a Hebrew *Vorlage* different from that used by the
Alexandrian translators, and the scroll of the Twelve Prophets furnishes an
example of such a revision. It is the fact that we are not dealing with various
translations of a constant *Vorlage* which supplies the foundation and justification for a text-critical treatment of the Septuagint in this special area. Thus,
with respect to the scroll of the Twelve Prophets, Kahle urges that it was
necessary for the Jewish Greek-speaking diaspora to have a Greek translation
founded on the Hebrew text with which Palestinian Rabbinical exegesis was
then exercised.[36]

This, however, is not the kind of textual criticism which is the principal
concern of the Göttingen Septuagint, in which Kahle's view of the textual
history of the Septuagint is challenged on a broad front. Here the textual
criticism of the Septuagint is largely concerned with inner Greek variants
unrelated to differing Hebrew *Vorlagen*. The Göttingen enterprise is described
by Tov as one which contains 'the best reconstructions of the original text of
the LXX',[37] and three examples from Ziegler's *Ieremias*[38] (an Old Testament
book in which Tov[39] has shown a special interest) will enable us to explore
its method and presuppositions:

(a) xxxix 33 (Hebrew, xxxii 33).[40] The only Hebrew *Vorlage* brought into play is לָקַחַת 'to accept' (Massoretic text) and criticism is focused on the variants in Greek manuscripts: ἔτι λαβεῖν B-S A; λαβεῖν, 87; ἐκβαλεῖν, 231; ἐκλαβεῖν, Q-VOLC etc. ἔτι and ἐκβαλεῖν are corruptions and the choice lies between λαβεῖν and ἐκλαβεῖν. Ziegler favours ἐκλαβεῖν because it is more impressively attested than λαβεῖν, and also because it offers an explanation of ἔτι as a corruption of ἐκ.

(b) xvi 18.[41] ἐπλημμέλησαν 'caused to err', 'led astray', is attested by B-SAQC, and ἔπλησαν by VOL. ἔπλησαν is a straightforward rendering of the Hebrew text (מלאו) which runs 'and they have filled my own land with their abominable images'. But the punctuation of the Septuagint is different from that of the Massoretic text and the choice is between 'with which they have caused my own land to err' and 'with which they have filled my own land' – with reference to idols mentioned earlier in the verse. Ziegler argues that the Greek translator rendered מלאו freely as ἐπλημμέλησαν and that he was influenced by the desire to supply a complementary expression for ἐβεβήλωσαν 'defiled' / 'caused to err' which occurs at an earlier point in the verse. The more original of the two readings is then ἐπλημμέλησαν and ἔπλησαν is a correction to provide a more exact rendering of the Hebrew text.

(c) x 13.[42] φῶς 'light' is attested by B-SA and ἀνέμους 'winds' by QOLC, where the Massoretic text has רוח 'wind'. The same state of affairs obtains at xxviii 16 (Hebrew, li 16). Ziegler holds that אור yielding φῶς was the original Hebrew *Vorlage* and that ἀνέμους derives from the influence of Ps. cxxxiv 7 (Hebrew cxxxv 7), where רוח is rendered as ἀνέμους.

When these examples are analysed, it will be seen that the criticism of each assumes a different relationship between the Septuagint and its parent Hebrew text. In the case of (a) the critical operation consists only of weighing up the Greek variants over against a Massoretic text which is assumed to be the *Vorlage*. In (b) only one Hebrew *Vorlage* is assumed and the Septuagint text which is judged to be more original is the one which is more loosely connected with it. The more exact correspondence of מלאו / ἔπλησαν is then a mark of a secondary correction. In (c) two Hebrew readings enter into the discussion, רוח (Massoretic text) and אור which is posited as the *Vorlage* of φῶς. Another factor which is introduced is influence from a parallel passage (Ps. cxxxiv 7) to which ἀνέμους in QOLC is attributed.

A special mark of Tov's textual criticism of the Septuagint, which differentiates his aims from those of the Göttingen Septuagint, is his concern with the use of the Septuagint in the textual criticism of the Hebrew Bible.[43] This is clearly going beyond the Göttingen undertaking which is defined by Kappler[44] as that of reconstructing the Septuagint text in its oldest recoverable form. Tov is exercised with the relations between the Hebrew and Greek texts and this brings into prominence the circumstance that the Septuagint is a translation from the Hebrew, that individual books were translated by different translators, and that, in a few cases, more than one translator operated within a single book. Hence a variety of types of translation is exemplified and these have to be analysed and appreciated in order that differences between the Massoretic text and the Septuagint which are explicable in translational terms may be separated from those which merit an explanation in terms of Hebrew readings deviating from the Massoretic text.[45]

Barthélemy describes the scroll of the Twelve Prophets as a Palestinian recension of the ancient Septuagint, that is, a recension of an earlier Alexandrian translation. It was done about the middle of the first century of our era, on the basis of the Hebrew text which had been established in Palestine and on which Jewish scholars were founding their exegesis. It was, according to Barthélemy, a part of the work of Jonathan ben Uzziel, a pupil of Hillel, to whom the Aramaic Targum of the Prophets has been attributed. Jonathan is identified by Barthélemy with Theodotion,[46] and the Greek translation of the Hebrew Bible associated with that name is then disengaged from the second century A.D. translations of Aquila and Symmachus and located in Palestine about the middle of the first century A.D. The contents of the leather scroll of the Twelve Prophets, and the fragments of Origen's Quinta which survive,[47] belong to a recension of the ancient Septuagint made in Palestine by Jonathan (Theodotion). The appearance of a Theodotionic text at 1 Cor. xv 54, where Isa. xxv 8 is quoted as κατέποθη θάνατος εἰς νῖκος, is evidence for the first century date of Theodotion's work, since the date of the epistle is A.D. 57.[48] On the speech of Peter in Acts ii, Barthélemy observes that at verse 18 the וגם of Joel iii 2 is rendered by καίγε, 'the touchstone of the recensional family to which Theodotion belongs'.[49]

For the purposes of our discussion the differences between Kahle and Barthélemy can be transcended. Having appealed to the palaeographical expertise of C. H. Roberts and W. Schubart, Kahle concludes: 'The scroll with the Greek text of the minor prophets was written in the closing decades of the pre-Christian era or at the beginning of our era.'[50] Both scholars agree that the leather scroll of the Twelve Prophets contains a Greek translation made by Jews in Palestine. In facing up to the question why such a translation should originate in Palestine, both answer in terms of the requirements of the Greek-speaking Jewish diaspora rather than those of Greek-speaking Jews in Palestine.[51] The new Greek translation is seen as a provision for Jews of the diaspora, a Bible which would give them an accurate indication of the Hebrew text on which exegetical developments among Jewish scholars in Palestine were founded and which would save or rescue them from error.

It is clear that there is no particular intention to connect Greek-speaking Jews in Palestine with the beginnings of Christianity by suggesting that among the earliest Christians there may have been those who used a Greek translation of the Hebrew Bible. Barthélemy's dating of the Greek recension represented by the leather scroll is not accommodated to this, and his position is made clear by his treatment of Acts ii 18. He identifies the Greek recension of the leather scroll in the quotation from Joel iii 2, but he makes the point that Peter was not speaking in Greek and reproducing this Greek rendering of Joel iii 2: 'The speech was not delivered in Greek nor was it taken down in writing, but it requires us to place earlier than the writing down of Acts the beginnings of the recension which interests us.'[52]

Sundberg[53] gives a new twist to the argument by supposing that the presence of a Greek translation of the Hebrew Bible, made by Jews for Jews in Palestine, is an indication that there were sufficient numbers of Greek-speaking Palestinian Jews to make such an enterprise worthwhile. Thus he views the translation as aimed at a Palestinian Jewish constituency rather than at Jews of the diaspora. On these assumptions we have a Greek Bible used by Greek-speaking Jews in Palestine, perhaps in the period of the beginnings of Palestinian Christianity. Here we have to reckon with the investigation of J. N. Sevenster[54] into the extent to which Greek was spoken in Palestine at that period and with his conclusion founded on an examination of the New Testament, Rabbinic and epigraphic evidence: 'It has now been clearly demonstrated that a knowledge of Greek was in no way restricted to the upper circles, which were permeated with Hellenistic culture, but was to be found in all circles of Jewish society, and certainly in places bordering on regions where much Greek was spoken.'[55] Hence the question is raised whether primitive Palestinian Christianity is correctly described as Semitic Christianity, if the intention is to exclude the use of a Greek Bible by the earliest Christians in a Jerusalem context.

The discussion can be sharpened by a consideration of the New Testament evidence as it is interpreted by C. F. D. Moule,[56] J. N. Sevenster[57] and M. Hengel.[58] In the first place it should be borne in mind that Jewish Christians in a Jerusalem context are Jews and that it is as Jews they have their associations with the synagogue and the temple. Acts vi 9 has been taken[59] to show that some Jewish Christians belonged to a synagogue whose services were conducted in Greek. These were the opponents of Stephen, described as 'members of the synagogue called the Synagogue of Freedmen, comprising Cyrenians and Alexandrians and people from Cilicia and Asia' (NEB). The conclusion to be drawn is that some Jews in Jerusalem spoke only Greek and had no Hebrew or Aramaic, and that there were synagogues in Jerusalem which catered for them. The opposition of Ἑλληνισταί and Ἑβραῖοι at Acts vi 1 concerns Jewish Christians who speak only Greek and those whose primary linguistic affiliations are Hebrew and Aramaic, but who may have some competence in Greek.[60] Hence the Ἑλληνισταί of Acts vi 1, and also those who debated with Paul at Acts ix 29 (NEB 'Greek-speaking Jews'), had no knowledge of Hebrew or Aramaic and used a Greek Bible in the synagogue. Moreover, as Jewish Christians, they also used a Greek Bible in the Jerusalem Christian community to which they belonged.

If we think in terms of the passages which according to Dodd and others were organized into a sub-structure of Christian theology, we should take into account not only the Hebrew Bible itself and Aramaic translations of it, but also a Greek translation of the Hebrew Bible. A selection of passages in Greek as well as in Hebrew and Aramaic, serving the ends of Christian theology, may have existed from the beginning of Palestinian Christianity.

The questions asked have not been completely answered, but the intellectual journey has been worthwhile and a kind of relative chronology can be set up. (a) A selection of passages and texts from the Hebrew Bible, expressed in Hebrew, Aramaic or Greek, whether oral or written, was the Church's earliest Bible and goes back to the beginnings of Palestinian Christianity. (b) Whether we think in terms of a 'Book of Testimonies' as the first literary product of the Christian Church or Dodd's organized body of texts constituting a primitive Christian theology, it is reasonable to suppose that a particularly high value would have been placed on the Greek version of these texts when the Christian Church broke through the limits of Palestinian Jewish Christianity into the Greek-speaking Gentile world. (c) This selective use of the Septuagint would then have been a prelude to the adoption of the Septuagint in its entirety as the Bible of the Church.[61] (d) When the New Testament writers contributed the Church's own writings in Greek, they integrated the primitive sub-structure, consisting of passages and texts taken from the Hebrew Bible, into their work. It is at this point that Dodd begins his enquiry and it is from here that he endeavours to penetrate to the primitive sub-structure. (e) It is only after the Church has conferred authority on this body of writings and made a canon of it that it is meaningful to refer to the Hebrew Bible or the Septuagint as an Old Testament. This is the terminology adopted by the Church in order to contrast the earlier Bible appropriated from the Jews with the new body of writings which it had generated – the New Testament.

Burkitt is persuaded that the recovery of the Semitic origins of Christianity can only be partial, even fragmentary:

To the student of general history Christianity makes its appearance as a Greek religion. The first Christian communities of any considerable size had their home in the great Greek cities on the eastern shores of the Mediterranean. In Alexandria, in Antioch, in Ephesus, in Smyrna, in Corinth – all near the sea, and in easy communication with one another – the little Churches came into being and developed their organization. The whole ecclesiastical vocabulary is Greek. Bishops, Priests, Deacons, the Laity, Baptism, the Eucharist, all the terms are Greek in origin.[62]

It is this dominant Greekness of the early Church which leads Burkitt to describe the religion of the Hebrew Bible as 'the alien religion out of which Christianity had sprung'. The other aspect of his grasp of the matter is that history unfolded in such a way as to make it difficult to catch even a glimpse of 'a very different world from that of Greek Christianity':

The Jewish state came to an end and with it perished the primitive Semitic Christianity. The Christians of Judaea fled to the mountains, and when the troubles were over the survivors seem to have mingled with the Greek-speaking urban population. Thus the one community which might have preserved the earliest traditions was swallowed up.[63]

It may be that the Greek factor has been overestimated by Burkitt in so far as it has been used to open up a gap between Palestinian and Greek Christianity. The reception of an enlarged Hebrew Bible into the Christian Church in a Greek translation or the writing down of the New Testament in Greek does not necessarily create such a gulf. It would be unwise to go as far as Philo who asserted that the Greek translation of the Torah which was the subject of the Letter of Aristeas achieved a perfect equivalence with the Hebrew,[64] but the degree of transformation which attaches to any translation should not be exaggerated, even a translation from Hebrew into Greek. Dodd[65] has noted two factors which make for imperfect equivalence: there are subtle differences between the semantic coverage and the nuances of words in different languages, and there is the degree of metamorphosis which is required to achieve intelligibility in a different intellectual climate. There may be a measure of truth in the claim that if the Hebrew Bible translated into Greek in Alexandria were to make sense to Jews living in that environment, there was a need to substitute a smooth Jacob-like quality for the Esau-like hairiness of the Hebrew Bible. Yet I suspect that the opportunities for such 'cultural translation' are not ample and that they are narrower in some books than in others. Some evidence of it can be found in the book of Proverbs,[66] but a close scrutiny of Jeremiah i – xxv,[67] where there are significant material differences between the Hebrew and the Greek texts, reveals little of it.

It is a fact that the early Christian Church was set at a distance from the Hebrew Bible, but the explanation of this is not to be found, for the most part, in the circumstance that the Church inherited the Hebrew Bible in a Greek translation. Matters would not have been significantly different if the Church had preserved an immediate contact with the Hebrew Bible. A translator, unless he is incompetent or irresponsible, is at the service of the book which he is translating, and the contents of the Hebrew Bible determine the outcome of the Greek translation in more fundamental respects than any elements of 'cultural translation'. Moreover, there is the counter-effect that the Hebrew Bible impresses its Semitisms on the Greek translation.

The reasons for the transformation which the Hebrew Bible underwent in the context of the Christian Church, whether in Hebrew, or in Aramaic or Greek translations, are mostly exegetical in character. They are not principally translational: they are connected with a new range of significance acquired by passages of the Hebrew Bible as a consequence of the conviction that these passages are illumined and fulfilled by Jesus Christ. Christianity, perhaps at its birth, transformed a Jewish Hebrew Bible into a Christian Bible and interpreted it accordingly. When the New Testament was created and the earlier Bible was made into an Old Testament, it was still a Christian Bible.

That this was a creative, exegetical achievement has been stressed by Dodd, but it is not clear that the antithesis of static and dynamic exegesis which he introduces in connection with this claim is entirely apposite.[68] It has been represented that the techniques which were used by Jews in Rabbinical modes of exegesis, in order to stretch the significance of their Bible and to widen its area of applicability, are discernible in Christian exegesis of the same Bible.[69] What creates the distance between Jewish and Christian exegesis is then not a mobility which is present in the one and lacking in the other, but the different goals to which the same or similar exegetical methods are directed, and the significant antithesis is that of Jewish and Christian. This is how the matter is generally set out by New Testament scholars, with a recognition that whatever parallelism may be discerned in the methods of interpretation employed by Rabbinical and Christian exegetes respectively, there is a disparity of content and objectives.[70] The transformation effected by Christian exegetes and the newness of their work arise from a vision that the scriptures are fulfilled in the coming of Jesus Christ and that this event is the key to their interpretation.

It may be, however, that Dodd's opposition of static and dynamic is particularly directed towards modern historical–critical exegesis of the Hebrew Bible and the assumptions with which it operates.[71] 'Static' would then refer to a type of enquiry which concentrates on the intention of the author and which seeks to elucidate this by applying textual criticism, lexicography and grammar to the text, and by attending to the particular historical circumstances which provide a setting for its interpretation. An enterprise of this kind may have the character of a search for what is regarded as the normative and only legitimate exegesis of the passage and this may be the target of Dodd's criticism. It is evident, however, that Dodd himself is concerned to establish that some Christian exegesis of the Hebrew Bible (whether the original or a translation) sets off from the intention of the text in its primary historical context and is the drawing out of a latent significance rather than the imposition of a new meaning which is divorced from the plain sense.[72]

The most important single feature of this Christian exegesis would seem to be the Promise – Fulfilment pattern which it assumes, and there can hardly be a more difficult task than an undertaking to explain the precise intentions of the New Testament writers with regard to this thought of fulfilment. We would like to know more about how they understood the relation between what they proclaimed as the final sense of a text or passage of the Hebrew Bible and the sense obtaining for that passage, in its primary historical and grammatical connections, in that Bible or in a Greek translation of it. To what extent were they aware that they were developing or enriching the primary historical exegesis of texts or passages of the Hebrew Bible? Did they not perhaps suppose that the only meaning which a text or passage had ever possessed was the one which they were now attaching to it?

This is a matter which is in Dodd's mind.[73] It can be put differently: did the Christian exegetes recognize that the final enrichment of sense had been supplied by them and that it had become manifest for the first time as the consequence of a Messianic fulfilment? Alternatively, did they hold a more esoteric doctrine that the Christian sense had been hidden in the text from the beginning as an inner meaning and that this was the only sense that had ever deserved consideration? We may not be able to answer these questions with any degree of assurance. Dodd does not entirely rule out the second of these alternatives, but he regards the first as deserving of the greater attention and as more generally operative. These are important questions, because on the answer which we give to them hinges our estimate of the extent to which the Christian interpretation was achieved at the expense of the plain sense of the Hebrew Bible. It is a defensible position that the sense of passages is open to the future and that new times and circumstances disclose new possibilities of significance. The view that the only sense which texts or passages of the Hebrew Bible ever had was a Christian one is indefensible.

Even, however, if this Christian exegesis of the Hebrew Bible, as it appears in the New Testament, is praised for its creativeness and perceptiveness and is given the rank of a sub-structure of Christian theology, there are important respects in which it sets a distance between the Hebrew Bible and the Christian Church. The exegetical gulf can be described as one obtaining between Jewish exegesis of the Hebrew Bible, especially but not only *peshaṭ* exegesis, and Christian exegesis of Greek translations of that Bible, as exemplified in the New Testament. In the light of the gradual emergence of critical biblical scholarship, the discrepancy which arises is between Christian exegesis, as exemplified in the New Testament, and historical–critical exegesis of the Hebrew Bible.

Origen and the Hebrew Bible

In Origen, a Greek-speaking Christian, probably a native of Alexandria and born about A.D. 185, the son of a Christian martyr, we encounter the first major biblical scholar produced by the Church. Already at the age of seventeen or eighteen he was teaching in a grammar school, an occupation which he gave up in order to devote himself entirely to the instruction of candidates intending Christian baptism, which task had been entrusted to him by Demetrius, Bishop of Alexandria. Subsequently he sought for himself a higher education in the intellectual climate of Alexandria, which may be described as Neo-Platonist, and he acquired the philosophical habits and mental frame of reference which shaped profoundly all that he afterwards said and wrote.

Before he finally left Alexandria in A.D. 215 he had already visited Rome and Trans-Jordan, and it was in Palestine, at Caesarea, a centre of Christian learning which rivalled Alexandria, that he was to spend the remaining years of his life. There, still a layman, he won the approbation of the Bishops of Caesarea and Jerusalem, and was occupied with the instruction of converts to Christianity as he had been in Alexandria. In A.D. 230 he was ordained to the priesthood by the Bishop of Caesarea, an event which awakened the sharp and persevering hostility of Demetrius, Bishop of Alexandria. In Caesarea Origen settled down to teach and preach, and the homilies which have come down to us belong to this setting and were crowded into the last period of his life.[74]

Origen's life is a story of unremitting scholarly labour and evangelical zeal. Although the impact of his philosophical categories on his biblical exegesis is not easily accommodated by the modern mind, in important respects he is all of a piece and the most technical aspects of his text-critical scholarship are brought to bear on his preaching. Our principal and almost sole concern is with the ruins of the impressive monument of his pure biblical scholarship, a synopsis of the Hebrew Bible and its Greek translations which is called the Hexapla. It has to be coupled with another work of the same kind called the Tetrapla;[75] it falls in the Caesarean period, between the years A.D. 230 and 240; it is arranged in six columns and takes its name from this circumstance. The first column contained the text of the Hebrew Bible, the second the transliteration of the Hebrew characters into characters of the Greek alphabet, and the third, fourth and sixth columns contained Greek translations already mentioned (Aquila, Symmachus, Theodotion) which had been done by Jews for Jews. The translation of Theodotion, generally assigned to the sixth column, has been regarded as a second-century A.D. translation like those of Aquila and Symmachus. However, in the Psalm fragments published by Mercati[76] the sixth-column contains another Greek translation mentioned by Eusebius,[77] the Quinta, and Barthélemy[78] has argued that 'Theodotion' is a first-century A.D. translator. Since he supposes that this Greek version forms the base of Origen's fifth column, he describes the text in the sixth column of the Hexaplaric remains of the Twelve Prophets as 'Pseudo-Theodotion'.[79]

If we accept the view that the Milan palimpsest, edited by Mercati, preserves the original format of Origen's Hexapla,[80] some light is cast on the presuppositions and objectives of this massive piece of scholarship. One assumption would appear to be that for every word in the Hebrew text there should be a corresponding word in a faithful Greek translation, and this is how the material is displayed. This is an extreme expression of literalism in translation, a quest after faithfulness which is self-defeating. The process of translation is not necessarily effected by such striving after word for word equivalence; it is a recipe for woodenness and a low level of intelligibility. There were special reasons, already indicated,[81] why the later Greek translations made by Jews were literal in character: where every word of the Hebrew text counted in the exegetical methods which were employed, it was thought necessary to have every word represented in a Greek translation of the Hebrew. But, as Soisalon-Soininen[82] has pointed out, the achieving of material or quantitative equivalence between the Hebrew text and a Greek translation of that text was also Origen's prime consideration. Different reasons have been given why he was so powerfully exercised by this concern, but it will be enough for the moment to say that it does not necessarily run counter to his taste for allegorical exegesis, because he might have thought it a matter of importance to know, at his point of departure, what the Greek text would look like if it were quantitatively equivalent with the Hebrew. In any case, it is this identity of parts rather than the synthetic capturing of the sense of one language in another language for which the format of the Milan palimpsest is designed.

The most important column of the Hexapla, and the one which is most difficult to interpret, is the fifth. The generally accepted opinion[83] has been that the work of 'healing'[84] the Septuagint was carried through by Origen in the fifth column of the Hexapla, and that this was effected by displaying, on the assumptions already noted, a Greek text which corresponded in every particular with the Hebrew text. This was done by enclosing the required additions to the Septuagint in asterisks and metobeli and the required subtractions in obeli and metobeli.[85] These signs are called Aristarchian, after Aristarchus, an Alexandrian philologist (217 – 145 B.C.), and they were in general use in Alexandrian textual criticism. Barthélemy's modification of this picture arises from his view that the Greek text at the base of the fifth column was not the 'ancient Septuagint' but the Palestinian recension of that Septuagint, attributed by him to Jonathan ben Uzziel (Theodotion).[86] The circumstance that in 2 Samuel – 1 Kings two forms of the Origenic text of the Septuagint are attested is explained by him in this connection: there is a text which agrees with the Greek translation of 'Theodotion' and has no Hexaplaric features and this is the text which is at the base of the fifth column of the Hexapla; there is another text corresponding with the finished product in the fifth column of the Hexapla, which has the additions associated with the asterisk and the subtractions associated with the obelos.[87]

Soisalon-Soininen[88] has urged that the manner of the ordering of the fifth column of the Hexapla reflects not only the objective of achieving quantitative equivalence between the Hebrew original and a Greek representation of it, but also the measure of respect which Origen had for the Septuagint, since the additions were made to this text and the subtractions referred to it. It was because Origen could not contemplate the jettisoning of the Septuagint that he achieved his quantitative equivalence with the Hebrew text in this round-about and unsatisfactory way. If he had been prepared to tolerate the idea that the Greek text generally received in the Church was expendable, he could have reached his objective simply by adopting one of the literal translations into Greek done by the Jews. On the assumption that Theodotion is a second-century A.D. translator, that his translation was in the sixth column of the Hexapla and that it was this which Origen chiefly used in making additions to or indicating deletions from the Septuagint, Soisalon-Soisinen[89] remarks that Origen could have achieved his end simply by adopting the translation of Theodotion.

A reinforcement of this line of thought is the observation that while Origen adds to his base text, and can do no other if he is to reach what must be regarded as his principal objective, he excises nothing from this text. Where subtractions from the Septuagint were required, simple deletion would have enabled him to reach the end of quantitative equivalence between the Hebrew and the Greek, but this is not the method which he adopts. Instead he preserves the text of the Septuagint entirely and indicates the need to subtract elements of its text which have no representation in the Hebrew by means of obeli. All of this may indicate that Origen was attached to the Greek text generally received in the Church, or that he thought it unwise not to take account of the depth of attachment to it which existed and the theology which declared it to be inspired. One should not, however, be swayed too much by considerations of this kind, even when support can be had from the utterances of Origen himself, but we shall return to this matter.

The argument which Soisalon-Soininen has used in order to demonstrate the regard which Origen had for the Greek text received in the Church is swept away by Barthélemy's account, since he has represented that the base text used by Origen in the fifth column of the Hexapla was a Palestinian recension of the Septuagint done by a Jew in Palestine around the middle of the first century A.D.[90] According to Barthélemy this Palestinian recension was used only by the Palestinian Church until it was inserted in the fifth column of Origen's Hexapla. The Churches of Alexandria and Antioch were faithful to the ancient Septuagint, but because of the influence of Origen's Hexapla the Palestinian recension which he had inserted in his fifth column subsequently supplanted the ancient Septuagint in Egypt and Cappadocia.[91] Kahle[92] has noticed that the tetragrammaton, written with square Hebrew characters (יהוה), appears in all five columns of the Milan palimpsest, and he has taken this as an indication that the provenance of all of the material assembled by Origen is Jewish. This produces a particular agreement with Barthélemy's account of the Greek version at the base of column five – a Palestinian recension of the Septuagint made by a Jew. One might enquire of Barthélemy whether, on general grounds, Origen's use of a text of the Septuagint widely received in the Church does not make better sense than his adoption of a Palestinian recension which was used only by the Palestinian Church. The observation that the Palestinian recension was nearer to the Hebrew text of the period than the ancient Septuagint is not an answer, because whatever basic text Origen used it still (*ex hypothesi*) required additions and subtractions to achieve quantitative equivalence with the Hebrew text. In that case there would seem to be a clear advantage in having a basic text which was generally recognized by the Church as the Septuagint rather than a Palestinian recension which had currency only in Palestine.

The Hexapla has not survived and it is commonly thought that it was destroyed at Caesarea during the Islamic conquest in the seventh century A.D. We have access to it principally through manuscripts of the Septuagint which have a Hexaplaric text or which have Hexaplaric readings in their margins, and through a Syriac translation of a Hexaplaric Greek text made by Bishop Paul of Tella at the beginning of the seventh century A.D., known as the Syro-Hexaplar. The Septuagint manuscripts which have a Hexaplaric text are derived from Origen's fifth column and the Syro-Hexaplar is a Syriac translation of the contents of that column. It is supposed, as already noted, that Origen used Theodotion mostly to supplement his basic Greek text in the fifth column.[93] The Hexaplaric marginal readings in manuscripts of the Septuagint can be explained as supplying information taken from the third (Aquila), the fourth (Symmachus) and the sixth (Theodotion) columns of the

Hexapla. Some Septuagint manuscripts with a Hexaplaric text do not employ, or do not employ consistently, asterisks and obeli. Jerome is a sufficiently important source of information about the contents of the Hexapla to deserve special mention.

Nothing has been said so far about the part played by the contents of the first and second columns of the Hexapla in Origen's synopsis. Eusebius[94] has informed us that Origen searched for Hebrew manuscripts as well as for Greek translations of the Hebrew, and Kahle[95] has urged that all the raw material of the Hexapla is to be traced to Jewish sources, the Greek translations in columns three, four and six, and others which Eusebius mentions,[96] but also the transcription of the Hebrew text in column two.[97] Kahle founds his opinion on words which occur at the beginning of a homily composed by Bishop Melito of Sardis in the second century A.D.: 'The book of the Hebrew Exodus has been read and the words of the mystery have been explained, how the Lamb was slain and the people saved.'[98] The editor of the facsimile of the papyrus (F. G. Kenyon)[99] remarked that these words might refer to a reading of the text in Hebrew and its translation into Greek which was then followed by the exposition contained in the homily. But a reading aloud of the 'Hebrew Exodus' (τῆς ἑβραϊκῆς ἐξόδου) is not necessarily to be construed as a reading aloud in Hebrew.[100] The connection which Kahle establishes between this reference and the second column of the Hexapla is indicated by the following: 'Not only for Christians but also for many of the Jews it was necessary to use a Greek transcription for the public reading of the Old Testament.'[101] Greek-speaking Jews needed a transcription of the Hebrew into Greek characters for the public reading of the Hebrew Bible and the Christian Church continued this liturgical use. It is Kahle's contention that this elucidates the function of the second column of the Hexapla and supplies an indication that Origen did not compose the transcription but acquired it from a Jewish source. 'It is difficult to think of any other useful purpose that the Second Column could serve. To a biblical student who knew Hebrew it would be superfluous; to one who did not, it would be unintelligible. But it could be very useful indeed for the purpose of liturgical reading of a sacred text, in a language no longer understood, as a preliminary to the reading of a translation.'[102] The argument is not irresistible. Would the transcription not be useful for a biblical student who knew a little Hebrew and who was helped by the transliteration of Hebrew characters into Greek characters? Moreover, while it is understandable that in a Jewish liturgical context the uttering of the sounds of Hebrew, even if they were unintelligible, might have been a requirement, the supposition that this also obtained in a Christian liturgical context is more difficult to accept.

This leads on to the more central question whether or not Origen knew any Hebrew. If we were to suppose that the transliteration of Hebrew characters into Greek characters in the second column of the Hexapla were his own, it might show that he was ill at ease with the Hebrew script or, more particularly, as Emerton[103] has argued, that the Greek transcription supplied him with a vocalization of the consonantal Hebrew text in column one. The received wisdom is that he had a limited knowledge of Hebrew.[104] If he had no knowledge of Hebrew, the first and second columns of the Hexapla make no contribution to his reconstructed Greek text in the fifth column. His objective is to secure a quantitative equivalence between Hebrew and Greek texts, but if he has no access to the Hebrew, he does not know at first hand that he is achieving his end. He has to make the assumption that the Greek translations which he has assembled possess this quantitative equivalence with the Hebrew text and that he can reach his goal through them. The view that this is how he proceeded, without any reference to the Hebrew text, is the one held by Nautin,[105] Kahle[106] and Soisalon-Soininen,[107] and Nautin[108] declares roundly that Origen had no Hebrew. If he had no Hebrew, and columns one and two were redundant in relation to the method by which he achieved his objective, we may ask why they were included in the synopsis. It is unlikely that he was guilty of window-dressing and his interest in Hebrew manuscripts, attested by Eusebius, is perhaps a sufficient reason for the inclusion of the first column, whether he knew Hebrew or not. It was an essential element of the structure of the synopsis and the result which it was intended to secure, even if Origen could not use it. If Origen had no Hebrew, it cannot be supposed that the transliteration of Hebrew characters into Greek characters in column two is his work, and Kahle's view that he had a Jewish source for this, even if the form of his argument is not convincing, deserves attention.[109]

Brock,[110] however, doubts whether the extent of Origen's knowledge of Hebrew is an important consideration and suggests that it may be misleading to represent him as a pioneer of *Hebraica veritas* or to suggest that he relied on Aquila, Symmachus and Theodotion because of his lack of Hebrew. This has to be related to Brock's view that Origen's principal concern was to be informed and equipped for controversy with Jews and that to acquire knowledge of the Greek texts used by Jews of his own day was his main objective: 'Origen uses the Three as a κριτήριον (a word which he himself employs in the commentary on Matthew), primarily because it is they that are the authoritative texts in Jewish Greek circles – and only incidentally because his knowledge of Hebrew was not very great.'[111] Brock holds that Origen assumed the supremacy of the authority of the Septuagint in the Church and that his chief interest lay 'in the ἐκδόσεις of the Old Testament current in the Greek speaking [Jewish] diaspora, that is to say, the Three, Aquila, Theodotion and Symmachus'.[112]

But Origen uses the Greek text of the fifth column of his Hexapla in his Christian preaching (as Brock remarks) and this shows that he placed an intrinsic value on it as scripture and that it was not simply a tool for Christian – Jewish controversy. The statement that he assumed the supremacy of the authority of the Septuagint in the Church has to be balanced against the circumstance that he sometimes used a Greek text quantitatively equivalent with the Hebrew in his homilies – in a context which had nothing to do with Christian – Jewish controversy.

I take up the contention that the main reason for the undertaking of text-critical operations in the Hexapla was Origen's concern to have a Greek text which corresponded quantitatively with the Hebrew text used by Jews and its Greek versions, and so to arm himself better for Christian–Jewish controversy. The following quotation bears on this:

I make it my endeavour not to be ignorant of their various readings, so that in my controversies with the Jews I may avoid quoting to them what is not found in their copies, and also may be able to make positive use of what is found there, even when it is not to be found in our scriptures. If we are prepared for our discussions with them in this way, they will no longer be able, as so often happens, to laugh scornfully at Gentile believers for their ignorance of the true reading which they have.[113]

The view that he was not really concerned to 'heal' the Greek text received in the Church, that he did not regard his work in the Hexapla as a search for a true Greek text, that there is nothing of Jerome's *Hebraica veritas* in his attitude, and that he is simply arming himself for controversy with Jews, is a natural ally of the assertion that it was not Origen's intention to cast doubt on the authority and complete adequacy of the text of the Septuagint which was in use in the Church. The fifth column of the Hexapla is not to be understood as a demonstration that the received Greek text is defective and has to be corrected through a comparison with the Hebrew Bible and literal Greek translations of that Bible. Words of Origen which are thought to justify this claim are these:

Are we when we notice such things [that is, divergences between the Septuagint and the Hebrew Bible] to reject as spurious the copies in use in the Churches, and to tell the fellowship that they should put away the sacred books current among them and should cajole the Jews into giving us copies which will be untampered with and free from forgery? Are we to suppose that providence which has provided for the edification of all the Churches of Christ through the medium of the holy scriptures has not taken proper care of the needs of those for whom Christ died?[114]

It is a mistake to suppose that victory can be won with a single stroke by producing a quotation of this kind. Origen does not speak with one voice and in another place he says about the state of the Greek text received in the Church:

Great differences have arisen in the transcripts, from the carelessness of some of the scribes, or from the recklessness of some persons, or from those who neglected the emendation of the text, or else from those who made additions to the text or omissions from it, as they thought fit. With God's help we were able to heal the disagreements in the copies of the Old Testament on the basis of the other [Greek] versions.[115]

There is a loss of touch with the detail of Origen's scholarly work in the Hexapla, and the objectives which he himself states, if it is baldly asserted that he accepted the view that the Septuagint was inspired and was a translation without blemish. Here is a scholar who searched for Hebrew manuscripts, who assembled translations of the Hebrew Bible done by Jews which displayed a quantitative equivalence with the Hebrew not possessed by the Greek text received in the Church, and who reconstructed that text in order to repair this deficiency. How can we suppose that someone who embarked on Herculean labours in order to 'heal' the Greek text received by the Church believed in the perfection of that text? In the context of the Hexapla Origen speaks the language of a textual critic; the reality of his enterprise and the ends which he pursued should not be dissolved or weakened by a declaration that he believed in the inspiration of the Septuagint.[116] Even the thought that Origen was inhibited by prudential considerations[117] rather than by his adherence to a high doctrine of the inspiration of the Septuagint, held within the Christian Church, should not be pushed too far. It is generally true that any change in settled translations of the Bible has awakened doubts and fears in the minds of churchmen. The consideration that the faithful were being needlessly disturbed lay behind Augustine's disagreement with Jerome,[118] and down to modern times the substitution of a new translation for an old one to which the faithful were attached has been regarded as a sensitive issue.

The weight of the other contention, that Origen was mainly occupied with securing parity in debates with the Jews by having a Greek text which agreed exactly with the Hebrew text on which they founded their arguments,[119] should not be exaggerated. Even the passage which lends support to it, also advances another reason for Origen's text-critical endeavours[120] and we shall now give further consideration to this aspect of the matter.

It would create a false impression if we were to suppose that Origen had his text-critical scholarship in one compartment of his mind and his doctrine that the perfection of the Septuagint was guaranteed by the Holy Spirit in another. There is evidence that he did not keep his scholarship hidden away, that it was not separated from his activities as a churchman, and that he used it in his preaching. He mentions that in the book of Jeremiah the differences between the Hebrew and Greek texts are notable,[121] and it can be shown that in his homily on Jeremiah he used the Greek text which he had reconstructed in the fifth column of his Hexapla to enrich his preaching. Nautin,[122] in the introduction to his edition of Origen's homilies on Jeremiah, has supposed that Origen preached to his flock in Caesarea with a Bible in his hand, employing the Greek text which he had reconstructed in the fifth column of his Hexapla. That he employed this text consistently is not borne out by an examination of the Old Testament quotations in Origen's homily on the book of Jeremiah. What such a scrutiny reveals is that he sometimes used such a text.[123]

If this evidence from the homily on Jeremiah is looked at in the round, it shows decisively that Origen valued the text which he had compiled in the fifth column of his Hexapla as a resource for preaching, but it does not tally with Nautin's suppositions that the Greek Bible which (*ex hypothesi*) he held open in his hands while he preached contained his Hexaplaric text of the Septuagint. Half of the examples considered show the text of the Septuagint without Hexaplaric additions, and Nautin's other point that

Origen sometimes quoted from memory ought not to be pressed in order to explain this pattern. We should have to assume that the text which was imprinted in Origen's memory was that of the Septuagint, without the Hexaplaric additions, whereas what Nautin has in mind are accidental deviations caused by an imperfect recollection of the texts which are cited.

A better explanation is suggested by Origen's remarks on Jer. xv 10,[124] where he compared the Hebrew text (לא נשיתי ולא נשו בי) with the Septuagint (οὐκ ὠφέλησα οὐδὲ ὠφέλησέ με οὐδείς). The Hebrew means, 'I have not borrowed and no one has borrowed from me'; the Septuagint, 'I have given no help and no one has offered help to me.' Origen describes the Greek text which accurately renders the Hebrew (οὐκ ὠφείλησα οὐδὲ ὠφείλησέ μοι) as more exact, but his conclusion is: 'It is necessary both to explain the [Greek] text which is traditionally received in the Churches and not to neglect the exposition of the [Greek] text which is derived from the Hebrew.'[125] The double concern, to 'heal' the Septuagint with reference to the Hebrew text and yet not to neglect the exposition of the Greek text which was established in the Church, perhaps helps to explain the distribution of his citations in the homily on Jeremiah between the Hexaplaric text which was the result of the 'healing' process and the text of the Septuagint without Hexaplaric additions.

A suitable conclusion to this particular study, an illustration of the use made by Origen of his Hexaplaric text in preaching, is his homiletical application of Jer. xvii 1.[126] Since xvii 1 – 4 are unrepresented in the Septuagint, this is part of a large Hexaplaric addition. The date is between A.D. 241 and 244, so that little more than ten years of his life is left to him. He has already had a taste of persecution, but he is about to be imprisoned and tortured, until broken by the hostility of the world his life ends at Tyre about A.D. 254. The text on which he is preaching reads: 'A sin of Judah has been inscribed with an iron tool, with a point of adamant it has been engraved on the innermost heart.'[127] This is what he has to say:

If my sin had been written in ink, I would have erased it, but it is written with an iron tool, with a point of adamant on my innermost heart, so that when I come to the judgement the prophecy will be revealed which says, 'There is nothing secret which will not be made manifest and nothing hidden which will not be revealed' (Mt. x 26). My breast and my heart will be uncovered to reveal the record of my sin, inscribed with an iron tool and a point of adamant ... Again it is said, 'Do not judge anything before the time when the Saviour will come who will illumine what has been hidden in darkness and will reveal the designs of men's hearts' (1 Cor. iv 5). To whom will he reveal them? Not to himself, for he already knows all things before they come to pass. Again I ask to whom will he reveal them? To all those who are able to discern because of their own purity the sin of those who sin, to the end that sinners may be raised to shame and eternal disgrace (1 Peter iv 11). From which may the God of all things save us, so that we may be raised to the glory which is in Christ, to whom be the glory and the power through all ages, Amen.[128]

A final answer which should be given to the question about Origen's motivation in his Hexapla is that it marks the beginnings of an interest in the Hebrew Bible within the Church. These are only small beginnings in so far as we are unsure about Origen's competence as a Hebraist, and have to give serious consideration to the possibility that he may not have known any Hebrew. Moreover, we have noticed that there are defects in his understanding of what constitutes a faithful translation of the Hebrew Bible into Greek. Translating from one language to another involves a degree of transformation, and the distinctive relational characteristics of the syntax of one language cannot simply be reproduced in translation into another language to establish a one – one correspondence of linguistic units. These are factors which cannot be taken care of when faithful translation is expressed principally as quantitative equivalence with the text which is translated. In addition to the myopic vision of word for word translation, there is the aggravation of the brokenness of Origen's translation caused by the circumstance that it is constituted by a basic Septuagint text patched with additions from other Greek translations. Nevertheless, he valued the text which he had obtained for the access which it gave him to the Hebrew Bible and he used it in his preaching. It is the beginning of a long road and the quest after *Hebraica veritas* is pursued in a more highly organized and scientific way by Jerome who was the first scholarly translator of the Hebrew Bible produced by the Church.

Jerome and the Hebrew Bible

Jerome was born about A.D. 346 of Christian parents at Stridon,[129] on the border of Dalmatia and Pannonia, close to Aquileia, at the northern end of the Adriatic. His material circumstances were comfortable,[130] his ardour for learning unhindered,[131] and he tells us that from the cradle he kept company with grammarians, rhetoricians and philosophers.[132] At the age of seventeen or so[133] he went to Rome with his friend Bonosus to further his education, and he was the pupil of Donatus, a noted grammarian.[134] His decision to learn Greek there, after he became a Christian,[135] must be regarded as one of the more important which he made in the course of his life, even if he did not appreciate its full significance at the time. He was on his way to becoming a trilingual scholar[136] and was eventually to settle down to a life of scholarship which depended on his mastery of Latin, Greek and Hebrew, an accomplishment which made him 'a near unique phenomenon at any period in the history of the early Church'.[137] He acquired Hebrew from a converted Jew during the years 375 to 377 or 378[138] when he practised asceticism living among the hermits in the desert of Chalcis, east of Antioch. When he was in Antioch his Greek was good enough to enable him to understand the lectures of Apollinaris of Laodicea.[139] He was comparing the Old Latin with the later Greek versions and the Hebrew Bible as early as 381,[140] but it was during his long period at Bethlehem that he improved his knowledge of Hebrew and acquired a commanding stature as a translator of the Hebrew Bible and a commentator on it.

In his earlier days it would have been more reasonable to predict a different kind of career for him, one which would have given him access to the corridors of ecclesiastical power rather than inclined him towards a monastery at Bethlehem. In Rome he had professed Christianity and received baptism,[141] and while travelling with Bonosus from Rome to Trier in Gaul, he met Rufinus in Northern Italy and completed the journey in his company. After three or four years at Trier the company returned to Italy, and at Aquileia Jerome was a member of a group devoted to the study of the Bible and the cultivation of the ascetic life. Rufinus and Chromatius, who subsequently became Bishop of Aquileia, were among its members, and Jerome's association with this group lasted until 373.

It was then that he experienced what he describes as a 'sudden disturbance' (*subitus turbo*) and set off for the East, violently wrenched from companionship, enclosed in darkness, and oppressed by a fearful ubiquity of sea and sky.[142] At Antioch he had a spiritual experience which is recorded in one of his letters.[143] In a state of fever, and with his life in danger, he was brought to the judgement-seat in the nether world and denounced as a Ciceronian (*Ciceronianus es, non Christianus*), but was allowed to return to the upper world when he took an oath that he would never again possess or read secular books. It was an oath which he interpreted with liberty, as we are informed by Rufinus,[144] who says that Jerome did not give up his attachment to 'our Cicero, our Horace, our Virgil' and larded his books with them. Why, asked Rufinus, does he not edify young females with quotations from scripture rather than supplying them with allusions to Latin authors? For his own part, Jerome confessed that he found the aesthetic attraction of Latin literature irresistible and could not bring himself to give up the library which he had acquired while resident in Rome. He fasted and kept vigil as a kind of penance for his inability to break his addiction to Cicero and Plautus. If he turned to the Hebrew Bible and the prophetic literature, he was repelled by the barbarism of the language.[145] Yet he had been reminded before the judgement-seat, *Ubi thesaurus tuus, ibi et cor tuum* (Mt. vi 21). Jerome found Semitic languages aesthetically uncultivated and harsh. He sweated over them[146] and they almost drove him to despair; he heard only a cacophony of uncouth sounds; the delight of symphony was not in them.[147] But Hebrew and Aramaic were a fountain of truth and an indispensable means to an end. After the grasp of Quintilian, the fluency of Cicero, the *gravitas* of Frontino and the smoothness of Pliny, the harshness of the sounds of Hebrew and the difficulty encountered in pronouncing them were all but unbearable. But thanks be to the Lord that from the bitter seed of this literature he plucked sweet fruit![148] Even if it be sackcloth, it is the vesture in which *veritas* has been clothed and it must be learned and mastered in order to gain access to that treasure.

The experience at Antioch which he relates is an indication of the complexity of his temperament, as is his period of two or three years in the desert of Chalcis. Back in Antioch his preoccupations were strikingly different: he was involved in ecclesiastical manoeuvres in connection with the three contenders for the Bishopric of Antioch and was writing letters to Pope Damasus explaining the difficulty in which he found himself, since all three claimed to be in union with St Peter's Chair ('My man is the man in union with St Peter's Chair').[149] It is this behaviour which draws the comment that Jerome was an incorrigible controversialist and had an 'almost grovelling respect for ecclesiastical authority'.[150] The Pope decided in favour of Paulinus, Jerome attached himself to Paulinus, was consecrated a priest by him and accompanied him to Constantinople for the meetings of the Second General Council. Afterwards they proceeded to Rome to take part in a council held by Damasus in 382,[151] and there Jerome acquired such a reputation as a biblical scholar,[152] and so waxed in favour, that he was regarded as a possible successor to the Chair of St Peter.[153] Not only did he become the confidential secretary of Damasus,[154] but he was commissioned by him to engage in biblical scholarship, and, in the first place, to revise the Latin Gospels on the basis of the Greek text.[155] At this period (381) he offered Damasus *On the Seraphim in Isaiah vi* as a sample of his work.[156] Whatever may have been the precise scope of the task which was laid on him, it is known that he undertook a revision of the Psalter[157] and worked on other Old Testament books.[158] In any case it was the beginning of an enterprise which proved to have a greater attraction for him than any other and in which he persisted to the end of his life.

The manner in which this outcome was achieved has an aspect of strangeness about it, because it is not directly related to his success in Rome and the ecclesiastical preferment which he had obtained there. The circumstance that he was not so highly esteemed by the new Pope (Siricius) as he had been by Damasus, nor so securely protected from his enemies,[159] are hardly adequate explanations of his resolve to leave Rome for ever. That it was, at least partly, his scholarship which had awakened opposition and hostility may have been particularly discouraging to him, but his own perception of this juncture is that he cut himself off from home and family for the sake of the Kingdom of Heaven and went to Jerusalem as a soldier of Christ.[160] The oddness of this second turn in his career is increased by the fact that his future flows not so much from the high connections which he had made within the Church at Rome as from what might be described as an extramural activity: his acceptability as a spiritual director and teacher in biblical studies to high-born and wealthy Roman women. Two of them, Paula and her daughter Eustochium, joined him at Antioch and together they toured the sacred sites of the Holy Land and went to Egypt. It may be said that Paula settled Jerome's future by founding a monastery at Bethlehem and installing him in it.[161] It was in the autumn of the year 386 and at Bethlehem, where he spent the rest of his life, that his dedication to sacred learning prevailed. Perhaps the victory of his scholarly interest, as much as his withdrawal from a world which disgusted him, is the best explanation of the unusual biographical pattern.

The first main phase of Jerome's activity as a translator involves contact with the Hebrew Bible, but its form and objectives are those which had earlier exercised Origen in his work on the Hexapla. Jerome's intention is to do for the Latin-speaking Church what Origen had done for the Greeks and to repair what he calls the Vulgate[162] by the same method as Origen had used for the Septuagint. To avoid confusion the Latin version to which Jerome refers when he uses the term 'Vulgate' will be called the Old Latin, a version which had been translated from a Septuagint text similar to the one to which Origen had made his additions by means of asterisks and indicated his subtractions by means of obeli.[163] This can be illustrated by Gen. xxxi 13, where the Hebrew text, 'I am the God of Bethel' is to be compared with the Septuagint ('I am the God who was seen by you in the place of God') and the Old Latin ('I am the God whom you saw in the place of God').[164] A sharp indication of the special relationship between the Septuagint and the Old Latin is given by the circumstance that in both cases בית אל ('house of God') is translated as 'place of God' rather than reproduced as a place-name. At Gen. xxxi 35 the words 'in every part of the tent' appear in the Septuagint and the Old Latin,[165] but not in the Hebrew, and the additional items at Gen. xxxv 4 are 'and desecrated them' and 'which can still be seen to-day'.[166] It is because the Old Latin is a translation from the text of the Septuagint similar to the one which Origen repaired that the two are so closely connected in Jerome's mind. Hence he associates his affirmation that he has not lost his regard for the Latin version received in the Church with his insistence that neither in his Latin imitation of the fifth column of Origen's Hexapla nor in his translation from Hebrew into Latin is it his intention to lay blame at the door of the Seventy.[167]

The prefaces to his 'Hexaplaric' Latin version contain explanations of his use of asterisks and obeli along the lines laid down by Origen,[168] and his versions of the 'Gallican' Psalter[169] and Job[170] are extant with asterisks and obeli. He had access to Origen's Hexapla at Caesarea[171] and he referred to the Hebrew Bible for purposes of comparison and control. His principal concern is to use the later Greek translations (Aquila, Symmachus and Theodotion), as Origen had done, in order to represent a Latin text quantitatively equivalent with the Hebrew Bible. He states that the additions made by Origen in his fifth column were adopted from Theodotion,[172] and supposes that a process of invisible mending is aided by the stylistic affinity of Theodotion to the basic 'ancient Septuagint' text of the fifth column.[173]

Jerome's primary assumption in all this is that the text of the Hebrew Bible which was available to him was identical with the one used by the Alexandrian translators, and that the representation of a Latin text corresponding quantitatively with the extant text of the Hebrew Bible amounted to a recovery of an original purity which had been lost through the corruptions suffered by the Greek text in the course of transmission.[174] This is a text-critical assumption which Jerome does not transcend when he moves on from a patching of the Old Latin to a new translation from Hebrew into Latin, because the possibility that the translators of the 'ancient Septuagint' may have had a Hebrew text different from that of *Hebraica veritas* is one which does not enter his mind. From what has been said it will be evident that his defence of the Seventy has an ostensible text-critical character rather than a theological one, even if his criticism lacks a scientific foundation. The view that the Seventy were inspired and that they should be regarded as prophets rather than scholars is one which he rejects.[175] In one place he does suggest that they may have exceeded their limits as translators and made additions to the text out of considerations of style or by the authority of the Holy Spirit,[176] but the prevailing emphasis is that they were scholars and not prophets and that the quality of their work was determined by their linguistic skill, not by the inspiration of the Holy Spirit. He dismisses the belief held in the Church that the Seventy did their work segregated in cells[177] and he describes the arrangements otherwise: they were congregated in one place and proceeded by conference.[178]

It is difficult to make sense of Jerome's text-critical defence of the Seventy. He knows that Origen used second-century A.D. Greek translations from the Hebrew made by Jews and he supposes that the additions in the fifth column were taken from Theodotion. If so, how can he say that Origen's Hexaplaric text in his fifth column preserves uncorrupted and unstained the translation of the Seventy?[179] The statement that later Greek translations, especially Theodotion, were used to recreate perfectly the original Greek text of the Alexandrian Septuagint seems to entertain a kind of miraculous coincidence, although it does not really have this character. It is explained by Jerome's assumption that the Alexandrian translators had the same Hebrew text as was available to Aquila, Symmachus, Theodotion and to himself, and also by the limited translational concerns which were dominant in Origen's reconstruction and in Jerome's Latin imitation of Origen. If the object of the exercise is to produce a Greek or a Latin version which has a word for word correspondence with the extant text of the Hebrew Bible, and if the later Greek versions translated the same Hebrew text on these principles, they can be used in order to achieve the desired end.[180] Moreover, if it is assumed that the Seventy translated this same Hebrew text and that they also aimed at a word for word representation of the Hebrew in Greek, it can be claimed that the work of the Seventy in its original form has been recovered. It may be that too much theorizing is misleading: it is better simply to appreciate that priority is being given to showing what a Latin text looks like when its material constituents are exactly those of the Hebrew, and that other considerations which enter into the achievement of a good translation are being deliberately sacrificed to this end.

Imitating Origen or translating *de novo* from Hebrew into Latin are presented by Jerome as alternatives and he invites his Christian critics to select the result which they prefer: either his use of old resources or his pioneer work as a translator of the Hebrew Bible into Latin.[181] The circumstance that his Hexaplaric venture is still much in his mind in the prefaces to his new translation from Hebrew into Latin may, perhaps, be associated with the perception that these are alternative methods of achieving a quantitative equivalence with the Hebrew text, but this parity of esteem should not be exaggerated. He is aware that his resolve to translate from Hebrew into Latin will draw criticism from the Christian side, but he anticipates that the deficiencies in the form of his Latin rendering with asterisks and obeli, which exposed him to Jewish criticisms, will be overcome in a work over which he will exercise complete control.

He is charged by his opponents within the Church of despising the ancients by translating *de novo* from Hebrew into Latin and he endeavours to repel this allegation. His aim is to make *Hebraica veritas* more easily accessible to men of his own language than it is through his Hexaplaric work.[182] The argument from tradition, that he was doing for the Latin Church what Origen had done for the Greeks, can no longer be used in its original form,[183] since he says of his new venture, *Haec autem translatio nullum de veteribus sequitur interpretem.*[184] The modified form is that if Origen used Greek translations done by Jews and heretics in order to achieve his Hexaplaric text of the Septuagint, and if this was granted wide recognition in the Greek-speaking Church, why should a translation from Hebrew into Latin done by a Christian, born of Christian parents, not be received in the Western Church?[185] Against the charge that there is a dangerous discontinuity in his innovation he prescribes the Hebrew Bible as the acid test. Wherever he departs from the 'ancient Septuagint' or the Old Latin it will be found that the reason for the divergence is his adherence to *Hebraica veritas*. Those Christians who do not have Hebrew should enquire of Jews who have both Hebrew and Latin and they will receive a confirmation that this is indeed the case.[186] The appeal to Jews, which is recommended by Jerome, has the disadvantage of providing fuel for the suspicion that he is a Judaizer, expressed in the taunt of Rufinus that he had preferred Barabbas to Christ,[187] and given substance by his resort to other Jewish teachers after he had settled in Bethlehem. His awareness of this particular background of Christian criticism is reflected in what he had said earlier (384) about his scrutiny of Aquila's translation to ascertain whether there was any evidence in it of alterations to the Hebrew designed to advance the cause of the Synagogue in its controversy with the Church.[188]

The other aspect of the matter is that Jerome was seeking to equip himself better for his conflict with the Jews, a consideration which he adduces in connection with his submission to the hard labour of learning Hebrew.[189] It was to overcome a position of weakness, where Christians quoted texts from the Old Latin unrepresented in the Hebrew Bible to advance their arguments and were greeted with Jewish derision, that Jerome produced his Latin rendering with asterisks and obeli.[190] He has gone a stage further in making himself an effective controversialist by translating directly from Hebrew into Latin:

Do I not have the right, after the version of the Septuagint which I gave many years ago to the people who speak my language, in an edition carefully corrected, to translate also to confound the Jews the exemplars which they hold as absolutely authentic, so that if ever Christians dispute with them, they will not be able to escape by side-roads, but will be felled with their own sword.[191]

Although the imitation of Origen had given Jerome a Latin text which was quantitatively equivalent with the extant text of the Hebrew Bible, and so equipped him better to engage in debate with Jews, it, nevertheless, exposed him to a new set of criticisms. He reflects bitterly on the failures of his Christian brethren to sustain him in his scholarly labours: in their worldliness and ignorance they are incapable of appreciating what he has done[192] and his 'Hexaplaric' Latin version has been wilfully misused.[193] Their attacks on him are poisonous;[194] their concern is to affect intellectual superiority, not to understand what he is doing;[195] as he confronts Jews he is stabbed in the back by Christians. Apart from these domestic complications it is obvious that his authority would be enhanced and his effectiveness as an opponent of the Jews would be increased considerably by the experience acquired in translating the whole of the Hebrew Bible into Latin. This would be ensured by the free exercise of his skills as a translator and by the circumstance that he could no longer be held responsible for renderings not his own.[196] From the narrow concern of representing in Latin, through Greek versions, a text quantitatively equivalent with the Hebrew Bible, he was launched into a work in which he was totally involved as a translator.

Jerome may have translated all the books of the Hebrew Bible into Latin on the model of Origen's fifth column. There is a progress report, which apparently refers to this phase of translation, in which he states that he has finished the Prophets, the books of Solomon (Proverbs, Ecclesiastes, Canticles), the Psalter, the four books of Kings (Samuel and Kings), that Exodus is at the point of completion, and that he is about to pass to Leviticus.[197] In a letter to Augustine he remarks that a large part of his Latin translation with asterisks and obeli has been lost through someone's deceit.[198] Once he had embarked on translation from Hebrew into Latin, the earlier phase must be regarded as a method which had been transcended. His statement that the two methods are optional is true only in the narrow sense that both are attempts to represent the Hebrew text faithfully in Latin. Even in this regard there are differences, because his translation from Hebrew into Latin is not wedded to a word for word equivalence with the Hebrew, nor to an undeviating preservation of the word-order of the Hebrew. Jerome criticizes the excessively literal translation of Aquila, its slavish adherence to Hebrew word-order and the absurdity of devotion to a word for word equivalence which results in the rendering of a marker for a determinate object (את) as σύν.[199] As will appear more fully presently, his continuing interest in Origen's Hexapla and his use of it in commentaries founded on *Hebraica veritas* are disengaged from his earlier use of it to represent the text of the Hebrew Bible. Since he is translating from Hebrew, he has no longer any need of Greek versions as intermediaries between the Old Latin and the Hebrew Bible.

Jerome now has the opportunity to realize his skills as a translator. The complexity of the process of translation had engaged him, and when he discusses the task of translating from Greek to Latin, he discerns it as a complicated transformation, related to the different syntactical structures of the two languages. These differences impose a word-order in Greek which is unsuited to Latin. He uncovers the fallacy of literal translation as a failure to grasp the degree of reorganization involved in turning one language into another.[200] It is difficult to make sense of his exclusion of the Scriptures from the general canons of translation: his view that a mysterious significance attaches to word-order in a biblical context and that a translator must have regard for this.[201] This may show that he is not entirely liberated from his Hexaplaric venture, but it is not a position which he consistently represents. Discussing his translation from Hebrew in a letter to Augustine, he states that his aim has been to express in Latin the true sense (*sensuum veritatem*) of the Hebrew rather than to preserve its word-order.[202] His clinging to *verborum ordo mysterium est* is perhaps to be associated with his exclusion of the translation of the Bible from the aesthetic canons which he otherwise applies. He combines the criticism of insensitive translators who have destroyed or obscured the sense of the original Greek or Hebrew with a caveat:

The eloquence of Cicero, which for Christ's sake you despise, is not required in small people like ourselves. The exegesis of the Church even if it possess beauty of style must conceal it and run away from it in order to address itself effectively, not to superfluous schools of philosophers and their coteries of disciples, but to human kind in its entirety.[203]

The need to make the product intelligible to all is an additional and compelling consideration for the translator of the Bible. For the most part Jerome is an honest translator, but he surrenders occasionally to bias, as when he renders Hab. iii 18 ('I will joy in the God of my salvation') 'I will joy in Jesus, my God'.[204] Another example, treated in detail elsewhere,[205] is the reading of במה (MT בָּמֶה) as בָּמָה, rendered *excelsus* in the interests of a Christological exegesis (Isa. ii 22).

At Bethlehem Jerome had the advantage of tuition from Jews who helped him with his study of Hebrew. One from Tiberias had reinforced his Hebrew scholarship in connection with his 'Hexaplaric' version of Chronicles,[206] and one named Baranina came to him by night 'like another Nicodemus' to improve his Hebrew.[207] Others were enlisted to advance his work of translation, and a Jew from Lydda, who came with a high reputation and was paid a substantial fee to unravel the linguistic complexities of the book of Job, draws from Jerome a comment which is both honest and cryptic.[208] What he seems to say is that he does not wish to overestimate the extent to which he grasped the scholarship of his tutor, but that without his help he could not have reached a level of understanding sufficient to enable him to complete the translation of Job from Hebrew into Latin.

In a letter to Pammachius (393) Jerome reports that he has translated sixteen books of the Prophets from Hebrew into Latin and that he has recently completed the book of Job.[209] All the books of the Hebrew Bible were eventually translated by him into Latin, and, with the exception of one book, it is the fruits of this enterprise which are gathered in what is now called the Vulgate. The exception is the book of Psalms which appears in our Vulgate in the 'Gallican' version. This was a second revision done from Greek versions compared with the Hebrew Bible[210] and is extant with asterisks and obeli.[211] Jerome explains that it was made necessary by the speed with which corruptions had infiltrated his first revision. The translation of the book of Psalms which Jerome made from the Hebrew is extant,[212] but it did not win acceptance in the Vulgate. It may be supposed that forces of conservatism, attaching to a book with such liturgical centrality in the Church, prevailed against Jerome's new rendering from the Hebrew. The term 'Vulgate', as applied to Jerome's work, does not appear until the thirteenth century[213] and the final ascendancy of his Vulgate or common edition (*editio vulgata*) was an outcome of the Council of Trent in the sixteenth century.

The thought of forsaking polluted streams and returning to the purest springs is one which occupies Jerome both in relation to the New Testament and the Old Testament.[214] The corrupt tradition of Latin New Testament manuscripts can be cured only by resort to the original Greek,[215] and he describes the Latin manuscripts of the Old Testament in similar terms: he learned Hebrew in order to elucidate obscurity and purify corruption.[216] All textual and translational problems are to be tested against a norm which is supplied by New Testament Greek and biblical Hebrew.[217] The poetic quality of the language ('returning to the fountain-head') lends itself to over-simplification, and, for Jerome, the textual complications of the Greek versions seemed to disappear in the presence of the textual stability of the Hebrew Bible, *the Hebraica veritas*. If he had known more, he would have seen matters differently. The Hebrew text, which he knew, had no rivals, because in the first century A.D. all of them had been suppressed. The explanation of the differences between the Hebrew Bible known to Origen and Jerome and the pre-Hexaplaric Septuagint is, in important respects, that the Greek translators had before them a Hebrew text different from the one which had ousted all rivals by the time of Origen and Jerome. Hence there is a flaw in-Jerome's *Hebraica veritas*, because it contains a wrong assumption that the Hebrew text, which he knew, was the only one that had ever obtained and that by virtue of this utter stability it gave access to the 'Hebrew truth'. Hence his statement that the Old Latin is *tertio gradu*[218] in relation to the original Hebrew loses some of its force, since the Old Latin was ultimately derived from a Hebrew text different from the one which Jerome knew. On the other hand, Jerome was right to enjoy the simplicity of translating from a form of the Hebrew text which was a sole survivor and whose authority was undisputed. Nor are modern scholars in a very different position. They are better informed about the history of the text of the Hebrew Bible, but they are largely dependent on the same Hebrew text as Jerome translated into Latin.

Jerome should not have been surprised that his enterprise awakened foreboding and opposition within the Church. It was such a novelty, so unconcealed a new beginning, that it inevitably appeared as the introduction of unsettling change and the insertion of a confusing discontinuity and instability. Augustine assigned the highest authority to the Septuagint,[219] and went to the extent of affirming that the translators were inspired prophets and that their work was the product of the Holy Spirit.[220] He pondered the full ecclesiastical consequences of adopting Jerome's new translation in the Western Church and foresaw that it would create a rift between the Eastern and Western provinces of the Church. In the East the Septuagint would continue to be the Bible of the Church, whereas in the West the Old Latin, which was a translation of the Septuagint, would no longer be used, if Jerome had his way.[221] At the more ordinary level of the Christian congregation Augustine anticipated that worshippers would be perplexed when their ears were assaulted with a new vocabulary and their expectations of hearing the familiar words and sequences of the old version were disappointed. He could discern neither wisdom nor advantage in this, only the unnecessary creation of disturbance and vexation.[222] He reported that a bishop at Oea in Tripolitania, who had been so bold as to read Jerome's new version of Jon. iv 6, had provoked a riot in the congregation.[223] It had been triggered by the disappearance of the 'gourd' (Septuagint κολόκυνθα; Old Latin *cucurbita*) from the verse and the substitution of 'ivy' (*hedera*) as a translation of קיקיון. No scholarly justification of *hedera*, even if it had been irreproachable,[224] could have made any impression on the kind of arguments which Augustine used. Nevertheless, Jerome's translation eventually prevailed, and one of the considerations which Jerome had advanced to recommend it to the Church in the face of opposition reappears in the estimate of Isidore of Seville (d. 636): it had more clarity than all others and, as the work of a Christian translator, it was more faithful.[225]

Although Jerome was subjected to Augustine's strictures about his lack of regard for the Old Latin translation, there is evidence in the commentaries which he wrote on the foundation of his translation from the Hebrew that he had not lost interest in it either as a translator or an exegete, and to this we may now turn. Jerome's commentary on Jeremiah, which was incomplete at the time of his death, will serve to establish that what is indicated by 'Septuagint' in his commentaries founded on *Hebraica veritas* is not the Hexaplaric text of Origen or Jerome's Latin expression of it. It is a pre-Hexaplaric Greek text which is not quantitatively equivalent with his Hebrew text and which, in all important respects, is the same as the Greek text in Vaticanus[226] or in Ziegler's Göttingen Septuagint.[227] From this observation it can be deduced that the Septuagint to which he refers is the type of Greek text from which the Old Latin was translated and that, in so far as he translates it into Latin when he is calling attention to it, we are brought close to the Old Latin translation. The usefulness of the book of Jeremiah in this regard is that there are many places where the Greek text is shorter than the text of the

Hebrew Bible,[228] and that at these points Jerome often, though not always, notices that the Greek text does not contain elements which are present in the Hebrew. *In LXX non habetur* is his standard way of recording this and its frequent presence in the commentary[229] demonstrates beyond all doubt that the Greek text which now captures his interest, for reasons other than text – critical ones, is a pre-Hexaplaric Greek text. A Hexaplaric Greek text has lost its significance for Jerome, because the textual concern to which it gave expression has been transcended by his translation from Hebrew into Latin. The interest which he now shows in the Septuagint and in the later Greek translations arises out of the attention which he gives to different nuances of translation and to lexicographical matters.[230]

It follows from Jerome's interest in the pre-Hexaplaric Septuagint, and so in the Old Latin, that he should be taken seriously when he professes his continued attachment to the Latin text of the Old Testament received in the Church. When he asks the question whether he is so stupid as to forget in his old age what he had learned as a child, this is more than a rhetorical flourish, and there is no reason to disbelieve the statement that in the company of his monks he kept up the practice of using the Old Latin in devotional exercises.[231] His continuing concern to bring out the sense of the Old Latin translation is shown by the attention which he pays to the Greek version from which it was translated in commentaries which are founded on his own trans-lation of the Hebrew Bible, including the Twelve Prophets which he mentions particularly in the passage just cited. He is still, as a translator, alive to the value of the nuances which can be captured from it, and as an exegete he still feels a duty to explain and interpret its renderings. So far as the other Greek versions are concerned, they have lost virtually all text-critical significance for him in his commentaries on *Hebraica veritas*, but they have an important lexicographical function to fulfil: he uses them as dictionaries of a kind and quarries meanings from them in considering problems of biblical Hebrew lexicography.

2

ANDREW OF ST VICTOR

Andrew's Old Testament scholarship is founded essentially on Jerome, on his Vulgate and on the learning available in his Old Testament commentaries. Andrew's grasp of Hebrew should not be exaggerated and such evidence as there is suggests that he did not know Greek. He conversed with Jews in French and may have had an elementary knowledge of Hebrew, but he was principally dependent on Jerome's Vulgate for his access to the Hebrew Bible.

He was a scholar of independent mind who expressed exegetical views which clashed with patristic exegesis in general and Jerome in particular. He is interesting and significant not because of the excellence of his fundamental biblical scholarship, whether as a Hebraist or a textual critic, but because of the novelty of his exegetical stance in the theological setting of the twelfth century, and because of the lively manner in which he expressed it. His concentration on the 'literal' sense of the Old Testament and the historical contexts which provide frameworks for it has a certain prophetic quality. There are intimations of issues whose outlines would appear more clearly in the future as critical biblical scholarship emerged. Already Andrew by his uncompromising pursuit of the 'literal' sense had pushed into the foreground an exegesis of the Old Testament which does not have a Christian content. In virtue of this he is an important figure in connection with the history of the Hebrew Bible in the Christian Church.

A biographical sketch

It is not known precisely when Andrew entered the Abbey of St Victor, but there is a statement by Boston of Bury that he was a canon of St Victor and a pupil of 'Master Hugh'.[1] This is supplemented by later information that he was of English nationality[2] and that he was born in England of English parents.[3] Hugh was resident at St Victor from *circa* 1118 to his death in 1141 and he taught there from *circa* 1125. The abbey of St Victor was a house of Augustinian canons regular whose rule was founded on that drawn up by Augustine for secular clergy. Though not a monk, the canon regular was cloistered and was especially devoted to sacred learning, and the abbey of St Victor, whose chief benefactors were the French royal family, had a splendid library and was a centre of vigorous intellectual life. Andrew's participation in this is evident from the appearance of his name in the *acta* of the house of St Victor in the middle of the twelfth century, where he is awarded a high place (*eminet Andreas*), and his activities as a biblical commentator are specifically mentioned.[4]

The information that Andrew was abbot of Wigmore is given in the annals of St Victor by John of Toulouse,[5] but the main source for his connections with this daughter-house of St Victor in Herefordshire is the Anglo-Norman account of the foundation of Wigmore[6] (hereafter *History*), supplemented by Annals of Wigmore (hereafter *Annals*) contained in a John Rylands Library manuscript.[7] The *History* begins with a description of the foundation of Wigmore in the reign of King Stephen (1135 – 54) and ends with the recording of a donation to the house by Roger de Mortimer I who died in 1214. In the prologue, the author of the work, an anonymous canon, claims that his account rests on traditions going back to the founder of Wigmore, Oliver de Merlimond, a steward of the Mortimers, to his son Simon, who was a canon of the house, and to others who had been connected with it. The beginnings of Wigmore were beset with difficulties: civil war created disturbed conditions in the vicinity, and its chief patron, Hugh de Mortimer, had problems in reaching an agreement with the canons about a site for the new house, so that they had unsettling experiences of moving from place to place.

They were still in this condition when they decided to elect an abbot and their choice fell on Andrew, 'a master of divinity', whom, we are told, they received with great reverence.[8] The appointment did not work out well for reasons which are obscure. It may be that Andrew did not have a head for business in relation to the needs of a new foundation, since we are informed that his successor, one Roger, a novice, was wise in managing temporalities.[9] When the canons were moved again to a site near Wigmore, they protested to their patron and he gave them permission to find a better one. At this critical juncture a difference arose between Andrew and the canons, and he left them to follow the course which they preferred (*a lor volunte*) and returned to St Victor.[10] The period in which Andrew's arrival and departure falls can be dated between the accession of Gilbert Foliot to the see of Hereford in 1147 and the struggle between Hugh de Mortimer and his new overlord, Henry II, in 1154 – 5.

Under Roger a new site was agreed between Hugh de Mortimer and the canons, and when Roger died, there was a desire to recall Andrew as abbot, a recall, we are told, which he accepted only after much persuasion by a delegation of three of the wisest of the Wigmore canons who waited on him at St Victor.[11] Andrew's return to Wigmore can be dated with the help of a letter written by Gilbert Foliot, Bishop of Hereford, to the abbot (Ernisius) and brethren of St Victor in which he lends his advocacy to the attempt of the Wigmore canons to persuade Andrew to return.[12] Ernisius was elected abbot of St Victor on the twenty-seventh of March, 1161, and Gilbert Foliot became Bishop of London on the twenty-eighth of April, 1163, so that the *terminus a quo* for the beginning of Andrew's second term of office as abbot of Wigmore is 1161 – 3. The *History* records the death of Andrew,[13] and the date of his death according to the *Annals* was 1175.[14] The foundation of the

abbey church had been laid in 1172,[15] and Andrew's successors are given as
Simon, previously prior, and Ranulphus, previously sacrist.[16] The dedication of the church in 1179 by Robert Foliot, Bishop of Hereford,[17] is
confirmed by the *History*, and Andrew's death, according to both the *History*
and the *Annals* took place between the laying of the foundation of the abbey
church and its consecration.

It can be established that Andrew commented on the Octateuch (Pentateuch, Joshua, Judges, Samuel and Kings)[18] before he worked on the
prophetical books, and that Proverbs and Ecclesiastes are the final stage of
his literary activity. Apart from the fact that he inserts references to his
commentaries on the Octateuch in his writings on the prophetical books,[19]
there is an explicit statement in his prologue to the prophets that his commentaries on the prophetical books are a resumption of what he had achieved for
the Octateuch.[20] The placing of Proverbs and Ecclesiastes last is supported
by the unfinished character of this part of his work, since it can be gathered
that he intended to comment on all of 'the books of Solomon' and these would
comprise Proverbs, Ecclesiastes and Song of Songs. Moreover, he tells us that
he undertook to write commentaries on 'Solomon's works' as a consequence
of pressure exerted by friends,[21] and there is the suggestion that at this point
he had thought his literary activity to be at an end and had been badgered
to do a little more.

The passages from Exodus and Isaiah, which feature largely in the
following sections of this chapter, are taken from the first and second phases
of his activity as an Old Testament commentator. His work on the Octateuch
probably precedes his first period at Wigmore and his work on the prophets
(and on Proverbs and Ecclesiastes) falls in the period between his return to
St Victor and his second term at Wigmore. There is a passage in his prologue to the prophets which Smalley[22] interprets as arising out of Andrew's
awareness that he might not always have the resources of a richly furnished
library to call on as he had at St Victor. His commentaries on the prophets
are then, to some extent, a compilation: with an ant-like foresight he selects
and lays up a concentration of literary treasures, reducing them to a form
which will enable him, wherever he may be in his personal poverty, to have
possession of them.

His environment and influence

We may think of Andrew as set between his master, Hugh, and his critic,
Richard, and ask what is special about him. Smalley[23] tells us that Stephen
Langton, glossing the Octateuch in lectures which he delivered in Paris in
the eighties of the twelfth century, quotes Andrew seventeen times in connection with the literal sense of passages in the Pentateuch, whereas Hugh
appears in his glosses only four times. Roger Bacon[24] was anxious about the
reputation which Andrew had acquired as an expositor of the literal sense and
was concerned to establish that he did not have the standing within the

Catholic Church to warrant the 'authority' which was attached to his name and his work.

In the opening decades of the twelfth century Hugh, as abbot of St Victor, acquired the reputation among his contemporaries of being a second Augustine.[25] He was not only or principally a biblical scholar and his concern with the Bible and the Hebrew Bible, to which he had access only through patristic sources and conversations with Jewish scholars in French, was only a subordinate part of the grand scheme of study to which he was committed. In this the Bible came second in importance, higher than the arts and sciences, but lower than doctrine and monastic contemplation. For Hugh the literal sense of the Old Testament was not a scholarly pursuit which could become an end in itself disengaged from the ultimate goal of the spiritual sense, that is Christian exegesis, to which it was expected to contribute. Sometimes the literal sense was a foundation for the higher reaches of exegesis, and in so far as it performed this service it deserved attention. In these circumstances it was important that the literal sense which was assumed should be correct, since the final product had to be manufactured from the appropriate raw material – the literal sense was the wax of the honeycomb.[26]

It would not be misleading to connect this emphasis with a greater willingness to admit a literal sense and to attend to it in a consideration of Old Testament texts, instead of leaping immediately to a Christian exegesis. A good example of Hugh's practice in this regard is afforded by Gen. xiv 18, where he remarks that the bread and wine given by Melchisedek to Abraham is a sign of peace *inter gentiles*, analogous to the offering of an olive branch. There is a history of exegetical controversy associated with this verse which has patristic foundations.[27] Hugh also connects Melchisedek's gesture with his priestly office: he offers (*proferens*) bread and wine to Abraham as a priest, and sacramental significance is to be attached to it, but Hugh does not advance a spiritual interpretation in terms of the Christian sacrament.[28]

In his criticism of Andrew Richard assumes that the preservation of the integrity of Hugh's exegetical structure is paramount, and that the study of the literal sense of the Old Testament must be subordinated to it and regulated by its grand intention and final outcome: the establishing of a Christian sense for Old Testament passages and a demonstration that they are an illustration and confirmation of Catholic doctrine. He finds in Andrew's explorations of the literal sense evidences of rashness and distance from Catholic exegetical sentiment, especially where Andrew is reproducing Jewish opinions, and he focuses his dissatisfaction on Andrew's methods with regard to Isa. vii 14 ('Behold a virgin will conceive and bear a son'); 'He gives the Jewish objections or questions without answering them; he seems to give the palm to them, since he leaves these matters unsolved.'[29]

Richard's chagrin is understandable for reasons which will be more particularly considered later in this chapter. His outburst indicates that Andrew has stepped out of line in crucial respects and has made a departure which appears intolerable to Catholic exegetical orthodoxy. The study of the literal sense of the Old Testament cannot be allowed such ill-considered or thoughtless freedom; it must remain leashed to the pursuit of Christian truth and must not rise above its lowly station within the exegetical system. From this point of view, Andrew's pupil who jumps to his master's defence, cuts little ice with Richard: 'Do not call it my master's opinion but the Jews', for, of course, he put it forward not as his own but as their's.'[30] To which Richard replies: 'It is precisely that matter which is unclear, whether he is giving it as his own opinion or as an alien [Jewish]one.'[31] The rejoinder that Andrew is without question simply reproducing Jewish opinions makes no impression on Richard. Andrew ought to have made perfectly clear when he was advancing a true opinion which was his own and when a false opinion which was Jewish.[32]

What is exceptional about Andrew does not reside in his knowledge of Hebrew, nor in the circumstance that he was in immediate contact with the text of the Hebrew Bible and made exegetical decisions on that basis. An attempt will be made later to justify this statement, but it will be convenient for the moment simply to consider it in general outline. In the light of it Roger Bacon's view of Andrew's significance and the nature of his contribution does not seem to be especially acute, although it should be granted that the text on which he focuses (Gen. ii 4–5) in pursuing his disagreement with Andrew is one of the more impressive fragments of evidence that Andrew might have had a particular knowledge of the Hebrew Bible.[33] It does not, however, demand such an explanation, but it is notable that in connection with Gen. ii 4–5 Andrew offers a Latin translation and a punctuation which accords with the Hebrew text and conflicts with the Vulgate, and it is on this that Bacon's disagreement with him turns.[34] It is Andrew's view of the punctuation with which Bacon expressly disagrees, maintaining that the sense runs on in verse 5 and that Vulgate *herbam* is correct, because it is the object of *fecit Dominus Deus* (verse 4). According to Bacon verse 5 has no element of negation in it and is sub specie affirmativa (*antequam* and *priusquam*). Thus Bacon rejects *et omne virgultum nondum fiebat in terra, et omnis herba regionis nondum germinavit*. Andrew explains verse 5 correctly: et est sensus sic per negationem: nullum virgultum agri adhuc oriebatur in terra; nulla herba regionis adhuc germinabat (cf. RSV, 'When no plant of the field was yet in the earth and no herb of the field had yet sprung up').

The passage is a celebrated exegetical crux, associated with the *simul* of Ecclus. xviii 1, on which Augustine, Bede and Andrew's master, Hugh, had expressed opinions.[35] Andrew explains 'day' in verse 4 not as a reference to 'instantaneous creation' but as 'period', and regards the verse as a brief recapitulation of what has gone before. Andrew's account of ii 5ff. has some resemblance to that of Bede and clearly differs from those of Augustine and Hugh. Moses 'from this verse onwards [referring to verse 5] explains more amply and clearly what before he ran through briefly [in i 1–ii 4], in order to show what was done on which day. He dwells, with especial care, on the things which concern the common use of man, and which the untaught, less gifted mind, can understand.'[36] Scholars have been misled by a wrong translation and by dragging in a text (Ecclus. xviii 1) which has no contribution to make and which distracts attention from what Moses is saying in the only passage which counts.[37] Gen. ii 4 is recapitulation, but not the kind of recapitulation which is incompatible with what precedes it: 'In a recapitulation something is often added, but not so as to destroy what goes before. It has been said above [i 1 – ii 3] that God made all things on six different days. Therefore, to say in a recapitulation that he made all things together (*simul*), this is not to add something to what is said above, but wholly to destroy it.'[38]

The making of a point by departing from the Vulgate and appealing to the Hebrew (secundum veritatem Hebraicam) in so effective a manner as this is not typical of Andrew, so far as can be gathered from the range of his exegesis which is available in Smalley[39] and Hadfield.[40] For the most part, despite the fragments of Hebrew lexicography which appear in his work, Andrew's basis is the Vulgate and it is this Latin text on which he is commenting. Hence, influenced by the case of Gen. ii 4 – 5, Bacon's suggestion, that the root of the matter is Andrew's forsaking of the Vulgate,[41] should not be accepted. It follows that the consolation prize which he awards to Andrew, with the stipulation that he does not possess authority and that the Church has not granted such authority to anyone subsequent to Bede,[42] is not one which enables us to reach the centre of Andrew's distinctiveness and significance. There are, says Bacon, unelucidated obscurities in the Vulgate and these have to be further investigated with the help of the Hebrew text. In so far as Andrew has provided an impetus for this kind of activity his influence has been salutary: 'Few would take thought for the true explanation of this passage [Gen. ii 4 – 5] and many others, unless they had seen how Andrew treats it.'[43]

We may, however, agree with Bacon that Andrew was a learned man and approve of the caution of his statement that he probably knew Hebrew,[44] while urging that the originality of Andrew and the impact which he made on the exegesis of the Old Testament in the Middle Ages were not principally connected with his powers as a Hebraist. The case of Gen. ii 4 – 5 (and there are others to be considered) does raise the question whether Andrew was capable of reading the Hebrew Bible. It will be seen that while there are a few pieces of evidence which might seem to demand a positive answer to this question, there are more weighty counter-indications that any knowledge of Hebrew which he had must have been exiguous. Hadfield[45] reconstructs a tutorial in which Andrew might have participated as a pupil and she supposes that he had the text of a Hebrew Bible before him. She pictures a scene in which he follows the Hebrew text laboriously from one word to the next, endeavouring to relate the exegesis which he hears from his Jewish instructor to the elements of the text.

The question about the nature of Andrew's distinctiveness, and the reasons for the impact which he made, has still not been answered, and it has to be recognized that an uncomplicated answer is difficult to achieve. Andrew is clearly unconventional, but he preserves some of the conventions of mediaeval

Christian exegesis of the Old Testament. For example, he is capable of outbursts against the Jews, of miscalling them and charging them with falsehood and obfuscation in their exegesis of the Hebrew Bible,[46] and yet one of his prime characteristics in his pursuit of the literal sense is the attention he pays to Jewish exegesis and the detailed treatment which he offers of it. It is true that his anti-Jewish polemic is infrequent, but its presence in any measure creates a problem which receives different explanations. Again, as an exegete devoted to the literal sense, he is sparing in his Christological exegesis of the Old Testament, but this does appear. It is apparently not a kind of interpretation which fires his enthusiasm and awakens his intellectual curiosity. Even when he represents it, he leaves it to pursue other paths.[47] Nevertheless, an unevenness is perceived and there are different ways of explaining or explaining away Andrew's inconcinnities.

In general, Smalley's view[48] of this is to be preferred to that of Hadfield: it is better to regard Andrew as having a somewhat low awareness of the system of Catholic exegesis of the Old Testament, within which he should have been operating, than to attribute to him a high degree of appreciation of the dangers which he was running. He is then not greatly bothered by anxiety or wariness. While he pursues the 'literal' sense, he does not nicely calculate the obligatory bows which should be made to Catholic exegetical authority in order to ensure his survival. Certainly he is not a 'spiritual anarchist'[49] who has set his mind on destroying the doctrines of the Church, and it would conflict with what has just been said to suppose that Andrew had any intention of engaging in controversy or undermining the foundations of Catholic exegesis of the Old Testament. He was not spoiling for a fight, trying to make a name for himself as a demolition agent, issuing a challenge to an exegetical system by claiming autonomy for one of its parts. We may suppose that the self-depreciatory tones in which he refers to his enterprise are overdone and that he thinks of himself more highly than his utterances would suggest, but there is something authentic about the offhand character of these: he has no wish to set himself up as a teacher or to acquire a reputation as an exegetical authority;[50] he follows the paths which awaken his interest and curiosity, and, squirrel-like, he amasses a store of knowledge which will always be accessible to him in the future.[51]

When Hadfield represents that Andrew is consciously and deliberately advancing the literal sense out of a Christian theological concern, that he has the objectives of Catholic exegesis always in mind and that he is breaking new ground as a pioneer in Old Testament theology, she is contradicting the account of his temperament and the cast of his mind which has already been given. Thus she has this to say:

Although he himself in his explanation concentrates very much on the historical side of the prophecies, he makes it clear all the same that these events are mentioned only because they are an expression of the divine purpose. That is to say, even when he is interpreting the historical sense of the book, he is not dealing with ordinary history, but with a history of a completely different nature, namely, the history of God's dealing with mankind, which is the history of salvation. It gives a deeper meaning to Andrew's understanding of what was regarded as 'the surface of the letter'. His historical interests enabled him in this way to acquire a more comprehensive view of what we are now used to call the 'theology of the Old Testament' than most of his contemporaries had.[52]

The reverse of all this would seem to be nearer the truth. What is special about Andrew's historical interest is that it is not cribbed or constricted by any theological scheme, that he has liberated history from such a confinement as is indicated by the tailoring which Hadfield describes. He has departed from such emasculated history, although not through a disavowal of it or a desire to destroy it. He still affirms it somewhere at the periphery of his mind, but what awakens his intellectual interest is precisely 'ordinary history', that is to say, the human scene and Israel's life in the ancient world. This had profound theological implications for the exegesis of the Hebrew Bible within the Christian Church, but Andrew was probably not aware of them and did not pursue his work in the light of the knowledge of them. We shall see that although he established, in new respects, a human dimension for the Old Testament within the Christian Church, his untendentious interest in the human and the historical does not make him into a 'higher critic' in the modern sense.

How far from the centre of his intellectual interest Christian theology lies may be illustrated by his treatment of Isa. xi 10, where he is absorbed in the problem created by 'root of Jesse' over against 'shoot of Jesse' in xi 1. He supposes that xi 1 requires both a historical and a Messianic interpretation, but he does not offer a Christological one.[53] When he comes to xi 10, he comments that 'root of Jesse' is a puzzling expression and his main concern is to address himself to its elucidation. In the course of this he introduces the possibility of a Christological exegesis (Messias sive Christus noster) which we would have expected to appear in connection with xi 1. It is as if he had recalled it from the edge of his mind as in item of Catholic affirmation which he ought to make.[54]

When all this has been considered, what ought to be said is that Andrew had a blessed amnesia which made him oblivious, for the most part, to the theological dangers which he might be running. It is a mistake to represent him (as Hadfield does) as a shrewd tactician covering his tracks with various devices, leaving out this and inserting that, seized with a care and anxiety not to give offence or topple over the edge of orthodoxy into heresy. He is not himself a critical, biblical scholar, but the autonomy of his humanism, pursued without any doctrinal impediments, was incompatible with the exegetical process of distilling a scheme of Christian truth from the Old Testament, disengaged from the historical and human connections of that book, although he was not aware of all these implications. Moreover, this investigation, which he pursues for its own sake, is a fundamental constituent of the critical attitude to the Old Testament which gradually emerged within the Christian Church in the succeeding centuries: an awareness that these are historical documents which have a time, a place and a setting, which were written by human authors and whose primary sense must be sought by bringing all these factors into play. It was the freshness of his work in the field of Old Testament study and the freedom with which he exercised his interest, not with a controversial intent nor burdened with any acute anxiety, which made such an impression on his successors. It was a new departure in the search for the literal sense. This is the heart of the matter, not his powers as a Hebraist (which he does not possess), nor his technical excellence as an exegete (since he does not always faithfully seek the sense of a text) and not even his plundering of the resources of Jewish exegesis. It is clear that he was fascinated by Jewish exegesis, but this was because he already had a thirst and was searching after a well at which to slake it. His concentration on the historical sense (ad historicum quidem spectantia sensum)[55] is a native bent determined by the cast of his own mind, rather than a copying of Jewish exegetical methods.[56]

Andrew and Hebrew scholarship

Among the different indications which Andrew gives of the influence exercised on him by Jewish scholarship,[57] only two (*secundum Hebraicum veritatem* and *in Hebreo habet*) need be construed as a claim for support from the text of the Hebrew Bible, while the others[58] may be associated with a more general kind of reporting of Jewish exegetical opinions. In assessing how much contact, if any, Andrew had with the text of the Hebrew Bible general features which should be considered are the absence of Hebrew script and the paucity of transliteration from Hebrew.[59] Not to mince words, it is plain that Andrew's text is, for the most part, the Vulgate and that he is not doing Jerome's work over again. He did not have the linguistic equipment necessary for a fundamental reappraisal of Jerome's translation from Hebrew into Latin, and there is a serious reason for doubting whether he knew any Greek. There is a lack of interest in the Septuagint, and such references to the later Greek versions as appear are probably mostly culled from Jerome, whether directly or indirectly.

Hence Andrew depends heavily on Jerome's translation for his access to the Hebrew Bible, and it is an advantage to establish this fact at the outset. He is not returning to the source, as Jerome did, and making up his own mind about the sense of the Hebrew text. He is, for the most part, launching his distinctive literal and historical exegesis of the Old Testament from the platform of Jerome's Vulgate. In what respects then is this dependence modified by Jewish influences? Since we are enquiring in this section specifically about Andrew's powers as a Hebraist and the degree of access which he had to the Hebrew text, more general kinds of Jewish exegetical influence may be left out of the reckoning. In so far as these are exegetical, have been conveyed in conversations with Jews, and do not turn on particular matters of Hebrew text, lexicography and grammar, they can make no contribution to the resolution of the questions which are being asked in this section.

We are thrown back on what purport to be references to the Hebrew text. The point has been made that a few of these betray a misunderstanding on the part of Andrew, and that he has mistaken an exegetical opinion conveyed to him verbally by a Jew for a lexicographical or translational one. In the case of Exod. xxvii 1 – 5[60] this may be too harsh a conclusion, and another reading of the evidence would be that Andrew is not undertaking to do any more than transmit Jewish descriptions of the object indicated by the word מזבח 'altar'. If so, Iudei ubicumque nos aram dicimus, dicunt aream ('Wherever we say "altar", the Jews say "cavity"') is not an assertion, as Hadfield supposes, that *parietes aree* ('walls enclosing a space') is a rendering of what appears in the Hebrew text, where the Vulgate rendering is *altare* ('altar'). Andrew is saying no more, probably, than that the rendering of מזבח by *aram* is misleading, because a מזבח is not an altar of the kind conjured up by the Latin *aram*. Hugh[61] had already connected this passage with Exod. xx 24 and had described מזבח similarly, but Hadfield is persuaded that Andrew is indebted to a Jewish opinion. There is no doubt that Rashi's account is in accord with Andrew's. Commenting on Exod. xxvii 1 – 5 he alludes to Exod. xx 24: 'For the earthen altar there spoken of is identical with the bronze altar described here, and it was called an earthen altar, because they used to fill the hollow space within it [that is, within its bronze walls] with earth, at every place where they camped in the wilderness.'[62] The outcome of this enquiry is that Andrew is seen to be explaining what kind of construction a מזבח actually is and that his comment is not a textual claim of the kind which Hadfield supposes. It is rather an exegetical note on *aram*: an attempt to tease out what is unelucidated and misleading in the translation of מזבח by *aram*.

Another example where Hadfield's interpretation of a reference by Andrew to the Hebrew text may be called in question is Exod. xv 13.[63] Andrew has a comment on *Quem redemisti*[64] and it should be noticed that he is not claiming (*ut aiunt*) that he has read the Hebrew text. He is, according to Hadfield, wrongly supposing that קנית 'buy', which appears at verse 16, is also the verb at verse 13, which, however, has גאלת 'redeem'. On *possedisti*[65] (verse 16) Andrew remarks, in Hebreo comparasti vel emisti ('In Hebrew "you have purchased or bought"'). In judging this, the almost identical character of the word-strings at verse 13 and verse 16 has to be noticed, and also the evidence from Ruth iv (verses 4, 5, 8, 9, 10) that גאל and קנה function as synonyms and that the 'buy' or 'ransom' nuance suits the Old Testament context of גאל. Hence Andrew's comment at verse 13, in all probability, does not rest on a mistaken supposition that קנית appears in the Hebrew text of that verse, but on an exegetical elucidation of גאל in terms of קנה.[66] The need for this is of the same kind as was discussed in connection with מזבח at Exod. xxvii 1 – 5.[67] Andrew is concerned that *redemisti* should be interpreted in the context of the obligations and functions of the Old Testament גָּאַל ('redeemer') and that 'redeem' should not be drawn into the sphere of Christian theology.

At Exod. vi 12⁶⁸ and Isa. xi 15⁶⁹ there are, on the other hand, signs of confusion between translation and exegesis in Andrew's comments. On *cum incircumcisus sim labiis* (Exod. vi 12) he has, ut obstrusis, quod in Hebreo est, labiis loquentem audire possit, and Rashi, 'tongue-tied',⁷⁰ interprets עֲרַל שְׂפָתִים 'uncircumcised of lips' similarly. Andrew's *quod in Hebreo est* creates confusion, because if he has a point against the Vulgate, it is that *cum incircumcisus sim labiis* is too literal a rendering of the Hebrew, not that the Hebrew text is misrepresented by the Vulgate. Hence he is mixing up a translational matter with a textual one, and his comment has significance only as an observation that a freer rendering than that of the Vulgate is needed to bring out the sense of עֲרַל שְׂפָתִים – that the Vulgate's literal translation is under-translation (cf. NEB, 'How will Pharaoh listen to such a halting speaker as I am?').

On *Et desolabit* (Isa. xi 15) Andrew has, in Hebreo planius: siccabit, and Hadfield notices Rashi's comment on וְהֶחֱרִים, 'To dry it up, so that the exiled of Israel returning from Egypt might pass over it.'⁷¹ It does appear that Andrew has mistaken an interpretation of וְהֶחֱרִים which he heard from Jews as a lexicographical comment. It could be argued that the sense of the verse is better served by *siccabit*, which is indicated by the Septuagint (καὶ ἐρημώσει) and other versions, and which points to וְהֶחֱרִיב, but these are considerations which are outside Andrew's range.

Thus, on closer examination Andrew does not come so badly out of this as Hadfield represents, but even where he is not in error or clouded by misapprehension, the quality of his notes do not, for the most part, inspire great confidence in his acuteness as a Hebraist. For reasons which will be readily understood references to grammar, syntax and punctuation are better indicators than lexicographical notes on single words of the Hebrew text. They enjoy this superiority, because it is a simpler matter for a non-Hebraist to report opinions which he has heard about the meanings of individual words than to make translational and exegetical points which depend on a grasp of the syntactical structure of a verse or a group of verses written in Hebrew. It should be said, however, that the grammatical comments which Andrew makes tend to have the same degree of isolation as his lexicographical notes and not to furnish a decisive indication that he was capable of reading Hebrew, as the following examples will show.

Exod. xx 3, 'You shall have no other god to set before me' (NEB); Isa. i 12, 'No more shall you trample my courts' (NEB): At Exod. xx 3⁷² Andrew comments on *non habebis* (לֹא יִהְיֶה לְךָ): idioma est Hebree lingue futurum indicativi pro presenti imperativi ponere. Again at Isa. i 12⁷³ on *non apponetis* (לֹא תוֹסִיפוּ) he remarks, More Hebraico futurum indicativi pro presenti imperativi et coniunctivi posuit. Sic et in lege frequenter invenimus: *non occides* (לֹא תִרְצָח 'You shall not commit murder', Exod. xx 13). Andrew does not reproduce any Hebrew, but the examples which he uses are correct. However, he does not state the principle correctly, since he neglects to say that the usage applies only to negative imperatives, and he is perhaps transmitting a piece of grammatical information which he has gathered from Jews, rather than explaining a feature of Hebrew which he knew at first-hand. In that case, when he says that he has found this usage frequently 'in the Law', he is referring to the Vulgate and not to his reading of the Hebrew text. He is saying that he has recognized that the *non occides* type of construction, as it occurs in the Decalogue, for example, is the equivalent of a negative imperative or prohibition.

Exod. xxv 4, NEB, 'and scarlet yarn', for Hebrew שני ותולעת: Commenting on *coccumque bis tinctum* Andrew remarks Lanam bis coccineo colore tinctam, ut multum rubea sit. In Hebreo tamen non habet bis tinctum.[74] Hadfield's supposition that the Vulgate text is 'a description of the Hebrew pleonasm' is wrong. She is referring to ותולעת שני taken as 'and crimson cloth dyed with scarlet', or the like, with which she connects Andrew's comment. But like Andrew she is unaware that *bis* is a rendering of שְׁנִי 'second' (Septuagint, καὶ κόκκινον διπλοῦν), as opposed to שָׁנִי 'scarlet'. This suggests that Andrew was not in touch with the Hebrew text. Someone had told him that the pointing of the Hebrew Bible indicated 'scarlet' for שני, but he had no insight into the reason for the Vulgate text – a different pointing of שני from that of the Massoretic text.

Isa. liii 2, NEB, 'whose roots are in parched ground': Andrew wrongly claims the support of the Hebrew Bible (sicut in Hebreo est) for *inhabitabilis* over against Vulgate *sitienti* 'parched' as a rendering of ציה.[75] Jerome[76] has a note on Aquila's translation of ציה (*invia*) and the semantic connection between 'trackless' and 'uninhabitable' can be discerned. The thought of regions unexplored where settlement had not been contemplated perhaps appeared to Andrew better accommodated to his exegesis than a drought-stricken land (ציה): Although treated with disdain by the Gentiles, Israel will grow swiftly in Yahweh's presence (*coram eo* interpreted as *coram Domino*) like a root planted in virgin soil. It is by such a train of thought that Jerome connects the verse with the Virgin Birth.[77]

The most interesting cases of this type of evidence are those where Andrew's lack of grasp appears in connection with textual or lexicographical particulars which have important exegetical implications and which have featured in the history of the exegesis of the Hebrew Bible. He fails to relate these to their source in a manner which one would have expected of a Hebraist. Two examples can be found in Andrew's handling of Num. xxiv 3(15) and Isa. ii 22, the second even more interesting than the first. In the case of the Numbers passage Andrew disagrees with the Vulgate (*cuius obturatus est oculus*) and claims support from the Hebrew and from Origen for *cuius revelatus est oculus* (NEB, 'whose insight is clear'). Andrew delivers his judgement in a rollicking style:

The Hebrew and Origen's translation has: *whose eye is opened*. The reading fits into the context, whereas the translation which we use is quite contrary to this same context. But to struggle with a false reading is not only idle; it is madness. Since all the rest of Balaam's speech is in praise of himself, why should he blame himself in this alone? Moreover when immediately afterwards he says that his eyes are *opened* [verse 16] why should he say here that they are *stopped up*, which is such a contradiction?[78]

The Septuagint (ὁ ἀληθινῶς ὁρῶν) is too far removed from the Hebrew text to help us very much with שתם העין, but it is clearly incompatible with *cuius obturatus est oculus*. Otherwise, the extent of Andrew's Greek scholarship is unclear, since the support which he claims from Origen could be attributed to a confusion: he may be referring to Hexaplaric material relating to Num. xxiv 4[79] in which καὶ ἀποκεκαλυμμένοι οἱ ὀφθαλμοὶ αὐτῶν is a translation of וגלוי עינים and not of ושתם העין (verses 3, 15). Moreover, Andrew's exegesis is not so self-evidently correct as he represents, and those who argued that Balaam's foresight is attributed to the eye of the mind rather than the eye of sense were not manifestly advancing an absurd opinion.[80] The principal matter, however, is that if Andrew had possessed the necessary linguistic knowledge, we would have expected him to elucidate the Hebrew readings from which the two different translations arise: that the vocalization שֻׁתֻם העין (שתם = סתם 'shut') is represented in the Vulgate and that שְׁתֻם העין is the source of *cuius revelatus est oculus*. This he fails to do.

Isa. ii 22, NEB 'Have no more to do with man, for what is he worth?': This verse contains one of Andrew's disagreements with Jerome; there is no doubt that he has much the better of the exegetical argument and that he uses the context skilfully to demolish Jerome's Christological exegesis, founded on *Quia excelsus reputatus est ipse* (Vulgate):

But according to the Jews, who for *high* (*excelsus*) read *in what*? (for the Hebrew word means either *high* or *in what*?) it can be read thus: Ye who in the day of the vengeance of the Lord, when Nabuchodonosor king of Babylon shall fight against us, shall put your trust in king Pharaoh, and your fleshly arm, that is Egypt, who is man not God, *cease from* him, that is: cease from your vain hopes in him, *for in what is he reputed*, either by God or men? As though to say: 'He is nothing and of no import, sufficing not even to himself. Pharaoh is a broken reed to all who put their hopes in him.'[81]

כי במה נחשב הוא is certainly an allusion to the ultimate frailty of men, however lofty their pretensions and is not 'a manifest prophecy of Christ',[82] but it is striking that Andrew is so coy or periphrastic in relation to a precise matter of Hebrew vocalization on which his exegetical argument turns. If he had had immediate access to the Hebrew Bible, we would have expected at least a transliteration. What is offered by Andrew has the appearance of a piece of information passed on by a non-Hebraist: 'But according to the Jews, who for *high* read *in what*? (for the Hebrew word means either *high* or *in what*?).' Anyone with a quite modest ability to read the Hebrew Bible would have been able to say that במה should be vocalized as בַּמֶּה and not associated with בָּמָה ('high-place' – Jerome).

There is a small group of examples, where Andrew's comments penetrate to the syntactical structure of the Hebrew and which must be regarded as containing the most positive indications that he may have had an elementary knowledge of the language. One of these (Gen. ii 4 – 5) has already been considered[83] and a few others merit examination.

Exod. iv 26, NEB 'So the LORD let Moses alone': Andrew's treatment of this verse is said by Hadfield[84] to hint at a basic knowledge of Hebrew, but it appears unnatural to a Hebraist reading his comments that he makes particular points about Hebrew lexicography, grammar and punctuation without reproducing or transliterating any Hebrew. In the first place he disagrees with *Et dimisit eum* 'And she left him' (Vulgate) as a translation of וילך ממנו, with the comment: In Hebreo *relaxavit eum*, id est cessavit ab eo. He also notices a difference of punctuation as between the Massoretic text and the Vulgate: the break in sense which is indicated by the *athnach* at ממנו is not observed by the Vulgate which renders אז wrongly as *postquam* and allows the sense to run on. Moreover, as Andrew notes, the Vulgate translation is incompatible with Hebrew grammar, because it presupposes a feminine subject (Zipporah), whereas the subject of וילך ממנו must be masculine (יהוה – verse 24). In all these matters Andrew's criticism of the Vulgate is just and the translation indicated by him is the one which appears in NEB: 'During the journey, while they were encamped for the night, the LORD met Moses, meaning to kill him, but Zipporah picked up a sharp flint, cut off her son's foreskin, and touched him with it saying "You are my blood-bridegroom". So the LORD let Moses alone.'

Exod. iv 25, NEB 'a sharp flint' (צר): Andrew's criticism of *acutissimam petram*[85] is less impressive, though it is not clear that he mistook an exegetical comment for a philological statement, as Hadfield maintains.[86] Andrew's *ferrum acutissimum* is wrong because the blade is flint and not iron, whereas his *cultrum acutissimum* is defective because it does not indicate that the knife is flint. Nor does his note on צר[87] repair these faults. If there is anything deficient about the Vulgate, it can only be that *petram* is too general a rendering for 'flint', but Andrew does not remedy this with *aciem* which gives no indication that צר is 'flint'.

Isa. xl 3, NEB 'There is a voice that cries: "Prepare a road for the LORD through the wilderness"': The Vulgate renders the Hebrew, *Vox clamantis in deserto: parate viam Domini*, and it is this understanding of the verse which is applied to the mission of John the Baptist in the New Testament (Jn i 23). On *vox clamantis* (קול קורא) Andrew comments,[88] vel secundum Hebreos: *clamans*. This is an interesting matter of punctuation, but the formula which Andrew uses here (*secundum Hebreos*) suggests that he had it at second-hand from Jews rather than that he discovered it himself through direct inspection of the Hebrew text. The punctuation of the Hebrew Bible gives the sense: 'A voice is crying out: "Prepare the way of the Lord in the desert"', while the Vulgate has, 'A voice of one crying out in the desert: "Prepare the way of the Lord".' This agrees with the Septuagint, and we may conclude that the form of the Old Latin has here been maintained in the Vulgate. Andrew offers three exegeses, and if we focus on two of them, we find that one (*vox clamans*) does not sustain the application of the verse to John the Baptist in the New Testament, while the other (*vox clamantis*) is compatible with it, although Andrew does not make the connection with John the Baptist.

Interesting negative evidence against the claim that Andrew was in some measure a Hebraist comes to light in connection with his comments on Isa.i 12, 14, 22, and the significance of it is not discerned by Hadfield.[89]

Isa. i 12, RSV 'Who requires of you this trampling of my courts?': Andrew comments on *Ut ambularetis in atriis meis*, In Hebreo planius: *calcare atrium meum non apponetis*.[90] Hadfield notices a rendering which appears in Jerome's commentary on Isaiah, *Calcare atrium meum non apponetis*[91] and suggests that this is the source of Andrew's alleged Hebrew text. In Jerome's commentary the translation of verse 12 agrees with the Vulgate (with the addition of *enim*) as far as *manibus vestris*, but, in disagreement with the Vulgate (*ut ambularetis in atriis meis*) רמס חצרי 'to trample my courts' is connected with what follows ('Do not continue to trample my courts') and not with what precedes. Hadfield's supposition[92] that Jerome has mistranslated הביא (verse 13) and that *non apponetis* can be explained on this assumption is mistaken. Jerome does not cite his rendering of verse 13 beyond *apponetis*, but a comparison with the Septuagint, which has the same punctuation, shows up the pattern of Jerome's translation clearly. It is evident that οὐ προσθήσεσθε is a rendering of לא תוסיפו and is to be equated with Jerome's *non apponetis* and that הביא is rendered by ἐὰν φέρητε.

Isa. i 14, NEB 'They have become a burden to me': The Vulgate renders the verse as *Facta sunt mihi molesta*, and *molesta* 'burdensome' represents Hebrew טרח, a word which occurs only here and at Deut.i 12 in the Hebrew Bible and which is usually translated 'burden' in agreement with the Vulgate. Andrew's comment runs, In Hebreo *facti estis mihi in satietatem*.[93] In his commentary on Isaiah Jerome produces the rendering, *Facti mihi estis in satietatem*,[94] so it is clear that the source of Andrew's ostensible Hebrew text is once again Jerome. Moreover, an examination of the Septuagint discloses the same text: the change from the third person plural of the Hebrew text (היו) to a second person plural (*estis*; ἐγενήθητέ) and the rendering of טרח as 'satiety' (*satietatem*; πλησμονήν). Thus the correspondences are exactly those noted at Isa.i 12.

Isa. 1 22, NEB 'Your liquor is diluted with water': Commenting on the Vulgate's rendering of this verse (*Vinum tuum mistum est aqua*) Andrew remarks, Huic sententie consonat alia translatio, que congruit Hebraice veritati: *Caupones tui miscent vinum aqua*[95] ('Your merchants mix wine with water.') מהול occurs only here in biblical Hebrew, and means 'circumcise' in post-biblical Hebrew. The Latin idiom *vinum castrare* has been noticed[96] and the likelihood is that the sense at Isa.i 22 is 'diluted' (NEB), as the Vulgate and Andrew suppose. The main matter, however, is the appearance of *caupones* in Andrew's rendering, to which nothing corresponds in the Hebrew text. Here again we find the same web of correspondences as at Isa. i 12 and 14. In his commentary Jerome offers the rendering, *Caupones tui miscent vinum aqua*,[97] and this accords with the Septuagint (οἱ κάπηλοί σου μίσγουσι τὸν οἶνον). Hadfield has noticed that this closely resembles a comment made by Rashi on the Hebrew ('Those who supply you with alcohol mix it with water'),[98] but Andrew's source is obviously Jerome as it was in the other cases.[99]

The Latin renderings offered by Jerome in his commentary on Isaiah at i 12, 14 and 22 agree with the text of the Septuagint and are unmistakeable translations of the Septuagint. This means that they are examples of the Old Latin text, which was a translation of the Septuagint, and that they are at two removes from the Hebrew Bible. Andrew, therefore, is committing a capital error in appealing to the Old Latin with such phrases as *in Hebreo planius* (verse 12), *in Hebreo* (verse 14) and *alia translatio que congruit Hebraice veritati* (verse 22). What Andrew presents as *Hebraica veritas* in his disagreement with the Vulgate is the condition of distance from the Hebrew text which dissatisfied Jerome and drove him to translate from Hebrew into Latin and so produce the Vulgate. Andrew forsakes Jerome's Latin expression of *Hebraica veritas*, ostensibly to be more faithful to the Hebrew, but he falls into absurdity because he cites a Latin text which was a translation from the Septuagint and so distant from the Hebrew. This can hardly be reconciled with the view that Andrew had direct access to the Hebrew Bible and was capable of reading it. Moreover, it is incompatible with a supposition that he knew Greek, since in that case we would have expected him to recognize the parentage of the Latin text for which he made false claims.

Andrew as an interpreter of the Vulgate

Enough has been done to show that Andrew was neither a 'twelfth-century Hebraist'[100] nor 'a second Jerome'.[101] It has become evident that he did not have the Hebrew scholarship to do all over again the fundamental work which Jerome did when he translated the Hebrew Bible into Latin. At best Andrew is doing no more than taking nibbles at the Hebrew Bible, probably on the basis of information acquired verbally from Jews, rather than by inspecting it himself, but otherwise his access to it is through Jerome's Latin version of *Hebraica veritas*. Hence his considerable achievements as a commentator, the interest which he awakens and the influence which he exerts, are not the consequence of his knowledge of Hebrew or his immediate access to the Hebrew Bible, but are compatible with his reliance, for the most part, on the foundation which Jerome laid – the Vulgate. We are still at a great distance from the Renaissance and from the emergence of Christian Hebraists capable of going behind Jerome's fundamental work and dealing with the Hebrew Bible *ab initio*. A consideration of Andrew's exegesis launched from the platform of the Vulgate is then one which merits some attention.

We may begin with linguistic comments which are made by Andrew on the basis of the Vulgate, whether or not he supposes that they relate to the Hebrew text. On Isa. i 7 (NEB 'Strangers devour your land before your eyes'), where the Vulgate has *regionem vestram coram vobis alieni devorant*, Andrew comments[102] that the present tense is used proleptically to convey the certainty that an event which still lies in the future will eventuate. The Hebrew form is participial (אכלים), but Andrew makes no claim that he is founding his opinion on the Hebrew text. Rather he is adopting an exegetical stance to the context as he gathers it from the Latin, and is maintaining, probably correctly, that the reference is not to events which are already taking place: the present tense is a device of literary style and is an instrument of the overpowering conviction that the events so described will inevitably unfold.

Another argument with linguistic connections can be inspected at Isa.i 9 (RSV, 'and become like Gomorrah'),[103] where Andrew appeals to the Hebrew text, but proceeds in a manner which shows that he is not in contact with the Hebrew. He is commenting on *quasi Gomorrha similes essemus* and he remarks that *similes* is superfluous, adding that there are many occurrences of such superfluous words in Hebrew. However, the three examples which he offers (Isa. i 9; Ps. cv 26; cxxii 3) reveal that he is not reading the Hebrew text in any of them and that what he has to say about superfluous words is founded on how the Hebrew comes out in the Vulgate.[104] There is nothing in the Hebrew which corresponds with *similes*; the superfluous item is in the Vulgate not the Hebrew, and Andrew would have noticed this if he had been reading לעמרה דמינו. The same holds for Ps. cv 26 and Ps. cxxii 3, where Andrew is drawing conclusions from excessively literal translations of Hebrew idioms in the Vulgate.[105]

Isa. liii 2 is a case where Andrew makes no claims on the basis of the Hebrew text, but where his exegetical presuppositions lead him to follow a punctuation which is different from both the Vulgate and the Hebrew and to make a semantic proposal which is without foundation. Instead of 'And when we see him, there is nothing about his presence which would make us desire him', for which the Vulgate has *et vidimus eum, et non erat aspectus, et desideravimus eum*, Andrew allows the sense to run on after *desideravimus eum: et desideravimus eum (quasi) despectum et novissimum virorum*. To this arrangement of the text he attaches his lexicographical comment on *desideravimus* which he endeavours desperately to justify: 'We sigh and grieve that he is despised and rejected of men; because sighing elicits desire, it is not absurd to write "we desire" for "we sigh".'[106] Smalley remarks, 'When Andrew says "without absurdity", it is a sign that he realizes himself to be on dangerous ground.'[107]

There are several instances which are not exactly comparable with this one, because no lexicographical conjuring appears in them, but which show how a general mode of elucidation which has taken hold of Andrew's mind may prove more powerful than his attention to the 'letter' of the text. Three examples produced by Smalley[108] in another connection, and from which she draws conclusions of a different kind, have a bearing on this. Andrew's comment on Dan. vii 16 approximates to homiletics focused on a single verse rather than exegesis which has regard to the context of Dan. vii. Daniel's wisdom is proverbial (Ezek. xxviii 3) and yet he enquires of another concerning the truth (NEB, 'I, Daniel, approached one of those who stood there and enquired from him what all this meant; and he told me the interpretation'). Truth, remarks Andrew, should be sought of the learned and the wise. Moreover, those who stand by, and not those who are busied with administrative tasks and are always in a hurry, are the possessors of wisdom. 'Wisdom is learnt from the leisured, in time of leisure, not from the hurried in time of disturbance.'[109] Again, Andrew's comment on Prov. xxxi 3 may, as Smalley suggests, reveal that he preferred the quietness of his study to the vexations of administering an abbey, but this has nothing to do with the text. The lack of connection between 'Do not expend your strength on women, *your semen on those who destroy kings*'[110] and 'Professed religious should be ashamed to ask for so many and such unnecessary things, yes and extort them from their dispensers',[111] is complete.

When Smalley observes that 'the search for truth in study was Andrew's ruling passion',[112] she is describing an attitude of mind which appears to exercise a heavier influence on him at both Dan. vii 16 and Eccles. i 13 than the particulars of these texts. In the latter Andrew is commenting on *Hanc occupationem pessimam dedit Deus filiis hominum*, which is rendered by NEB as, 'It is a sorry business that God has given men to busy themselves with.' There is no doubt that this is a questioning of the value of 'research' and of the pursuit of wisdom, as what precedes and follows it makes clear, and one which arrives at the conclusion, 'For in much wisdom is much vexation, and the more a man knows the more he has to suffer' (verse 18, NEB). The thought which dominates Andrew's exegesis, that God has endowed the soul with an insatiable intellectual curiosity, and that truth is fugitive and difficult to capture, is distant from the text.[113] That this was a leading thought which fascinated him, and could distract his exegetical concentration and overpower the claims of the 'letter' of the text, receives confirmation from an examination of his prologues to the prophets[114] and to the book of Isaiah.[115] Here again a sense of the elusiveness of the truth, the relentlessness with which the search for it must be conducted and the correlation of its profundity and its inaccessibility, exercise a powerful influence on him and affect the formation of his attitudes.

Passages in which Andrew is clearly founding his exegesis on the Vulgate, and breaking new ground with his originality are distinguishable from some of those just considered, and examples are found at Jer. i 5, Gen. vii 2 and Isa. liii 4.

Jer. i 5: NEB 'Before I formed you in the womb I knew you for my own; before you were born I consecrated you, I appointed you a prophet to the nations': The parts of the Vulgate text on which Andrew[116] focuses special attention are *novi te* and *sanctificavi te*, and he opposes Jerome's interpretation of *novi* as 'foreknew'[117] on the ground that it produces too general an exegesis, since God's foreknowledge is applicable to all his human creatures, whereas what is needed is a sense of *novi* which has a special bearing on Jeremiah's prophetic vocation. Pursuing this train of thought, Andrew urges that the nuance of 'know' which is required is 'approve' and that this pre-natal 'approval' is the earnest of the unfailing support which the prophet will subsequently enjoy.[118] Andrew leans on nuances of 'know' in Exod. xxxiii 12 and Mt. xx 12, but he would have done better to invoke ידעתי in Amos iii 12 – 'known' in the sense of 'chosen': 'You only of all the nations of the earth have I chosen.'

Smalley is impressed by the extent to which Andrew is unshackling himself from Jerome and from the allegorical exegesis of the verse, but the extent to which he is still attached to a tradition of interpretation is even more striking, and her comment that Andrew has interpreted 'sanctification' as 'preparation' and 'pledge'[119] does not take all of his exegesis into account. The allegorical interpretation which Andrew rejects involves the equation of *womb* with the purificatory rite of circumcision, and so the conclusion that Jeremiah, being already cleansed before his formation in the womb, was immune from original sin. If Andrew had looked harder at הקדשתי, he could have disposed of the exegesis flowing from *sanctificavi te* and interpreted the second part of the verse as a 'setting apart' to the prophetic office. Instead he remains more heavily under the influence of *sanctificavi te* than Smalley's statement indicates. On *Et antequam exires de vulva, sanctificavi te* Andrew comments, 'I granted you such sanctity, that nothing but the holy and pure could please you after your passing to birth. Through the sanctity vouchsafed him, Jeremias is believed to have kept a perpetual virginity.'[120] If this does not express a view that in a pre-natal state Jeremiah was made immune from original sin, it is not far removed from such an assertion.[121]

Gen. vii 2, NEB 'Take with you seven pairs, male and female, of all beasts that are ritually clean': This is less complicated and is a good example of Andrew's refusal to be distracted from the text of the Vulgate in order to sustain a traditional exegesis which hinges on an odd number of clean animals, and on the number *seven* in particular, and which will not countenance seven pairs of animals, that is, *fourteen*. On *Ex omnibus animantibus mundis tolle septena et septena, masculum et feminam*, Andrew comments, 'But we who try to expound the letter, not twist or destroy it, expound the text thus ... "Take *seven* males and take *seven* females".'[122]

Andrew's collective exegesis of Isa. liii, in following which he identifies the sufferer as Israel in exile, is conducted entirely on the basis of the Vulgate, and this is especially noticeable at verse 4, where *et nos putavimus eum quasi leprosum*, which serves as an element of his exegetical scheme, is an interpretation rather than a translation of ואנחנו חשבנו נגוע (NEB, 'While we accounted him smitten'). On the Vulgate text Andrew remarks, 'Here the prophet is numbering himself among those who supposed that the people of the captivity was to be taken captive for its own sins, and that its own sins required it to be separated as a leper from God's people, struck and humbled by God.'[123] Apart from the special 'leper' feature of this exegesis, Andrew is reflecting a view which overturns an adverse verdict on the exiles and declares in particular that those deported in 597 B.C. are the good figs (Jer. xxiv 1–10). Thus on *Pro eo quod tradidit in mortem animam suam*, 'Because he surrendered his soul to death (Isa. liii 12), Andrew comments, 'This can refer only to those who went into exile willingly, by the counsel of the prophets, as Jechonias and those who submitted to the Babylonians.'[124]

Andrew's treatment of Gen. i 1 (*In principio creavit Deus caelum et terram*, 'In the beginning God created heaven and earth') will serve as a bridge to the next section in which consideration will be given to the statement that he displays rationalist tendencies. On Gen. i 1 Smalley says of Andrew, 'He excludes the spiritual exposition on the one hand and theological questions on the other. He has no time for homiletics or for doctrinal discussion.'[125] It has been shown that Andrew does not invariably have an unerring nose for the text, but it may be granted that matters are, for the most part, as Smalley describes them. The task which Andrew sets himself is to recover the intention[126] of the author of the text and he will not easily be turned aside from this. In particular, he will resist any attempt to use the text merely as a peg on which to hang doctrinal opinions, since this is symptomatic of a lack of interest in the 'literal' sense and of serious purpose in pursuing it. It is such a resistance to arbitrary exegesis, rather than a rationalist reductionism which seeks to dissolve angelology, by which Andrew's attitude to Gen. i 1 is determined. There is nothing about angels in the text and what possible justification can there be for the introduction of a discussion about angels into its interpretation? Andrew begins with his perception of the intention of the author whom he supposes to be Moses. The author deliberately excluded any consideration of angels that he might deal with matters which had a particular human usefulness. 'We too, of set purpose, shall omit what others think should be said about the angels on this passage, even should we have views.'[127] The stand which Andrew is taking is on the ground of strict exegetical relevance.

Andrew and 'rationalism'

Smalley[128] remarks that Andrew is not a rationalist in the sense of having a religious faith which seeks understanding, that he does not have the logical mastery or the theological interest to set reason to work in the interests of faith, and that he is consequently not a twelfth-century rationalist of the stamp of Abelard. The positive side of Smalley's task, the indicating of the sense in which Andrew is a rationalist or has rationalist tendencies, is not so clearly done and gives rise to some perplexity. It is understandable that Andrew's rationalism should be elucidated as naturalism, as a 'preference for natural to supernatural explanations', and that this should be described as a cult of 'common sense' having some affinities with eighteenth-century rationalism. Examples of Andrew's exegesis which display these tendencies can be produced, but the degree to which Andrew reduces or dissolves the supernatural by rationalist explanations should not be exaggerated.

The principal lack of clarity in Smalley's account of Andrew's rationalism is caused by the introduction of Jewish exegetical categories into the discussion and by her assumption that *peshaṭ* exegesis can be equated with a rationalist tendency: 'Rashi added a third method of exposition: the literal or rational.'[129] She urges further that he 'had directed Jewish exegesis into new channels; he had made it "literal" in the sense that it kept closely to the text and preferred rational to allegorical explanations.'[130] Confusion is created by this representation that there is an intrinsic connection between *peshaṭ* exegesis and rationalism, while the examples which Smalley selects from Joseph Bekhor Shor demonstrate a conflict between *peshaṭ* and rationalist interpretation.[131]

There are no inherent rationalist implications in the exegetical method which is called *peshaṭ*: it is the pursuit of the plain sense of a passage as given primarily by lexicography and grammar; it is the sense which arises from the faithful translation of a passage. The view that rationalist tendencies of interpretation are necessarily present in *peshaṭ* exegesis, or must lurk behind it, has no justification. If we regard a translation (in Andrew's case the Vulgate) as constituting the essence of a *peshaṭ* exegesis, we shall see that Andrew's essays into rationalism are associated with a further stage of interpretation. The implication of this is that there is no necessary connection between *peshaṭ* and rationalism and that, far from complementing each other, the achievement of a rationalist elucidation of the Hebrew text may involve conflict with the *peshaṭ* or its overthrow. The equation of rationalism with *peshaṭ* exegesis is a confusion, because if there are supernatural elements in the Hebrew text, these should be represented faithfully by the *peshaṭ*, whereas it is the aim of a rationalist elucidation to explain away references to supernatural agencies. Hence Andrew was not misled into thinking that 'literal' should be equated with non-mystical or rational.[132]

In order to salvage anything valuable from Smalley's remarks, we have to concentrate on Andrew's relation to the Christian exegetical scheme of Old Testament interpretation. Her case would then be that because Andrew equated 'literal sense' with *peshaṭ*, he had an understanding of 'literal sense' which was too restrictive to do justice to Christian exegetical orthodoxy. 'Literal sense' for Andrew was the sense given by lexicography, grammar and the historical setting of the text, and he founded his enquiry, for the most part, on the Latin translation provided in the Vulgate. According to the Christian exegetical scheme, on the other hand, a Christological sense could be the 'literal sense' of passages of the Hebrew Bible. These considerations, however, have nothing to do with an essential connection between Jewish *peshaṭ* exegesis and rationalism, and a review of some of the examples taken by Smalley from Joseph Bekhor Shor will make this clear.

At Gen. xix 26[133] it is not disputed that the Hebrew represents that Lot's wife was changed into a pillar of salt (NEB, 'and she turned into a pillar of salt'). Joseph disposes of the supernatural associations of the *peshaṭ* by explaining that Lot's wife was the victim of a volcanic eruption and was overwhelmed by a flow of lava. Similarly at Exod. iv 24[134] there is a plain statement in the Hebrew text that Yahweh confronted Moses with a view to killing him, but in the sequel let him go. The confrontation is rationalized as a serious

illness which struck Moses, and his being let go is explained as a recovery from
that illness. In his exegesis of the plague of boils (Exod. ix 8)[135] Joseph
changes the 'dust' of the Hebrew text into 'hot ashes'. The plague, which
according to the Hebrew text was miraculously or magically produced by
Moses on Yahweh's instructions, is explained as the production of blisters
by hot ashes, with the concession that the widespread effects described
constitute a supernatural feature: 'God does not alter the laws of nature and
therefore effected the miracle partly according to natural laws. For this reason
he commanded Moses to cast the ashes. And so you will find with the majority
of miracles that God does not alter natural laws.' The limitation which Joseph
places on his rationalism in this case deserves notice, since it can be shown
that Andrew too may reduce the supernatural content of a passage without
completely dissolving it.

The principal observation which has to be made on these examples from
Joseph Bekhor Shor is that they contradict Smalley's equation of *peshaṭ* exegesis
with a rationalist tendency. They show that the supernatural is embedded
in the Hebrew text and must therefore be represented by the *peshaṭ*; the
rationalist explanation can make progress only by explaining away the *peshaṭ*.
Hence far from lending any support to the view that the *peshaṭ* method has
a rationalist bent, they display a situation of conflict between *peshaṭ* and
rationalism.

Ezek. i 1, NEB 'The heavens were opened and I saw a vision of God':
Andrew's comments on *Aperti sunt caeli, et vidi visiones Dei* are offered by
Smalley[136] as an example of Andrew's rationalist exegesis: 'If anyone would
like to argue that *the heavens were opened* for the prophet's gaze to pass through
them, that he might see God and the things above, we in no way hinder him;
let him abound in his own sense. But let him ask whether reason or the nature
of things allow what he wishes to argue. If he resort to the argument that divine
omnipotence can do what nature cannot, enable a man to direct his gaze
through the heavens and beyond them, we know that with God nothing is
impossible and in no wise gainsay it. But he should realize this: in expounding
Scripture, when the event described admits of no rational explanation, then
and then only should we have recourse to miracles.' The outcome of Andrew's
stated method, as it is applied to Ezek. i 1, lacks boldness. In urging that the
prophet does not see into the heavenly places with the eye of sense, but with
the mind's eye, and that his vision is interior and intellectual, he is following
Augustine[137] and the marginal gloss.[138] Otherwise his exegesis is anti-literal
rather than rationalist in character, since it reduces the details of the representation not to a rational explanation but to a statement that the prophet was
divinely inspired and had a special access through revelation to God and the
divine world.

Thus on *vidi visionem a Deo*[139] Andrew comments: 'The sense is: the fact
of my having *seen a vision*, and understood what will come upon you, upon
the rest [of the people] and upon the City, is not from me but *from God*. In
these words the prophet both shows his humility, and plainly teaches his

readers that they must assent to what he will say as divinely inspired. According to this opinion what else does the *opening of the heavens* mean, but that a heavenly gift is vouchsafed him?'[140] Closer inspection has shown that Andrew's explanation of Ezek. i 1 is not a rationalist one. It includes supernatural assumptions (an inspired prophet with revealed knowledge) and its function is to reduce an excessively literal attachment to a form of imaginative representation: the opening of the heavens is not to be taken literally, and we are not to suppose that Ezekiel saw through a gap into the heavens in the same way as he would see into a room when the door was opened.

Andrew's attitude is here associated with a linguistic judgement, a distinction between the literal and metaphorical functioning of language. Since, in agreement with the mediaeval terminology, he is said to be an exegete devoted to the literal sense, it is all the more important to appreciate that this does not make him slavishly or woodenly literal. He recoils from the supposition that supernatural descriptions of the kind found in Ezek. i 1 are to be interpreted in a matter of fact way, and he probes the metaphorical functioning of language employed rather than taking it seriously as literal description. Moreover, there are passages where Andrew's comments on the literary effects achieved by metaphor are related to a general exegetical style rather than to any rationalist tendency. When he comments on *Lavamini* (Isa. i 16) and *Si fuerint peccata vestra ut coccinum* (Isa. i 18), he is concerned to elucidate the literary ends which are served by 'scarlet', 'crimson' and 'white': 'He [Isaiah] expresses the filth of sin by scarlet and crimson, purity by snow and wool. Nothing looks filthier on vessel or vesture than the red stain of blood; it shows up more than any other; and we know when a thing is cleaned by its turning white.'[141] Andrew introduces the further thought that red is the colour of blood, that bloodstains have a particular association with pollution, and that 'scarlet' and 'crimson' contain an allusion to blood (cf. i 15, 'There is blood on your hands'): 'He [Isaiah] has chosen to compare the redness of blood to *scarlet* and *crimson*, because they express redness with such intensity.'[142] In connection with a reference to books in which the sins of all men are recorded (Dan. vii 9) we find a reduction of literal description comparable to what is found at Ezek. i 1: 'When sins are said to be written in books, what else does it mean but that God remembers as though they were written?'[143] The details of the portrayal are not to be taken literally, but they point to the infallibility of God's memory.

Exod. xv 10, NEB, 'Thou didst blow with thy blast; the sea covered them': One may detect a movement towards rationalism in Andrew's assertion that God achieves his ends by harnessing a natural power (the wind) and not a mysterious supernatural power, but the affirmation that the wind is the servant of God's purposes has, nevertheless, the character of a supernatural belief rather than a rational explanation. Moreover, Andrew is accepting *spiritus tuus* as a correct translation of רוּחֲךָ; he is not holding that רוּחַ in this verse means 'wind', and he is suspended in a mentally uncomfortable, half-way position, where he justifies *spiritus tuus* as a rendering of רוּחֲךָ, although he grants that it is the wind to which reference is made. The wind is named 'spirit', because it was sent by God and executes his will.[144] Hence there is little evidence of a rationalist boldness in Andrew's treatment of this verse.

Isa. xi 15, NEB 'The LORD will divide the tongue of the Egyptian sea and wave his hand over the River to bring a scorching wind; he shall split it into seven channels and let men go across dry-shod': This is another verse where Andrew's rationalism moves within narrow limits. He is commenting on *Et levabit manum suam super flumen in fortitudine spiritus sui* and he remarks that the raising of God's hand is indicative of threat, explaining *spiritus sui* either as God's anger or as a burning wind – an instrument of his anger (vel ire vel urentis venti).[145] In the same verse, in a comment on *Et percutiet eum in septem rivis* Andrew chides the Jews for attaching a too literal interpretation to a description of the Messianic age and for nursing extravagant expectations. In any case, he adds, the Nile had already been divided into seven rivers by Alexander the Great on the occasion of his entry into Egypt. This is not so much a rationalist debunking of literalism as it is an attention to historical detail which might be expected from Andrew. It is what he regards as a historical fact that demonstrates the wrongness of putting a literal interpretation on a description of what will happen in the Messianic age. However, all of this is anchored to a wrong exegesis, and Andrew's alternative exegesis that *et percutiet eum in septem rivis* refers back to *super flumen* (river = Euphrates) is the correct one. It is those returning from Assyria who will cross the Euphrates dry-shod, when Yahweh splits it into seven channels.[146]

A final example, showing how Andrew reacts to the literalism of the Jews, and the expectation of miracles which it arouses, is Isa. xl 4 (NEB, 'Every valley shall be lifted up, every mountain and hill brought down; rugged places shall be made smooth and mountain-ranges become a plain'). This is a description of the road along which the Jews will journey from their Babylonian captivity to Jerusalem, and Andrew's concern is that the functioning of the linguistic components of the verse should be properly appreciated. The intention of the imagery is to indicate that the Jews will return expeditiously and victoriously, unhindered by physical obstacles, along roads prepared for their progress. The Jews who suppose that hills are to be miraculously lowered and valleys miraculously raised, that twisted tracks are to be straightened and irregular terrains levelled, are naïve and fatuous.[147]

To sum up, a clear statement of a rationalist principle appears in connection with Andrew's comments on Ezek. i 1, where he expresses his preference for the most economical hypothesis – the application of Occam's razor. Supernatural or miraculous causes should be disposed of, if an elucidation can be achieved in terms of what is natural and rational. His rationalism, however, is not rigorous, but where the tendency is present it is characteristically associated with his evaluation of imagery used in descriptions of heaven or other supernatural matters, or of the Messianic age and future deliverances of the Jews. This evaluation rejects literalism and by a freer interpretation or transformation of descriptive detail comes to another understanding of how

non-literal descriptions work to secure literary effects. Moreover, his interest
in the non-literal use of language can assume an independent status in his
work, disengaged from his rationalism.

Andrew's exegesis and the intention of Old Testament authors

The purpose of this section is to investigate in what respect Andrew's exegesis
purports to represent the intention of biblical authors, to indicate how this
is dissociated from what modern scholars would regard as a critical attitude
to scripture, and to show that Andrew's concern to supply a historical setting
for his exegesis is also clearly distinguishable from a historical – critical
interpretation of the Old Testament. The lack of clarity about these matters
in Hadfield is partly associated with a confusion of Jewish and mediaeval
Christian exegetical categories, and, especially, with the use of the term
'spiritual' in connection with Jewish Messianic or eschatological exegesis. This
is an illegitimate interchange of Jewish and Christian exegetical terminology:
there is no Jewish 'spiritual' exegesis in the sense in which 'spiritual' is used
in the Christian scheme of Old Testament exegesis, because spiritual exegesis
means Christian exegesis of the Old Testament.

Andrew is linked by Hadfield with Ibn Ezra, but the latter has a grasp of
'intention' which is much nearer to modern critical scholarship than Andrew's
position. The coupling of Andrew and Ibn Ezra appears in the following
passage:

When Andrew, for example, clearly sees the prophet behind the prophecies in these
chapters (Isa. xl ff.), and pays attention to the historical situation in which Isaiah
addressed his people, or when Ibn Ezra states that the prophecies concerning the
Babylonian exile were not really 'prophecies' predicted long beforehand, but had been
put down only to encourage faith in the final redemption of the Messianic age, then
they establish themselves as independent, critical commentators of the sacred text.[148]

But, having represented Andrew and Ibn Ezra as pioneers in the historical –
critical interpretation of the Old Testament, and having apparently credited
them both with the postulation of a Deutero-Isaiah, Hadfield goes on,
unaccountably, to say:

These and such-like considerations will make it obvious that the best way to come to
a fair appreciation of a medieval exposition of Isaiah xl – lxvi is to discard, for the
moment, all one's knowledge about a Deutero- or even a Trito Isaiah, and to read
the prophecies as the medieval commentators themselves did.[149]

There is no way in which sense can be had out of this, but there are other
indications, perhaps not entirely decisive, that, in Hadfield's view, Andrew's
exegesis of these chapters assumes that the Isaiah in question is a prophet of
the exile. This seems the most reasonable conclusion to draw from the
statement that Andrew's concern was to explain 'what Isaiah's words meant
to the people to whom they were actually spoken'.[150] This is hardly compatible with Isaiah of Jerusalem addressing an audience about distant exilic

conditions of life, and it would be a puzzle why Hadfield should make such a point, unless her intention was to assert that Andrew's Isaiah was addressing an exilic audience.

Hadfield's view of Ibn Ezra is that he was postulating a Deutero-Isaiah on the ground that Isaiah of Jerusalem, active in the eighth and seventh centuries B.C., could not have possessed such a detailed knowledge of the exilic period as is supplied in Isa. xl ff.[151] She is building on a passage at the beginning of Ibn Ezra's commentary on Isa. xl and is following Friedländer.[152] Ibn Ezra remarks, 'In my opinion the whole (of Isaiah xl – lxvi) refers to our exile', and he follows this up with 'Except that there are passages in the middle of the book referring to the Babylonian exile, to bring to mind that it was Cyrus who set the exiles free. But in the last part of the book the (prophet's) words refer to the future.'[153]

Ibn Ezra is apparently not allowing two levels of prophetic reference: he is not saying that in chapters xl – lv an exilic prophet predicted the end of the Babylonian exile, but that there is a further reference to the end of the exile which mediaeval Jews are suffering and that the fulfilment of this is still awaited. His position is rather that the context of the Babylonian exile is no more than historical illustration, the recall of an earlier deliverance in which Cyrus, the Persian king, played an important part, and that the only exegesis which requires serious consideration is an eschatological one.[154] 'Our exile' is the exile of mediaeval Jews, and the contents of Isa. xl – lxvi relate to a restoration of the dispersed of Israel which the future will bring forth.

If this is a correct understanding of Ibn Ezra, all he intends by his remark about 'the last part of the book' is that the illustrative, historical material is no longer present there and that these chapters are manifestly eschatological. At any rate it is plain that the Isaiah whom Ibn Ezra has in view emerges at the end of the exile and is not Isaiah of Jerusalem. Similarly directed are Ibn Ezra's remarks that since the death of Samuel is recorded at 1 Sam. xxv 1, he could not have been the author of the two books of Samuel,[155] and that there are certain expressions in the Pentateuch which it would be unnatural to attach to Moses himself and which are pointers that he was not the author of the entire Pentateuch.[156]

These are genuine critical perceptions, but nothing of this kind should be attached to Andrew. The Isaiah to whom he refers in his commentary on Isa. xl ff. is none other than the Isaiah whose biography he sketched in his prologue to the book of Isaiah: a prophet of royal blood, the father-in-law of Manasseh by whom he was subsequently persecuted.[157] Andrew explains Isa. l 4 as a reference to this Isaiah, who contrasts his knowledge and vigilance with the ignorance and disobedience of those to whom he is sent[158] (cf. Isa. vi 9 f.). Isa. l 6 is explained in connection with the persecution suffered by Isaiah at the hands of Manasseh,[159] and on Isa. lii 13 – 14 Andrew comments that Israel's restitution will be a vindication of Isaiah's sufferings.[160] When he remarks at the end of Isa. liii, that some Jews substitute the prophet Isaiah for the 'Israel' of the collective interpretation, there is no reason to suppose that the prophet whom he has in mind is other than Isaiah of Jerusalem.[161]

Hence in his commentary on Isa. xl ff. Andrew does not have in view an exilic prophet immersed in the experience of his contemporaries, one who speaks with the immediacy of a Jew of that period. On the contrary, he feels no mental discomfort in supposing that Isaiah of Jerusalem, in virtue of his predictive powers as an inspired prophet to whom Yahweh had revealed the details of a distant future, had access to the history of the Jews in the exilic period before it eventuated. In this entire area he is pre-critical and he has no intellectual difficulty in assenting to the opinion that such a detailed preview of historical events lying in the distant future is contained in the 'intention' of Isaiah of Jerusalem.

An important implication of this is that there is no significant relation between Andrew's understanding of 'intention' and the historical exegesis to which he is devoted in Isa. xl ff., because the 'intention' which he is recovering is that of Isaiah of Jerusalem, while the historical background he is assuming is that of the exilic age. If the critical assumption is made that the intention of a biblical author can be elucidated only against the background of his own times, and cannot be stretched to take in historical detail of a distant future, a view of 'intention' more credibly human than that of Andrew has been adopted, and a significant connection has been established between intention and historical exegesis. These are in fact the presuppositions of the historical–critical method of biblical exegesis.

Andrew is far removed from this, but it is perhaps misleading to suppose that his concern was to make much of the predictive power of Isaiah of Jerusalem or that his mind was full of such a theology of prophecy. This was not the centre of his interest, and the best account of the matter is that it never occurred to him to question the predictive power of a prophet: this rather than the supposition that he had a zealous, dogmatic attachment to it. He may have given scant consideration to the relation between the intention of Isaiah of Jerusalem and the historical detail of Isa. xl ff. by which his interest was so thoroughly aroused. It was the text itself, the evidences of historical background supplied by it, and the exegesis demanded by the chosen historical framework which excited him and dominated his enquiry.

If Andrew's historical exegesis has critical connections and is an important step on the road to modernity, it is because it enhances the humanity of Old Testament literature by interpreting it in a historical context and a human world. In so far, however, as it assumes an Old Testament prophet super-naturally endowed and discoursing on the distant future with full historical detail, it does not make a decisive contribution to the discovery of the humanity of the Old Testament prophet. It is the concentration on his humanity and the illumining of his prophetical perceptions in relation to his life and times which is most characteristic of the historical–critical method.

The persistence with which Andrew employs a collective interpretation in Isa. xl ff., and particularly in the 'Servant' passages, is striking evidence of how committed he is to historical exegesis. 'Reading Andrew', says Smalley, 'one sometimes has to rub one's eyes!'[162] She makes her remark with special reference to Isa. liii, but throughout these chapters Andrew's tendency is to assume that the experience of the Jewish community in Babylon provide the historical context for their exegesis,[163] that the sufferer is Israel in exile, and that this suffering has a vicarious significance. Smalley's comment is particularly pointed towards the absence of a Christological exegesis of Isa. liii and so she continues, 'It is extraordinary to think that this was written at St Victor, by a pupil of Hugh, that he was begged to continue his work, begged to resume his abbacy, and finally buried with "great honour". The twelfth century is full of surprises.'[164] Thus on *Virum dolorum* (Isa. liii 3) Andrew comments, 'The prophet is speaking of the people as though of one man, whom he calls *a man of sorrows*.'[165] And on *Vere languores nostros ipse tulit*, 'Yet on himself he bore our sufferings' (NEB, Isa. liii 4), he comments: 'By these words the prophet means that the people who were to suffer in the Babylonian captivity were to expiate not only their own sins, but also the sins of the unrighteous: "Surely that *man of sorrows* will carry out infirmities and sorrows, which we, for our sins, ought to bear".'[166]

Andrew's mind, however, is not so fixed on supplying a historical background for his interpretation of Isa. xl ff. that he abstains from eschatological or Jewish Messianic exegesis in these chapters. It may be that his preference is for interpretation in a historical setting, and this would be consistent with his human, this-worldly interest in Old Testament literature, but he does not shut his eyes to the fact that there are some passages which relate to an ideal future: a future which has had no historical realization and which is described in terms alien to historical experience. He explains Isa. xi 6–7 in Jewish terms, as a depiction of a Messianic age which lies in the future,[167] and his two interpretations of Isa. xi 9 have a similar future reference. According to one the Messianic hope will be realized in the Promised Land, while, according to the other, the fulfilment will encompass the whole earth.[168] Isa. xi 10 is a portrayal of an event still unfulfilled, the flocking of the Gentiles to a Jewish Messiah of the future,[169] and the subject of Isa. xi 11 is a hope of restoration yet unborn, which lies beyond the fall of Jerusalem to the Romans, when God will gather dispersed Jews to Palestine from the four quarters of the world.[170] With this may be connected Andrew's comments on Isa. lii 1, which he locates in the last days, and with which he associates the thought that the uncircumcised and unclean will never again enter Jerusalem.[171] Finally, Isa. li 5 is explained in Jewish terms as a reference to the salvation of the Gentiles, and in li 6 Andrew detects an allusion to a new heaven and a new earth.[172]

We may regard Ibn Ezra[173] as a Jewish commentator whose exegesis of Isa. xl–lxvi is tilted towards eschatology, so that there is a polarity between him and Andrew whose exegetical tendency is historical. Hadfield[174] transposes 'historical' and 'eschatological' into Christian exegetical terminology and equates them with 'literal' and 'spiritual'. The right way to explain this state of affairs is to say that in such a case Andrew and Ibn Ezra are offering different *peshaṭ* interpretations of these passages. That they differ from each other in what they understand by 'intention' has already been argued.[175] Making allowance for this we can say that both are aiming to recover the intention of the biblical author: Andrew assumes, where his exegesis is historical, that this will be achieved by interpreting the passages against the background of the Jewish community exiled in Babylon, whereas Ibn Ezra assumes that the prophet is referring to an age which is strikingly discontinuous with historical existence as hitherto experienced, which does not relate to recognizable historical trends, and which must be located in the future. Both are practising *peshaṭ* or plain-sense exegesis, and from a modern, critical point of view there is less offence in Ibn Ezra's supposition that a prophet towards the end of the Babylonian exile imagined and described distant eschatological events than there is in the assumption that Isaiah of Jerusalem foresaw the historical circumstances of the Babylonian exile. Hadfield is wrong in two respects: Andrew's 'literal' exegesis is not identical with the 'literal' exegesis of the Christian scheme of Old Testament interpretation, and Jewish eschatological or Messianic exegesis is not analogous with the 'spiritual' or Christological exegesis which functions within that scheme.

From a different angle, it should be noticed that Andrew does not confine himself to a kind of exegesis which is broadly equivalent to *peshaṭ*, and that there are examples of a freer mode of exegesis in his work, identifiable with Jewish *midrash* or *haggadah*. In his second exegesis of Isa. xi 10 he reproduces a story that the Jewish Messiah was born on the day when Nebuzaradan burnt down the Jerusalem temple (2 Kgs xxv 8 – 9; Jer. xxxix 8 – 9). He will die full of years, will be greater than David, and is called a 'root of Jesse' rather than a 'root of David', because Jesse rose above the foibles of David who gravely offended God in the matter of Uriah[176] (2 Sam. xi – xii). In his comment on Isa. xi 13 Andrew refers to a Jewish tradition about two Messiahs, a Messiah of Ephraim and a Messiah of Judah, who do battle with the Antichrist. The latter is identified with Gog, prince of Mosoch and Thubal (Ezek. xxxviii 2; xxxix 1), who slays the Messiah of Ephraim.[177] Hadfield supposes that Andrew is not aware that there are different kinds of Jewish exegesis, that he does not draw any distinction between *peshaṭ* and *midrash*, but lumps them together. The introductory formula *Fabulantur Hebrei*, which Andrew uses at xi 10, is then an item in Andrew's collection of polemical vocabulary directed against Jewish exegesis.[178] It is not certain, however, that *Fabulantur Hebrei* is merely or principally a pejorative remark. It may be an indication that Andrew is aware that he has made a transition to a different mode of exegesis. It may rest on information that he has received from Jews that there are kinds of interpretation other than the single-minded pursuit of the plain sense. In that case he is not so much engaging in a polemic against the Jews as providing an example of exegesis different from *peshaṭ*.

The next section is devoted to a consideration of the conflict between Andrew's exegetical style and the assumptions of the Christological exegesis of the Old Testament which obtained in the Church. The final part of this section will prepare the ground for it. Disagreement has already been expressed with one account of Andrew's tactical dispositions, how he walked a tight-rope, maintaining a precarious balance, alive to the danger of incurring ecclesiastical censure or falling into heresy.[179] If Andrew was doing what Hadfield represents, her account of the prudential considerations which weighed with him would not have provided him with an effective defence. The gist of the argument is that Andrew limits his operations, for the most part, to the 'letter' of the text and that he has no intention of challenging the significance of the higher levels of interpretation of the Old Testament which were installed in the exegetical scheme of the Catholic Church. He was in accord with the orthodox Christian interpretation of the Old Testament; it was simply that, for his own part, he was content to concentrate his efforts on the pursuit of the literal sense.

The problem which this account overlooks is that Andrew and the Church were not agreed about the scope of the literal exegesis of the Old Testament, and here again we are in the presence of a confusion of Jewish and Christian exegetical terms. If what Andrew meant by literal interpretation was, more or less, Jewish *peshaṭ* exegesis,[180] there is a crucial difference between its scope and that of the 'letter' within the Christian scheme. For that reason Andrew would not be mounting an effective defence if he were saying that he would confine himself to the 'letter' and leave the Christian interpretation of the Old Testament to those who had a better head for heights than he had. According to Andrew's practice there were no Old Testament texts immune from literal, that is, from *peshaṭ* or plain-sense or historical exegesis; according to the Church there were some texts which had no literal sense of that kind and whose literal sense, and only sense, was a Christological one. 'The whole meaning intended by the sacred writer'[181] in the mediaeval Christian scheme of things may be construed as only and entirely Christological, in which case the intention of the sacred writer, as a definition of the literal sense, produces an entirely different result from the intention of the sacred writer as expressed in *peshaṭ* exegesis.[182] This is the centre of the conflict.

Andrew and Christian exegesis of the Old Testament

Isa. vii 14: NEB 'Therefore the Lord himself shall give you a sign: A young woman is with child, and she will bear a son, and will call him Immanuel': It will be recalled that the purpose of Richard's treatise on *De Immanuele* was to establish that Isa. vii 14 refers to the Virgin Mary, that this is its literal sense, and that Andrew's Jewish interpretations of it contradict the exegetical doctrine of the Church.[183] Jerome[184] notices that the Hebrew word used is עלמה not בתולה, as also does Richard,[185] in dependence on Jerome. The last mentioned sums up the pattern of translation in the Septuagint and assumes wrongly that the sense 'hide' is given by the same Hebrew root from which עלמה derives.[186] Only at Gen. xxiv 43 (Rebecca) and Isa. vii 14 is

עלמה rendered as παρθένος and the sense 'young woman' (*adolescentula*),
which Jerome notices, is represented in the Septuagint and the Vulgate at
Exod. ii 8, Ps. lxviii 26, Prov. xxx 19, Cant. i 3 and vi 8.[187] One of these
passages (Ps. lxviii 26), which is obscure, should almost certainly be associated
with the equally obscure עלמות of the psalm titles which are connected by
the Septuagint and the Vulgate with עלם 'hide'.[188] Jerome uses the sense
'hidden', which he derives from the psalm titles, to establish that עלמה
means not simply 'young woman' or even 'virgin' (*non solum puella vel virgo*),
but *virgo abscondita*: she is an adolescent virgin (*virgo junioris aetatis*) who has
been hidden away from men and whose chastity has been carefully guarded.
Jerome remarks that he has no knowledge of עלמה being used of a married
woman, and, on the linguistic foundation which he has laid (an unsound one),
he deems that the only tenable exegesis of the verse is Christological.[189]

It is because Richard accepts both Jerome's linguistic argument and his
view that the 'literal' sense of this verse is Christological, that he is so vexed
by Andrew's treatment of it. Andrew[190] sets off with the assertion that Isa. vii
14 refers to the Virgin Mary and to her son Jesus Christ, and he attacks the
Jews who challenge this interpretation as enemies of the truth (*veritatis inimici*).
Andrew does not engage seriously with Jerome's linguistic argument, but he
picks it up in so far as he provides transliterations of עלמה and בתולה, and
seizes on Jerome's idea that 'hiddenness' is a nuance of עלמה.[191]

The thought that if the verse has a primary Christological significance the
sign must have an extraordinary character (a Virgin Birth) was one which
exercised Jerome and influenced his conclusions.[192] Andrew raises this
question, how an ordinary event, the bearing of a child by a married woman
in the normal course of things, can take on the character of a sign,[193] and the
mediaeval Jewish exegete, Rashi, was occupied with the same problem. The
answer which Rashi offered was that the name 'Immanuel' ('God with us')
was given to the child by Isaiah's wife, and that it is the revelatory content
of this name which constitutes the sign. She is described as a prophetess
(הנביאה) at Isa. viii 3, and the bestowing of the name 'Immanuel' is supposed
to have marked the opening of her prophetic career, the first occasion on which
she was inspired by the Holy Spirit. Rashi considers another account of the
extraordinary character of the sign: the mother would bear the child before
she had reached the age of child-bearing.

Hadfield's supposition[194] that Rashi is presenting a Jewish version of a
'Virgin Birth' exegesis is founded on a misunderstanding. The matter turns
on the meaning of ואינה ראויה לילד ('and she had not reached the age of child-
bearing'). There is no doubt that what Rashi intends is that the extraordinary
nature of the sign is discerned by some in the circumstance that the mother
of the child was a young girl (נערה) who had not reached the age of menstruation. This is clear from the Mishnah, where תינקת שלא הגיע זמנה לראות
is rendered by Slotki as 'A young girl whose age of menstruation has not yet
arrived'.[195] לראות is explained as 'seeing blood'. In the Gemara Rabbi
Meir uses the phrase ראויה לראות in the sense 'capable of a menstrual

discharge',[196] and the right conclusion is certainly that by ואינה ראויה לראות
Rashi means a young girl who has not yet menstruated. Hence the extraordinary nature of the sign is the circumstance that the mother in question
bears a child before she has reached the age of menstruation.

Andrew, having made his bow to the Christian exegesis of Isa. vii 14, and
registered his awareness of the discussion which had gone on about the nature
of the sign, applies himself to the Jewish interpretation of the verse which he
states without comment or criticism of his own. The עלמה is Isaiah's wife and
the name 'Immanuel' has to be linked with that of 'Maher-shalal-hash-
baz' whose birth is recorded at the beginning of Isa. viii. The defeat of the
hostile coalition mounted against Judah by Syria and the northern kingdom
of Israel is portended by both 'Immanuel' and 'Maher-shalal-hash-baz'
('Speed-spoil-hasten-plunder'), and so the sign in Isa. vii 14 is constituted
by the revelatory and prophetic content of the name 'Immanuel'.

Andrew prefaces his own comments on Isa. vii 14 with a statement of his
intention to pursue and capture the literal sense,[197] but it is evident that his
literal sense cannot be contained within the exegetical orthodoxy of the
Catholic Church. In his comment on *Ecce virgo concipiet* Andrew does not
employ *virgo*, but combines *iuvencule* and *abscondite*. He does not, however,
make much of *abscondite* in his exegesis, the main point of which is that the
deliverance which was promised, when either the mother or the House of
Judah was instructed to bestow the name 'Immanuel', will take place when
the child is born. The context of Andrew's literal sense is historical, and he
explains the promise and its realization in the birth of Immanuel with reference
to a historical deliverance experienced by Judah in the pre-exilic period.[198]

Isa. l 4: RSV 'The Lord GOD has given me the tongue of those who are
taught, that I may know how to sustain with a word him that is weary': Here
Jerome rejects a Jewish interpretation which Andrew follows: the prophet
Isaiah is contrasting his knowledge and vigilance with the ignorance and
disobedience of those to whom he is sent.[199] Jerome remarks that the verse
is referred by the Jews to Isaiah and that in their misplaced and perverse
cleverness they stop at nothing to overthrow prophecies of Christ and twist
them to another meaning.[200]

Isa. l 6: NEB 'I offered my back to the lash, and let my beard be plucked
from my chin, I did not hide my face from spitting and insult': Andrew has
both a Jewish and a Christian interpretation, but this would still have merited
Jerome's censure, judging from his comments on Isa. l 4, since he would not
have allowed Andrew's literal (Jewish) sense. According to Andrew, Isa. l 6
contains a reference to a persecution suffered by Isaiah in the days of
Manasseh,[201] but it also alludes to the sufferings of Christ, though the details
recorded of Isaiah's persecution do not correspond exactly with the New
Testament accounts of the violence meted out to Jesus. Andrew notices
particularly that nothing is said of the plucking out of the beard of Jesus, but
his intention is to minimize the difference between Isa. l 6 and the New Testament – we are not to suppose that all the indignities and cruelties perpetrated

against Jesus have been recorded in the Gospels: 'Our Saviour himself perhaps suffered the removal of his beard by the plucking of his cheeks, which, however, to be sure, is not recorded, for not everything is recorded. But that he suffered all these things we teach, when we give instruction in the Gospel.'[202]

An exacerbation of this type of disagreement between Jerome and Andrew can be seen in the unusual case where Jerome's translation is itself a Christological exegesis, so that the Christian sense, which is held to be the only sense possessed by the verse, is already embedded in the translation. *Quia excelsus reputatus est ipse* at Isa. ii 22, which was discussed earlier,[203] is an example of this. The more usual circumstance is the one which has been set out in the immediately preceding examples, and another case of this kind is Isa. xli 2–4. Jerome's translation makes room for both a 'Cyrus' and a Christological exegesis, but he explicitly rejects the 'Cyrus' exegesis.[204] Andrew, on the other hand, uses the future tenses which are a feature of the Vulgate (*dabit, obtinebit, dabit, transibit, apparebit*) to establish the superiority of an interpretation of the verse in connection with Cyrus over one which associates it with Abraham.[205]

What emerges from this enquiry is that conflict always arises between Andrew and the mediaeval scheme of Catholic exegesis of the Old Testament, wherever Andrew allows a historical, Jewish exegesis for passages which, according to the Church, had only one sense, that is, a literal sense which was Christological. It was only in relation to passages which were allowed to have Andrew's type of literal sense, as well as a Christian sense, that Andrew could defend the absence of Christological exegesis in his work by stating that he was concentrating on the literal sense and would leave the higher order of exegetical activity to those more theologically gifted than himself.[206] The steadfastness of Andrew in pursuing the kind of Old Testament exegesis which awakened his interest is admirable, whatever degree of awareness he may have had of stepping out of line and advancing interpretations which the Church could not tolerate. It was suggested earlier that he may not have had a high awareness of this,[207] that his work was not intended to make a theological point against the exegetical orthodoxy of his time, that he was in no sense an agitator or a person with an appetite for conflict.

He is, however, and this too has already been said,[208] concerned to find a historical and so a human context for his Old Testament interpretation, and the truth is perhaps that he loses interest in the subject when this context is denied to him. His approximation to a critical attitude is connected with his dislike of a system of exegesis which supposes that there are some passages which do not have a human context, and cannot be explained against a background of time and place. Old Testament texts whose literal meaning is alleged to be Christological exist in a world which he cannot take seriously, because it offends against the robustness of his grasp of a human world and the historical experience which it generates.

Passages which are located in a dehumanizing vacuum, which were never caught up in the flow of history, but emerged inexplicably and long before they were needed as timeless Christian truths, are a kind of obfuscation to which he will not yield.

3

WILLIAM FULKE AND GREGORY MARTIN

Between Andrew of St Victor and William Fulke there lies the Renaissance and the Reformation. Both contribute to Fulke's attitudes to biblical scholarship in which a pursuit of the original languages of the Bible is mixed with a theological concern: to possess in an English translation made from Hebrew and Greek the best approximation to the mind of the Holy Spirit. A scientific temper directed to textual and linguistic matters is taken up into a theological view that the authority of the Bible is supreme, that it should be given to the people, and that the Church should be reformed in agreement with it. The Bible is a powerful agent of change to which the Church must yield where it is at variance with it.

The reaction to this movement and mood appears in Gregory Martin. For the most part his Catholic conservatism does not match the Renaissance ideals of Fulke's textual and linguistic scholarship. He has a distaste for vernacular versions of the Bible and he rests on the authority of the Vulgate, though he has both Hebrew and Greek. He regrets the necessity of having to supply an English translation from the Vulgate, but he concludes sadly that the missionary situation of the Roman Catholic Church in England makes it imperative. He is suspicious of Protestant translations of the Bible into English which make Christian theology popular rather than learned. His preference is that the world might stand still or return to yesterday, and that the scriptures might be available only to those with a mastery of Latin, the international language of learning. Yet he is able to get the better of Fulke in places where Fulke's normal linguistic sanity is impaired by theological prejudice. Martin shows that a devotion to the original languages of the Bible does not solve all the problems. In particular, in the area of Old Testament citations in the New Testament he succeeds in uncovering the deficiencies of Fulke's interpretation of *Hebraica veritas*.

Biographical sketches

Gregory Martin entered St John's College, Oxford, in 1557, where he is said to have rivalled Edmund Campion 'in all the stations of academic learning',[1] graduating B.A. in 1561 and M.A. on the 19th February, 1565. Thereafter he served the Duke of Norfolk, and when the Duke was committed to the Tower in 1570, he could no longer delay his choice between his loyalty to

Rome and his acceptance of the reforming tendencies of the Church of England. Since he could not conscientiously conform to Protestantism, he accepted the consequences of exile at Douai, where an English College had been newly established, was ordained as a priest and engaged in teaching Hebrew and biblical interpretation. In 1577 he was in Rome, assisting the foundation of the English College, but after a short interval he returned to Douai and moved with his colleagues to Rheims in 1578. During the remainder of his life he was largely occupied with the translation of the Bible from the Vulgate into English, the New Testament appearing in 1582,[2] the year of his death, and the complete Bible in 1609–10.[3]

We are told that 'he was a most excellent linguist, exactly read and vers'd in the sacred scriptures and went beyond all his time in humane literature, whether in poetry or prose'.[4] He was the author of a dictionary[5] and his interest in philology and lexicography is evident in the book which was the target of William Fulke's criticism.[6] In a letter written to his sisters, and attached to *A Treatise of Christian Peregrination and Relics* (1583) he sets his life in the context of the religious faith which he refused to renounce: 'It pleased God to stay me so with his grace, that I chose rather to forsake all, than do against my belief, against my knowledge, against my conscience, against the law of almighty God. For a time I lay secretly in England, afterwards I came beyond the seas into these Catholic countries, out of schism and heresy, for the which I do thank almighty God much more, than for all the estimation I had or might have had in England. Whatsoever my estate is here, I do more esteem it, than all the riches of England as it now standeth.'[7]

William Fulke[8] went from St Paul's School to St John's College, Cambridge, graduating B.A. in 1557–8 and M.A. in 1563. His father intended him for the law and he was at Clifford's Inn for six years, but he made his way back to Cambridge to study mathematics, languages and divinity. He was elected a Fellow of St John's College in 1564 and appointed Lecturer in Hebrew in that College in 1567. His career at Cambridge was stormy and was punctuated by setbacks, but the fact that despite his tempestuous nature he continued his ascent of the academic ladder to become Master of Pembroke Hall in 1578 and Vice Chancellor of the University of Cambridge in 1581 is an indication of his intellectual power. Hardly had he become a Fellow of St John's College than his involvement with Thomas Cartwright (1535–1603)[9] brought him to the fore in a controversy about vestments, a foray which cost him his Fellowship and in connection with which he had been summoned to appear before Cecil, the Chancellor of the University, 'by a special commandment', as a chief author of the dissension.[10]

The controversy arose out of the 'Advertisements' of Matthew Parker, then Archbishop of Canterbury, instructions which were designed 'partly for due order in the public administration of common prayers and using the holy sacraments, and partly for the apparel of all persons ecclesiastical, by virtue of the queen's letters commanding the same'.[11] Parker, with his prescription of cope, surplice and square cap was striving after a middle way which, however, was unacceptable to the Puritan wing of the Church of England and gave rise to the Cambridge disturbances. Fulke is said to have 'beat into the heads of younger sort such a persuasion of the superstition of the surplice'[12] that nearly three hundred at one time discarded it in the chapel of St John's College, and the movement spread to other colleges. Fulke and others were charged with having made 'Robin Hoodes pennyworths of their copes and other vestments',[13] that is, with having sold them dirt cheap. It is understandable that in 1569, when Fulke was shaping to be Master of St John's College, his progress was barred by Archbishop Parker,[14] and his extremism may be thought to have done him a disservice when he was a candidate for the Regius Chair of Divinity in 1579.

Fulke bounced back quickly after the controversy over vestments, was restored to his Fellowship in St John's College in March 1566–7 and was Senior Fellow in April 1567–8. On two further occasions he resigned his Fellowship: first when he was alleged to have connived at an incestuous marriage, but was subsequently acquitted, and again in connection with feuding within St John's College. He retired to livings which he enjoyed through the patronage of the Earl of Leicester, who favoured the Puritan party in the Church of England, until with Leicester's help he became Master of Pembroke Hall in 1578. The book which he wrote to confute the opinions of Gregory Martin was published in London in 1583.[15]

Without any implication that his procedure is unfair, it can be said that Fulke has a distinct advantage over Martin in so far as he determines the ground on which the battle is to be fought by selecting passages from the book of an opponent who is deceased. This aspect of the matter would hardly need to be mentioned were it not that the form of Fulke's book easily creates the illusion of a running debate between himself and Martin, with the latter actually having the opportunity to counter Fulke's arguments. By creating the art form of a debate, which in some way resembles a Socratic dialogue, Fulke has made his book more interesting and dramatic than it would have been if he had simply offered a critical review of Martin's work in the manner of a modern scholar. It is arguable that what Fulke does is as intellectually defensible, in principle, as a rigorous review of the work of a scholar who is deceased, provided we are aware that we are inspecting a work of art whose creator is Fulke, in the context of which Martin is Fulke's creature, though he speaks his own words.

Vernacular translations of the Bible

We have to attempt to locate Martin and Fulke on a kind of ecclesiastical grid, with special reference to new translations of the Bible from Hebrew and Greek. Martin is not ignorant of Hebrew and Greek, he was the compiler of a dictionary in which these two languages featured, and yet he presides over a translation of the Bible which was done from the Latin Vulgate and not from Hebrew and Greek. This puts him at a disadvantage which Fulke is able to exploit, because it can be shown that the attitude of Catholic scholars in Europe to new translations of the Bible from Hebrew and Greek into Latin in the period before the Council of Trent was different from the one which Martin now represents. The conclusion that Martin was an ultra-conservative individual may not be entirely beside the point, but more important is the recognition that the Council of Trent, whatever precise nuance of interpretation is given to the subtleties of its attitude to new translations from Hebrew and Greek, constituted a watershed. It had reinforced the authority of the Vulgate and had established, at least, that new translations of the Bible from Hebrew and Greek did not have the status of the Vulgate in relation to the tradition or dogma of the Roman Church.

The question of the relation of new translations of the Bible from the original languages to Church order and dogma is one which exercises Martin seriously and urgently. This was also a matter of concern to Church of England bishops and may have inclined them to caution if not to procrastination in connection with the English translation projected by Cranmer. Burnet's statement that Stephen Gardiner, Bishop of Winchester, wanted a translation 'so daubed all through with Latin words, that the people should not understand it much the better for its being in English'[16] is disputed by Mullinger,[17] and he may be right in holding that Gardiner's objective was not so much to create unintelligibility, and so defeat the designs of a popular Bible, as to safeguard technical theological vocabulary on which authoritative, ecclesiastical formulations had been founded. If indeed he saw the dangers 'of attempting to supply exact English equivalents for [Latin] words which learned divines had found it necessary to define with laborious and painful precision, and to whose definitions the decisions of the Church had given the highest doctrinal importance', he was not simply declining to turn into English certain words deemed 'safer to retain in their Latin form', but he was also hindering the advance of biblical scholarship and guarding against the possibility that better translations from Hebrew and Greek might reveal the wrongness of the technical Latin vocabulary on which ecclesiastical authority rested.

This is the complaint which Fulke lays against Martin, though it is true that he supposes Martin to have compounded the felony. Martin's position is different from that of the English Bishops, since he, as a matter of principle, does not go to the Hebrew and Greek,[18] but the translation itself, which he makes from Latin into English, is, according to Fulke, too Latinized[19] and even amounts to deliberate obfuscation:

But now you see you cannot prevail against the translation, you have begun so to translate the scripture, as in many things it were as good not translated, for anything the people shall understand by it. For you have not explicated the fourth part of the feigned ink-horn terms that you have used. And that St Augustine saith, Cresconius went fondly about to terrify him with the Greek word *anticategoria*, you do the like with parasceve, azymes, scandals, neophyte, yea, with the Latin words *gratis*, *depositum*, and such like, seek to bring the ignorant in great admiration of your deep knowledge.[20]

Similarly Fulke charges Martin with affecting 'new terms, unused or not understood', and avoiding 'common and usual terms of the same signification'.[21] Among the examples which he gives are evangelizing for preaching the gospel, the advent of Christ for the coming of Christ and scandalizing for offending.

Martin's complaint about the 'profanity' or 'secularity' of the language in the new English versions[22] is not only or principally a linguistic or aesthetic one. It acquires its importance for him because the vocabulary which is disappearing has a technical, ecclesiastical significance, or is related in other respects to crucial aspects of biblical interpretation. Vocabulary, present in the Vulgate, which sustains Christological interpretations of Old Testament texts is a particular cause of concern to Martin, and in these cases 'profanity' in English translations is seen by him as an erosion of the Christological content of the Old Testament. The aesthetic question is, however, an interesting one in its own right, largely independent of the particular historical context in which it is raised, and still with us. It is a question about the kind of language which is appropriate to a religious book, and an appreciation that a conflict may arise between 'plainness' and 'weight' or 'gravity', between the demand for popular access to the scriptures and the danger of trivialization through banality. Or it is a realization that language which will be a fitting bearer of the mystery must have a poetic, allusive quality, and that a too single-minded pursuit after plainness of communication may be self-defeating. There are echoes of this problem in the debate between Fulke and Martin, but they are incidental. The more fundamental issue is the special authority which Martin claims for the Vulgate and the circumstance that from it he has made his translation of the Bible into English.

His claims for the Vulgate are well represented in a paragraph written in an ironical vein and directed against all translators who have forsaken the Latin and translated from the Hebrew and the Greek:

Lastly and principally is to be noted, that we will not charge them with falsifying that which indeed is the true and authentical scripture, I mean the vulgar Latin bible, which so many years hath been of so great authority in the church of God, and with all the ancient fathers of the Latin church, as is declared in the preface of the New Testament:[23] though it is much to be noted, that as Luther, only in favour of his heresies, did wilfully forsake it, so the rest followed, and do follow him at this day, for no other cause in the world, but that it is against them. And therefore they inveigh against it, and against the holy Council of Trent, for confirming the authority thereof, both in their special treatises thereof, and in all their writings where they can take any occasion.[24]

Biblical science

The differences between Fulke and Martin are not understood adequately in ecclesiastical or doctrinal terms: it is not enough to say that Martin is a traditional Catholic and Fulke an Anglican of the Puritan persuasion, unless it is appreciated that such a statement also embraces a divergence of intellectual temper. It is not an accident that Fulke has a background of preoccupation with science and rational enquiry. In 1560 he had written a book against astrology, opposing the light of reason to the occult and superstitious, and his interest in natural philosophy is shown by his book on meteorology, published in 1563.[25] He asserts the autonomy of biblical science, of which textual criticism, lexicography and translation are elements, in a manner which is foreign to Martin's appreciation of the status of biblical scholarship. That Fulke does not always observe and achieve scientific rigour in practice can be shown, but in his theoretical attitude to the translation of the Bible from Hebrew and Greek into English his principles are those of a humanist scholar who makes scholarship the only test of the rightness or wrongness of the process of translation. What he hopes to arrive at by a right translation of the scriptures is nothing less than the mind of the Holy Ghost, but the means of achieving this end are entirely contained within the limits of humanist scholarship and linguistic science. Hence as a biblical scholar he is much more flexible and functional than Martin, and he regularly destroys Martin's generalizations, whether on the connections between new English translations and heresy, or the unanimity of the patristic consensus, or the infallibility of the Septuagint, by a more particular scrutiny and a greater attention to detail.

Martin makes large claims for the inspiration of the Seventy, but Fulke's interest lies in the use that can be made of the Septuagint as a scholarly aid in places where the Hebrew text is obscure: 'We reverence it for the antiquity, and use it for interpretation of some obscure places in the Hebrew.'[26] That new translations are an autonomous activity, disclosing more perfectly the mind of the Holy Ghost, and therefore a powerful agency for reforming ecclesiastical structures, doctrinal and institutional, is eagerly embraced by Fulke, but is regarded as anathema by Martin. For him the contribution which scripture has to make to the doctrines and institutions of the Church, the reciprocity obtaining between Bible and Church, has been defined or will be defined with reference to the Vulgate. That is why the Vulgate must not be superseded. To countenance the obsolescence of the Vulgate is to place in question structures whose stability and immunity from radical change are taken for granted. Moreover, a plurality of new translations differing from each other would introduce disagreement and discord in areas where the Vulgate in its singularity presented a reassuring uniformity and served as an unambiguous reinforcement of the doctrinal and institutional *status quo*. It is this uncompromising, conservative function which Martin assigns to the Bible, but its translation from Hebrew and Greek into English is for Fulke an agent of change, a radical activity which is capable of rocking the foundations of ecclesiastical institutions.

That such translations into English might in some cases and certain respects produce heresy or promote sectarianism is a contention which Fulke does not deny: 'It is very true, that so many heretics as pretend the authority of the holy scriptures, abuse the same to their own destruction.'[27] It would be ill-advised to attempt to refute such a blanket charge, but this is a different matter from accepting Martin's view that translations into English from Hebrew and Greek, in so far as they differ from the Vulgate and from each other, are necessarily heretical and sectarian in their tendency:

If the puritans and grosser Calvinists disagree about the translations, one part prefer-ring the Geneva English bible, the other the bible read in their church; and if the Lutherans condemn the Zwinglians' and Calvinists' translations, and contrariwise; and if all sectaries reprove each another's translation; what doth it argue, but that the translations differ according to their diverse opinions?[28]

Fulke's answer, in short, is that the only test which matters is that of scholarship. If new translations into English from the original languages have promoted heresy or sectarianism, the most fundamental and the only necessary criticism which need be made of these translations is that they break the rules of sound linguistic science and must be corrected by better scholar-ship. For his own part, and over against Martin, he tends to see such errors as issuing from bad biblical science rather than from a heretical or sectarian intention:

We crave no pardon, if it can be proved that we have wilfully translated another thing than is contained in the Hebrew and Greek, to maintain any false religion or wicked opinion. Provided always, that if any translator, or all the translators, have ignorantly erred in misunderstanding any word or phrase of the Hebrew or Greek text, that if it may be plainly shewed unto them, they acknowledging the fault, they may not be charged with heretical corruption, from which it is certain their intention was most free.[29]

This has to be connected with a recognition by Fulke that there are areas of obscurity in the Hebrew Bible, and that much remains to be done in the future by the application of a more refined and better informed linguistic science to the problems of translating the Hebrew Bible into English. From this point of view English translations of the Bible will be subject to change in the future, will approximate ever more closely to the mind of the Holy Ghost, and will, therefore, continue to have a reforming potential in the Church.

A different matter is the positive view which is taken by Fulke of differences in English translations. Various renderings are not necessarily or principally evidences that one rendering is correct and the other erroneous. This rests on a view of translation which is too mechanical and literal, which fails to appreciate the complexity of the relation between the language which is translated and the translation, and the degree of reshaping or creative trans-formation which is involved in the process.

The different translations should be seen as complementary rather than as in conflict, one compensating for the deficiencies of the other and, in sum, disclosing the possibilities of nuance which are present in the original:

If you were of St Augustine's judgment, you would acknowledge that the multitude and diversity of translations is for the benefit of them that be ignorant in the tongues, yea, and of them also that be learned in them oftentimes, that of divers men's translations they may judge which is the aptest.[30]

A measure of the divergence of intellectual temper between Fulke and Martin is the circumstance that Fulke is able to enlist European Catholic scholars of earlier periods, such as the Italian Dominican, Sanctes Pagninus (1470–1536),[31] Isidore Clarius,[32] a Benedictine monk, subsequently Bishop of Foligno, born in 1495, and the Spanish Erasmian, Arias Montanus (1527–98)[33] who superintended the preparation of the Royal Polyglot Bible, printed in Antwerp by Christopher Plantin and published in 1572 under the auspices of Philip II of Spain. This is an indication of the nearness of Fulke to the intellectual values of the Renaissance from which Martin was more remote. A fundamental expression of this humanist scholarship is the effort to recover original sources by forms of learning which have a scientific character, whether textual criticism, philology or lexicography, and which achieve a consummation in new translations of ancient texts. This is precisely the contribution which was made by Catholic scholars inspired by Renaissance ideals, and since they share with Fulke a devotion to Hebrew and Greek and make strenuous efforts to recover the sense of these languages as they are used in the Hebrew Bible and the New Testament, it is not surprising that he makes common cause with them.

In contrast with the sense of intellectual adventure possessed by these Catholic scholars Martin can only be described as excessively conservative. They produced critical editions of the Vulgate, combined in great works of comparative biblical scholarship like the Complutensian Polyglot (1522) and the Royal Antwerp Polyglot (1572), compiled dictionaries of biblical Hebrew, and made new translations into Latin from the Hebrew Bible and the Greek New Testament. Martin accepts the boundaries drawn by the Council of Trent and perhaps puts too severe an interpretation on them. At any rate he is resolved to abstain from any exploration beyond the limits of the 'authentical scripture' (a Council of Trent formulation referring to the Vulgate), and so a new beginning from the original languages is a 'new-fangled singularity of teaching and translating otherwise than all antiquity hath done'.[34] The passage of a century and a half had brought about a great change in mental attitude, and there is a need to remember that Pagninus had made his new translation from Hebrew and Greek into Latin with the approval of Pope Adrian VI and Clement VII, and that the work was financed by Leo X.

Fulke has the learning to demonstrate that there is a gulf between Martin and the Catholic scholars of the Renaissance. With regard to the textual criticism of the Vulgate he knows of a critical edition prepared by Isidore Clarius[35] in which many errors in 'the vulgar Latin translation' were corrected according to the 'Hebrew verity', while some were left uncorrected because the divergence was so great:

Therefore in many places he retaineth the accustomed translation, but in his annotations admonisheth the reader, how it is in Hebrew. And, notwithstanding this
moderation, he acknowledgeth that about eight thousand places are by him so noted
and corrected. This epistle [the preface of Isidore Clarius] the deputies of the Council
of Trent could not abide; and therefore in the later edition of this bible, set forth with
observation of their censure, 1569, it is clean left out.[36]

Fulke is making polemical points against Martin and is endeavouring to
undermine the authority of the Vulgate. Moreover, there are limits to his own
text-critical science, because he is assuming that the Hebrew text which was
available to Isidore Clarius, and with which he himself was familiar, can be
equated simply with the 'Hebrew verity', whereas the Hebrew text from which
the Seventy translated is another and different 'Hebrew verity'.[37] Nevertheless, if we stand back from the polemic, we find evidence of an interest in
the textual criticism of the Vulgate which is no longer part of the furniture
of Martin's mind.

In an explanation of the attitude of the Council of Trent to new translations
of the Bible which had been made by Catholic scholars Sutcliffe[38] observes
that 'the Vulgate was not declared intrinsically superior to other Latin
versions, nor were these others in any way condemned. As far as they are
concerned the decree is purely negative. They are left in exactly the condition
in which they were. Only to no other was given the juridical recognition of
authority which was accorded to the Vulgate.' The somewhat obscure
'juridical recognition of authority' is spelled out by Crehan:

The sense of the declaration was to make the Vulgate a reliable source of dogmatic
arguments for theological teaching and debate. The ground of this reliability was not
its relation to the originals, close or otherwise, but the fact that it had been for so many
centuries in constant use for this purpose by the Church, which could not have used
it for so long without engaging thereby its supreme teaching authority.[39]

A similar judgement is made by Loewe[40] who holds that the affirmation of
the 'authenticity' of the Vulgate was on grounds of its embodiment of a linkage
with patristic exegesis and not by way of depreciation of the greater accuracy
of the new translations.

From the point of view of the ideals of Renaissance linguistic scholarship
this is not entirely reassuring. It cannot be regarded as having offered
unequivocal support to biblical scholars who were devoted to the object of
effecting a progressive refinement of Latin translations of the Bible through
a continuing advance in textual and linguistic science which allowed them
an ever improving access to the original languages. The implication of the
interpretation of 'authenticity' offered above is that such a search for greater
accuracy would not be taken with the utmost seriousness by the Church and
would not be a power for change in ecclesiastical contexts. Scholars might
pursue their tasks provided they appreciated that no notice would be taken
of their results, wherever these conflicted with exegesis or doctrine or matters
of Church order resting on the Vulgate which could not now be disturbed.

The Vulgate had been given a special status and had been removed from the field of advancing linguistic science. It could not be regarded simply as a great feat of scholarship by Jerome who was the first Christian scholar to have a commanding access to the Hebrew Bible. The Vulgate was not permitted, without reservation, to suffer an assessment which made its approximation to scholarly accuracy relative. It was not to be threatened with obsolescence by the argument that it was now being overtaken by the advance of biblical scholarship and that this process would continue into a future to which no limit could be set. Hence in certain crucial respects the Vulgate was exempted from the accidents of history and was invested with an authority on which linguistic scholarship could not impinge. There could be a provision for refining the text of the Vulgate itself by applying text-critical principles to its manuscripts, but in this ecclesiastical context there could be no question of replacing the Vulgate with 'better' Latin translations done afresh from the Hebrew and the Greek, since that might produce unacceptable consequences of uncertainty, instability, doctrinal and institutional change.

Even if we were to conclude that the attitude of the Council of Trent to biblical scholarship, issuing in new translations, was not harsh, but rather, within limits, benevolent, or, at least, permissive, its historical effects, if we are to judge from Martin's stance, were to produce a further hardening. We might suppose that it is the particularity of the English situation, a distinctive insular acerbity, which gives such intensity to Martin's dislike of English translations done by Protestants from the Hebrew and Greek. At any rate he is not disposed to avail himself of the latitude allowed by the Council of Trent and, in principle, the only scripture which he acknowledges is the Vulgate. In translating the Vulgate into English he is concerned about the surrender of principle which is involved,[41] but he does it out of a sense of missionary necessity for the sake of English Catholics inundated with Protestant translations.

The authority of the Bible

It is clear that the question of the seat of authority is raised sharply by the disagreements between Martin and Fulke and that this has to be related to the differing forms of churchmanship which the two men represent. The debate is especially concentrated on translation and Fulke's case is founded entirely on humanist ideals of linguistic scholarship and is tidy and coherent. The only authority which a translation of the Bible from Hebrew and Greek can possess consists in its representing the best textual, lexicographical and philological science available at the time when it is done. Bad translation may be expressive of heretical or sectarian tendencies, but, essentially, bad translation is due to defective scholarship and its remedy is the emergence of better scholarship. The scope of Fulke's humanism and scientific temper in relation to the scriptures is not to be exaggerated. It would not be seriously misleading to say that it does not go beyond the acquisition of an English translation of the Bible: it is limited to areas of textual criticism (of which he does not have a great deal), lexicography, philology and theory of translation. What is then obtained is the best approximation possible in English to the mind of the Holy Ghost, given the present state of linguistic science and the acknowledgement that there are obscure passages which await further elucidation.

The entrance of the Holy Ghost at this point seems to mark the exit of humanism. We are still, for the most part, removed from any 'higher criticism' of the Bible, that is, from any recognition that the translation supplied introduces us to the idiosyncrasies of human authors and to the differing textures of the societies out of which they spoke and wrote. The ownership claimed for the Holy Ghost takes the translation achieved by humanist scholarship out of human hands, removes it from our world and makes it an approximation to eternal truth unrelated to the changes and chances of our historical existence.

This needs only a little qualification, but it is important to say that there is an indication in Fulke's attitude to the authorship of the Epistle to the Hebrews[42] that he had an awareness of diversities of literary style in biblical books which could only be pursued on humanist assumptions and which he had the intellectual openness to confront with historical arguments. Eusebius, Jerome and other ancient writers had questioned Pauline authorship, and these early doubters were influenced by differences between vocabulary, literary style and methods of reasoning in the Epistle to the Hebrews as compared with other Pauline epistles. Fulke himself enters a different consideration: the words in Hebrews ii 3, 'Those who heard him (Jesus) confirmed it to us' are inapplicable to Paul, since he (Gal. i 12) did not receive his gospel from men but only 'through a revelation of Jesus Christ'. Fulke urges that the authority of the Epistle to the Hebrews is not thereby diminished and falls back on Tertullian's opinion that it was written by Barnabus or Luke or Clement. Hence he says to Martin, 'But I marvel greatly why you write, that to be Paul's or not Paul's maketh great difference of credit and estimation.'[43] The phrase which throws most light on Fulke's attitude to these matters is, 'seeing it is out of controversy that it was written by the Spirit of God'.[44]

The final understanding of Fulke which we may achieve is that his belief in the authorship of the Holy Ghost co-exists with his awareness that the biblical books are attributable to human authors and that humanist, literary techniques may be employed for the evaluation of certain aspects of them, always provided that a thoroughgoing humanism does not enter into their interpretation. In the last analysis the circumstance that the authors were human does not shape or otherwise influence the content of truth which they possess.

When we turn from translation to what Martin calls 'voluntary expositions', the issues are more difficult to disentangle. It has been customary to refer to Fulke, and to other Cambridge Anglicans in the same theological camp, as Puritans or as Anglicans leaning towards Puritanism and I have not avoided this. It is, however, a designation which Fulke dislikes and which he would not have applied to William Whitaker, a Cambridge scholar elected to the Regius Chair of Divinity in 1579. The passage about to be cited turns on Whitaker's attitude to the Apocrypha in the Book of Common Prayer. Fulke follows Jerome in making a qualitative distinction between the contents of the Hebrew Bible and the apocryphal books, just as he appeals to 'the rule of Augustine and testimony of the ancient fathers'[45] in affirming the canonicity of the Epistle of St James. He remarks:

These ancient writers shall answer for our service-book, that although it appoint these writings to be read, yet it doth not appoint them to be read for canonical scriptures. Albeit they are but sparingly read, by order of our service-book, which for the Lord's day, and other festival days, commonly appointeth the first lesson out of the canonical scriptures. And as for superstition, although M. Whitaker say, that some one thing savoureth of I know not what superstition, he doth not by and by condemn the whole book for superstitious, and altogether unworthy to be read; neither can he thereby be proved a puritan, or a disgracer of the order of daily service.[46]

It is evident from this that Fulke is not opposed to the Book of Common Prayer and the liturgical order which it establishes, and that he draws a distinction between Anglicans like himself and Puritans on this ground. The ordering of public worship is not a matter for individual discretion, and so he affirms his attachment to a particular expression of ecclesiastical order, the Book of Common Prayer. In this respect he has a sense of the Church which inclines him towards a common pattern of public religion and not towards the making public of private effusions of piety. In another passage he declines the 'nick-name' Calvinist[47] and describes himself as a Christian and a Catholic. When he counters Martin's claim that the substitution of 'general' for 'catholic' in the title of the Catholic Epistles is a deliberate derogation of the Holy Catholic Church, he says:

I do not know where the name of 'catholic' is once expressed in the text of the bible, that it might be suppressed by us, which are not like to bear malice to the catholic church or religion, seeing we teach even our young children to believe 'the holy catholic church'.[48]

Here we are in touch with another aspect of Fulke's churchmanship: his attachment to the creeds. His belief in one, holy, catholic and apostolic Church surfaces in a controversy over the translation of Cant. vi 9,[49] where Martin supposes that the rendering 'My dove is alone' (Geneva Bible) has a reductionist intention over against the Vulgate *una est columba mea*. Fulke does not question Martin's assumption that there is an allusion to the Christian Church, and he argues persuasively that the rendering 'My dove is alone' (cf. NEB, 'But there is one alone, my dove') is a stronger statement of the unity of the Church than the one which appears in the Vulgate: the sense of alone is that she is the only child (NEB, 'her mother's only child').

Although Fulke is not a simple biblicist and does not press *sola scriptura* too hard, it follows from the degree of primacy which he accords to the Bible that he does not have so high a doctrine of the Church or so firm a commitment to its hierarchical structure as Martin. He does not affirm resoundingly that the hierarchical order of the Church of England is a matter of doctrine or of the substance of the Church: archbishops and bishops with their chancellors, archdeacons, commissaries and officials are elders of government to exercise discipline 'in whom if any defect be, we wish it may be reformed, according to the word of God'.[50] To this should be added the following, 'And although we have not such a consistory of elders of government, as in the primitive church they had, and many churches at this day have; yet have we also elders of government to exercise discipline'.[51] Fulke's view of the arrangements for governing the Church of England, in so far as there are distinctions of ecclesiastical rank, is functional and not doctrinal. The distinction between 'bishop' and 'priest' or 'bishop' and 'minister' is not of the essence of the Church, and within his framework of interpretation 'apostolic succession', concentrated on the office of bishop, could not be a crucial test of catholicity.

Yet Fulke is aware that the fathers established a difference of rank between *episcopus* and *presbyter*, but he places the authority of scripture above that of early Church tradition:

The name of *presbyter* in the scripture signifieth one thing, and in the fathers another. For in the scripture it is taken indifferently for *episcopus*, and *episcopus* for *presbyter*: but in the fathers these are two distinct degrees.[52]

The apparently simple and clear-cut opposition of scripture and patristic authority which appears here is not altogether representative of Fulke's position, and if we return to the matter of 'voluntary expositions' and to the question of how the seat of authority in biblical exegesis is to be defined, we encounter more refined accounts of the relation between the Bible and ecclesiastical tradition:

We expound not the scriptures after our own private conceit and fantasy; but, as near as God giveth us grace, according to the plain and natural sense of the same, agreeable unto the rule or proportion of faith, which being approved by the ancient fathers, and catholic church of Christ, in all matters necessary to eternal salvation: not bringing a new and strange sense, which is without the scriptures, to seek confirmation thereof in the scriptures (as the manner of heretics is rightly noted by Clemens); but out of the scriptures themselves seek we the exposition of such obscure places as we find in them, being persuaded with St Augustine,[53] that nothing in a manner is found out of those obscure and dark places, which may not be found to be most plainly spoken in other places. And as for the approved sense of the holy ancient fathers, and catholic church of the eldest and purest times, if the papists durst stand unto it for the deciding of many of the most weighty controversies that are between us, there is no doubt but they should soon and easily be determined, as hath been shewed in divers and many treatises, written against them.[54]

A number of matters arise from this, first the principle founded on Augustine of elucidating obscure passages of scripture by a 'conference' or comparison of similar passages whose sense is plain. Another expression of this is:

And the scriptures themselves, where they are so obscure, that neither by common-sense, knowledge of the original tongue, grammar, rhetoric, logic, history, nor any other human knowledge, nor judgment of any writers, old or new, the certain understanding can be found out, they are either expounded by conference of other plainer texts of scripture, according to the analogy of faith; or else they remain still in obscurity, until it shall please God to reveal a more clear knowledge of them.[58]

Another matter to be explored is the amount of weight which Fulke attaches to an ecclesiastical consensus in the history of biblical exegesis, and whether in dealing with obscure passages such a unanimity might take precedence over the indications which would be given by conference or comparison, following a method which operates entirely within the Bible. The answer to this does not emerge with perfect clarity, but it is likely that in the case of obscurity priority is assumed for the method of comparison of texts. Moreover, Fulke does not suppose that biblical exegesis must be so authoritative that divergence of opinion is avoided. He notices that Jerome and Augustine differed in their respective interpretations of Gal. ii 11–14, and he urges that 'voluntary expositions' are inescapable in respect of many texts of scripture.

Addressing Martin in another place, Fulke makes what might be regarded as a more fundamental submission to patristic authority and conciliar decrees in respect of biblical exegesis:

If therefore you had the spirit of the ancient fathers, you would be content to be tried by the scriptures, for reverence you owed to God's most holy and perfect writings; and not because we will have it so, who are content in many controversies to be tried by the judgment of the ancient fathers, or general councils, or universal custom of times and places; and in all controversies, wherein all the ancient fathers, all councils, and universal custom of all times and places do consent, if any think such things can be brought against us, as it is falsely and sophistically bragged.[56]

As an Anglican, and with special reference to English translations of the Bible which had been placed in the hands of the common people, Fulke defines the part which is to be played by Church instruction:

He hath the word of God expounded by catechising, sermons, and lectures, in which he may learn the substance of christian religion ... He hath at hand every where learned divines, unto whose counsel he may resort, if he be offended with anything that he readeth in his bible, sounding contrary to the publicly received doctrine of the church.[57]

The most profound difference between Fulke and Martin is that a selective approach to ecclesiastical tradition, such as Fulke adopts, accepting what is earlier but rejecting what is later, is entirely foreign to Martin. The tradition of the Catholic Church is for him one which has no brokenness throughout its course, which has brought the Church to its present position and which is irreversible. Fulke has a view which allows him to embrace the earlier reaches of tradition, and to bow to it where there is patristic unanimity, but to dissociate himself from later developments of it by positing a process of degeneration and departure from the authority of the scriptures. Moreover, the precedence which he gives to the Bible in its original tongues permits him to entertain a jettisoning of tradition and a *de novo* reconstruction which is incompatible with Martin's understanding of the relation between tradition and scripture. According to Martin, where scripture has been taken up into tradition on the basis of particular senses, the question whether these are supported by the Hebrew and the Greek cannot be pressed in such a way as to undermine the tradition and initiate a revolutionary discontinuity. Of the later course of Roman tradition in the periods of alleged degeneration Fulke says:

And when they have discoursed never so much of the catholic church's interpretation, they reduce and submit all men's judgments to the determination of their councils, and the decrees of the councils to the approbation of their pope; which, as he is often-times a wicked man of life, so is he ignorant and unlearned in the scriptures; to whose most private censure the holy scriptures themselves, and all sense and exposition of them, is made subject, under colour that Christ, praying for Peter that his faith should not fail in temptation, gave all popes such a prerogative, that they could not err in faith.[58]

Textual criticism

In the principles of textual criticism which he enunciates Fulke is more scientific and nearer to our modern understanding than Martin, even if he does not always put his principles into effect and is not flawless in practice. Given the ecclesiastical context of his engagement with Martin it is to be expected that he would dwell on the defects of the Vulgate and the obscuranticism involved in maintaining a 'corrupt vulgar translation against the truth of the original texts of Greek and Hebrew'.[59] This is a sin against the fundamentals of textual science, but, on a more empirical level Fulke observes:

For the authors of that vulgar translation might be deceived, either for lack of exact knowledge of the tongues, or by some corrupt and untrue copies which they followed, or else perhaps that which they had rightly translated, by fault of the writers and negligence of the times might be perverted.[60]

The commitment to the original sources of Hebrew and Greek, a Renaissance intellectual fervour for the primary documents, is the most general premiss of Fulke's textual criticism and it finds frequent expression:

We can well enough with good conscience and sound knowledge, that may abide the judgment of all the learned in the world, defend both the Hebrew text of the Old Testament and the Greek text of the New: not of purpose to discredit the vulgar Latin translation and the expositions of the Fathers, but to fetch the truth, upon which the hope of our salvation is grounded, out of the first fountains and springs, rather than out of any streams that are derived from them.[61]

So far as the Old Testament is concerned, Fulke leans on Jerome in maintaining a qualitative distinction between the books contained in the Hebrew Bible and those in the Greek Apocrypha. This definition of the Old Testament canon is sharpened by remarks which he makes about Daniel and Esther, books which appear in the Hebrew Bible and are added to in the Greek Bible. For one thing he takes account of the Aramaic parts of Daniel (ii 4b – vii 28) and Ezra (iv 8 – vi 18; vii 12 – 26) and makes explicit reference to them.[62] For another thing, he focuses his distinction between the Hebrew Bible and the Apocrypha on two books which, from his point of view, have both canonical and non-canonical elements:

As for pieces of Daniel and of Esther, we reject none; but only we discern that which was written by Daniel in deed from that which is added by Theodotion the false Jew, and that which was written by the Spirit of God of Esther, from that which is vainly added by some Greekish counterfeiter.[63]

The Septuagint, though not a primary source and therefore subordinate to the Hebrew Bible, has its usefulness as a supplementary tool of biblical scholarship. Fulke remarks in this connection:

We always hold, as near as we can, that which the Greek (of the New Testament) and Hebrew signifieth. But if in places of controversy we take witness of the Greek (Septuagint) or vulgar Latin, where the Hebrew or Greek (New Testament) may be thought ambiguous; I trust no wise man will count this a flight from the Hebrew and Greek, which we always translate aright, whether it agree with the Seventy or vulgar Latin or no.[64]

An example of how Fulke uses the Greek in the presence of an ambiguous text is furnished by Ps. xcix 5 (NEB 'Exalt the LORD our God, bow down before his footstool; he is holy'), where Martin, following the Vulgate (*quoniam sanctum est*), renders, 'Adore his footstool, because it is holy', commenting:

And yet at another time you follow the determination of the Greek for another advantage, as Psalm xcviii (Vulgate). 'Adore his footstool, because he is holy.' Whereas in the Hebrew it may be as in our Latin, 'because it is holy'.[65]

Fulke[66] appeals to the Septuagint's resolution of the Hebrew (קדוש הוא), namely, ἅγιός ἐστιν, 'He is holy', but reinforces this with a consideration drawn from a 'conference' of Hebrew texts: the first stichs of xcix 5 and 9 are the same (רוממו יהוה אלהינו) and the final stich of xcix 9 (כי קדוש יהוה אלהינו ; 'For the LORD our God is holy') resolves the ambiguity of קדוש הוא (xcix 5).

Martin, for his part, holds that the Seventy 'were inspired with the Holy Ghost in translating the Hebrew bible into Greek'[67] and has a much higher view than Fulke of its independent authority. This difference comes to a head principally in discussions about Old Testament citations in the New Testament. Martin's particular authority in his affirmation of the inspiration of the Seventy is Augustine, and Fulke attacks the doctrine at this source. The representation, found in Philo,[68] that the seventy-two translators were closeted and yet all arrived at an identical translation, is reproduced by Augustine[69] and is dismissed by Fulke, on the authority of Jerome.[70] Another line of argument pursued by Fulke following William Lindanus, a sixteenth-century Catholic apologist, is that 'some parts of the Old Testament in Greek, which we now have, are not the same that were counted the Seventy translation in the ancient fathers' time'.[71] This is separate from Fulke's other contention, founded on Jerome, that the Seventy translated only the Pentateuch at Alexandria:

Your argument of the number of the seventy interpreters, all Hebrews, is very ridiculous and childish. Jerome himself will laugh you to scorn in it, who acknowledged for certainty no more than the books of the law translated by them.[72]

It is notable that in respect of the Septuagint the pro-Jewish and anti-Jewish attitudes normally adopted by Fulke and Martin respectively are reversed. Martin remarks that the Seventy who were 'Jews and best learned in their own tongue' are more authoritative translators of the Hebrew Bible than those who come after them. 'Is not their credit, I say, in determining and defining the signification of the Hebrew word, far greater than yours?'[73] Theodotion, on the other hand, is labelled by Fulke as 'the false Jew'[74] in connection with the Greek additions to the book of Daniel.

Martin digs below the textual foundations of Fulke's original sources in Hebrew and Greek and gives precedence to 'the ancient approved Latin text' with his phrase 'the Hebrew and Greek that now is'.[75] The implication of this is that the extant Hebrew and Greek texts of the Hebrew Bible and the New Testament respectively do not correspond with the originals. If we ask how this has come about the answer given by Martin is that they have suffered through processes of corruption. The principal cause of corruption in the Hebrew Bible, according to Martin, is a deliberate tampering with the text by Jewish scholars in order to eradicate Christological allusions.[76] Fulke's response is to express his confidence in the ability of 'the Jewish rabbins' to interpret 'words of their own tongue' and to establish their superiority as Hebraists over 'ancient Christians ignorant of the Hebrew tongue'. He does concede, however, that the Jews 'do sometimes forwardly contend about the signification of a word or two, against the truth of the gospel'.[77] He appeals to the Massoretic scholarship of Arius Montanus and adopts the point of view expressed in his preface to the Royal Antwerp Polyglot.[78]

Other agents of corruption alluded to by Martin are heretical Christians, ancient and modern, including Marcion, *Mus Ponticus*, who gnawed at the text of scripture,[79] and Beza whose practice of conjectural emendation is a form of biting at the text.[80] Fulke's defence of Beza's arbitrariness in the cases of which Martin complains shakes one's confidence in his judgement as a textual critic. There is no question of producing textual evidence to support Beza's conjectures. These guesses were made by Beza in the hope that manuscript evidence would support them at some future date. They are founded on 'some ground or similitude of reason'.[81] When Martin refers ironically and sceptically to additions which are alleged to have 'crept out of the margin into the text',[82] Fulke replies lamely:

As for creeping out of the margin into the text, which you say is his common and almost only conjecture, why may it not come to pass in writing out of the books of the scripture, as it hath in other writings of other authors?[83]

Fulke's view[84] that the original text of Mk i 2 (NEB 'In the prophet Isaiah it stands written') is ἐν τοῖς προφήταις ('in the prophets') is no doubt influenced by his persuasion that to admit a lapse involving a confusion between Isaiah and Malachi would be an affront to the inerrancy of the New Testament. In any case his text – critical judgement is bad and ἐν τῷ ᾽Ησαΐᾳ τῷ προφήτῃ (followed by the Vulgate) is the better text. Fulke, however, does conduct the argument in text – critical terms: 'But the more part of best Greek copies leave out the name of Isaiah.'[85] The more correct reasoning is that the citation from Isa. xl 3 in Mk i 3 has resulted in the attribution of both citations to the prophet Isaiah. The observation that the citation in verse 2 comes from Mal. iii 1 has led to the secondary rectification ἐν τοῖς προφήταις.[86]

Attitudes to Jewish scholarship

As a preface to a consideration of the manner in which Jewish learning is employed by these two scholars,[87] we may investigate a little further the principles which guide and regulate their approach. There is no question that Fulke is bolder than Martin and that his positive attitude rests on linguistic principles which are clearly expressed and which go a long way towards dispelling prejudice. He holds that the scriptures are normally accessible through 'knowledge of the original tongue, grammar, rhetoric, logic, history',[88] and so it is a humanist linguistic science backed by broader humanist disciplines which he regards as the fundamental equipment of the biblical scholar. Moreover, he is not disposed to call in question the excellence of Jewish scholarship in these departments. The high philological and lexicographical competence of the 'rabbins' is to be anticipated and accepted, and Christian scholars must yield to its truth, rather than searching for ulterior motives in it or, otherwise, kicking against the pricks.[89]

Fulke has a strong sense of the hollowness of arguments, however devious or sophisticated, which fly in the face of sound linguistic judgement, and of the uselessness of standing on such insecure ground in any controversies with Jews. At fundamental levels of Hebrew scholarship he is content to accept their findings, because he is impressed with their profound knowledge of Hebrew, and that is the only test which he will apply. He does not seek victories where linguistic science would be a casualty, nor does he believe that prejudice or obscurantism will finally defeat scientific elucidation:

We must say in English, as the prophet hath said before us in Hebrew, and so truly translate the scripture, that never a Jew in the world may have just cause to accuse our falsehood or partiality.[90]

At the level of exegesis all is not so plain sailing, particularly with texts which were thought to have a Christological content. Yet Fulke insists that he is not a 'Judaizer', nor has he any antipathy, in principle, to the assumption of the Church that there are Christological texts in the Hebrew Bible:

If we followed the Jews in exposition of the scriptures against Christ, we were not so much to be pitied as to be abhorred: but if we be content to learn the propriety of Hebrew words of the learned rabbins, as Jerome was glad to do of his rabbin ... there is no cause why any man should pity us.[91]

The bone of contention between him and Martin is his considered judgement that a Christian exegesis of the Hebrew Bible has gone much too far and that a severe culling of the stock of Christological texts is necessary in the interests of biblical science.[92]

The sharpest way of indicating the scope of the Jewish learning possessed by Martin and Fulke is to examine two individual cases where it is employed. One example is Ps. xxii 17 which is rendered by RSV (xxii 16), 'They have pierced my hands and feet.' Martin[93] had alluded to כארי 'like a lion' as a deliberate Jewish corruption of כארו ('They have pierced'), intended to suppress a reference to Christ on the cross. Fulke[94] says that Martin is ignorant of 'what is written concerning this word in the Masoreth'. He apparently has in mind the note in the *masora parva* that the כ of כארי is pointed with *qameṣ* (כָּאֲרִי) and on the basis of this he argues that the meaning cannot be 'like a lion' which requires כָּאֲרִי.[95] He has also scrutinized Jewish and Christian Bibles: on the Christian side he has looked at the Complutensian and Antwerp Polyglots and has found not כארי but כארו (= כרו 'dug').

Fulke notices the rendering of the Targum in the second Rabbinic Bible,[96] 'Wounding my hands and feet as a lion would'. Whatever be the correct explanation of the text, whether it is conflate or periphrastic,[97] it should be noticed that 'wounding' here makes its appearance in Jewish exegesis. 'Wounding' is nearer to 'piercing' (Jerome in his translation of the Psalms from the Hebrew)[98] than is 'dug' in the Septuagint and the Vulgate. 'Piercing' is the sense which facilitates a Christological exegesis of the verse.

Another example is the semantic disagreement between Martin and Fulke over שאול (Sheol). This is narrow and it is the polemical setting which exaggerates its significance. Martin is arguing that the primary sense of Sheol is 'hell' and not 'grave', and that English translations of the Hebrew Bible do not acknowledge this. They allow 'hell' as a rendering of Sheol only where there is an assumption that the sense is metaphorical, as at Jon. ii 3, where 'hell' is a metaphor of 'whale's belly', just as 'when we say in English, "It is hell to live thus"'.[99] According to Martin, 'hell' as a rendering of Sheol is deliberately avoided by English translations in all places where it lends support 'in the questions of limbus, purgatory, Christ's descending into hell'.[100] In setting out the contrary view Fulke appeals to the judgement of such Catholic lexicographers and philologists as Pagninus and Isidore Clarius and he addresses Martin:

You may in time to come, if you apply your study, prove learned in that language, wherein as yet you are but a smatterer, not worthy to be heard against so many, so learned, so famous professors of the Hebrew tongue, Jews and Christians, protestants and papists, authors of grammars, dictionaries, and translations.[101]

It is not Fulke's intention to deny that Sheol can refer to 'hell' in the Hebrew Bible and so have a penal nuance:

I have shewed before divers times, that although the Hebrew word *sheol* do properly signify a receptacle of the bodies after death, yet when mention is of the wicked, by consequence it may signify 'hell'.[102]

The implication of this is that Fulke ought not to contest the rendering 'hell' in any verse where he admits that Sheol has a penal nuance. He does not allow such a nuance at Ps. lxxxvi 13,[103] and so he resists the translation, 'Thou hast delivered me from the depths of hell.'

Martin,[104] for his part, approves of Augustine's exegesis of this verse, 'Thou hast preserved me from mortal sins, that would have brought me into the lower hell, which is for the damned.'[105] Fulke argues that the point of Ps. lxxxvi 13 (and this is almost certainly correct) is the threat of death rather than the threat of punishment for sin. Hence the translation ought to be, 'Thou hast delivered me from the underworld where the dead are' (cf. NEB, 'depths of Sheol').

Another expression of Fulke's semantic understanding of Sheol runs:

So for the receptacle of the reprobate souls, in the Hebrew tongue *topheth* or *gehinnom*, which properly are the names of an abominable place of idolatry, are used; and *sheol* sometimes figuratively may signify the same.[106]

The Jewish mediaeval scholars to whom both Martin and Fulke appeal complicate rather than clarify this dispute, because the understanding of Sheol which they represent has a developed penal nuance. This is not the sense which it has, for the most part, in the Hebrew Bible. Fulke could have made his point more sharply against Martin, if his argument had been that Sheol does not have a penal nuance in the Hebrew Bible but is the underworld of the dead into which all must pass at the end of their span of historical existence. Since this was not his stance, he no less than Martin was removed from the lexicography of Sheol in biblical Hebrew, and this diminishes the significance of his advocacy of 'grave' as the primary sense of Sheol. There is one verse in the Hebrew Bible whose extant text certainly represents a heaven–hell antithesis (Prov. xv 24), but where למעלה and מטה or למטה (haplography) should be regarded as secondary elements, not represented by the Septuagint, which produce this effect.[107] Since Fulke does not doubt the originality of the extant Hebrew text, there is no point in his defending 'grave' at Prov. xv 24, which he does by saying of משאול מטה that 'if it were translated "the grave", that declineth or is downward, it were no inconvenience'.[108] This is all the more pointless in that there is a consensus of 'hell beneath' in English translations.[109]

It also conflicts with the principle which he has laid down that the rendering 'hell' is permissible where Sheol has a penal nuance.

Patristic scholarship

This section is designed to justify a statement made earlier[110] that Fulke destroys Martin's generalizations about patristic agreements by a more particular scrutiny and by greater attention to detail. In an argument which arises over the absence of any mention of 'Canaan' in the genealogical list of Gen. xi in the Hebrew Bible and the presence of such a reference in the Septuagint (xi 13) and at Lk. iii 16, Fulke tackles Martin on the solidity of the patristic testimony that the Seventy-Two were inspired, by setting Augustine at odds with Jerome:

First St Augustine[111] ... of their agreement, notwithstanding they were separated into several cells, gathereth, that those Septuagints were inspired with the same prophetical spirit of interpreting, that the prophets were in foreshewing. But this doth St Jerome[112] utterly deny, and derideth the ground of this imagination, those seventy two cells at Alexandria, as a fable and a lie.[113]

The remark of Ambrose, 'We have found that many things are not idly added by the seventy Greek interpreters',[114] is explained by Fulke as a recognition that the Septuagint may throw light on the correct sense of the Hebrew, and not as an assertion that 'they had authority to add anything which Moses had omitted'.[115] In other words, where there are textual differences between the Hebrew Bible and the Septuagint, the *Hebraica veritas* is always to be preferred.

The same type of argument is used by Fulke in order to impair the claims which Martin makes for the authority of the Vulgate.[116] Fulke refers to Augustine's initial resistance to Jerome's proposal to translate from the Hebrew into Latin and to supersede the Old Latin version which had been translated from the Greek:

Neither would he be dissuaded by St Augustine, who although he misliked that enterprise at the first, yet afterward[117] he highly commended the necessity of the Greek and Hebrew tongue for Latin men, to find out the certain truth of the text in the infinite variety of the Latin interpretations.[118]

That Augustine refers here to Latin versions translated from the Septuagint, and so to what is now called the 'Old Latin', is clear from the continuation of his remarks which Fulke translates:

For they that have interpreted the scriptures out of the Hebrew tongue into the Greek tongue may be numbered (the Seventy), but the Latin interpreters by no means can be numbered. For in the first times of the faith, as a Greek book came into every man's hand, and he seemed to have some skill in both the tongues, he was bold to interpret it.[119]

Are we to conclude, asks Fulke, that 'neither the churches of Greece, Syria, Aremenia, Aethopia, nor any other in the world, which have not the vulgar Latin, had not the true and authentical scriptures'?[120] He continues:

And though your vulgar Latin hath for many years been of great authority in the Latin church, from the time when the knowledge of the Hebrew and Greek tongues have decayed; yet is it utterly false that you say, that it hath been of great authority with all the fathers of the Latin church; whereas there is not one that lived within 400 years after Christ that knew it, but almost every one followed a several translation.[121]

There are several prongs to Fulke's argument. The Vulgate was the product of Jerome and did not exist in the earlier period of the Church. In translating from the Hebrew Bible and the Greek New Testament Jerome returned to 'the Hebrew and Greek fountains',[122] but it is these and not Jerome's translation of them which constitute 'the true and authentical scriptures'. Then again there was a Latin version of the Old Testament prior to Jerome's Vulgate, translated from the Septuagint and marked by great textual variety, and it was this which was used by the fathers of the Latin Church 'that lived within 400 years after Christ'. Hence there is no Latin Bible that is 'the true and authentical scriptures': the earlier one is not because it did not return to the first fountains, and the Vulgate of Jerome is not because it existed only from the end of the fourth century or the beginning of the fifth. A further and different defect in 'catholicity' is that there were other provinces of the early Church which had translated the original Hebrew and Greek into languages other than Latin (Greek, Syriac, Armenian, Ethiopic). The only true and authentical scriptures are the Hebrew Bible and the Greek New Testament, and although Jerome translated them, his translation must not be accorded such authority that it blocks access to them.

Gen. xiv 18, NEB 'Then Melchizedek king of Salem brought food and wine. He was priest of God Most High': Concerning this verse Martin complains ironically:

What shall I speak of the Hebrew particle *vau*? which must in no case be translated *because*, lest it should prove that Melchisedec offered sacrifice of bread and wine, as all the fathers expound it.[123]

The point is that if והוא כהן לאל עליון is rendered 'because he (*Melchizedek*) was a priest of God Most High', support is found for the contention that הוציא in the earlier part of the verse means 'offered as a priest'. Fulke grants that 'the Hebrew particle *vau* is sometimes to be taken for a causal conjunction', but he contests Martin's statement that 'all the fathers expound Melchisedec's bringing forth of bread and wine to be a sacrifice'. 'I grant that many do', says Fulke, 'but not all: yet do not they ground upon the conjunction causal'.[124] Martin's interpretation in respect of *waw* and הוציא ('offered as a priest') agrees with the Vulgate (*At vero Melchisedech rex Salem, proferens panem et vinum, erat enim sacerdos Dei altissimi*), but not with Jerome's exegesis of the verse in another place: 'Victori Abraham obviam processerit, et in refectionem tam ipsius, quam pugnatorum ipsius, panes vinumque protulerit.'[125] Fulke translates: 'Melchisedec came forth to meet Abraham the conquerer, and for refection, as well of him as of his warriors, brought forth bread and wine.'[126] On this view the verse refers to Melchizedek's hospitality and not to the discharge of a priestly function. Fulke cites Cyprian[127] in support of *autem* (rather than *enim*) and *protulit* (rather than *proferens*), and Ambrose[128] and Augustine[129] in support of *protulit*.

The process of translation

What kind of appreciation is there of the process of translation and its problems in Fulke and Martin? Martin supposes that the corrections in later English translations over against earlier ones destroy confidence in the reliability and authority of these translations. Fulke, with his sense of the progress of linguistic scholarship, regards corrections as necessary and inevitable, and does not assume that a final perfection can be achieved in any translation from the original Hebrew and Greek:

But it is a common and known fashion, you say, used of us, that not only in trans-lations, but in other books and writings of ours, we alter and change, add and put to , in our later editions. And who useth not so to do, if by later cogitations that often are wiser, he find anything meet to be changed?[130]

Martin[131] discerns in new translations, which elicit a sense from the Hebrew and the Greek different from that of the Vulgate, evidence of tendentious translation or heretical intentions, but Fulke will have these questions settled entirely in terms of scholarship, without denying that bad scholarship has issued in mistranslation in English versions. On the other hand he does deny that such errors have been wilful or influenced by a motive 'to maintain any false religion or wicked opinion'.[132]

When Martin resumes the charge of 'wilful corruptions',[133] Fulke again makes the matter hinge on competent scholarship:

Now, if some of our translators, or they all, have not attained to the best and most proper expressing of the nature of all words and phrases of the Hebrew and Greek tongues in English, it is not the matter that I will stand to defend, nor the translators themselves, I am well assured, if they were all living: but that the scriptures are not impudently falsified or wilfully corrupted by them, to maintain any heretical opinion, as the adversary chargeth us, that is the thing that I will (by God's grace) stand to defend against all the papists in the world.[134]

To drive home this point Fulke tells a story about Henry VIII and 'divers bishops' in connection with Coverdale's Bible (1535). The bishops had been asked by the king to scrutinize it and they had dragged their feet, until Henry thrust a decision on them:

And being demanded by the king what was their judgment of the translation, they answered that there were many faults therein. 'Well', said the king, 'but are there any heresies maintained thereby?' They answered, there were no heresies, that they could find, maintained thereby. 'If there be no heresies', said the king, 'then in God's name let it go abroad among our people.'[135]

This reveals Fulke's conviction that even imperfect vernacular versions of the Bible, which are honest attempts to capture the sense of the Hebrew and the Greek, can do nothing but good. More than this, he views variety in translations not as a defect or a failure but rather as in one sense unavoidable and in another an enrichment. Hebrew and Greek words do not exist in the Bible in grand isolation; their sense or nuance is supplied by their context and regard for the context may require that more than one English word should be used in translation to comprehend all the occurrences of a Hebrew or a Greek word. From this point of view a mechanical uniformity in translation should not be demanded. In claiming that variety in translations is an enrichment Fulke appeals to Augustine:

Which thing truly hath more helped the understanding than hindered, if the readers be not negligent; for the looking upon many books hath oftentimes made manifest sundry obscure or dark sentences.[136]

It is to this that Fulke[137] refers when he says that variant translations represent a range of scholarly opinions and attack problems from different angles; that scholars no less than those who do not have access to Hebrew and Greek are thereby better informed to make balanced judgements.

Another matter, the kind of language which is appropriate in English translations of the Bible, cannot be disengaged from the function envisaged for such translations, and this aspect of the subject has already been touched on in the context of the differences between the churchmanship of Martin and Fulke.[138] Where there is a fear that giving the Bible to the common people may present difficulties to the maintenance of a proper ecclesiastical authority and promote sectarianism and faction, there is a tendency to make the translation of the Bible more technical and less popular. A vocabulary which, in some respects, defeats the comprehension of the common people is then employed, one which keeps the Bible in line with ecclesiastical dogma and tradition, which preserves biblical interpretation for the experts and accommodates biblical language to the technical language which they use.

A different antithesis from popular versus technical or ecclesiastical vocabulary is that of 'profane' versus 'holy' vocabulary. Here we may recall that one factor which impelled Origen towards an allegorical interpretation of the Bible was a concern to provide sufficient philosophical interest and spiritual refinement to support the claim that it was revealed truth.[139] The case against the plain sense of scripture was simply that it was too pedestrian and could not be regarded as conveying the ultimate significance of the Hebrew Bible. There is something of this in the complaints which Martin lays about the 'despiritualizing' of the Bible, especially the Hebrew Bible, in its English translations, the disappearance of renderings in the Vulgate which were edifying and their replacement by more earthy translations of the Hebrew.

This has a link with the age-old difficulty of the Church in coming to terms with the Hebrew Bible, the conviction that to yield too much to the plain sense was to incur the peril of 'Judaizing'. The 'secularizing' of Canticles, according to Martin, is indicated by a new English title, 'The ballad of ballads of Solomon', 'so terming that divine book, *Canticum Canticorum*, containing the high mystery of Christ and his church, as if it were a ballad of love between Salomon and his concubine'.[140] The New English Bible renders Isa. xxvi 18, 'We have been with child, we have been in labour, but have brought forth wind.' Martin's complaint is that new English translations have destroyed the spirituality of the verse as it is preserved in the Vulgate (*Concepimus, et quasi parturivimus, et peperimus spiritum*) and the Septuagint:

But you say more profanely thus: 'We have conceived, we have borne in pain, as though we should have brought forth wind.' I am ashamed to tell the literal commentary of this your translation: why might you not have said, 'We have conceived, and, as it were, travailed to bring forth, and brought forth the spirit?'[141]

Martin mourns what he regards as a wilful and unnecessary debunking of the verse: flatulence instead of spirit. Fulke's answer could hardly be bettered. The rendering of the Vulgate into English offered by Martin cannot be reconciled with the grammar of the Hebrew, and the context requires 'wind' not 'spirit' as a rendering of רוח: 'The prophet's purpose was to shew that people were in desperate case, without hope of help.'[142] The only detail with which one might quarrel is Fulke's supposition that the reference to bringing forth wind is to be explained as 'torment' rather than 'emptiness' and utter ineffectiveness: not the birth of a child but merely wind. In suggesting that 'the similitude is taken of a travailing woman, whose womb if it be full of wind, she is in great torments', Fulke misjudges the way in which the imagery functions.

The disappearance of the Spirit (Holy Ghost) and its replacement by 'wind' is also a matter of complaint at Ps. cxlvii 18 (ישב רוחו יזלו מים) rendered by the King James version as 'He causeth his wind to blow and the waters flow'. It is evident that theological anxieties are clouding Martin's linguistic judgement in this verse. Fulke replies tartly, 'What need we here to cause the Holy Ghost to be sent to melt the ice?'[143]

Martin is unwilling to countenance 'profane' translations of texts which he regards as bastions of spirituality with an indispensable Christian content. There are other cases where his suspicions of tendentious translation into English are similarly unfounded. ἀδελφὴν γυναῖκα (1 Cor. ix 5) is an odd expression, but there is little doubt that Paul is referring to his right to take a wife if he so chose (NEB, 'a Christian wife'), and Martin is unreasonable in supposing that the departure from Vulgate *mulierem sororem* ('woman, a sister'; cf. KJV, 'a sister, a wife') is directed against the celibacy of the priesthood.[144] One has to suppose that ἀδελφὴν γυναῖκα is a kind of hendiadys and aim at an idiomatic rendering in the manner of the New English Bible.

Martin holds that the Hebrew of Mal. ii 7[145] should be translated, 'The priest's lips shall keep knowledge, and they shall seek the law at his mouth.' He objects to, 'The priest's lips should preserve knowledge and they should seek the law at his mouth' (cf. RSV). He alleges that an attempt is being made to call in question, 'a marvellous privilege given to the priests of the old law, for true determination of matters in controversy, and right expounding of the law'.[146] The dispute is an empty one in the context, because even if verse 7 is still setting out the ideal rather than the actual state of affairs, verse 8 leaves us in no doubt that the point of the passage is priestly failure and dereliction of duty.[147]

Fulke's awareness that translation is not a mechanical process has already been mentioned,[148] and the general statements which he makes on this topic command respect:

For to translate out of one tongue into another is a matter of greater difficulty than it is commonly taken. I mean exactly to yield as much and no more than the original containeth, when the words and phrases are so different, that few are found which in all points signify the same thing, neither more nor less, in divers tongues. Wherefore, notwithstanding any translation that can be made, the knowledge of the tongues is necessary in the church, for the perfect discussing of the sense and meaning of the holy scriptures.[149]

But his practice does not always match his general principles.

Eph. v 5, NEB, 'or the greed which makes an idol of gain'; Col. iii 5, NEB 'and the ruthless greed which is nothing less than idolatry': At these verses Fulke's response to Martin is so ill-judged that it is evident that a determination to find pejorative references to 'images' is disturbing his customary linguistic judgement. In connection with Eph. v 5 (ἢ πλεονέκτης, ὅ ἐστιν εἰδωλολάτρης) and Col. iii 5 (καὶ τὴν πλεονεξίαν, ἥτις ἐστὶν εἰδωλολατρεία), Martin remarks:

If the Greek be *idololatria* and *idololatra*, and they translate not *idolatry* and *idolater*, but, worshipping of images, and worshipper of images; and that so absurdly, that they make the apostle say, 'covetousness is worshipping of images'; this none would do but fools and madmen, unless it were of purpose against sacred images.[150]

Martin appreciates the idiomatic character of the language in these verses:

We say commonly in English, Such a rich man maketh his money his god; and the apostle saith in like manner of some, 'whose belly is their god' (Phil. iii 19); and generally every creature is our idol, when we esteem it so exceedingly that we make it our god. But who ever heard in English, that our money, or belly, were our images, and that by esteeming them too much we become worshippers of images?[151]

Fulke vainly defends his form of the idiom:

The apostle calleth the covetous man a worshipper of images, and covetousness, worshipping of images; and not properly, but because their money is to them the same occasion of departing from God, that the images was to the worshipper of them.[152]

Martin's[153] objection to the use of 'image' as a rendering of מצבה in some places and not in others in English translations is not satisfactorily answered by Fulke: 'image' is avoided at Gen. xxviii 22 and Isa. xix 19 (KJV 'pillar'). Fulke's claim that 'images' rather than 'pillars' is a legitimate rendering at 2 Kgs x 26 and xvii 10 (KJV 'images'), because there is a reference to idolatrous objects, should not be allowed. If a מצבה is a pillar, it remains a pillar wherever it occurs. Whether it is regarded as a legitimate or an idolatrous cult object should make no difference to its translation.

The Christian interpretation of the Hebrew Bible

The intention in this part is to explore the measure of agreement between Fulke and Martin, and also the differences between them, with regard to the Christian interpretation of the Old Testament. Martin's concern to maximize the Christian interpretation of the Old Testament finds expression in his disapproval of the tradition of Antioch as represented by 'Theodorus Mopsuestites' of whose view Wiles says, 'the direct prophetic message always stays ... restricted to the period before the coming of Christ'. Theodore allows predictions in Old Testament prophecy, but not Christological or Trinitarian predictions. Why does he impose this limitation? Wiles says:

The answer would seem to lie in his strong theological conviction of the radical nature of the break between the two ages or dispensations before and after Christ, which we shall meet as a prominent element also in determining the character of his New Testament exegesis.[154]

Martin describes Theodore's emphasis as an expounding of the scriptures after 'private conceit and fantasy, not according to the approved sense of the holy ancient fathers and catholic church'. He continues, 'So did Theodorus Mopsuestites affirm of all the books of the prophets, and of the Psalms, that they spake not evidently of Christ.'[155]

. Fulke, who shows more reserve than Martin in his Christological exegesis of the Hebrew Bible, finds himself in a position occupied by Christian scholars before and after him. Where he accepts plain exegesis and rejects Christological interpretations, he lays himself open to the charge of being a 'Judaizer'. His rejoinder in brief is that if and when he follows Jewish scholars, he does it not because the scholarship is Jewish but because he judges it to be accurate.[156] It is not that Fulke banishes Christological interpretation from the Old Testament; on the contrary, it is an exegetical area which he regards as vital. This appears from a sentence already quoted in another connection, 'If we followed the Jews in exposition of the scriptures against Christ, we were not so much to be pitied as to be abhorred.'[157] Yet he is clearly nervous about an indiscriminate, expansionist Christian interpretation of the Old Testament. He believes that there is a body of Old Testament texts which refer to Christ, but he reacts against an obsession with predictions of Jesus Christ in the field of Old Testament exegesis:

I have told you in the beginning of this chapter, we must not, neither is it safe for the strengthening of our faith, to draw places of scripture unto Christ, which by the Holy Ghost had another meaning: so shall the Jews laugh us to scorn; and the faith of the ignorant, which is grounded upon such translation, if it shall be opened unto them that it is untrue, shall be mightily shaken, and brought in doubt of all other places of scripture, applied to the like end. God be thanked! there be plain and evident testimonies of Christ in the scripture, which no malice of Jewish or heathenish enemies can wrest out of our hands, which are sufficient for instruction and confirmation of our faith.[158]

The expression 'which by the Holy Ghost had another meaning' is the one on which attention should be focused, because it appears to show that Fulke made no concession to an ancient tradition of exegesis, elaborated in the Middle Ages, according to which different levels of exegesis could be applied to the same text. Fulke leaves no room for a distinction between 'literal' and 'spiritual' exegesis, with its implication that the same text could be treated according to differing exegetical modes. Only one normative exegesis, decreed by the Holy Ghost, is acknowledged, and, if so, a text cannot be both non-Christological and Christological. The measure of actual agreement between Fulke and the canons of mediaeval exegesis comes about fortuitously rather than through any convergence of principle. According to the mediaeval principles there were some texts in the Hebrew Bible which were Christological through and through and which did not have a 'literal' sense.[159] The texts which Fulke identifies as Christological are nothing but Christological, yet it would be inappropriate to say, from the point of view of his principles, that they had no 'literal' sense. It would be correct rather to say that the Holy Ghost had conferred on them a Christological sense, just as it had conferred a non-Christological sense on those texts in respect of which Fulke resists Martin's Christological exegesis.

Ps. xxii 17, RSV (xxii 16) 'They have pierced my hands and feet': The disagreement between Martin and Fulke on this verse is narrow and its relation to the Hebrew text and the Targum has already been examined.[160] Neither scholar pursues the lexicography of כרו = כארו . The meaning 'pierce' is given by Jerome's translation of the Psalms from the Hebrew (*fixerunt*; cf. Vulgate, *foderunt* 'dig' = Septuagint, ὤρυξαν). Aquila, ἐπέδησαν and Symmachus, ὡς ζητοῦντες δῆσαι, 'bind', are apparently employing a different lexicography, and Koehler-Baumgartner shows as a conjecture IV כרה 'bind' (Arabic *kwr*, 'to wind a turban'):[161] 'They have bound my hands and feet.' Both Fulke and Martin[162] are content with 'pierce', because they are agreed that there is an allusion to Christ on the cross, and 'bind' would not be of service to them. But the semantic development of כרה from 'dig' to 'pierce' (also in KJV) is left unexplained.

Gen. iii 15, NEB 'I will put enmity between you and the woman, between your brood and hers. They shall strike at your head, and you shall strike at their heel': Both scholars hold that this verse has a Christian content, but whereas Martin elucidates it in terms of Vulgate *ipsa*, Fulke founds his case on MT הוא which he correctly relates to זרעך: it is the 'seed' of Eve (NEB 'they') which will bruise the serpent's head. But αὐτός (Septuagint) is not capable of this interpretation, because σπέρμα is neuter gender and requires αὐτό. Hence the reading of the Greek is more explicitly Christological, as Fulke points out: 'And the Greek translateth the pronoun in the masculine gender, (he) meaning Christ.'[163] It is supposed by Martin that the intention of Vulgate *ipsa* is to make the text refer to the Virgin Mary: the Hebrew text would have to be היא תשופך ראש and היא would refer to the third feminine singular suffix of זרעה. Fulke's theological point is that the serpent's head will be 'bruised' not by the mother of Jesus but by the seed of a woman, by Jesus born of Mary. Both are interpreting the text in the same theological area and the exegetical cleavage is not too deep, but Martin, whose case rests entirely on the Vulgate, is convinced that Protestant exegesis is directed against the Virgin Mary.

Ps. xvi 10, NEB 'For thou wilt not abandon me to Sheol nor suffer thy faithful servant to see the pit': Both scholars offer a Christian interpretation of the verse and the controversy blows up because of Martin's concern to attach it particularly to Christ's descent into hell and to doctrines of the Church, *limbus patrum* and purgatory. Fulke's exegesis is directed unswervingly towards the resurrection of Jesus, and it is He who affirms in the psalm, 'Thou wilt not abandon me to Sheol'. Fulke notices that this is how Ps. xxii 8 – 11 is interpreted at Acts ii 25 – 27, where the Old Testament citation is introduced by the rubric, 'For David says of him', that is to say, David puts words into the mouth of Jesus.[164]

In other cases Martin emerges as a Canute-like figure, defending the Christological interpretation of the Old Testament against the advancing tide of 'profane' exegesis, but all the while doomed to defeat, because he cannot prevail against the grammatical and philological sanity of Fulke. That this holds for Isa. xxvi 18 and Ps. cxlvii 18 has already been shown.[165]

Prov. ix 2, NEB 'She has killed a beast and spiced her wine.' Prov. ix 5, NEB 'Come dine with me and taste the wine that I have spiced.' Martin objects to the renderings of מסכה and מסכתי at these verses: 'She hath drawn her wine' and 'Drink of the wine that I have drawn' (Geneva Bible, 1560). He appeals to the Septuagint (ἐκέρασεν; ἐκέρασα) and the Vulgate (*miscuit*; *miscui*) and denies that 'draw' or 'pour out' is a possible sense for מסך:

Gentle reader, if thou have skill, look the Hebrew Lexicon of Pagnine, esteemed the best: if thou have not skill, ask, and thou shalt understand, that there is no such signification of this word in all the bible, but that it signifieth only mixture and mingling.[166]

On the translation 'poured out' or 'drawn' Fulke remarks:

I confess, our translators should more simply, according to the word, have said, 'mingled his wine' and 'the wine that I have mingled'; but because that speech is not usual in the English tongue, it seemeth they regarded not so much the property of the word, as the phrase of our tongue.[167]

Fulke is urging that 'drawn' or 'poured out' is preferred to achieve an idiomatic translation, but 'mingled' appears in both verses in the King James Version. Fulke anticipates the rendering 'spiced' (NEB) and, against Martin's point that mixing is a dilution of the wine with water, he cites Isa. v 22 (למסך שכר 'in mixing strong drink') and says, 'not to mingle it with water for sobriety, but with some other delectable matter to provoke drunkenness'.[168]

Fulke has no difficulty in disposing of Martin's attempt to show that Wisdom's mixing of wine to prepare for a banquet is a 'foreshewing' of 'the immolated host of bread and wine'.[169] Martin appeals to Jerome,[170] Augustine[171] and Cyprian:[172] the two verses in Proverbs are 'a manifest prophecy of Christ's mingling water and wine in the chalice at his last supper'.[173] Fulke describes this as 'watery exposition':

And if a mixture be granted in the place you require, how prove you a mixture with water rather than with anything else? Verily the circumstance of the place, if there must needs be a mixture, requireth a mixture of spices, honey, or some such thing to make the wine delectable unto which wisdom doth invite, rather than of water only, to abate the strength of it.[174]

Old Testament texts in the New Testament

Fulke rejects the possibility that Old Testament passages appearing in Greek in the New Testament may have a text or a sense which does not derive from the Hebrew Bible. This is an *a priori* theological assumption which cripples him as a textual critic and a linguist. Martin discerns that Fulke's premisses cannot be reconciled with the New Testament evidence and he probes the flaw in Fulke's reasoning:

To maintain the Hebrew verity (as they call it) in the Old Testament, he careth not what become of the Greek in the New Testament, which yet at other times, against the vulgar Latin text, they call the Greek verity, and the pure fountain, and that text whereby all translations must be tried.[175]

Martin presses home his advantage:

Will you be tried by the vulgar ancient Latin bible, only used in all the west church above a thousand years? No. Will you be tried by the Greek bible of the Septuagint interpreters, so renowned and authorised in our Saviour's own speeches, in the evangelists' and apostles' writings, in the whole Greek church evermore? No. How then will you be tried? They answer, only by the Hebrew bible that now is, and as now it is pointed with vowels. Will you so? and do you think that only the true authentical Hebrew, which the Holy Ghost did first put into the pens of those sacred writers? We do think it (say they), and esteem it the only authentical and true scripture of the Old Testament.[176]

If the Greek of the New Testament is a fountain of truth must this not also hold for citations from the Old Testament appearing in Greek in the New Testament? But if so, the mind of the Holy Ghost, expressed through the

Hebrew Bible, does not always coincide with the mind of the Holy Ghost expressed through the Old Testament citations in Greek in the New Testament. Fulke resists such a conclusion and he has several lines of defence. The conjecture that the New Testament text in such cases has been corrupted by scribal error is used only sparingly.

At Mt. xxvii 9 (Zech. xi 12) a wrong attribution (διὰ 'Ιερεμίου) appears in the New Testament. Fulke says, 'Corruption hath happened to all copies that at this day are extant, both Greek and Latin, in naming Jeremiah for Zechariah'.[177] But on strictly text-critical grounds διὰ 'Ιερεμίου is unassailable[178] and the discrepancy has to be tolerated (cf. NEB, 'The prophetic utterance of Jeremiah').

A second example (Lk. iii 36; Gen. xi 11 – 13) gives rise to a long and tedious dispute between Martin and Fulke: the point is a text-critical one and Martin has the better of the contest. καὶ ἐγέννησαν τὸν Καϊνάν (Gen. xi 12, Septuagint) is reflected in τοῦ Καϊνάν (Lk. iii 36), but in the Hebrew Bible at Gen. xi 11 – 13 there is no mention of 'Canaan' in the genealogy of Shem. The correct explanation of this is that the New Testament writer is following the Septuagint and not the Hebrew Bible, but Fulke first asserts the principle that 'whatsoever is cited out of the LXX. in the New, is not contrary to the Hebrew in the Old'. He continues: 'Therefore the way of reconciliation is easily found, without discrediting both, or either of both, in those places'.[179] He is consequently driven to assume (following Beza) that τοῦ Καϊνάν at Lk. iii 36 is 'a mere corruption, borrowed out of the corruption of the Septuagint, or a Judaical addition'.[180] For a simple and clean explanation that the New Testament is following the Septuagint, he substitutes the rigmarole of a corrupt Septuagint (perhaps derived from corrupt Hebrew) by means of which a New Testament text which originally agreed with the Hebrew Bible has been corrupted. Martin replies:

Let them tell us whether they will discredit the New Testament because of the Septuagint, or credit the Septuagint because of the New Testament; or how they can credit one and discredit the other, where both agree and consent together; or whether they will discredit both for credit of the Hebrew.[181]

Martin is prepared to tolerate differences between the Hebrew Bible and Old Testament citations in Greek in the New Testament, although he is not hungry for a critical exploration of them, and, depending on Augustine,[182] has his own form of theological reconciliation. On the proposed deletion of τοῦ Καϊνάν he says:

Alas! how far are these men from the modesty of the ancient fathers, and from the humble spirit of obedient catholics, who seek all other means to resolve difficulties, rather than to do violence to the sacred scripture; and when they find no way they leave it to God. St Augustine, concerning the difference of the Hebrew and the Greek, saith often to this effect, that it pleased the Holy Ghost to utter by the one that which he would not utter by the other.[183]

Fulke, however, seldom takes the path of emendation, and his main defence against Martin's attempt to corner him (as in the passage above) is indicated by the following:

Neither our Saviour, nor his apostles, citing any place out of the Old Testament, do bring anything disagreeing in sense and substance of matter ... from the truth of the Hebrew text. Therefore there is no need that the LXX. in those places should be rejected. Although our Saviour Christ, speaking in the Syrian tongue, is not to be thought ever to have cited the text of the LXX., which is in Greek. And his apostles and evangelists, using that text, regard the substance of the sentence, and not the form of words.[184]

The suggestion that because Jesus spoke Aramaic we should expect his citations from the Hebrew Bible which appear in the New Testament to be paraphrases is an interesting one, but the passages which are discussed do not, for the most part, have a bearing on this. The general proposal which Fulke makes is apparently that Hebrew texts are already converted into Aramaic paraphrases by Jesus and that, therefore, with such citations we now have a paraphrase in New Testament Greek at two removes from the Hebrew.

Mt. xiii 14f. (Isa. vi 9f.), which is discussed by Fulke, lends no support to his hypothesis: Mt. xiii 15, NEB 'For this people has grown gross at heart; their ears are dull and their eyes are closed.' Isa. vi 10, RSV 'Make the heart of this people fat, and their ears heavy, and shut their eyes.' The New Testament text is almost identical with the Septuagint. The Greek translators, in all probability, read the same consonantal text and assumed the same vocalization as is found in the Hebrew Bible, but הַשְׁמֵן, הַכְבֵּד and הָשַׁע are taken as infinitive absolutes rather than imperatives. NEB has done the same thing with Isa. vi 10: 'This people's wits are dulled, their ears are deafened, and their eyes blinded.' 'And I shall heal them' (καὶ ἰάσομαι αὐτούς) probably derives from a free translation of רפא לו rather than from a different Hebrew text read by the Seventy: 'and one heals him (them)' is equivalent to 'and there is healing to them'[185] which is converted into 'and I will (would) heal them'. Hence Fulke's comment on these verses is without substance: 'Beza knoweth that Christ and his apostles always keep the sense of the Hebrew verity, although they do not always rehearse the very words.'[186]

Gal. iii 13, NEB 'Cursed is everyone who is hanged on a tree': A precise textual explanation rather than the assumption of a paraphrase is again appropriate for Gal. iii 13 (Deut. xxi 23). It is true that the New Testament text (ἐπικατάρατος πᾶς ὁ κρεμάμενος ἐπὶ ξύλου) deviates from that of the Septuagint (κεκαταραμένος ὑπὸ θεοῦ πᾶς κρεμάμενος ἐπὶ ξύλου), but the crucial agreement is ἐπὶ ξύλου 'upon a tree' which is not represented in the Hebrew text. Even if it were argued that there is an element of paraphrase at Gal. iii 13, there could be no doubt that the text which has been paraphrased is that of the Septuagint. Hence Fulke's remarks are unreasonable: 'You shew either gross ignorance or intolerable forwardness, for these words "upon a tree" are in that verse (23), and in the verse next before'.[187] He is urging that the sense is the same whether or not עץ על 'upon a tree' appears after תלוי 'hanged', because of the previous occurrence of עץ על (verse 22) and העץ על (verse 23). But this overlooks the essential text-critical consideration, since the Septuagint also has ἐπὶ ξύλου (verse 22) and ἐπὶ τοῦ ξύλου (verse 23). The point on which to seize is that the Septuagint and the New Testament (ἐπὶ ξύλου) represent עץ על after תלוי and the Hebrew text does not.

Ps. xl 7, NEB 'Thou wouldst have given me ears to hear' (literally, 'dug ears for me'). Heb. x 5, NEB 'But thou hast prepared a body for me': Fulke's comment on Ps. xl 7 (Heb. x 5) is also weak and amounts to a refusal to grasp the nettle:

Likewise, where the Psalmist saith in the Hebrew, 'Thou hast opened mine ears', the apostle doth rightly collect, that Christ had a body, which in his obedience was to be offered unto the Father.[188]

This suggests that אזנים כרית לי has become σῶμα δὲ κατηρτίσω μοι in the New Testament by an exegetical process, in the course of which 'ears' were taken as a synecdoche for 'body', but the evidence does not lead to such a conclusion. It is not only the change from 'ears' to 'body' which needs an explanation, but also the rendering of כרית 'dug' as κατηρτίσω 'prepared'. In fact the text of Heb. x 5 is very close to that of the Septuagint and demands a text-critical explanation on this basis. It cannot be elucidated as an exegetical process founded on the Hebrew Bible. In Ps. xl 7 – 9 the Septuagint follows the Hebrew text closely, except that σῶμα is substituted for אזנים and כרית is rendered by κατηρτίσω. It is obvious that the Septuagint is the foundation of the Greek text at Heb. x 5 – 7.

Ps. xvi 10, NEB 'For thou wilt not abandon me to Sheol (KJV "my soul") nor suffer thy faithful servant to see the pit.' Acts ii 27, NEB 'For thou wilt not abandon my soul to Hades, nor let thy loyal servant suffer corruption'. The semantic difficulties in which Fulke is involved as a consequence of his premiss that the sense of an Old Testament text cited in Greek in the New Testament must coincide with its sense in the Hebrew Bible, is well shown by the case of נפש in Ps. xvi 10 (Acts ii 27). נפש[189] is not so much a bone of contention between Martin and Fulke in the field of Hebrew lexicography proper, as it is a problem which arises in comparisons of the Hebrew Bible with the Septuagint and the Vulgate, or with Old Testament citations produced in Greek in the New Testament. On Ps. xvi 10 Martin asks, 'Is not the one Hebrew word as proper for *soul*, as *anima* in Latin?'[190] He pokes fun at Beza's translation of נפש (*cadaver*) which he gives as 'carcase', and teases those who 'are loth to say soul' and would rather say 'life', 'person'.[191] Fulke will have nothing to do with 'soul' as a rendering of נפש and sums up the lexicographical evidence competently:

The Hebrew word in the Old Testament may be translated, according to the circumstance of the place, life, person, self, yea, or dead body, and in some place perhaps carcase.[192]

Fulke's difficulties arise when he tends to impose on the Greek ψυχή a sense agreeable with that of Hebrew נפש. The Greek text at Acts ii 27 (ὅτι οὐκ ἐγκαταλείψεις τὴν ψυχήν μου εἰς ᾅδου) is almost identical with that of the Septuagint (εἰς ᾅδην), and so the Septuagint has to be interposed between כי לא תעזב נפשי לשאול and the New Testament text. In that case the first question is not what נפש means in biblical Hebrew, but what the Alexandrian translator intended when he translated נפש by ψυχή, since it is his translation which has been transplanted into the New Testament. 'Yea, there be that hold', says Fulke, 'that it (נפש) is never taken for the reasonable immortal soul of a man, as *anima* is, specially of ecclesiastical writers.'[193] Further, Fulke has this to say:

But to our English translation, where in the margin they say 'life' or 'person', when in the text they say 'soul'; what doth this offend you? They render the usual English word for the Greek word, but they admonish the reader that the word 'soul' in this place signifieth not the soul separated from the body, but either 'the life', or 'the whole person'; because that, although the body only be laid in the grave, yet according to vulgar speech and sense the whole man is said to be buried, and his life seemeth to be inclosed in the grave, according to which popular and humane conceit the prophet in that psalm speaketh; as appeareth in the latter part of that verse, which is all one in sense with the former, 'neither wilt thou give thy holy one to see corruption', where corruption, which is proper only to the body, is there spoken generally of the whole man.[194]

The entire argument is concentrated on נפש and Fulke is urging that נפש does not denote the soul separated from the body, that the parallelism of the poetry of Ps. xvi 10 is incompatible with such a separation, and that, consequently, ψυχή at Acts ii 27 does not denote the soul as distinct from the body. Martin[195] is also extending the lexicographical chain unnecessarily by arguing from נפש to the sense of ψυχή at Acts ii 27 in the interests of the opposite conclusion, namely, that נפש means 'soul'. Both Martin and Fulke, although their conclusions are at different poles, share the assumption that the lexicography of נפש determines the sense of ψυχή in the Septuagint. It is true that ψυχή means 'life' in Homer,[196] but in the Alexandrian context ψυχή is perhaps a 'cultural translation' of נפש which assumes a Platonic or Neo-Platonic opposition of body and soul, the one perishable and the other immortal. Neither Martin nor Fulke takes this factor into account. Finally there is another consideration: how the New Testament writer understood ψυχή in the text which he took from the Septuagint and what nuance he intended for it. In any case it is the nuances of ψυχή which matter and not those of נפש in the Hebrew Bible.

The examples which have been treated, and others which could have been added,[197] show that Fulke's attachment to the 'pure fountain', the original Hebrew and Greek, does not serve him well when he attacks the problems raised by the presence of Old Testament texts in the New Testament. He applies the principle of *Hebraica veritas* in so rigid a way that it becomes a recipe for linguistic error and leads him consistently to wrong conclusions. The dogma that the only sense which these Old Testament texts can have in a New Testament context is the sense which they have in the Hebrew Bible becomes a source of error.

4

RICHARD SIMON

Richard Simon (1638–1712) combines critical boldness with Catholic conservatism. He shares with Gregory Martin the view that vernacular translations of the Bible should be made from the Vulgate and that attention should be focused on the definitions of the Council of Trent. The differences between them are more striking and Simon is intellectually adventurous in ways which set him at a great distance from Martin.

There are two principal respects in which Simon cast doubt on Fulke's description of the vocalized text of the Hebrew Bible as the 'first fountain', one critical and the other theological. On the critical front he advanced the claims of the Septuagint. The most significant critical observation which he made was not that the Hebrew text which was translated by the Seventy differed quantitatively from the text of the Hebrew Bible. Simon's point was rather that where the consonantal texts were identical, the vocalization of the Seventy sometimes differed from that of the Hebrew Bible. The consonantal text has to be interpreted (vocalized) before it is translated and different interpretations can be offered. When the Seventy indicate a different vocalization of the Hebrew from that of the Hebrew Bible, is it the vocalization of the Seventy or the vocalization of the Massoretes which gives access to the 'first fountain'? Fulke's idea which seemed so fundamental and untroubled by ambiguity lost some of its sharpness.

On the theological side Fulke's view that a competent translation of the Bible gives access to the mind of the Holy Spirit is countered by Simon. Even a translation which largely succeeded in reproducing the plain sense of the Hebrew Bible would not possess theological transparency nor constitute a supreme rule of Faith. The Hebrew Bible translated into a vernacular language and widely accessible to Christian believers is not an authority which establishes theological truth and detects error. The Christian content of the Hebrew Bible is not intrinsic. It is an external interpretation which has to be supplied by the theologians of the Roman Catholic Church. Simon's concept of the 'theological obscurity' of the Hebrew Bible was not only directed against the Protestants, but, as we shall see, served his own critical ends.

Simon's environment and the nature of his biblical scholarship

Born in Dieppe in 1638, the son of an artisan, Richard Simon was educated
at the Oratorian college in Dieppe and then by the Jesuits at Rouen. In 1658
he became a novice of the Oratory in Paris, but made a stuttering beginning
in his progress towards membership of the Oratory, terminating his novitiate
in 1659. He then studied at the Sorbonne from 1659–62, but returned to the
Oratory in September 1662 and completed his novitiate in 1663. Thereafter
he was occupied with various assignments, as a teacher and librarian in and
out of Paris, a period when he had opportunities to consolidate his learning
in general, and his Semitic learning in particular,[1] and which achieved a
kind of culmination with his consecration to the priesthood in 1670.

The opportunities for intellectual discourse which he enjoyed within the
community of the Oratory were considerable,[2] and he was on his way to
becoming an established trilingual scholar by producing a fundamental piece
of Old Testament scholarship which appeared in 1678 and was published in
Paris with the title *Histoire Critique Du Vieux Testament*. By the decree of the
king (Louis XIV) and at the instance of Jacques Bénigne Bossuet, later Bishop
of Meaux, the edition was suppressed, and the long shadow of ecclesiastical
and political authoritarianism, never subsequently to be lifted, fell on Simon's
career as a biblical scholar.[3] It was an environment in which Simon's
scholarship could not flourish. His attempts to overcome it and secure the
degree of intellectual freedom which he needed were never successful and
eventually he succumbed to it.

There were times when it seemed that some accommodation might be
reached, but the final outcome showed that the gulf between Simon and
Bossuet was always too great to be bridged. The version of Trévoux, a translation of the New Testament from the Vulgate into French, with an elaborate
critical apparatus, may be regarded as Simon's last endeavour to gain
recognition and acceptance. It appeared in 1702, ten years before his death,
and it drew the opposition of Bossuet. In the ensuing exchanges between
Simon and the bishop, the translator was, as Auvray has it, 'defeated, reduced
to silence, annihilated'.[4] Steinmann[5] has supposed that the design of the
Trévoux version was settled by prudential considerations rather than by
Simon's critical principles, according to which he should have translated from
the Greek. 'A wise translator', says Simon, 'who proposes to make intelligible
to the people the scripture which is read in church will always be obliged to
translate from the Latin rather than from the Greek and Hebrew.'[6] In any
case the bow which Simon is supposed by Steinmann to have made to
ecclesiastical authority did not avail, and he lost his last battle with Bossuet
just as he had lost the first crucial encounter in 1678.

Is it simply a case of a biblical scholar, who is principally a textual critic
and linguist, exercising an intellectual freedom incompatible with the rigid
political and ecclesiastical structures of his age and country? Was Simon born
at the wrong time in the wrong regime and predestined to a hard fate?

Or were there some individual traits, perhaps deficiencies or quirks in his personal make-up, which invited suspicion and created distrust? There is no doubt that his deviousness is odd and that it becomes more and more extravagant and pathological. It may be a kind of thrashing about, an effort to escape from an intellectual imprisonment of which he is aware. It is already present in the preface and notes of the 1685 (Rotterdam) edition of *Histoire Critique Du Vieux Testament*, contributed by Simon, but represented as the work of a Dutch Protestant.[7] It is present also in *Critical Enquiries into Various Editions of the Bible*, a work which appeared in London in Latin and was translated into English, both in the year 1684, where a dedication to J.H. (John Hampden?), ostensibly the work of the editor, R. Denison, was written by Simon.[8] John Hampden was a friend of Simon and either he or his father, Richard Hampden, may have translated *Histoire Critique Du Vieux Testament* into English in 1682.[9]

It would be helpful to be able to say firmly at the outset what it was in Simon's work on the Old Testament that appeared particularly false or menacing in the eyes of the Church. John Dryden[10] finds Simon's cavalier treatment of the Bible unacceptable and suspects that the reverence which he professes for Catholic tradition is just a smoke-screen behind which he conducts his destructive operations against Holy Scripture. Dryden objects to the divorce of faith and biblical criticism which is achieved, when inerrant tradition is conjured up in order to allow a critical freedom which shows that 'Scripture, though derived from heavenly birth, has been but carelessly preserved on earth'. Dryden smells a rat and is convinced that Simon's principal concern is with his corrosive criticism rather than with Catholic tradition.

It is not easy to reconcile the various utterances which Simon makes on these matters. On scripture he makes a distinction between errors in general and errors which 'could bring about some change in Faith and Morals'.[11] Thus he affirms: 'One cannot doubt that the truths contained in Scripture are infallible and of Divine authority, since they come immediately from God who makes use of men only as his interpreters. Also, there is no one, whether Jew or Christian, who does not acknowledge that this Scripture, being the pure word of God, is at the same time the first principle and foundation of Religion.'[12] But then he also says: 'The Catholics who are persuaded that their religion does not depend only on the text of Scripture, but also on the Tradition of the church, are not at all scandalized to see that the misfortune of times and the negligence of copyists have brought about changes in sacred books as in profane works.'[13]

It appears from this that there can be nothing in scripture concerning faith and morals which would conflict with the testimony of Catholic tradition, and even that a priority is assigned to scripture: it is 'pure word of God', 'the first principle and the foundation of Religion'. Further investigation will awaken doubt whether scripture can have such an autonomy for Simon in the definition of faith and morals, whether it does not await an interpretation imposed by Catholic tradition before it achieves dogmatic status. In any case, the relation which obtains between scripture and tradition in Simon's scheme is still vague and requires further elucidation. Whether or not Dryden's suspicions are justified, we are on the right track when we ask questions about the boundaries which Simon fixes for critical biblical scholarship. How does he understand the relation between the Bible, which he studies almost exclusively as a critical scholar, and Catholic tradition in which authoritative ecclesiastical teaching on dogma and morals is encapsulated?

It would be easy to gather a wrong impression of Simon's book from the statement that he is 'the father of Biblical Criticism', coupled with the observation that he limited Mosaic authorship of the Pentateuch to the laws which are contained in it.[14] It is generally true that one is not well prepared for an encounter with the *Histoire Critique* by summary references to it in other books. A reason for this is the prominence which is given to Simon's denial of Mosaic authorship of the entire Pentateuch, for one discovers that this is a minor item, that it occupies only a small part of the book and that it is not a clue to the principal concerns and tendencies of Simon's criticism. Moreover, this is not an area in which he is impressively original: the degree of his dependence on Abraham Ibn Ezra is admitted,[15] and the examples which he produces to show that Moses did not write the whole of the Pentateuch are those which appear in Ibn Ezra's comment on Deut. i 1.[16]

A concentration on this higher-critical foray at the beginning of the book distracts attention from the scale and plan of his work which reveals that he is not operating, for the most part, in the area of higher criticism. If he has a right to be regarded as a father of biblical criticism, it is because of his textual and linguistic expertise, his exploration of the relations between the Hebrew Bible and the ancient versions, his views on Massoretic scholarship, on Hebrew grammar and lexicography; and the bearing of all this on critical biblical scholarship as expressed in translation and exegesis. The gist of his argument is that in this entire area biblical scholarship may be granted independence without any damage being done to Catholic tradition.

This is somewhat distant from the contents and considerations of what is usually regarded as higher criticism of the Old Testament, and Steinmann[17] has overstated the degree to which Simon, with his hypothesis of archives and archivists or 'public writers'[18] has anticipated a documentary hypothesis for the Pentateuch. No doubt to some of his contemporaries denial of Mosaic authorship of the 'annalistic' parts of the Pentateuch was one of the more shocking aspects of his work, but he did not make a great advance on what Ibn Ezra had already said in the Middle Ages.

His interests are certainly aesthetic as well as textual, philological and semantic, but his are not the source-critical pursuits of higher critics, because the historical and literary problems which arise for them are hardly at all in his sights. He apparently does not find any difficulty in accommodating all the material in the Pentateuch, excepting the laws, to his hypothesis of archives and archivists, even the book of Genesis and the contents of chapters i – xi of that book. The different literary genres represented[19] are, therefore, not part of his critical perception and concern, nor the consideration whether all the contents of the Old Testament can credibly be regarded as the kind of literature which would be gathered into archives. He is working with a crude idea of historicity, according to which all the material in the Old Testament is historiographical. All that needs to be demonstrated is that it has been safely conserved in archives, and transmitted and edited by reliable archivists.

It is true that he describes these archivists as 'divine writers' and 'inspired prophets', and that the prophets, in a narrower sense, are said to be not only recorders, but also preachers and unveilers of the future whose harangues are deposited in archives.[20] On the whole, however, he is reducing inspiration to professional competence in the selection, abridgement and expansion of archives, and so he gives the palm to Ezra,[21] the scribe *par excellence*, whose editorial superintendence was the most crucial and far-reaching in the entire process of transmission. He observes that these editors, who are preserved from error by a special divine endowment, sometimes indicate the archives from which they are selecting.[22]

It is a matter of some difficulty to establish how these higher-critical observations are to be related to Simon's text-critical opinions on the Hebrew Bible. Simon makes much of the imperfections of the Hebrew text and of the circumstance that the originals (autographs) are not preserved and that only defective exemplars (copies) are available. The most reasonable interpretation[23] is that the process of transmission which he describes, involving archives and archivists or scribes, is not intended to convey any suggestion of defect or imperfection and that it goes beyond the limits of textual criticism proper. It is described as an organic process of selection and modification of existing archives. This implies that in such a process of weeding out and supplementation the representation of the raw archives in the biblical text is constantly changing, and that this transformation goes on until the text is fixed. Then, and only then, will it be possible to speak of autographs and copies and to describe the transmission of the text in text-critical terms. This, in the post-Ezra period, will bring us into the area of mechanical defects in the copying of the text, in a word into the sphere of scribal errors.[24]

This point has been reached when Simon observes that the Hebrew text available to the Seventy was different from the Hebrew text 'of to-day', and that the Jews corrected the Hebrew text in the period after the Septuagint translation.[25] Connected with this is the view that manuscripts copied for use in synagogues achieved a higher degree of accuracy than those copied for private use[26] and that the Septuagint was translated from the latter class of Hebrew manuscripts.[27] This is an effort to explain the deviations of the Hebrew *Vorlage* of the Septuagint from the Hebrew text 'of to-day'. Simon[28] supposes that faulty mechanical transmission is partly due to the disappearance of Hebrew in the post-exilic period, its replacement by Aramaic, and the consequent tendency of copyists to introduce Aramaisms. It was one of the tasks of Massoretic scholarship to correct these, but some have survived.[29] He holds[30] that the interchangeability of א and ה is also related to Aramaic influence, originating with copyists who confused the two phonemes after the return from Babylon.

The feature which demands most attention in a drawing together of the threads of this discussion is located in the higher-critical sphere. An activity which is described as the exercise of a human intellectual capacity (judicious editing) and seems, therefore, to be disengaged from ideas of divine endowment or inspiration or prophecy, is, nevertheless, supposed to enjoy a freedom from error because of such divine enabling or participation. This combination of editorial judgement exercised on archives, on the one hand, and inspiration, on the other, is intellectually uncomfortable. On the assumption that נביא means 'public speaker' these 'public writers' can also be represented as נבאים.[31] But they are not men who would claim, given Simon's description of them, that the 'word of Yahweh' had been revealed to them in an immediate way, and so they are not prophets in that sense. Auvray[32] describes Simon's view of inspiration as Molinist and indicates that the concern of Molinism was to correct a failure to do justice to the human dimension of the Bible. The precise problem, however, is that Simon does not combine the divine and human aspects which he allows to the Bible in a credible way. Two disparate and apparently incompatible modes of cognition are being combined, and the only sense that can be made of this is that these editors or public writers are unaware of any divine reinforcement as they undertake their tasks and that it does not enter into their intellectual reckoning. It is a separate, parallel process which does not interlock with their mundane competence – a kind of special, over-arching providence.

It follows from this that Simon's higher-critical theory is better understood in the total context of his critical history of the Old Testament and the shape which it assumes, rather than as an anticipation of documentary hypotheses which subsequently appeared, especially in connection with the Pentateuch. His interest in the study of the Bible is almost entirely a critical one and he seeks complete intellectual freedom on the ground that such scholarship does not impinge on the authoritative teaching of the Catholic Church in relation to dogma and morals. He concentrates his scholarship on textual and linguistic problems associated with translation, and in his exegesis he focuses on the so-called literal sense. This is an outline which requires refinement and qualification, but it is nonetheless true that what Simon is doing, for the most part, is to carve out for himself a field of biblical scholarship in which he can work, unfettered, with humanist assumptions. He asserts that the Bible is 'the first principle and the foundation of Religion',[33] but he is hardly at all exercised to show that it serves this end.

For most of the time it is Catholic tradition which must support the truth of religion. Simon smuggles God and divine truth into the Bible, but he makes no use of them: his own brand of biblical scholarship does not need such theological support. He is trying to preserve a tenuous link between his critical scholarship and the Bible as divine truth, but the purest form of his understanding is perhaps that the Bible only becomes divine truth when it is interpreted authoritatively by Catholic tradition. The defect is that he does not display convincingly the interpenetration of scripture and tradition, because he is almost exclusively taken up with the literal or plain sense of the Old Testament. These are matters to which we shall return.

Simon and Jewish scholarship

Simon distances himself from the often repeated Christian claim that the Jews had maliciously corrupted their scriptures. This was particularly associated with allegations that Christological allusions in the Old Testament had been suppressed. Such Christian exegesis is almost entirely absent from Simon's book, and so he has no exegetical goals which would incline him to entertain seriously a charge that corruption of the Hebrew text of this kind was ever perpetrated by Jews. For example, when he deals with Ps. xxii 17, a verse over which Martin and Fulke quarrelled,[34] he rejects the Christian allegation that it has been deliberately corrupted by Jews.[35] In assessing the attitude of the ancient Fathers factors to be borne in mind (according to Simon)[36] are that their Bible was the Septuagint, that the Jews confronted them with a Hebrew text different from the Septuagint, and that they did not have a knowledge of Hebrew which enabled them to explore the significance of these differences for themselves. Of Justin Martyr Simon[37] says that he knew neither Latin nor Hebrew, so that his views on the question of Jewish corruption of the scriptures rest solely on his comparison of the Septuagint with Aquila, where Aquila is textually different from the Septuagint. Thus Justin[38] notices that עלמה (Isa. vii 14), rendered by the Septuagint as παρθένος 'virgin', appears in Aquila as νεᾶνις 'young woman', and the charge of corruption boils down to bad translation or interpretation. The assumption of the ancient Fathers,[39] is that the Septuagint is inspired and that whatever does not agree with it in the newer Greek translations made by Jews, is to be regarded as corrupt: 'Now, since this principle is not true, one must necessarily conclude that all the consequences which the Fathers drew from it were not true.'[40] Origen's Hexapla was, therefore, according to Simon,[41] a convenience for disputation with Jews, since by means of it the Greek versions could be read *tout d'un coup* and compared with the Septuagint.

On the subject of Jewish corruption of their scriptures the authority of Origen and Jerome is pre-eminent, but in this as in other matters they present us with a troublesome ambiguity, now apparently concurring with the popular view and now resisting the charge of deliberate corruption. When they speak of corruption, they go against *leur véritable sentiment, pour s'accommoder à l'opinion des autres*.[42] Origen[43] accommodates himself to the people by urging that the process of comparing the Hebrew text with the Septuagint is too *recherché*, while elsewhere[44] he accords primacy to the Septuagint. Jerome[45] supposes that Origen adhered to the 'common version' (i.e., the Septuagint) in his *Homilies*, but not in his more learned works.[46] It was a case of horses for courses, and

Jerome[47] represents that he is following the practice of Origen and other Fathers who do not always express in their disputes what they think, but what they judge to be most pertinent (*le plus à-propos*).[48]

Jerome had espoused *Hebraica veritas* and yet on occasions he accuses the Jews of having corrupted their text. He replies to Rufinus,[49] and others who complain, that they ignore the laws of dialectic: in a dispute one speaks now in one way, now in another. A further complication discerned by Simon is that Jerome may, on one side, simply be reporting Jewish opinion and, on the other, transmitting patristic views, in neither case allowing his own opinion to emerge.[50] Jerome does not decide whether the verse (Josh. xv 59a – Septuagint) containing 'Ephrathah, that is, Bethlehem', has been removed by the Jews or added by the Seventy, influenced by Mic. v 1. It is easy, however, according to Simon,[51] to discover Jerome's true opinion, since he asserts elsewhere that the Jews did not corrupt their text. This is a case where the Jews are alleged to have suppressed 'Ephrathah, that is, Bethlehem' at Josh. xv 59 because of its Christological significance at Mic. v 1: 'But you Bethlehem in Ephrathah are small among Judah's clans, yet out of you shall come a governor for Israel.'

Morin's[52] resolution of the ambiguity of Jerome, that his different views are to be correlated with different periods of his life, is rejected by Simon.[53] Morin holds that Jerome praised the Septuagint as a prophetic product and as inspired when he was a young man and accused the Jews of having corrupted their scriptures; then he changed his mind, fraternized with the Jews and denounced the Septuagint. Jerome had replied to a similar charge by Rufinus.[54]

In Augustine[55] differences between the Hebrew Bible and the Septuagint are attributed to providence rather than to a corruption of their own scriptures by the Jews. The Seventy were enabled by God to translate in a manner which would best suit the needs of Gentile Christians when they emerged. Despite his preference for the Septuagint, Augustine, according to Simon,[56] did not fail to do justice to the Hebrew Bible and the Jews against the common sentiment of the Fathers. He was capable of preferring the Hebrew to the Greek, as in the case of Jon. iii 4 (Septuagint, 'three days'; Hebrew, 'forty days').

Simon's[57] own conclusion is that there is no compelling evidence that the Jews have corrupted their scriptures, and his attitude invites comparison with that of Fulke[58] whose tendency was to reject or, at least, minimize charges against the Jews made by Martin. There is, however, a significant divergence of opinion between Fulke and Simon. Fulke's reliance on Jewish scholarship is less reserved than that of Simon, and Fulke has an interest in the Christological exegesis of the Hebrew Bible almost entirely outside the limits set by Simon for his critical scholarship. The consequence of this is that the reservations made by these two scholars are different in kind and are located in different areas of Jewish scholarship. Simon challenges Rabbinic and Massoretic scholarship whereas Fulke is inclined to accept it and declare the opinions of the Rabbis 'froward'[59] when they do not support his exegesis in texts which he regards as Christological. Simon does not engage in such exegesis of the Hebrew Bible and does not confront Jewish scholarship on these matters.

An opinion which is one-sided but which is characteristic of Simon[60] is that the concern of the Jews with the plain sense of the Hebrew Bible was a response to Christianity and to the Christian appropriation of the Septuagint. He supposes that the production of Greek translations which were closer to the text of the Hebrew Bible than the Septuagint belongs to the same pattern of Jewish reaction. This is supplemented by the statement that Jewish opposition to the Septuagint is to be set in the context of a conflict between Palestinian and Hellenistic Jews.[61] Simon does not adequately appreciate that inner-Jewish accounts of the new Greek translations can be given, especially in relation to the Pentateuch and to authoritative interpretations of the law with which these new translations agreed. The impression given by Simon that we have to reckon simply with Jewish reactions to Christian initiatives is misleading. Similarly Simon's view that freer forms of Jewish exegesis take a back seat for apologetic reasons and that there is a concentration on plain exegesis (*peshaṭ*) in order to counter Christian interpretations of the Septuagint should be treated with scepticism.

More generally, Simon is urging that scholars should not be overawed by Jewish biblical scholarship. The Jews have laboured to refine and correct the Hebrew text and they have armed themselves against a Christian interpretation of the Septuagint by concentrating on the plain sense of scripture, but it should not be thought that their textual criticism, as expressed in Massoretic scholarship, is the last word.[62] Moreover, the 'new grammars and dictionaries', which are generated by Massoretic learning and rest on its assumptions, should not be thought to embody a perfect acquaintance with the Hebrew language. Simon[63] has some expectation that a collation of Hebrew manuscripts will advance the textual criticism of the Hebrew Bible, and in this connection he tends to regard the Massoretic device of Q^{e}re – K^{e}tib as essentially a setting out of variant readings. Many of these variants, he urges, are superfluous, and a scrutiny of Hebrew manuscripts combined with intelligent conjectures will enable us to reduce their number.

By 'variant readings' Simon means principally cases of Q^{e}re –ʾK^{e}tib, but he gives one or two examples which go beyond this. ילד (1 Chr. ii 48) is read as יָלְדָה (MTʾיָלַד), since, for the sake of the sense, Maacah (feminine) must be the subject of the sentence.[64] Simon reports that he has read ילדה 'in an ancient Spanish manuscript'[65] and explains the form ילד in terms of his general view that the caprice or carelessness of copyists has produced a situation where in the Hebrew text 'of to-day' vowel letters (here ה) are sometimes represented, sometimes omitted. Moreover, a possibility of confusion[66] exists between the function of א, ו, and י as vowel letters and their consonantal function, so that מלאכי (Isa. xiv 32) can be read as 'envoys' (א a consonant) or 'kings' (א a vowel). Hence Jerome[67] ought not to have criticized adversely βασιλεῖς ἐθνῶν 'kings of the nations' (Septuagint). Simon apparently assumed that the Greek translators read מלכי, but his point would have been better made if he had concluded that they equated מלאכי with מלכי, supposing that א was a vowel letter.

Simon's main discussion of textual variants is linked to his account of Qᵉre – Kᵉtib and there are perplexing features about it. He recognizes that this device has to be associated with the scrupulous preservation of the consonantal text by the Massoretes, and yet, for the most part, he neglects this aspect of the matter. If weight is attached to it, the Massoretes are seen not to be supplying textual variants. His statement, 'The Massoretes gave the names Qᵉre – Kᵉtib to the different readings of manuscripts'[68] deepens our perplexity, because he suggests, at the same time, that the Qᵉre is sometimes to be regarded as the correction of a copyist's error, and a correction has a different status from a textual variant founded on manuscript evidence. Certainly Qᵉre and Kᵉtib cannot be regarded as representing textual variants of equal standing, because the Kᵉtib is the consonantal text and the Qᵉre a modification of the consonantal text. Simon[69] proposes to deal critically with Qᵉre – Kᵉtib by correcting the text (that is, inserting the consonants required by the Qᵉre into the text) in many places where the Massoretes have been too scrupulous in keeping the old reading (that is, the Kᵉtib). His programme[70] is to eliminate by critical decisions 'variants' which are a consequence of copyists' errors and to preserve only those instances of Qᵉre – Kᵉtib which represent 'real variants', locating the better variant in the text and the inferior one in the margin.

One aspect of the superfluousness of the Qᵉre which Simon does not consider is a failure by the Massoretes to understand an unusual morphology or orthography in the Kᵉtib, where the critical decision which is needed is an affirmation of the Kᵉtib. It is difficult to resist the conclusion that a defective grasp of the subject impairs the discussion and that Simon's proposals, because they would obscure the distinction of status between Qᵉre and Kᵉtib intended by the Massoretes, would have bad critical consequences and would amount to a suppression of textual evidence.

There is an oddness in the state of affairs which is disclosed by this criticism of Simon. It is founded on a distinction between the consonantal text and the text as constituted by the Massoretic vocalization (the Massoretic text), and this is a distinction to which, in other respects, Simon attaches importance. He notices[71] that vowel points were not in existence in the time of Jerome, so that one has always to be aware of the possibility that Jerome's translation may rest on a vocalization of the Hebrew consonants different from that of the Massoretic text. Simon's purpose is to make a clear, qualitative distinction between the consonantal text and the much later apparatus of vowel points, and he praises Louis Cappell's book[72] for having set this out clearly. The 'patriarchs' of Protestantism (Luther, Zwingli, Calvin) appreciated this distinction, and Robert Olivet, Calvin's cousin, gave many proofs of it in his translation from Hebrew into French, but the bad influence of Buxtorf had led more recent Protestants to suppose that raising the vowel points to the same status as the consonants was necessary to the principle of *sola scriptura*. The prolegomena to Walton's Polyglot show that more judicious Protestants prefer Cappell to Buxtorf.[73]

The vowel points are then to be understood as imposing a particular interpretation on the consonantal text which does not exclude other interpretations. The Tiberian system of vocalization is not to be thought of as a *creatio ex nihilo*, but rather as a fixation of time-honoured usage. In this Simon follows Ibn Ezra's view that the Rabbis of Tiberias read the Hebrew text in the same way as Ezra and the members of the Great Synagogue had done in their time, adding points and punctuation in order to transform an oral tradition of synagogue reading into a written system.[74]

This consideration of consonantal text and vowel points has an important bearing on Simon's general view of the Hebrew Bible, particularly on his contention that it is obscure and indeterminate in respects which the Protestants do not weigh when they insist that the Bible is the supreme rule of Faith. Into this context can be fitted his views on the Samaritan Hebrew Pentateuch which, he notes,[75] is unpointed and to which he gives a text-critical precedence over the ancient versions. The Samaritan Pentateuch, written in Hebrew with ancient characters, is an exemplar (a manuscript of the Hebrew text) and not a version. Hence it has the same standing as the consonantal text of the Hebrew Bible, and its variants are genuine text-critical variants. 'Let us see now', says Simon, 'if their exemplar is to be preferred to that of the Jews, or if we should follow both as two exemplars of the original, each of which has its perfections and defects.'[76]

He notices the different ways in which this enquiry can be pursued: one can suppose that variants in the Samaritan Pentateuch are the consequence of a partisan, schismatic stance (for example, the substitution of Gerizim for Ebal) or of copyists' errors, and that the better text of the Pentateuch is preserved in the Hebrew Bible. Alternatively, it may be thought that the text of the Samaritan Pentateuch is superior, but the arguments for this presented by Morin[77] do not convince Simon. These are that *plene* spelling is more consistently represented in the Samaritan Pentateuch than in the Massoretic text, and that the Q^ere – K^etib differentiation, which simply preserves textual corruptions, is absent from the Samaritan Pentateuch. Simon's interpretation of the latter point is that the Samaritans were readier to alter the consonantal text to achieve evenness than the Jews. He prefers the scrupulousness of the Q^ere – K^etib method of the Massoretes, even if it is sometimes mistaken, because it preserves a greater openness of interpretation than the Samaritan Pentateuch.

Simon has a view that *plene* spelling always involves a double representation, one by means of vowel letters and the other by vowel points. The implication of this is that *plene* spelling ought in principle to preserve the consonantal text as it was before the acquisition of vowel points. The extant mixture of *scriptio plena* and *scriptio defectiva* is due to the unsystematic practice of copyists who have sometimes preserved both vowel letters and vowel points and sometimes only vowel points. Thus he urges[78] that if we had older manuscripts, we should discover many *yodhs* and *waws* which the Jews have deleted, principally since the points were invented. The conclusion demanded by this theory would seem to be that the Samaritan Pentateuch preserves the ancient consonantal text, but Simon, nevertheless, traces the practice of consistent *scriptio plena* in the Samaritan Pentateuch to a secondary imposition of the uniformity.[79] In any case the view that *scriptio plena* is a more ancient form of Hebrew orthography than *scriptio defectiva* conflicts with the evidence provided by Hebrew inscriptions.[80]

Simon examines the instances where the Samaritan Pentateuch agrees with the Septuagint. The correct conclusion, he holds, is not that it has been translated from the Greek, but that the Septuagint has been translated from the same Hebrew *Vorlage* as is represented by the Samaritan Pentateuch. He remarks, however, that the possibility of secondary additions to the Samaritan Pentateuch from the Septuagint should not be ruled out, since the Samaritans had connections with Alexandria and had a Greek version of the Pentateuch.[81] A few of Simon's examples will show how he orders his discussion:

(a) Gen. ii 2: According to the Massoretic text God finished his work of creation on the seventh day, but the Samaritan Pentateuch, with the Septuagint and the Syriac, reads 'sixth day', *ce qui semble faire un meilleur sens*.[82]

(b) Gen. iv 8: The Samaritan Pentateuch, along with the Septuagint and the Vulgate, has the additional words, 'Let us go into the field'. Simon notices that Jerome[83] preferred the shorter Massoretic text, but that 'he treated the Samaritan Pentateuch as if it were a version rather than an exemplar'.[84] The New English Bible has the longer text.

(c) Deut. xxvii 26: Simon rightly dismisses the allegation that כל, 'all', 'every', which appears in the Samaritan Pentateuch and is represented by the Septuagint, has been deleted by the Jews in order to exclude themselves from the curse of the law. He observes that its absence or presence makes no difference to the sense.[85] The Septuagint has πᾶς ἄνθρωπος ὅς οὐκ which can represent אשר לא (Hebrew Bible) or כל אשר לא (Samaritan Pentateuch).

One feature which raises doubts in Simon's mind about the purity of the Hebrew text of the Samaritan Pentateuch is its tendency to fill out the sense of certain passages by means of insertions from parallel passages. He does not suppose that an enhanced explicitness in the Samaritan Pentateuch over against the Hebrew Bible is a valid reason for urging the textual superiority of the Samaritan Pentateuch. Examples of this type of supplementation are supplied by Exod. xii 40 and Gen. ii 24: at Exod. xii 40 the 430 years of the Massoretic text is harmonized with the conventional chronology by the addition of ואבתם, 'and their fathers'; at Gen. ii 24 והיו לבשר אחד ('and they will be as one flesh') is supplemented by שניהם, 'both of them'.[86] In the Samaritan Pentateuch Gen. xlii 16 is supplemented by Gen. xliv 22, 'The youth may not desert his father, for if he deserts him, his father will die.'[87]

Simon's conclusion is that where variants in the Massoretic text and the Samaritan Pentateuch both make good sense, they should be noted as significant variants of the same original.[88] The scrupulousness of the Massoretes has been overdone and the number of examples of Q^{e}re – K^{e}tib can be considerably reduced, but the elimination of all these alternatives in the Samaritan Pentateuch is a foreclosing of the openness of the sense of the consonantal text. The very excessiveness of the textual conservatism of the Massoretes inspires confidence in their conscientiousness and integrity. Hence, while Simon would use the Samaritan Pentateuch to correct the Massoretic text, if he expresses any preference it is for the consonantal text preserved by the Massoretes.[89]

The final important element in Simon's textual criticism of the Hebrew Bible is the Septuagint, and there are two aspects to this. The first is connected with his awareness that the Hebrew text which was available to the Greek translators is not identical with the Hebrew text 'of to-day'.[90] This is related to his terminology of originals (autographs) and exemplars (copies), about which he makes too much fuss.[91] The possession of autographs is not a normal expectation of a textual critic of ancient documents, and he would not necessarily despair of reconstructing the original text simply because he had no 'originals' in Simon's sense. The important consideration would be whether the 'copies' were accurate, or, to dispense with Simon's language, whether there were manuscripts available on the basis of which a critical reconstruction of the original could be undertaken.

Simon is attempting to show that the readings of the Hebrew text are not 'constant and assured', and he compares not only a reconstructed Hebrew *Vorlage* of the Septuagint with the Hebrew text of his time, but also Jerome's Hebrew text with the Hebrew text of his time. He argues[92] that although Jerome was aware of evidences of a Hebrew text different from the one which he had, in practice he tended to equate the exemplars of his time with *Hebraica veritas*: 'He did not always have sufficient regard to readings founded on the ancient versions and the nature of the Hebrew language.' Nevertheless, he could on occasions prefer the indications of the Septuagint, as at Zeph. ii 14, where *corvus* 'raven', which agrees with κόρακες, represents ערב over against חרב. 'drought' of the Hebrew Bible.[93]

The main thrust of Simon's argument is that by the time the Septuagint came into existence there was already a 'diversity of exemplars' attributable to careless copying in an earlier period, 'when the study of criticism was entirely neglected'. He does not, therefore, propose to correct the Hebrew text 'of to-day' on the basis of the Hebrew *Vorlage* of the Septuagint 'because the Seventy did not have the true original (*le véritable original*) any more than we have and their copy of the Hebrew text had as many errors as ours'.[94] The outcome of Simon's deliberations is somewhat disappointing. He might have shown another kind of interest in the material differences between the Massoretic text and the Septuagint, and raised questions about the Hebrew *Vorlage* of the Septuagint different from those which occupy his attention.

In the presence, for example, of a Greek text in the book of Jeremiah significantly shorter than the Massoretic text he might have enquired whether the shorter text was founded on a *Vorlage* which represented a more original Hebrew text than that of the Hebrew Bible.

His argument is a very narrow one and is entirely devoted to a demonstration of the imperfection of the extant Hebrew text. It was already in disarray at the time when the Hebrew Bible was translated into Greek, and the Jews made subsequent efforts to refine and correct it, but, even so, the text 'of to-day' has many imperfections. This is not a conclusion with which any textual critic would disagree, but one has the impression that Simon has used a sledge-hammer to crack a nut. The detail into which he goes is, however, understandable in connection with his general theme of 'obscurity'. He is urging against the Protestants and their principle of *sola scriptura* that the Hebrew Bible is not the model of intelligibility which they represent, and that one of the reasons why it is not plain sailing to translate the Bible into any language is the corruptness of the Hebrew text. This defeats elucidation more frequently than is generally appreciated and is especially severe in books like Psalms, Micah, Hosea, and, more broadly, in poetry rather than in prose. This is a relevant contemporary matter, for it is still only dimly perceived outside the circle of those who engage in the translation of the Hebrew Bible.

The second aspect of Simon's text-critical use of the Septuagint is the more important and is nearer to his principal concern, to contest the authority of Massoretic scholarship. The emphasis falls not on the differences between the Hebrew text of Simon's time and the Hebrew *Vorlage* of the Septuagint, but on a demonstration that the same consonantal text can be differently interpreted and that the interpretation imposed by the Massoretic vocalization is not necessarily the right one in every case. Simon is concerned to remind his readers that the Seventy were translating an unvocalized Hebrew text into Greek and that where their translation implies a vocalization of the Hebrew consonants different from that of the Massoretes it deserves serious critical consideration. One of the reasons why the Septuagint should not be cast aside in favour of the Massoretic text is that it may represent a better understanding of the Hebrew consonantal text than that conveyed by the Massoretic vowel points. Part of Simon's textual skill is his ability to show in particular cases how the Septuagint translation is explicable in these terms. In this area he shows a keen awareness of the fineness of judgement which is needed to elicit the right decisions, and, particularly, to discriminate between merely translational as opposed to textual phenomena. What appears on the surface to be an indication of a Hebrew *Vorlage* different from the Massoretic text may, on closer examination, be explicable as a free translation, or even as a kind of transformation unavoidable in the process of turning Hebrew into Greek and possessing no textual significance.

A final drawing together of the contents of this section must concentrate on Simon's concept of the 'obscurity' of the Hebrew Bible and the damage which this does to the Protestant principle of *sola scriptura*. To some extent this obscurity is the consequence of an imperfectly preserved Hebrew text, but it also derives from grammatical uncertainties and lexicographical problems[95] which darken the counsel of translators and interpreters. 'Obscurity', however, is more importantly related to the possibilities of differing interpretations associated with the Hebrew consonantal text. Simon is urging that the clarification of this obscurity achieved by the Massoretic vocalization of the consonantal text is not always to be accepted. Other ways of reading the text have to be taken into account and this approach leads to a rehabilitation of the ancient versions, especially the Septuagint, and to a demonstration of the wrongness of always preferring the interpretation imposed by the Massoretes to that which lies behind the translations of the ancient versions.

It is this fundamental perception that the sense of the Hebrew consonantal text is not narrowly defined which principally governs Simon's attitude to the Septuagint over against the Hebrew text 'of to-day', and to Jerome's *Hebraica veritas* over against the Old Latin which was translated from the Septuagint. He thus seeks to puncture the claim that the Hebrew Bible has a simple and unqualified primacy over the ancient versions. His distinction between the consonantal text and the text vocalized by the Massoretes and the function which he assigns to the ancient versions in textual criticism bring him close to the principles which are set out in the preface of the Old Testament part of the New English Bible. Simon will have nothing to do with extreme views which aim to discredit either the Massoretic text or the Septuagint.[96] We are not to say 'only the Hebrew' with the Jews, or 'only the Septuagint' with some Christians; or 'only the Vulgate'. Both the Hebrew text and the versions are to be used and judgements are to be made 'according to the rules of criticism'.[97] The Hebrew text takes precedence, but it should not be severed from the versions and allowed a sole supremacy.[98]

The Septuagint

The importance of the ancient versions in Simon's critical scheme[99] arises from the circumstance that he does not make such a simple and clear-cut distinction between the Hebrew and the ancient versions as would accord to the Hebrew, in the form of the Massoretic text, an absolute priority. The degree of indeterminacy which he attaches to it is such that the reading or vocalizing of it is an interpretation. Consequently between the Hebrew and any translation of it into another language, an interpretation, which may not preclude another interpretation, has been inserted. The different status of primary and secondary versions has to be taken into account, but even the Latin version (now called the Old Latin), which preceded Jerome's Vulgate and was a translation from the Septuagint, and therefore at two removes from the Hebrew, is within the scope of what is special about Simon's perception. The translation of the Seventy, having set out from an unvocalized text, is an interpretation of the Hebrew consonantal text independent of the interpretation imposed by the Massoretic vocalization and earlier than it. Hence the Septuagint is both an interpretation and a translation, and the form of determinacy imposed by the Seventy on the Hebrew consonantal text is preserved in any faithful translation of the Septuagint, and so is present in the Old Latin. The Old Latin reaches back to the Hebrew consonantal text in so far as it is a transformation into Latin of the vocalization of the Hebrew consonantal text determined by the Seventy.

If this is so, the distinction between primary and secondary versions is more complicated than might be supposed, because of the need to consider the aspect of interpretation of the Hebrew consonantal text as well as that of translation into a language other than Hebrew. Thus the Aramaic Targums are primary versions in so far as they are translations from the Hebrew, but because they are translations of a Hebrew text which, for the most part, follows the tradition of vocalization which was finalized in the Massoretic text, they do not make the independent contribution to the interpretation of the Hebrew consonantal text which Simon ascribes to the Septuagint. It is against this background that Simon is to be understood, when, denying that the Seventy were inspired, he, nevertheless, holds that the Septuagint was 'authentic' in the Church for several centuries:[100] it embodied an interpretation of the Hebrew consonantal text, and the Old Latin, in so far as it preserved the same interpretation, was likewise authoritative.

The differences between the Septuagint and the Hebrew text of Simon's time are, however, not all disagreements over the vocalization of an identical consonantal text. They extend to differences of consonantal text. Thus Simon remarks[101] that the Hebrew *Vorlage* of the Septuagint should not be supposed to have coincided with the Hebrew text 'of to-day', and that the Septuagint should be highly esteemed as an independent witness to the Hebrew text. Neither Origen nor Jerome appreciated this adequately and both tended to reform the Septuagint with too much liberty.[102] Origen's knowledge of Hebrew was mediocre,[103] but his textual criticism of the Septuagint was too much influenced by literal, Greek translations of a Hebrew text which was different from the Hebrew *Vorlage* of the Septuagint. Hence he corrupted the text of the Septuagint where he supposed that he was refining it. Similarly Jerome's equation of the Hebrew text of his time with *Hebraica veritas* did not dispose him towards a correct understanding of the textual criticism of the Septuagint. The worst consequences of the supposition that the original text of the Septuagint is to be recovered through a correlation with the extant Hebrew Bible are to be seen in the Complutensian Polyglot,[104] and this is 'corruption' not textual criticism.[105]

Whether or not the Seventy were inspired is to be decided by critical enquiry and not by counting the heads of the Fathers who said that it was.[106] A biblical critic is not bound by authorities, if their common view is at variance with the truth. Origen conformed with the estimate of the Septuagint which was generally held in the Church, and the Septuagint was located centrally in the Hexapla with the intention that it should serve as a rule for the faithful.[107] Jerome could accommodate himself to the ecclesiastical consensus,[108] but he expresses clearly and trenchantly his critical opinion that the Seventy were not inspired, and he pours scorn on 'the Seventy and their cells', which Justin Martyr said that he had seen in Alexandria, and on the claim that the Seventy had worked independently of each other and had achieved an identical result. The Letter of Aristeas is an aetiological legend, but the historical core is that the Law of Moses was translated in an Alexandrian context under one of the Ptolemies.[109] Neither in the Letter of Aristeas nor in Josephus is the story of the Seventy and their cells narrated in order to show that the translators were inspired, but it appears in Philo[110] for whom they were 'prophets', because they understood the sense of Moses with a special spiritual penetration. But, according to Simon, Philo applied himself more to the study of eloquence than to criticism and, not knowing Hebrew, was disqualified from passing judgement on the matter.

The positive attitude which Simon adopts towards the Septuagint is founded on critical considerations and does not depend on the doctrine that the translators were inspired. He avoids extremes of partisanship and his intention is to give both the Hebrew and the Septuagint the attention they deserve and to hold them together in a critical tension. He touches on the question of the use of the Septuagint by the apostles in their quotations from the Old Testament and concludes that this was a matter of missionary tactics: they were preaching to Jews in synagogues where the Septuagint was the Bible in use.[111] On the particular case of Acts vii 14 (Gen. xlvi 27), where the Hebrew Bible has 'seventy' and the Septuagint 'seventy-five', he notices that the New Testament verse follows the Septuagint. Stephen, he remarks, must have cited the Hebrew Bible when he was in a Jerusalem context, but Luke followed the Septuagint because he composed his history for the Gentiles.

Simon is aware that the view of the Septuagint held by the Fathers is influenced by their ignorance of Hebrew. When Justin Martyr cites 'the Hebrew', he is citing Aquila and is relying on a one–one correspondence between that translation and the Hebrew text.[112] The Fathers who declare Aquila to be 'false' did not have the Hebrew to judge the matter. By 'false' they did not intend that the Hebrew text had been corrupted but that it had been interpreted in a manner which disagreed with the Septuagint. The Fathers recognized only the Septuagint as scripture; they associated the Hebrew with the synagogue and had no regard for it.[113] Simon, for his part, attaches to the Greek versions a lexicographical value which arises from their literalness. His statement that the Septuagint is a literal translation[114] is more true of some books than of others, but it is not generally true. The Psalm fragments of the Hexapla published by Mercati,[115] in which the glossary or word-book aspect of the work is suggested by the format, shows that it is more difficult to set out a one–one correspondence of the Hebrew text with the Septuagint than with the other, more literal, Greek versions. Moreover, Simon's subsequent remarks[116] that the Septuagint has a periphrastic character and functioned as a Greek Targum on the Torah in Hellenistic synagogues, where the Hebrew text was also read, cannot be reconciled with his statement that the Septuagint is a literal translation. Jerome, according to Simon,[117] attacked the concept of literal translation as non-translation when he was replying to criticisms that his own translation (the Vulgate) was too free, but he praised Aquila as a kind of dictionary which reproduced the correct sense of Hebrew words.

Simon's view of the function of Origen's Hexapla, which he repeats frequently, is too narrow. It had no other purpose than to be useful to Christians in their disputations with Jews.[118] It has been shown in an earlier chapter[119] that this assessment of the Hexapla is sometimes associated with the claim that Origen believed firmly in the inspiration of the Septuagint. Although Simon attaches doctrinal significance to the central position accorded to the Septuagint in the Hexapla, he does not thereby pin on Origen an unequivocal affirmation that the Septuagint is inspired. Origen does not speak with one voice and what he says depends on the context in which his remarks are made. Jerome[120] too was capable of bending to popular sentiment as when he said that his translation from Hebrew into Latin was not directed against the Septuagint, but was made to facilitate disputations with Jews and to give to the West what Origen had given to the Greeks in the fifth column of his Hexapla.[121] But, Simon notes, this is in marked contrast with his express devotion to *Hebraica veritas*. In any case the homiletical use which Origen makes of a Hebrew text longer than the text represented in the Septuagint, whether his Hebrew was good enough to give him direct access to the original or whether he relied on literal translations of the Hebrew into Greek, shows that he valued these additions as an enrichment of the sense and that he took account of the contents of the fifth column of the Hexapla in his preaching.[122]

Simon argues[123] that Origen was misled by his assumption that the text of the Septuagint ought to have a close correspondence with that of the Hebrew Bible of his time. Simon is not arguing that the objective of Origen's textual criticism was to produce a perfect correspondence between the two. The displaying of what the Greek text would look like if it corresponded *exactly* with the Hebrew text, which is achieved in the fifth column of the Hexapla, with the safeguards of text-critical symbols, is another and separate matter. But, according to Simon, Origen's critical edition of the Septuagint is influenced in more subtle ways by his knowledge of the form of the Hebrew text, perhaps principally gathered from Aquila, Symmachus and Theodotion. The 'common' text of the Septuagint (that is, the text in use in the Church) is called the κοινή or Vulgate by Simon, and it was this text which Origen reformed. He discerned that it needed a critical reconstruction, because textual differences in manuscripts which he scrutinized were evidence that it had suffered from the negligence of copyists, or from the recklessness of those who had added to or taken away from the original.

Simon notices Jerome's[124] statement that the κοινή had suffered from accidental and deliberate corruption and that Origen's edition is purer.

Simon also reviews the attempts of Lucian and Hesychius to refine the κοινή text, and remarks that Origen's 'Palestinian' text of the Septuagint was extracted from the fifth column of the Hexapla by Eusebius and Pamphilius.[125] Jerome,[126] however, suspects that Origen is working from defective text-critical principles and that he has reformed the text with too much liberty under the influence of a false criterion: by bringing the Septuagint closer to the Hebrew text he has introduced confusion into the ancient version of the Septuagint.

Another source of the corruption of the Septuagint which Simon discerns arises from the format of the fifth column of the Hexapla. The text of the Septuagint which appeared there was Origen's reformation of the older κοινή edition, but copyists lacked accuracy in reproducing the text-critical symbols and there was a tendency to supplement Origen's critical text of the Septuagint with the additions which he had marked with asterisks and metobeli and which were originally no part of it. Hence the error of the original text-critical approach[127] was magnified by accidents of transmission arising from the way in which Origen's critical text of the Septuagint was encapsulated in the fifth column of his Hexapla.[128]

On the contents of the fifth column Simon remarks, 'Origen added to the version of the Septuagint, which was in the Hexapla and not in a separate volume, the marks of which we have spoken, so that one could see at a glance what was superfluous and what was defective in the Septuagint over against the Hebrew, without having recourse to the other versions which were in the Hexapla.'[129] There can be little doubt that Origen's principal aim in his manner of reconstructing the fifth column is to show what the Greek text would look like if it conformed quantitatively, in every respect, with the Hebrew. In Simon's words[130] the aim was to provide a bird's-eye view of variations between different Greek versions, but Simon's description presupposes not only the contents of the fifth column, but also critical notes in the margin showing how Origen's text of the Septuagint differed from the κοινή text and also from the Greek versions of Aquila, Symmachus and Theodotion. Simon[131] makes the assumption that Origen used Theodotion exclusively within his fifth column to indicate with his critical apparatus where the Hebrew text differed from his critical text of the Septuagint. The implication of this is that all the material from Aquila and Symmachus used for the same purpose was located outside the fifth column in the form of marginal variants to the material from Theodotion within the fifth column. Thus he remarks, 'Origen's text of the Septuagint is in the Hexapla, since it could easily be copied without the additions of Theodotion, and one can say in this sense that the Greek Vulgate was in the Hexapla, but corrected and more pure than the ancient Vulgate [κοινή].'[132]

Simon makes a point of emphasizing, as the quotation at the beginning of the previous paragraph shows, that the composite representation of a Greek text exactly corresponding with the Hebrew text, with a critical apparatus of asterisks and obeli, was contained in the Hexapla and was not a separate work. A special interest attaches to this, because in recent times Kahle,[133] with reference to the Psalm fragments of the Hexapla published by Mercati, has argued that Origen's text-critical work with asterisks and obeli was separate from his Hexapla. In that case the fifth column of the Hexapla contained no more than Origen's critical text of the Septuagint. A careful scrutiny of the Mercati fragments does not support Kahle's conclusion. One cannot say that it refutes his conclusion, only that it does not supply the kind of evidence which is needed to make a decision one way or the other.[134]

The examples which Simon[135] uses to illustrate his attitude to the Septuagint, and its value as an independent interpretation of the consonantal Hebrew text, are associated with a plea that a monopoly of wisdom should not be accorded to Jewish grammars and dictionaries, and a statement that the Rabbis have too limited a view of biblical Hebrew.[136] His review of passages broadly confirms his claim that he is not attached as a partisan either to the Massoretic text or the Septuagint. He does not set out to show that the Septuagint is always right, and some of the passages selected are illustrations of misunderstandings of the Hebrew by the Seventy, or of a Hebrew *Vorlage* which was corrupt and is inferior to the Hebrew text 'of to-day'. His critical perceptions are often sharp, but they are sometimes disappointing, and his treatment of these examples can fairly be described as uneven in quality. An examination of samples will throw some light on the kind of problems which he is attacking. His work can be classified under the following heads:

A. Translational: Gen. iii 14; xlix 21.
B. Variants and copyists' errors: Gen. xlix 5; Ps. xxii 9, 27, 30.
C. Lexicographical: Gen. vi 14; xxv 18; xlix 9; Ps. xxii 2.
D. Pointing and punctuation: Gen. iv 26; vi 3; xlix 6; Ps. xxii 4.

A. Simon illustrates neatly by means of ἀπὸ παντῶν τῶν κτηνῶν καὶ ἀπὸ πάντων τῶν θηρίων τῆς γῆς (Gen. iii 14) that a so-called literal translation may amount to a mistranslation. The comparative function of Hebrew מן is not fulfilled by Greek ἀπὸ, and so the sense 'You are the most accursed of all cattle and wild beasts' is lost.

Gen. xlix 21, NEB, 'Naphtali is a spreading terebinth putting forth lovely boughs': The purpose of Simon's comments on Gen. xlix 21 and 22[137] is to show that differences between the Hebrew and the Septuagint are not necessarily traceable to textual causes and may arise rather from transformations associated with free or idiomatic translation. In this instance Simon has apparently not recognized the lexicographical basis of στέλεχος which is the identification of אילה with אלה 'terebinth' and not with 'hind'. On this foundation the New English Bible has 'a spreading terebinth'.[138] Thus Simon's remark[139] that the Septuagint has translated according to the sense rather than the grammar lacks insight.

B. Gen. xlix 5, NEB 'Simeon and Levi are brothers, their spades (RSV 'swords') became weapons of violence': Simon's explanation[140] of συνέτελησαν ἀδικίαν ἐξ αἱρέσεως αὐτῶν ('They consummated injustice by means of their conquest') as a translation of כלי חמס מכרתיהם is only partial. He supposes that the Greek translators read כֻּלּוּ and that כלי ('utensil', 'weapon') is a copyist's error for כלו, but he does not clarify how ἐξ αἱρέσεως αὐτῶν ('by means of their conquest') arises from מכרתיהם. It is clear that מ has been identified with מן (ἐξ), but how the sense αἵρεσις is to be had from כור or כרה remains obscure, and Barr[141] favours 'their plans' (מכר 'to plan').

In the following three instances Simon's textual judgement[142] coincides with that of the New English Bible:

(a) Ps. xxii 9, NEB (xxii 8), 'He threw himself on the LORD for rescue': Simon[143] remarks that the indicative mood represented by the Septuagint (ἤλπισεν) makes better sense than the imperative (גֹּל).

(b) Ps. xxii 27, NEB (xxii 26), 'Let those who seek the LORD praise him and be in good heart for ever': Simon[144] holds that αἱ καρδίαι αὐτῶν ('their hearts') yields better sense than לבבכם ('your heart') and NEB agrees with this.[145]

(c) Ps. xxii 30, NEB (xxii 29), 'But I shall live for his sake': Simon's insight[146] that לא = לו, or that לו has been corrupted to לא, is followed by NEB.[147] This and נפשי (also adopted by NEB) are indicated by the Septuagint (καὶ ἡ ψυχή μου αὐτῷ ζῇ) over against the Hebrew Bible (ונפשו לא חיה).

C. Gen. vi 14, NEB 'ribs of cypress' for עצי גפר. גפר. occurs only here in the Hebrew Bible and has been identified with a type of wood. Simon[148] does not explain the lexicography of גפר, but he springs to the defence of the Septuagint rendering of עצי גפר (ἐκ ξύλων τετραγώνων) with which he compares the Vulgate *de lignis laevigatis*, 'planks which have been made smooth'. He urges that the interpretation of גפר in the Septuagint should be taken seriously and that the reference is to planks cut or sawn to a regular shape, suitable for shipbuilding. He notes that Jerome (*Quaest. in Gen.*) has preferred כפר to גפר (*de lignis bituminatis*),[149] but holds that כפר arises from textual corruption or is a conjectural emendation by Jerome.[150]

Simon's judgement[151] at Gen. xxv 18, where he maintains that the Septuagint has correctly taken the sense of נפל (κατῴκησεν 'settled'), is supported by the rendering of the New English Bible, 'having settled to the east of his brothers'. This is superior to 'died' (Vulgate, *obiit*), and Simon is aware that both the Targum (שרא) and the Peshiṭta (*šrʾ*) agree with his lexicography. An interesting feature of his argument in relation to modern practice is his appeal to the word – string at Gen. xvi 12 (על פני כל אחיו ישכן) which is in all respects identical with על פני כל אחיו נפל, except that ישכן 'dwell' is substituted for נפל.

Gen. xlix 9, NEB 'You have returned from the kill, my son': This is a case where Simon[152] explains the rendering of the Septuagint (which he does not prefer) in terms of a homonym. מטרף בני עלית is correctly rendered by the New English Bible, but the Greek translator has taken טרף to mean 'foliage', its sense at Ezek. xvii 9 (cf. טרף at Gen. viii 11), and has supposed the point to be that Judah had small beginnings (ἐκ βλαστοῦ, υἱέ μου ἀνέβης).

Ps. xxii 2, RSV (xxii 1) 'My God, My God, why hast thou forsaken me? Why art thou so far from helping me, from the words of my groaning?': Simon[153] sets out to explain why שאגתי 'my groaning' is translated as παραπτωμάτων μου 'my transgressions'. The problem is bound up with the double function of *aleph*: it is both a consonantal phoneme and a vowel letter. If it is the former, the correct rendering of דברי שאגתי is 'the words of my groaning', but if it is the latter, שאגתי has to be derived from 'to go astray', and this is how it has been taken by the Greek translator. But the form שגה (a noun) is not attested in biblical Hebrew, whereas שגגה is.

D. Simon's distinctive insight is that the consonantal Hebrew text has to be 'interpreted' (vocalized and punctuated) before it can be translated, and this section has a special bearing on that critical contribution.

Gen. iv 26, NEB 'At that time men began to invoke the LORD by name': Simon[154] notices that הוחל is vocalized in the Massoretic text as הוּחַל and is derived from חלל 'begin' (Vulgate, *coepit*), whereas the Septuagint has read הוחל as הוֹחֶל (ἤλπισεν) and associated it with יחל 'to hope'. Some have supposed that the Hiphil (הֶחֵל) rather than the Hophal of חלל ('a beginning was made') is desiderated, but in any case 'began to call on the name of the LORD' is better than 'hoped to call on the name of the Lord God'.

Gen. vi 3, NEB 'My life-giving spirit shall not remain in man for ever': BDB[155] remarks that 'strive' (KJV and RV) for ידון is unjustifiable and notes the conjecture ידור 'remain' (an Aramaism) or ילון 'lodge'. Both the Septuagint (καταμείνῃ) and the Vulgate (*permanebit*) represent ידון as 'remain', as does NEB, without any indication of a change of text. Simon[156] remarks that new interpreters with 'most of the Rabbis' favour 'dispute', 'judge' and that Jerome in *Quaest. in Gen.*[157] (cf. Vulgate) declared for this meaning. Simon observes that 'remain' gives better sense, that it is supported by the Septuagint, the Vulgate and the Targum (יתקיים) and that καταμείνῃ does not derive from a textual variant (ילון) but from נדן (נדן) יְדוֹן[158] 'remain').

Gen. xlix 6, NEB 'My heart shall not join their company': Simon[159] perceives that τὰ ἥπατά μου (כבדי) provides an expression which is parallel to ἡ ψυχή μου (נפשי) and that the vocalization of כבדי adopted by the Greek translators (כְּבֵדִי 'my liver') is better than the Massoretic text (כְּבֹדִי 'my glory'). In this he is followed by NEB.

Ps. xxii 4, NEB (xxii 3), 'And yet thou art enthroned in holiness, thou art he whose praises Israel sings': Simon[160] argues that the Septuagint has construed the Hebrew consonantal text correctly: אתה קדוש יושב תהלות ישראל is rendered as συ δὲ ἐν ἁγίοις κατοικεῖς, ὁ ἔπαινος Ἰσραήλ ('You dwell with the saints, the one who is praised by Israel'). This is a reference to worship offered in the Jerusalem temple. Jerome's translation from the Hebrew which is given by Simon (*Et tu sancte, habitator laus Israel*)[161] follows the punctuation of the Massoretic text, as does KJV ('But thou *art* holy, *O thou* that inhabitest the praises of Israel'). It is evident that the punctuation assumed by the Septuagint is correct: קָדוֹשׁ יוֹשֵׁב constitutes a phrase and NEB's translation is essentially the same as that of the Septuagint.

The Vulgate

It will be convenient in considering what Simon has to say about Jerome's Vulgate to make a distinction between his critical assessment of Jerome as a Hebraist and a translator, and his clarification of what is intended by the 'authenticity' of the Vulgate in the formulation of the Council of Trent. The criteria of authenticity take us beyond the boundaries of critical scholarship into the sphere of tradition where 'authenticity' is defined by the institutional and dogmatic structures of the Catholic Church. On the one hand, the Vulgate is to be viewed as the achievement of the first Christian scholar with un-disputed trilingual competence, and this will take the form of a critical essay, a balancing of Jerome's strengths and weaknesses. On the other hand, the Vulgate is to be described in the context of the Catholic Church, as a trans-lation on which a singular authority was conferred by the Council of Trent, which is integrated into the structures of the Church, and whose status is not properly appreciated when it is disengaged from its ecclesiastical matrix and judged purely in terms of critical, biblical scholarship. Simon's argument, in general, is that, with these stipulations, there is no embarrassment in combining the claim of authenticity with a candid acknowledgement of the critical defects of the Vulgate. The question which arises is whether the embargo on linguistic scholarship in the area where the Vulgate is authentic is tolerable, and whether the assertions which are made in this area are amenable to critical challenge.

In his estimate of Jerome as a translator, devoted to *Hebraica veritas*, Simon notices[162] the criticism of Rufinus[163] that he betrayed Judaizing tendencies and preferred what he gathered from a Jew called Barabbas to what the Church had received from the apostles. Peter would not have been so deceived into supposing that corrupt Hebrew scriptures were true; only Jews and apostates translate from Hebrew. Simon is more judicious than Rufinus, but he does not exempt Jerome from criticism and censure. Unlike Rufinus he does not suppose that the Seventy were inspired, nor is he given to accusing Jews of having corrupted their scriptures. He does not doubt Jerome's view that the Septuagint is defective in many places, nor that the Hebrew Bible has an indispensable part to play in critical, biblical scholarship. He does, however, say that Jerome sometimes abandoned the Septuagint without sufficient grounds,[164] that he distanced himself too much from it and that his translation from the Hebrew should not be praised too highly.[165] It is Simon's view that Jerome's *Apology*[166] is not entirely adequate to deal with the matters raised by Rufinus. For example, his assertion that the apostles did not prefer Greek to Hebrew in principle, but were influenced by tactical considerations related to their missionary design: Greek was spoken in the

synagogues of dispersed Jews and there was a Greek version (the Septuagint)
to hand. Further, Jerome's answer to the charge of Judaizing was deficient:
that the Jews were the best teachers of Hebrew and had been consulted
by Clement of Alexandria and Origen.[167]

On the positive side Simon says of Jerome that he avoids the literalism
of Aquila and that he reproduces the sense of the Hebrew without a slavish
regard for a one–one correspondence with the words of the Hebrew text.[168]
All the versions ranged in Origen's Hexapla served him as a dictionary,
and he supplemented this lexicographical material with opinions which
he elicited from learned Rabbis and to which he attached great weight.[169]
His freedom and flexibility as a translator demonstrate his grasp of Hebrew
idiom, and he is to be praised for the modifications which he made to
the Old Latin in many places. He succeeded where a more literal type
of translation was in effect a non-translation or an under-translation which
failed to eradicate ambiguity and achieve clarity.[170]

On the negative side Simon holds that Jerome was sometimes too free,
and that the failure to observe a distinction between translation and paraphrase has led to an unacceptable restriction of the sense of the Hebrew,
so that a one-sided interpretation has been substituted for the greater
openness of the original.[171] Moreover, Jerome was too much under the
influence of Jewish lexicography and interpretation, and even the lexicographical use of Aquila, Symmachus and Theodotion promoted this
tendency, in so far as these translations had a Jewish character.[172] The
more general charge that he diverged too much from the Septuagint and
the Old Latin is thought to have a connection with his Judaizing leanings
and his exaggerated emphasis on *Hebraica veritas*. The critical foundation
of this is Simon's view that the Septuagint is an independent witness of
the first rank, offering an interpretation of the Hebrew consonantal text
different from the interpretation offered by the vowels of the Massoretic
text. All this has been explored in a previous section,[173] and, given this
perception, Jerome's *Hebraica veritas* is seen to be question-begging in
two respects: there is the assumption that the Hebrew text available to
Jerome, which is not identical with the Hebrew *Vorlage* of the Septuagint,
is *Hebraica veritas*; and there is the assumption that the Jewish vocalization
of the Hebrew consonantal text, which influenced Jerome, is correct where
it differs from the vocalization assumed in the Septuagint. Fundamentally,
it is on these critical grounds that Simon taxes Jerome with having departed
too much from the Septuagint and the Old Latin (which was a translation
from the Septuagint).

The examples of Jerome's work produced by Simon are taken from
Genesis and Ecclesiastes. We have to consider not only Simon's description
of what Jerome is doing, but also his own critical judgements which he
inserts from time to time. First of all, however, here is a classification
of samples chosen to illustrate Simon's approach to his subject:

A. *The Vulgate and the Old Latin*: Gen. ii 8; Eccles. i 7.

B. *Jewish Influence on Jerome*: Gen. xxv 8; Eccles. i 14.

C. *Textual Matters*: Gen. ii 2; iv 8; xxiii 2; xv 15; xxi 22; xxvi 32.

D. *Pointing*: Gen. iii 17; xv 11.

E. *Translation*: Gen. ii 17; xix 14; iv 7; Eccles. i 8; i 11; i 15.

It may be said of Simon's examples in the round that they do not, to the extent that one might have expected, illustrate the thesis that Jerome was too prone to depart from the Septuagint and old Latin in order to follow his *Hebraica veritas*. A few make this point and some aim to show that Jerome fell too much under the influence of the Rabbis, but a large number, surprisingly, give an indication for which Simon's previous remarks have not prepared us. There is evidence of Jerome's conservatism in not departing so far from the Old Latin as he would have done if he had had regard only to *Hebraica veritas*. Moreover, there are a number of cases where Simon gives his own verdict that the Hebrew text 'of to-day' is better than the Hebrew *Vorlage* of the Septuagint.

A. Gen. ii 8, NEB 'Then the LORD God planted a garden in Eden away to the east': Simon[174] holds correctly that παράδεισον ἐν Ἐδεμ ('a garden in Eden') is a better rendering of גן בעדן than *paradisum voluptatis* ('a garden of delight') in the Vulgate which supposes that עדן is a common noun rather than a place-name. Simon approves of Jerome's decision in *Quaest. in Gen.*,[175] where he interprets the Hebrew in the same way as the Seventy had done. In the same verse Simon prefers κατὰ ἀνατολάς / *ad orientem* (Old Latin) to the Vulgate *a principio* as a rendering of מקדם. This gives the sense 'away to the east' rather than 'at the beginning' (Vulgate).

Eccles. i 7, NEB 'All streams run into the sea, yet the sea never overflows': This is one of a number of verses in Ecclesiastes where Simon[176] maintains that Jerome has abandoned the Septuagint without sufficient grounds. He holds that ἐμπιμπλαμένη (*impletur*) is an entirely adequate rendering of מלא 'be full' and that there was no need for Jerome to introduce the sense of the sea not overflowing (*mare non redundat*) in the Vulgate. This is a somewhat carping criticism and it is arguable that the renderings of והים איננו מלא preferred by the Vulgate and NEB bring out the sense better than καὶ ἡ θάλασσα οὐκ ἔσται ἐμπιμπλαμένη, 'and the sea will never be full'.

B. Gen. xxv 8, RSV 'Abraham breathed his last and died in a good old age, an old man and full of years': According to Simon[177] Jerome is so attached to Jewish exegesis that he fails to pay sufficient attention to a Hebrew text which does not support his conclusions. In *Quaest. in Gen.*[178] he quarrels with ἐκλείπων, the Septuagint rendering of ויגוע 'breathed his last', because it ought not to be said that Abraham 'diminished'. Simon describes this as 'pure allegory': Jerome translates the Hebrew faithfully in the Vulgate (*Et deficiens mortuus est*) and gives a spurious reason for omitting *deficiens* in *Quaest. in Gen.*

Eccles. i 14, NEB 'I have seen all the deeds that are done here under the

sun; they are all emptiness and chasing the wind': Jerome[179] 'on the authority of his Jewish doctor' renders רעות רוח in the Vulgate as *afflictio spiritus*,
'affliction of the spirit'. Simon records a doublet for רעיון רוח ('chasing
the wind') at Eccles. i 17 in the Old Latin: either *pastio venti* 'a pasturing
of the wind', or *praesumptio spiritus* 'a wilfulness of spirit', the latter agreeing
with προαίρεσις πνεύματος (Septuagint). Simon notices that Aquila, Symmachus and Theodotion follow the Septuagint, but he says that προαίρεσις
is a Syriac rather than a Hebrew sense of רעות or רעיון.[180] The Septuagint
elucidation of רעות determines the sense of רוח as 'spirit' rather than
'wind'. Modern dictionaries[181] give the sense of רעות and רעיון as 'longing',
'striving'.

C. The textual examples adduced by Simon are not easily summed up,
but it can be said at the outset that they do not embody a single-minded
endeavour to demonstrate that the Hebrew *Vorlage* of the Septuagint is superior
to the Hebrew text from which Jerome translated.

Only Simon's comments on Gen. ii 2,[182] and perhaps on iv 8[183] and xxiii
2,[184] aim to establish the superiority of the Hebrew *Vorlage* of the Septuagint.
At Gen. ii 2 'on the sixth day' (τῇ ἕκτῃ) is deemed better than 'on the seventh
day' (השביעי; Vulgate, *die septimo*), and this is the view of the New English
Bible. At Gen. iv 8 διέλθωμεν εἰς τὸ πεδίον (NEB, 'Let us go into the open
country') is represented in the Vulgate (*Egrediamur foras*), but Jerome (*Quaest.
in Gen.*)[185] noticed that nothing corresponded to it in the Hebrew text and
remarked that it served no useful purpose. It is not altogether clear what
Simon's view of this is, but he notes that נלכה השדה appears in the Samaritan
Pentateuch, and it follows from this, given his text-critical principles, that
נלכה השדה was in the Hebrew *Vorlage* of the Septuagint. In view of Jerome's
remarks in *Quaest. in Gen.*, we must suppose that his conservatism in relation
to the Old Latin has influenced his rendering in the Vulgate.

At Gen. xxiii 2, on the other hand, Jerome's Hebrew text is reflected in
the Vulgate which does not represent אל העמק 'in the valley', although
this is present in the Samaritan Pentateuch and appears in the Septuagint (ἐν
πόλει Ἀρβόκ, ἥ ἐστιν ἐν τῷ κοιλώματι, 'In Kiriath-arba which is in the
valley').

The tendency of the other textual examples is to establish the superiority
of Jerome's Hebrew text or the Hebrew text 'of to-day' over the Septuagint
and the Old Latin. Thus at Gen. xv 15[186] *nutritus* 'nourished' (Old Latin) is
traced to an inner Greek corruption (τραφείς for ταφείς),[187] while the
Vulgate (*sepultus*) is shown to represent correctly תקבר (NEB, 'and be buried
in a good old age').

The longer text of the Septuagint at Gen. xxi 22[188] is a consequence of the
insertion of καὶ Ὀχοζὰθ ὁ νυμφαγωγὸς αὐτοῦ from xxvi 26, and the Vulgate
shows that Jerome's Hebrew text agreed with the Hebrew 'of to-day'.
Simon[189] traces οὐχ εὕρομεν ὕδωρ, 'We have not found water' (Gen. xxvi
32) to a confusion of לו and לא and notices that the Vulgate *atque dicentes
invenimus aquam*, 'Moreover, they said, "We have found water"', takes the

correct sense of the Hebrew (וַיֹּאמְרוּ לוֹ מָצָאנוּ מָיִם, 'And they said to him, "We have found water"').

D. Only a few of Simon's examples turn on differing vocalizations of the Hebrew consonantal text. At Gen. iii 17 (NEB, 'Accursed shall be the ground on your account') Jerome[190] prefers the Hebrew (בעבורך, 'on your account') to the Septuagint (ἐν τοῖς ἔργοις σου, 'in your works'), and the Vulgate (in opere tuo). According to Simon, Jerome's desire to conserve the Septuagint and the Old Latin has led him into error, and he is wrong in taking ἐν τοῖς ἔργοις σου as a reference to 'sinful works' by associating it with עבר 'transgress'. A matter which Simon does not consider is whether ἐν τοῖς ἔργοις σου does not arise from בעבודך in the Hebrew Vorlage of the Septuagint: 'Accursed shall be the ground when you cultivate it.' The continuation of this thought may have been discerned in 'with labour you shall win your food from it all the days of your life' (NEB).

On Gen. xv 11 (NEB, 'Abram scared them away') Simon[191] shows that Jerome's rendering in the Vulgate (abigebat eas Abram) is derived from the same vocalization as appears in the Massoretic text (וַיַּשֵּׁב אֹתָם אַבְרָם), whereas καὶ συνεκάθισεν αὐτοῖς ᾿Αβράμ ('And Abram sat down with them') indicates that the Septuagint has assumed a different vocalization (וַיֵּשֶׁב אִתָּם אַבְרָם).

E. A scrutiny of Simon's translational examples confirms the trend which has already appeared and increases the element of surprise that he is, on the whole, demonstrating Jerome's conservatism in relation to the Old Latin rather than his neglect of the independent weight of the Septuagint and the Old Latin. Thus in several instances Simon explains the character of Jerome's translation in the Vulgate in terms similar to those used for Gen. xxiv 63,[192] namely, that he was unwilling to change the Old Latin too violently because in his time it was in use in 'all the church of the West'. Simon[193] remarks that only what was too distant from the sense of the Hebrew was corrected in the Vulgate, whereas Jerome's design in Quaest. in Gen. was 'to conform with Hebrew exemplars and to follow the indications of Jewish doctors as far as possible.' Thus Jerome asserts (Quaest. in Gen.)[194] that מוֹת תָּמוּת, 'You will certainly die' (Gen. ii 17) is best translated with Symmachus, mortalis eris ('You will be mortal'), but he allows the more literal rendering of the Septuagint (θανάτῳ ἀποθανεῖσθε) to stand in the Vulgate (morte morieris).[195]

Gen. xix 14, NEB 'So Lot went out and spoke to his intended sons-in-law': Simon[196] notes that Jerome retains generos (Old Latin) in the Vulgate, although he departs from the sense of the Septuagint and the Old Latin. Two possible renderings are indicated by the New English Bible: 'to his intended sons-in-law' (in the text) or 'to his sons-in-law who had married his daughters' (in a footnote). It is the former which is represented by the Vulgate (Egressus itaque Lot, locutus est ad generos suos qui accepturi erant filias eius) and the latter by the Septuagint (καὶ ἐλάλησεν πρὸς τοὺς γαμβροὺς αὐτοῦ τοὺς εἰληφότας τὰς θυγατέρας αὐτοῦ). But Jerome allowed generos 'sons-in-law', suitably qualified, to stand in the Vulgate,[197] while in Quaest. in Gen.[198] he substituted sponsos 'men who are betrothed'.

For the most part, differences between the renderings of the same passages in the Vulgate and in *Quaest. in Gen.* are explained by Simon in the manner indicated above, but he has another form of elucidation which he employs in two places. He suggests that these variations are indications that the extant Vulgate is not entirely from Jerome, 'although, speaking in general, he is the only author of it'.[199] Of Gen. iv 7 Simon remarks that Jerome's translation in *Quaest. in Gen.*[200] is verbally different from the Vulgate, although the sense is the same: 'One should not imagine that one will find in the observations of St Jerome [that is, in the translations which he offers in his commentaries and other works] exactly the same words as in the Vulgate which we presently use.'[201] This should be compared with another statement that Jerome did not claim infallibility for his version. He was aware of the uncertainties of Hebrew lexicography and it is this which accounts for the differences between his renderings of scripture in his commentaries and his renderings in the Vulgate.[202]

Simon praises Jerome for the idiomatic character of his translation, and he illustrates the danger of literal renderings which are deficient in their grasp of idiom, but also of renderings which are too free and distant from the original. At Eccles. i 11[203] the Septuagint, because it is too literal (οὐκ ἔστιν μνήμη τοῖς πρώτοις, 'There is no memorial to the men of old') is not an adequate translation of the Hebrew (אין זכרון לראשנים) whose sense is captured by Jerome, *Non est priorum memoria* (NEB, 'The men of old are not remembered'). The Septuagint renders כל הדברים too literally at Eccles. i 8,[204] where 'things' rather than 'words' is the translation required (Jerome, *cunctae res*).

Eccles. i 15, NEB 'What is crooked cannot become straight; what is not there cannot be counted': Simon[205] criticizes Jerome's translation (*Perversi difficile corriguntur. Et stultorum infinitus est numerus*) as too free. He ought not have limited the Hebrew (מעות לא יוכל לתקן) to a moral sense in the first stich, and this tendency is still present in his rendering of וחסרון לא יוכל להמנות which, however, should have a wider reference (cf. NEB). In this second stich Jerome has understood חסרון as 'lack of wits', associating it with חסר לב, 'one who lacks good sense'.

Criticisms of translators and commentaries

Simon's qualifications to make aesthetic judgements about translations of the Hebrew Bible, or more comprehensive critical evaluations about commentaries on it, are impressive. He makes them stylishly with a wit which is sometimes mordant. He gives away his *bons mots* without any fuss as natural products of his mastery of words and of his unfaltering modulation of many gradations of sensibility and irony. They emerge in the course of his review of biblical scholarship and they are of a kind to make those who read them wish that they had written them.

Of Jerome, Simon says that he had a better nose for the plain sense of the

Hebrew Bible than any other ancient writer, but that seventeenth-century scholars engaged in the pursuit of sacred learning show little interest in him. He adds, not innocently, 'Moreover, since they have neglected the study of Hebrew and Greek, they cannot read his works.'[206] When Simon criticizes the ascendancy of scholastic theology in the Middle Ages, he complains not only of the neglect of biblical scholarship in that a potted work, Petrus Comestor's *History of the Bible from the Creation of the World to the Ascension of Our Lord*, was substituted for the study of the sacred languages. He also complains of the deadening effect of philosophical and theological terminology on literary sensibilities and the loss of feeling for good writing – a carelessness about *les belles lettres*.

Of Paul, Bishop of Burgos, a converted Jew, Simon remarks that he was too disputatious: 'He has filled his book with uselessness, so that there is much time to be wasted if one wishes to read it from cover to cover.'[207] Père de la Haye, who edited his *Biblia Magna* in five volumes, and followed it up with a *Biblia Maxima* of nineteen volumes, is derided as a conceited ass: 'In this latter collection he was more concerned to satisfy his vanity than to be useful to his readers.' The merriment is increased by repeating the author's own boast: 'La Bible d'Alcala ne contient que trois volumes; celle de Londres, six; la Royale, huit; celle de Paris, dix; au lieu que mon Édition en contient dix-neuf.'[208] Simon thinks very poorly of Calvin as a Hebraist, and it is a puzzle what evidence could have driven him to the conclusion that Calvin knew little more than the characters of the Hebrew alphabet. In general, however, he has more time for Calvin than for Luther: Calvin knew less Hebrew than Luther, but he used the scholarship of others more judiciously: 'He touches the heart, whereas most of Luther's thoughts are nothing but vain speculations and ridiculous debates.'[209] Calvin overdid 'total depravity', and as a commentator he was frequently carried away by his theological prejudices. He is summed up in a dismissive sentence, 'If he had been less pig-headed and had not been consumed with a desire to be the big chief, he could have done very useful work for the church.'[210]

Simon reserves a similar comment for Jean Mercerus, who followed François Vatable as Professor of Hebrew in the Collège de France, and whose scholarship he praises highly. He was 'one of the most learned and judicious interpreters of scripture'.[211] He had a mastery of Greek and Hebrew and could read the commentaries of the Rabbis; he was devoted to the plain sense of the Hebrew Bible and consulted Hebrew manuscripts and ancient versions in the Royal Library. His best commentaries are on Job, Ecclesiastes and Song of Songs, and these are among the most difficult books in the Hebrew Bible. Economy of expression and compactness of style are their characteristics, and it is difficult to penetrate to their sense unless one has a thorough grasp of Hebrew. 'He would be worthy of still more praise, if he had not abandoned the religion of his fathers to follow the novelties of Calvin.'[212] Another who had abandoned the religion of his fathers after having been a student at the trilingual College of Louvain was John Drusius, who came from the

Netherlands to England and taught Hebrew at Magdalen College, Oxford from 1572–6, when he became Professor of Hebrew at Leiden.[213] Simon puts him at the top of his list: he was a good Hebraist and could read Rabbinic commentaries; he was acquainted with the ancient Greek versions and had patristic learning.[214]

Simon grumbles about the irrelevancies into which Ludovic de Dieu[215] is led by his erudition; he forgets what he is doing and does not pursue the plain sense of the Hebrew Bible with a single-minded constancy: 'It nearly always happens that persons who have some erudition fill their books with it, without examining whether this erudition has any relevance.'[216] Grotius[217] lacked critical judgement, but is to be praised for his comparisons of the ancient Greek translations with the Hebrew and for not being too preoccupied with Massoretic learning.[218] He receives a withering comment for making too great a show of his erudition in profane literature: 'I could have wished only that, following the rules of criticism, he had not cited from profane authors except in places where there was a need for these elucidations. It was not, for example, necessary in order to explain the Latin word *signa* (Hebrew, אתות 'signs') to cite two verses of Homer and five of the poet Aratus.'[219]

Of Andreas Masius, whose commentary on Joshua[220] awakened ecclesiastical opposition and for whom he had a fellow-feeling, Simon says, 'One cannot, in truth, give too much praise to Masius for this excellent work, but that did not prevent envious people from denouncing him and raising such a stir by their slanders and calumnies that his book was put on the Index.'[221] His dislike of swank comes to the surface again in his criticism of Liveleius (Edward Lively)[222] who had written a commentary on five of the minor prophets (Hosea, Joel, Amos, Obadiah and Jonah): 'He affects too much to be learned, where there is no necessity, a pose which agrees better with a rhetorician than a critic who must explain in a few words the text of scripture, without embellishing his discourse with authorities which have no bearing on his subject.'[223] This opposition of critic and rhetorician recalls his assessment of Don Isaac Abravanel whose lucidity is counted a virtue, but whom Simon regards as a rhetorician rather than a commentator.[224]

Simon disagrees with Walton when he opposes the view, expressed in the *Prolegomena* to the London Polyglot,[225] that God created language (Gen. i 3, 'And God said') or that he speaks Hebrew. Simon has no stomach for such fastidious theological speculation, 'Man would resemble God more, if he could express his conceptions and understand those of others by means other than words, in the same way as angels who do not resemble God less though they do not speak.'[226] And, alluding to the same subject, 'It is necessary, as far as possible, to reconcile reason with faith, philosophy with theology, and not to multiply in a facile way things miraculous and extraordinary.'[227] And a final, crushing rejoinder to Walton, 'I pass over in silence certain arcane questions of too prying a kind which Walton considers, following certain theologians who believe that the Blessed speak Hebrew in heaven.'[228]

On Christian scholars who had made new translations of the Hebrew Bible

Simon's general criticism is that they are not good enough Hebraists to be wholly or largely successful. If they succeeded in some places, it was more by chance than by design. Those who had some claim to competence in Hebrew were under the sway of Rabbinic scholarship, and all the translators were in too much of a hurry. Moreover, command of the language into which Hebrew is being translated forms an indispensable part of the translator's equipment, and his skill consists in matching nicely the texture of his vocabulary and the qualities of his style with the kinds of literature which he finds in the Hebrew Bible. He should avoid archaisms, and if he is a practitioner of *les belles lettres*, he must beware that he does not impose too much aesthetic delicacy and refinement on his originals, depriving them of their plainness and sinewy strength and making them ornate and flaccid.[229] Sebastian Châtillon (Castellio),[230] who translated into both Latin and French, is praised for the measure of success which he achieved with his Latin, but is said to have affected too much a purity and elegance of style, and by this aesthetic miscalculation to have weakened the sense of the Hebrew in some places.[231] Other Christian translators are more heavily censured. Pagnini's[232] translation into Latin, supported by 'quelques Papes' is criticized for its lack of faithfulness and for being barbarous and obscure, because 'it is attached with too much affectation to the rules of Hebrew grammar'.[233] Arius Montanus,[234] who claimed to have refined the translation of Pagnini for the Antwerp Polyglot, in fact coarsened it and exaggerated its obscurities, besides filling it with many faults.[235] Leon of Judah,[236] who observed the mean between the pedestrianism of Pagnini and the aestheticism of Châtillon, was, nevertheless, too free and did not have enough regard for the literary shape of the original.[237]

Simon's general criticism of Jewish translations of the Hebrew Bible is that they are too literal.[238] Something has already been said about his view that literal translation is defective translation,[239] and in this connection he remarks that the Greek Fathers (St Cyril and Theodoret) would have achieved a better grasp of the Hebrew if they had relied on the Septuagint rather than Aquila ('an excessively literal translation') to gain access to it.[240] The order of words in the Hebrew should not be slavishly kept in translation, but there is an antinomy that when the order of the words is changed a danger arises that some aspect of the sense of the original will be lost. Doubts begin to be awakened whether any translator will ever succeed in steering through the narrow channel between Simon's Scylla and Charybdis. He does, however, hold out the prospect that the historical books are easier to translate than the others 'which can hardly at all be translated into another language'.[241] He supposes that the order of difficulty is highest in Proverbs, Ecclesiastes, Job and Canticles, poetic books with so compressed a style and with such obscure expressions and comparisons that their sense is difficult to make out. The obscurity of prophetic books, from which Isaiah 'the most polished writer in the Old Testament' is exempted, arises not only from their figurative language, but also from their subject matter.[242]

A critical faculty so awakened as that of Simon is difficult to please and its balance is perilously maintained. Its demands tend to become unreasonable, its appetite for perfection insatiable, and it can hardly allow a degree of generosity higher than that of damning with faint praise. It is a niceness of appraisal which slides into captiousness and it litters the path of the would-be translator with such an assembly of gins and traps that it threatens to become a counsel of despair.

The concept of 'obscurity'

The principal task of this section is to come to grips with Simon's contention that the Hebrew Bible is obscure. Some attention has already been devoted to this, but it requires further elucidation. When he discusses the translation and exegesis of the Hebrew Bible, Simon states that a primary objective is to show to what extent the Bible is obscure.[243] The analysis of this idea of obscurity is complicated by the circumstance that it is both critical, or scientific, and theological in its content. Moreover, Simon does not always succeed in distinguishing the one sense from the other.[244]

There is no necessary connection between Simon's idea of textual and linguistic obscurity, and the other idea of theological obscurity. Let us suppose that there was no textual or lexicographical or grammatical obscurity attaching to the Hebrew Bible, that all these technical problems had been overcome and that a translation with a high degree of competence and transparency had been achieved. This would not make a significant impact on what Simon intends by the theological obscurity of the Hebrew Bible. The theological idea of obscurity is not properly directed against the Protestants as textual critics or lexicographers or grammarians; it is properly directed against Protestants only in so far as they believe that the Bible itself has a luminous, internal theological content and does not need external, ecclesiastical, dogmatic definition.

When the burden of these complications is laid down, it is a relatively straightforward task to deal with what Simon means by obscurity in a critical context. Parts of this task have been accomplished, but it will be an advantage to recall what these were and to draw the whole together in a concise way. At the beginning of his third book Simon[245] sums up his account of the relation between the Hebrew consonantal text and the Massoretic vocalization: there is an interpretation of the consonantal text which precedes translation, the Massoretic vocalization is such an interpretation, and the Septuagint, for its part, incorporates an independent interpretation. From this he moves to a consideration of the difficulties of Hebrew lexicography. These are problems not easily solved and sometimes insurmountable, so that progress in the translation of the Hebrew Bible is not assured. Translators should not behave as if they were full of assurance, when their minds should be full of doubt. If there is an absence of doubt and tentativeness, this is a mark of superficiality or lack of candour, rather than the condition of a profound scholarship which has achieved mastery. Since the Protestants make scripture the only rule in matters of doctrine, they have to pretend to certainty and to reject the device of locating alternative renderings in the margin, but there is no reason why Catholics should not admit the degree of uncertainty which is implied by allowing alternatives, or be perturbed by it.[246]

That there is considerable lexicographical obscurity in the Hebrew Bible would be generally agreed. One way of indicating it is to call attention to the large number of *hapax legomena* distributed through a small corpus. The Hebrew Bible is estimated to contain about 300,000 words[247] and the vocabulary consists of 7,000–8,000 words.[248] The *hapax legomena* are counted as 1,500 or, by another method, as 2,440 (about a third of the total vocabulary), and 500–600 words are estimated to occur only twice. Simon does not say very much about possible ways of mitigating this state of affairs. He deprecates a too great dependence on Jewish lexicographical and grammatical scholarship,[249] and he urges reasonably that the ancient versions and Jerome have lexicographical contributions to make. He says nothing about the value of comparative Semitic philology as a means of eking out the meagre resources of biblical Hebrew, though he notices its use by Ludovic de Dieu.[250] This is a method which has been dominant in modern times, references to Arabic, Accadian and Ugaritic having become a commonplace in dictionaries of biblical Hebrew, not only in a preliminary setting out of the phonemic equivalences of roots, but also as a way of getting at the meanings of rare Hebrew words.

What Simon[251] has to say about scripture and tradition in the context of Judaism will serve as a bridge to the most central aspects of his idea of theological obscurity. He refers to Ibn Ezra's account of five different methods of interpreting scripture in the introduction to his commentary on the Pentateuch. He is especially concerned with the fifth method which is Ibn Ezra's own and which is directed particularly against the Karaites whom Simon views as proto-Protestants. The Karaites supposed that the Hebrew Bible could be interpreted without the assistance of Rabbinic tradition and this (the second method in Ibn Ezra's arrangement) is described by Simon as a reliance on reason and a rejection of authority. Louis Jacobs says of the Karaites in this connection:

Ibn Ezra as a staunch Rabbinic Jew takes the strongest exception to the second method of Biblical interpretation, that of the Karaites. This ignores entirely all that the Rabbis had taught by tradition and tried to discover unaided the meaning of the Biblical verses … Ibn Ezra retorts that without traditions many of the Biblical verses are obscure.[252]

Ibn Ezra's most important dictum, which Simon notes, is that the plain sense must never be neglected 'except where to accept the plain meaning would contradict a law as handed down by the Rabbinic tradition'.[253] An analogy is discerned by Simon between the Karaites, who suppose that they have immediate access to the sense of the Hebrew Bible without any framework of interpretation supplied by Rabbinic tradition, and the Protestants who claim that they can discern and expound the 'Word of God' in the scriptures without having any recourse to *les véritables Traditions*.[254]

Simon's case is that the Protestants deceive themselves, that they do not have immediate and unerring access to the 'Word of God' and that the theological conclusions which they draw from the Hebrew Bible derive from human opinions which they have interposed.[255] They have rejected a system of theological interpretation (*les véritables Traditions*), whose truth is assured by a church which is kept from error, a system which enjoys a universal recognition or catholicity, and they have foisted an individualized, private, fragmented and, from Simon's point of view, erroneous theological interpretation on the Hebrew Bible. Although Simon sometimes describes this as a taint of rationalism, it clearly requires a more careful and diverse analysis, even if we allow that rationalism in Simon's time 'was not a system of beliefs antagonistic to Christianity, but an attitude of mind which assumed that in all matters of religion reason is supreme'.[256]

The products of Protestant exegesis of the Hebrew Bible have an appearance of theological complication; they display an interest in the creation and elaboration of doctrine rather than in any rationalist simplification and reductionism. Hence it would have to be recognized that the human opinions of which Simon speaks, and which he says Protestants unknowingly interpose when they interpret the Hebrew Bible, might be analysable, on his terms, as theological prejudices of a rigidly dogmatic kind, or as a style of private piety. For the most part, they are not interpretations which flow from humanist assumptions or from an economy of explanation which reason is thought to demand. In one place, where he lumps together Protestants and Socinians, Simon does refer explicitly to religious prejudices as a source of error: 'What is astonishing is their claim that Scripture is clear and easy to understand. In saying this they show clearly that they speak according to the prejudices of their religion and not according to truth, since they cannot agree between themselves touching the explication of the principal passages on which they found their belief.'[257] Detection of a rationalizing tendency, the eliciting of a religion from the Bible thought to be more amenable to reason than orthodox Christianity, the claim that the scriptures support Unitarianism rather than Trinitarianism, would more properly apply to the tendency and concerns of Socinian reinterpretation.[258]

The form of Simon's argument is not, however, what some of these observations may have led readers to suppose. There is only slight evidence that he is interested in the theological interpretation of the Hebrew Bible, with the guiding principles of *les véritables Traditions* brought into play. There is more evidence that he is concerned to fix the limits of the critical study of the Hebrew Bible and to establish the autonomy of criticism within these limits.

The slight evidence that he is concerned with senses of the Hebrew Bible other than the 'literal' or plain sense consists of a few statements of a general kind and a more detailed treatment of one or two verses of the Hebrew Bible. Simon says that the earliest Fathers favoured mystical explanations of the Old

Testament rather than the literal sense which seemed to them 'suited only to the Synagogue' and that in so doing they followed a pattern of allegorical exegesis set by the apostles.[259] Elsewhere he remarks that the Fathers acknowledged senses of the Old Testament other than the plain sense and that in so far as allegorical exegesis was practised by the apostles they had a right to imitate them.[260] It is. not clear that Simon recognizes allegorical exegesis or other ways of pursuing the 'higher senses' of scripture as exegesis in a strict sense. 'We must then', he says, 'seek the truth of the Christian religion in the commentaries of the earliest Fathers on scripture rather than a literal exegesis of the Bible.'[261]

The texts in which Simon appears to countenance a sense other then the plain sense are Gen. i 26,[262] xlix 10[263] and Ps. xxii 17.[264] Gen. i 26 (NEB, 'Let us make man in our image and likeness') is the most explicit indication which he gives of a kind of interaction between scripture and tradition: the sense which we attach (according to Simon) to the words צלם 'image' and דמות 'likeness' depends on their context and on the interpretative framework which is supplied by theology, 'and so it is impossible to explain Scripture except with reference to ideas which Tradition has given to Religion'. With this should be compared his comment on the periphrastic citing of Old Testament texts in the New Testament: the apostles do not reproduce the words of scripture exactly when they cite them, 'supposing that Religion depends more on the assumptions of Tradition than on the simple words of Scripture which are subject to diverse interpretations'.[265]

Gen. xlix 10, NEB (footnote), 'The sceptre shall not pass from Judah, nor the staff from his descendants, until he comes to Shiloh': Simon explains שילה ('Shiloh' in NEB footnote) as שֶׁלּוֹ and urges that 'kingdom' has to be supplied, 'to whom is the kingdom'. The text is Messianic and has been acknowledged as such by Jews and Christians (Targum Onkelos, 'Until the Messiah comes to whom belongs the sovereignty').[266] Simon's attitude to the Christian appropriation of Davidic (Messianic) texts is expressed more fully in a passage where he criticizes Augustine for making too much of the different senses of Old Testament texts and warns against the danger that 'man's word will pass for God's word'. He pleads for a strict control over the Christological exegesis of the Hebrew Bible, and he accepts it for Davidic texts not as a higher sense but as an alternative literal sense:

One cannot deny that many passages contained in the Old Testament may be applied, even according to the literal sense, both to David and to our Lord, and that rests on the idea which we have of the Christian Religion. Since these two Religions do not differ in substance and the latter is the perfection of the first, it follows that what is said of David or Solomon, in literal terms for the time in which they lived, will also be said in literal terms of our Saviour, but in an enhanced sense.[267]

Over against these passages have to be placed a few others on which conflict between Christians and Jews had been focused and which had been associated with Christian claims that the Jews had corrupted their scriptures. Simon's handling of them is remarkable in so far as he takes no account of their polemical aspects and concentrates on the critical problems which they pose. He apparently allows a Christian content to Ps. xxii 17, since he refers to it as 'prophetic',[268] but he dissociates himself from the claim that the Jews have deliberately changed כארו to כארי in order to obliterate a Christological allusion. His main concern is to explain ὤρυξαν 'dug' (Septuagint) as a rendering of כארו: א has the status of a vowel not a consonant and כארו is an orthographical variant of כרו. The Massoretes supposed that א was a consonant and the confusion of *waw* with *yodh* is a copyist's error.[269] Similarly on Isa. vii 14 he explains what Justin Martyr intends when he alleges that the rendering of עלמה by νεᾶνις 'young woman' (Aquila) instead of παρθένος 'virgin' (Septuagint) is a falsification. Simon gives no indication of the theological ramifications of these different renderings,[270] and the point which he is concerned to make is simply that by 'falsification' Justin Martyr meant 'bad translation'.[271] When he deals with Gen. iii 15, Simon[272] has nothing to say about the Christian exegesis attached to *ipsa* in the Vulgate or to αὐτός in the Septuagint,[273] and he has no other interest than to elucidate how these readings arose. Augustine and some of the ancient Fathers had *ipsa* in their Latin manuscripts; it derives from a more ancient error in the Septuagint, αὐτός for αὐτό: αὐτός was rendered as *ipse* and *ipse* was corrupted to *ipsa*. 'The doctors of Louvain testify that they have found *ipse* in many manuscripts of the Vulgate.'

John Dryden disliked Simon's cavalier treatment of the Bible, but he agrees with him that scripture does not contain its own theological interpretation:[274]

> Must all tradition then be set aside?
> This to affirm were ignorance or pride.
> Are there not many points, some needful sure
> To saving faith, that Scripture leaves obscure,
> Which every sect will wrest a several way?
> For what one sect interprets, all sects may.

It is a question how serious Simon is about an interaction of scripture and tradition as a means of realizing 'the truth of Religion'. If this is not his main preoccupation, although, as we have seen, he makes concessions to it,[275] it may be beside the point to criticize his lack of success. Instead of grumbling that the critical study of the Hebrew Bible and the pursuit of the truth of religion fall apart, we should appreciate that this is principally what Simon is driving at: that his concern is not to explain how scripture and tradition interact, but to secure autonomy for the critical study of the Hebrew Bible. There are two ways of investigating this further: by producing statements which he makes about the theological priority and self-sufficiency of tradition over against scripture, and by examining his comments on kinds of exegesis which go beyond the limits of the plain sense of the Hebrew Bible.

He notices Augustine's view[276] that it is not an absolute necessity for a Christian to read the sacred scriptures, and he observes that Tertullian makes the truth of scripture dependent on the truth of religion, preserved in its purity in the apostolic churches: 'The establishment of Religion in the first churches by the apostles is the true rule of faith, and is so before there were any New Testament Scriptures. That is why we need not be too exercised whether we still have the ancient Originals of Scripture precisely preserved, since Religion does not depend entirely on the books of Scripture.'[277] Simon contrasts scripture and tradition in the manner to which Dryden[278] took exception: 'The Church has always kept the truths contained in Scripture, but to achieve this she has not given the spirit of sincerity to copyists who wrote down the exemplars of the Bible and has not prevented them from introducing corruptions into their copies.'[279]

A clearer expression of the priority and self-sufficiency of tradition comes in a passage where Simon is discussing the theological obscurity of the Bible:

It is necessary to have recourse to another principle, a digest (*abrégé*) of Religion which has always been in the Church, independent of Scripture, in terms of which one resolves the difficulties which are found in the Bible. This is what is meant by Tradition, which Tradition was present in the Church before there was any Scripture, and she never neglected to conserve it at a time when there was no book of Scripture.[280]

The second method of investigation has regard to Simon's lukewarm attitude to senses of the Hebrew Bible other than the plain sense, and the disparaging remarks which he makes about these modes of exegesis. He has serious doubts whether the 'mystical explanations' of the Fathers constitute legitimate biblical exegesis,[281] and he dislikes Augustine's tendency to impose a philosophical system on scripture.[282] In particular, he criticizes Augustine for living in a world of perfect Platonic ideas and for attempting to accommodate his interpretation of the Bible to them. The Bible belongs to the realm of the contingent and the historical about which Augustine knew too little: 'He sometimes accommodated Scripture to his ideas, rather than forming his ideas on the basis of Scripture.'[283]

Similarly Origen is criticized for being at too great a distance from the simplicity of the Bible. He resorted to allegorical exegesis because the plain sense was too pedestrian and materialistic to satisfy his demand for philosophical subtlety and spirituality: 'He valued only the sense which was sublime and the interpretation which he called spiritual, hardly being able to suffer the literal sense which he thought was too ordinary and simple.'[284] Or he may have been driven to seek a higher sense in scripture by homiletical considerations, as other Fathers were. Of St Hilary and others Simon[285] says that they were inexact with regard to criticism and the literal sense, and of St Cyril of Alexandria that he offers lessons in theology rather than biblical exegesis.[286] His conclusion about patristic commentaries is, 'One must seek the truth of our Religion in their commentaries on Scripture, rather than the pure literal sense of the same Scripture.'[287]

This brings Simon back to the subject of tradition and to what is perhaps his most complete exposition of the theological primacy of tradition. It occurs in a passage on patristic exegesis of which he seems to be saying that the theological content is derived from tradition and that scripture is used as a homiletically effective way of illustrating and communicating these ideas: 'The Fathers are always much more subject in matters of Faith to a reliable Tradition which was spread throughout all the Church than to the grammatical and literal sense of the Bible.'[288] He continues:

In effect it is impossible to find Religion entirely in Scripture without calling to one's assistance the ancient and divine Tradition which the first Fathers consulted, not only in what obtained to the discipline of the Church, but also in respect of its belief. In every age there has been in the Church a summary of Religion independent of Scripture, by means of which one may decide on what is obscure in Scripture. Conciliar decisions, where bishops reported the belief received in their churches, followed this method. They did not suppose that to find the sense of some difficult passage of the Bible it was necessary to have recourse to grammarians and learned critics. They consulted the common belief of the Church. Hence the explanations [of Scripture] given by most of the Fathers are applications rather than literal explanations.[289]

The implication of this is that whereas all the resources of biblical science are to be employed in order to ascertain and enrich the plain sense of the Bible, this science or criticism has no part to play in determining how the Bible relates to tradition. The scholars must provide the Church with a translation, but, having given authority to a translation, the Church will necessarily interpret it so that it agrees with 'true Religion', a system of beliefs and morals independent of the translation. The critical study of the Bible and tradition or theology are separated, and it was this separation which Simon sought to achieve in the interests of critical autonomy.

It should be accepted that Simon is concerned to reject Protestant claims that the Bible is theologically self-explanatory and that his concept of 'obscurity' has this design: for its theological elucidation the Bible depends on definitions of true religion contained in a system which is external to the Bible. What is now being suggested, however, is that in separating the critical study of the Hebrew Bible from theology Simon is also fighting his own cause as a biblical critic. We might have supposed initially that his intention in criticizing the Protestants was to establish that the theological obscurity of the Hebrew Bible could only be relieved by a Christian exegesis which arose from an interaction between the biblical text and *les véritables Traditions*. We find, however, that other interests are engaged and that he is concerned to peg out an area of biblical scholarship, free of theological implications, where critical autonomy will be allowed.

Simon quotes a statement of the fourth session of the Council of Trent, 'It is not permitted to Catholics to have recourse to interpreters of Sacred Scripture who are not Fathers.'[290] He argues against an interpretation of this which would disallow all biblical exegesis subsequent to the age of the Fathers and which would condemn all those who had criticized patristic exegesis.

One must draw a distinction between critical study of the Bible and what concerns the belief received universally in the Church ... The fathers of the Council [of Trent] did not condemn the first way [critical] of explaining Scripture, but only the innovators of that period who opposed their new explanations of Scripture to the doctrine received and approved in the Church.[291]

The error, in Simon's view, would be to combine critical scholarship with theology, because one would then fall foul of the Council of Trent. Provided that integration is avoided, and biblical science is kept separate from Catholic belief, the resolution of the Council is not contravened.

There is also a liberty to disagree with critical defects in patristic exegesis, but not to criticize the Fathers when they express or define belief received universally in the church. Simon cites Cardinal Cajetan: 'One should not attach the [critical] interpretation of Scripture to the explanations of the Fathers; one should interpret the words of the text as literally as possible.'[292] The way out is to hold the critical pursuit of the plain sense of scripture apart from patristic theology. In this connection Simon defends the orthodoxy of Cajetan: his view is in conformity with the doctrine of the Church which has always permitted interpreters of scripture the liberty to seek after the plain sense without making them subject to the interpretations of ancient doctors; they are subject only to the doctrine received and approved in all the Church.[293]

The direction in which all this points is a study of the Hebrew Bible whose assumptions are humanist and scientific and whose goal is the ascertaining of the plain sense. The Hebrew Bible is to be studied using the same scholarly equipment and methods as would be applied to any other set of ancient documents, a view with which Hobbes and Spinoza would have agreed.[294] The linguistic sciences, textual criticism, lexicography and grammar are brought into play in order to achieve a translation, and other disciplines like extra-biblical history, geography, anthropology, mythology, elucidation of the *fauna* and *flora* of ancient Palestine, and so on,[295] enlarge the area of biblical science and contribute to an exegesis which is an enrichment of the plain sense. The objective is to locate the Bible in as rich and comprehensive a human context as can be constructed.

It is not difficult to discern that this is a highway along which Old Testament scholarship has in fact advanced and that Simon, in so far as he mapped out this route, showed remarkable prescience. There is nothing precisely theological about this type of scholarship, and Christian credal affirmations ought not to be engaged. They belong to different forms of discourse. There is no reason, in principle, why Catholics and Protestants should not co-operate in it. The circumstance that before the publication of his *Histoire Critique* Simon had shown an interest in a projected translation of the Bible into French in which Catholics and Protestants would participate should not be overlooked.[296] It is even more significant that in his *Histoire Critique*, despite what he has said about the incapacity of Protestants for a dispassionate criticism of the Bible, he returns to the perception that common ground exists.

Commenting on Cajetan's view noted above he remarks: 'There, in a few words, is the method which must be followed in the explication of the Bible, and by this means it will be easy to reconcile Catholics with Protestants on this subject.'[297] It is, however, a reconciliation which excludes theology.

5

ALEXANDER GEDDES

A century separates Richard Simon and Alexander Geddes, but they have much in common. Both were Roman Catholics with a Paris education which gave them mastery in the same departments of critical biblical scholarship. Both were biblical critics of the same kind; both were Hebraists and applied the ancient versions to the study of the Hebrew Bible. They were familiar with patristic literature and, in particular, were steeped in Jerome. They had decided aesthetic opinions on the translation of the Hebrew Bible and they regarded translation as a consummation of textual and linguistic scholarship. They set the same limits to the critical exegesis of the Hebrew Bible and neither was interested in the Christian exegesis of the Old Testament.

When the differences between them are reckoned, it ought to be said that whereas Simon holds that vernacular translations of the Bible for ecclesiastical use should be made from the Vulgate, Geddes sees virtue only in translations which are done from the original languages. Moreover, Geddes provides more evidence than Simon that he has wrestled with the practical problems of translating the Hebrew Bible: he has an awareness of the craft of translation as opposed to the theory. He discusses difficulties which arise for the workman at his bench; he knows the pinpricks which are associated with the job, the little problems which emerge and clamour for decisions.

The most important difference between Simon and Geddes lies in the range of their scholarly ambitions. Simon is the cool scholar who seeks freedom to pursue his critical investigations into the Hebrew Bible. Far from having any concern to convert his humanist, critical scholarship into a biblical theology, he argues that it has no theological implications. Geddes, on the other hand, has a sense of vocation for a Christianity which is agreeable with rational principles, and is concerned to convert the results of his criticism into a new formulation of Christianity.

The environment of Geddes's biblical scholarship

The story of Alexander Geddes awakens curiosity, and in any consideration of his scholarly work the pattern of his life thrusts itself upon the notice of the investigator. He came out of a farming community, the son of a tenant farmer, and hailed from that area of north-east Scotland, comprising parts of Banff and Moray, where there is an unbroken tradition of Scottish Catholicism. Yet the piety of his home bore some resemblance to Scottish Presbyterian piety of the period, in so far as it would appear to have been founded on the reading of the King James Version of the Bible. 'Although my parents were Roman Catholics', wrote Geddes, 'they were not bigots; and the Bible was the principal book in their scanty library. They taught me to read it with reverence and attention, and before I had reached my eleventh year, I knew all its history by heart.'[1]

After his elementary schooling, received from the tutor employed by the local laird, he went a little further afield to Scalan, some forty miles south of Elgin, a more advanced school and also a seminary, where, at least, a preliminary training for the priesthood was offered. When he went to Scalan in 1751 Geddes was fourteen and he remained there until 1758. He then moved on to the Scots College in Paris, where he pursued his studies for a further six years, returning to Scotland in 1764.

It would be difficult to exaggerate the effect exercised on Geddes by the intellectual and cultural influences which he absorbed during his six years in Paris. Certainly when he returned to Scotland in 1764 a distance had been set between his mental habits and way of life, and the mould of the Scottish Catholic piety in which he had been formed. He writes particularly warmly of the scholarship and humanity of Ladvocat, who was the first occupant of the Chair of Hebrew in the Sorbonne, a Chair which 'was erected in the year 1751' by the Duke of Orleans, 'for the purpose of reviving Oriental learning in the University of Paris, and of explaining the Hebrew Scriptures'.[2]

Scottish Catholic bishops nursed a long-standing dissatisfaction with the Scots College in Paris, a kind of disagreement between academics and ecclesiastics as to what constitutes the right theological education for priests or ministers which is still with us. Bishop Hay, of whom Geddes was subsequently to fall foul, featured prominently in these representations, and Geddes[3] was the translator of a memoir in which John Gordon of Auchentoul, Principal of the Scots College, replied to Bishop Hay's strictures.

It is clear that Geddes had found the intellectual freedom and the cultural opportunities of his Paris experience entirely congenial and that he had been singularly fitted by nature to receive these influences and be transformed by them. Later, there is evidence that his view of Christianity had become immoderately élitist, but there are indications that in the period 1764–80 he still retained the common touch. Of Geddes's eleven years in his calf country, when he had pastoral responsibilities at Auchenhalrig, Fochabers and the chapel of Tynet between Cullen and Fochabers, Fuller says: 'He got on well with everyone around him, regardless of religion or social distinction.' But he adds, 'With his Paris education, vivacious personality, exceptional intelligence and ready wit, he was a welcome guest in the houses of the nobility, who were, for the most part, Episcopalian. Chief among these were the Duke and Duchess of Gordon, and Geddes enjoyed their friendship for many years.'[4]

Geddes spent his first years as a priest (1764–8), apart from a few months in Dundee, at Traquair House, Peebles, as a member of the household of the Earl and Countess of Traquair. Fuller's account is that the Countess asked Bishop Hay to remove Geddes in 1768, because his Catholicism was not sufficiently strict to satisfy her scruples.[5] The author of the article on Geddes in the Dictionary of National Biography supposes that Geddes's removal arose from the need to put an end to an affair of the heart in which he had become involved.[6] The statement of the same author that the final break with Hay, which resulted in Geddes forsaking his native countryside and heading for London, arose out of his attendance at a Presbyterian service and his participation in hunting[7] is, perhaps, a kind of parable rather than a sober, factual account. The service, attendance at which gave the offence, was Episcopalian rather than Presbyterian.[8] Nevertheless, one can distil the truth that Geddes was not made to be a country priest in the north-east of Scotland, and that for a man of his intellectual sharpness, critical learning, literary finesse and social graces the situation would hardly have been tolerable had he not had the *éntree* to the houses of the nobility and opportunities for conversation with professors of the University of Aberdeen. The University recognized the merit of his translation of *Select Satires of Horace* (1779)[9] by conferring on him the degree of Doctor of Laws *honoris causa* in May, 1780.

When he left Auchenhalrig for London, it was the beginning of the end of his life as a practising Catholic priest, although his disenchantment with the Roman Catholic Church and his alienation from it apparently proceeded by stages. On his arrival in London he found employment at the Imperial Chapel in Portman Square, but this lasted only until the end of the year 1781. After Easter 1782 'he gave up all ministerial functions and seldom officiated'.[10] We learn from John Disney and Charles Butler, in a posthumous publication of Geddes's translation of the book of Psalms, that in 1781 his patron, Lord Petre, had furnished him with a complete biblical library and promised to allow him an annuity of £100, 'double the amount of which he regularly paid him'.[11] When Lord Petre died in 1801 he bequeathed Geddes £100 in his will, and the next Lord Petre granted him an annuity of £100 'to continue his father's patronage of the work',[12] that is, the work of preparing a new translation of the Hebrew Bible into English on which Geddes had embarked.

In 1782 Geddes still viewed his project for a new translation of the Bible in the context of the Roman Catholic Church, as is evident from his *Idea of a New English Edition of the Holy Bible for the Use of the Roman Catholics of Great Britain and Ireland* published in that year. What he is proposing is in effect a replacement of the Rheims-Douai version: not a new translation from the Hebrew and the Greek, but a further advance on the basis of Bishop Challoner's revision:[13] 'It was then his intention to translate from the Vulgate, and to make the Douay version, with Bishop Challoner's amendments, in some respects the basis of his own; but he soon abandoned this plan.'[14] Geddes informs us that he had in his possession 'a manuscript New Testament, prepared for the press, by the late Mr Robert Gordon of the Scotch College at Paris; in which some considerable mistranslations of all the preceding versions are noted and rectified'.[15] The manuscript presumably contained a translation into English from the Vulgate rather than from the Greek, although this is not explicitly stated. Gordon[16] was unsuccessful in his efforts to have the version approved at Rome (1743) and subsequently (1753) returned to Paris, where he lived for a time in the Scots College. He had earlier (1705–12) been 'a prefect of studies and procurator' in Paris.

No trace of a distinctively Catholic scheme of translation survives in the *Prospectus* of 1786. The 'vulgar version'[17] to which Geddes refers, and which he regards as the antecedent of his projected translation of the Bible, is the King James Version.[18] The Douai Version of 1609, which has almost disappeared from view, is described as 'literal and barbarous'.[19] The notion of translating from a Latin translation of the Hebrew into English is dismissed as unscholarly and unreasonable: 'A translator, who works on the originals, can derive but little help from versions made from the Vulgate; and therefore I will not detain the reader with a long enumeration of them.'[20]

There is no institutional, Roman Catholic framework to which Geddes's proposals for a new translation of the Bible, as they appear in the *Prospectus*, can be related. Such ecclesiastical connections as there are link him with the Church of England rather than the Roman Catholic Church, but he is essentially a scholar giving birth to what he hopes will be a literary success. He seeks out the most influential allies he can find in the world of biblical learning, and he depends on a munificent patron in Lord Petre, whose Catholicism was sufficiently liberal to tolerate his intellectual boldness. Geddes salutes him as the one who had provided financial backing for his work 'after twenty years of frustration': 'It was his great love for religion, and his extreme desire of seeing Scriptural knowledge more generally promoted among those of his own communion; that suggested to him the idea of procuring a new translation, before he knew that I had ever entertained a similar idea, and at a time when I had almost despaired of seeing it realized.'[21] It was to Lord Petre that Geddes dedicated the first volume of his new translation (Genesis–Joshua) in 1792. The second volume, which appeared in 1797 and contained Judges, Samuel, Kings, Chronicles and the Prayer of Manasseh, was dedicated to the Duchess of Gloucester.

We may sometimes feel that Geddes's expressions of admiration and deference for Anglican scholars are too unctuous, but an unfavourable construction should, perhaps, not be put on them. The Petre family maintained its liberality to him and its regard for him to the end of his life. The son of his original patron instructed Disney and Butler to examine Geddes's papers after his death and they report:

We did it as far as our avocations allowed; but, to our great surprise, we did not find a single manuscript line which related to his biblical pursuits. We signified this to his lordship, and recommended a further search might be made by some person who could bestow more time upon it: this was done, but was equally unsuccessful. From the Doctor's own declarations, and other circumstances, there is every reason to suppose he had made great progress in his work: it seems therefore probable, that in the view of his approaching dissolution, of which he had long been sensible, he had committed all his manuscripts to the flames.[22]

This may be a right conclusion, but it is a puzzling one. Why should Geddes have committed such an act of destruction?

Disney and Butler form an odd alliance, the one an Anglican clergyman who had given up his preferments in 1782 to become a Unitarian minister,[23] and the other a barrister and a Catholic, a champion of the Catholic laity against the hierarchy and of English Catholics against the Pope.[24] As the kind of friends whom Geddes still had at the end of his life, and who had a care for his reputation after his death, they tell us something about his intellectual and spiritual pilgrimage. His growing ecclesiastical isolation during his period of residence in London has to be kept in mind, and it must have meant a great deal to him to be admitted to a fellowship of learning by scholars of the calibre of Benjamin Kennicott and Robert Lowth. Nor have we any reason to doubt the sincerity of the regard in which he professed to hold them. They were masters of kinds of biblical learning which he admired. He considers that Walton's London Polyglot has 'a decided superiority over all the rest',[25] and of the edition printed from the Alexandrian manuscript of the Septuagint in the British Museum he says, 'Until the Romans are pleased to give us more correct copy of their manuscript (Vaticanus), this edition must be our text book of the Greek version; and all future collations of manuscripts should be made relatively to it.'[26] He praises 'Professor White of Oxford' and notices that in a letter to the Bishop of London (Lowth) he has laid down 'some excellent rules for having a good new edition of the Septuagint; a work very much wanted; and which we wish the learned professor's other avocations would permit him to undertake'.[27]

Kennicott, in particular, had established the textual foundation which appeared to justify the enterprise of a new translation of the Hebrew Bible into English. His great collation of mediaeval Hebrew manuscripts was thought by Geddes, and also by Lowth, Newcome and Blayney to have opened the door to a decisive advance in the understanding of the Hebrew Bible. All these names are mentioned by Geddes:[28] William Newcome's work on the *Minor Prophets*[29] was published in 1785, when he was Bishop of Waterford, and Benjamin Blayney's on *Jeremiah and Lamentations*,[30] appeared in 1784. But it is on Robert Lowth that his laureations are concentrated, and he appeals to him especially in his *Letter* of 1787 as an authority on English grammar,[31] no less than on the structure of Hebrew poetry and the translation of the Hebrew Bible into English.[32] It is all summed up in a great crescendo of praise and deference at the end of his *Letter*, a feature which is at once an indication of his great facility with words and of the danger of fulsomeness to which he was exposed:

These, my Lord, are a part of the principal doubts and difficulties that have occasionally presented themselves during the course of my present labours. I lay them before your Lordship with all the confidence which your former encouraging countenance so naturally inspires. If health and leisure shall allow you but to glance them over, I am persuaded that a great portion of the mist will be dissipated by so clear and keen a ray. I wish not to give your Lordship the trouble of writing long remarks. The shortest hint of approbation or the contrary; a single *yes* or *no* on the opposite page, relative to any query I have put, or opinion I have ventured to give, will be a sufficient indication of your sentiment and go a great way to make me cherish or abandon my own. Before next Michaelmas I hope to have the honour of submitting to your perusal a whole volume of my translation. How happy shall I esteem myself, if it should have the good fortune to merit the same flattering approbation you were so kind to express of my Prospectus. Whether that be in my fate, or not, I eagerly seize this opportunity of testifying to the Public, with what respect and veneration I have the honour to be, My Lord, Your Lordship's much obliged, and most obedient, humble servant.[33]

We learn from Disney and Butler that Geddes had sent a manuscript copy of his *Prospectus* to Lowth, with a letter 'desiring his lordship would mark with a black theta whatever passage might appear objectionable'. Lowth returned the manuscript with a note in which he said 'that he had read it with some care and attention, and with the fullest approbation; that he found no room for black thetas; and that he doubted not it would give general satisfaction'.[34] The *Letter* addressed to the Bishop of London is dated 15th January, 1787. It was the year in which Lowth died, and so little time remained for an answer to the many questions on matters of theory and practice which had arisen in the hard school of experience, when Geddes knuckled down to his task of producing a new translation of the Hebrew Bible into English.

Kennicott died in 1783, so that it was only during the earliest period of his residence in London that Geddes had the benefit of his friendship, encouragement and influence, but he remembers him fondly:

The late Dr Kennicott, on whose tomb every Biblical student ought annually to strew the tributary flower, has a peculiar claim to my grateful remembrance. I had hardly made known my design, when he anticipated my wishes to have his advice and assistance towards the execution of it, with a degree of unreserved frankness and friendship, which I had never before experienced in a stranger. Not contented with applauding and encouraging himself, he pushed me forewards from my obscurity to the notice of others: he spoke of me to Barrington, he introduced me to Lowth. The very short time he lived after my acquaintance with him, and the few opportunities I had of profiting from his conversation, are distressing reflexions; but still I count it a happiness to have been acquainted with a man, whose labours I have daily occasion to bless, and whose memory I must ever revere.[35]

The new name which appears here is that of Shute Barrington who, as a sometime Canon of Christ Church, had been a colleague of Kennicott, and who was successively Bishop of Llandaff (1769), Salisbury (1782) and Durham (1791).

Although Geddes rarely ventures on an open disagreement with the Anglican scholars whose work he notices and acclaims, he has more independence of mind than might appear on the surface and is capable of expressing dissent. He parts company with Lowth, Blayney and Newcome on the question whether 'Jehovah' should appear in an English translation, and in his *Letter* to Lowth he remarks, 'Jehovah is a barbarous term, that was never heard of before the sixteenth century ... Bate, your Lordship, Green, Blayney and Bishop Newcome have all adopted it.'[36] Geddes favours 'Lord' (cf. NEB, LORD) in line with the Greek, Syriac, Latin and Arabic versions. He tempers his disagreement with Newcome's rules for translating by making a handsome gesture of deference to him:

At the same time his great judgment and taste, and his established character as a writer, make me hesitate and doubt about the propriety of some of my own. I shall consider both at more leisure and with new attention; and weigh his Lordship's reasons with all possible care and impartiality.[37]

Geddes disagrees with Lowth about how Hebrew poetry should be set out in an English translation. Lowth had argued[38] that the poetry of the prophetic books is of the first rank,[39] and had offered a metrical representation of the poetic sections of the book of Isaiah in 1778.[40] Blayney and Newcome in turn had been influenced by Lowth. Newcome remarks that he has followed Lowth 'in translating the prophetical books according to their supposed measure' and adds, 'Many will think that I have carried this hypothesis too far in some parts of my translation. But I followed it when there appeared a remote probability of its truth; and readily grant that some parts may be prosaic to which I have given a metrical form.'[41] Lowth knows that the prophetic literature is interspersed with prose, but he takes pains in his *Isaiah*[42] to show that a metrical arrangement of prophetic poetry in English is an indispensable contribution to interpretation. He sets out to convince the reader that 'this branch of Criticism, minute as it may appear, yet merits the attention of the Translator and of the Interpreter of the Holy Scriptures; so large a part of which is entirely Poetical, and where occasional pieces of Poetry are interspersed through the whole'.[43]

Geddes disagrees deferentially and elegantly with Lowth, but there is no escaping the conclusion that he is overturning Lowth's sustained argument that a metrical setting-out of Hebrew poetry in English is a necessary stage of criticism and an essential aspect of interpretation. He urges that such dispositions make for stilted English, for unnatural divisions of sense, and that they hinder rather than assist comprehension. He accepts that the difference between poetry and prose must be marked in an English translation, but he has in mind a special kind of English prose as a medium for Hebrew poetry and not a metrical simulation of it. He heaps praise on Lowth and his successors and grants that a translator should make a distinction between Hebrew poetry and Hebrew prose. 'And here it is, I think, that modern translations, our public one (KJV) not excepted, are the most susceptible of further improvement. Your Lordship set the example; which has been successfully followed by Mr Blayney and Bishop Newcome; and after which I also have attempted to form my imperfect copy.'[44] But Geddes is against setting out Hebrew poetry 'in lines or hemistichs' in an English translation and prefers 'the sober garb of measured prose'.[45] 'You, my Lord, of all men know best, how little we are acquainted with the measure and mechanism of Hebrew verse; and how capricious, for the most part, are the divisions that have been made of them, even by the most learned Hebraists.'[46] He continues:

Were the text for public service to be thus divided, the best readers would, I believe, make but an awkward appearance in delivering the most sublime oracles of religion. The eye and the ear would be at continual variance; the tones and cadences would be perpetually confounded, and grating disharmony attend the pronunciation of almost every period ... On the whole, then, may I not appeal to your Lordship's judgment, even from your own practice; that in giving a version for general reading, such a division of those parts which are supposed to be poetry, would be attended with manifest inconvenience; and with no visible advantage; and that, therefore, a plain prose-like version, which should preserve as much as possible of what your Lordship has so ably proved to constitute the essence of Hebrew poetry, would be greatly preferable.[47]

In a further reference to Lowth's *Isaiah* praise is again mingled with criticism: 'Let this version be taken out of its present form, and divided and arranged like plain poetical prose; and the least intelligent reader will, I think, be struck with the difference.'[48]

In the *Prospectus* there is a reference by Geddes to his cousin 'Bishop Geddes of Edinburgh'[49] with whom he shared his early education and corresponded regularly, certainly up to 1791, the year prior to the publication of the first volume of his translation.[50] It closes with an expression of his awareness that the path of criticism on which he was set might not commend itself to the Roman Catholic Church and that his future ecclesiastical standing was touched with uncertainty. Geddes says of his cousin:

His prudent advices and seasonable encouragement have often given a new stimulus to my spirits in the midst of my labours, and sometimes supported me under their almost oppressive load. I trust, from his long uninterrupted friendship, that he will continue the same good offices, until I shall have fairly discharged myself of the heavy burthen; and I foresee I shall yet stand in need of such good offices.[51]

Geddes could ill afford to lose Kennicott and Lowth so soon, and the bad effect that his feelings of isolation and of being surrounded by adversaries had on his scholarship and on the reasonableness of his temper appears in the second volume of his translation and, especially, in the preface to his *Critical Remarks*. Already in the first of these there is evidence of a lack of composure, of an inner turbulence which is producing deterioration, and of a tendency to rant. Thus, having denied that Moses was 'inspired' as a historian, he allows that 'in some sense' he was 'inspired' as a legislator, and continues, 'Were there no middle option left me, but either literally to believe all that is written in the Pentateuch, by whomsoever written; or to deny the divine legation of Moses; I should not long hesitate in forming my determination:

I should deny the divine legation of Moses.'[52] So far his tone is reasonable, but then he anticipates a fury of dissent and denunciation:

What torrents of illiberal abuse and obloquy this honest declaration will draw upon my head, I can readily preperceive; at least, if, from past experience, I may conjecture future contingency. Whatever superstitious credulity has of bitter zeal, whatever gloomy fanaticism of spiteful asperity, whatever canting hypocrisy of pious fraud, will be employed to misrepresent, traduce, calumniate and blacken my character. I shall be called *apostate*, *heretic*, *infidel*, and every other odious name. My work will, most probably, be proscribed, and my person persecuted; as far as proscription can take place, and persecution dares be avowed, in a land of liberty. Protestant will contend with Papist, which shall throw the first stone at me: and both, forgetting here their mutual antipathies, will agree in contributing their respective portion of wormwood and venom, to embitter and poison the cup to be presented to my lips: but I am not obliged to drink it. – All this I foresee without the gift of prophecy: but, I thank God, I am grown insensible to injuries: and although I am by no means indifferent about honest fame, I am perfectly disregardful of ungenerous and unmanly censure. As I write to please no party,[53] I trust there are, in every Christian sect, some persons of superior discernment, candour and probity; who, before they pass sentence on me, will read me with patient attention, weigh my arguments in the scale of reason; and then, will either ultimately acquiesce in my opinion, or confute it in the language of temperance and charity.[54]

The contrast between this tirade and the cool, scholarly proposals of the *Prospectus*, the precise discussion of translation problems in the *Letter* to the Bishop of London, or the moderate tone of the preface to the first volume of the translation, is very striking. It is clear that this anxiety and inner disquiet arise from a continuation of his work beyond the stage of translation and his entanglement with questions about the historical accuracy of sections of the Hebrew Bible and its 'inspiration'. In the earlier books, on the contrary, Geddes is entirely occupied with a range of fundamental critical considerations which were preparatory to translation: textual criticism in relation to the Massoretic text and the ancient versions, the lexicography of biblical Hebrew, and translational matters of principle and detail. The new Geddes would not have commended himself either to a Canon of Christ Church or a Bishop of London, and his own Church had moved against him soon after the publication of the first volume of his translation: 'An ecclesiastical interdict, signed by Drs Walmesley, Gibson and Douglass, as vicars apostolic of the western, northern and London districts, was published, in which Geddes's work was prohibited to the faithful.'[55] Geddes issued a remonstrance, but was suspended from all ecclesiastical functions.

Geddes had ventured into a different kind of biblical criticism, necessarily less precise than textual criticism, and potentially more contentious. Even so, had he remained no more than a critic, as Richard Simon was content to do, and not attempted to construct a new religion out of his criticism, he might have preserved a kind of scholarly calm which he had lost by 1797. There are issues here which require a more detailed consideration, but the particular ways in which his higher criticism and his theology interact can be left for later examination. His sense of isolation and rejection must have contributed to the darkness of his mood, and to the extravagance of his imperious sweeping away of all extant forms of institutional Christianity. He was now nursing an élitist hope of a gathering of thoughtful Christians from all the sects to embrace a new Christianity in a temple of reason, where only religious belief recommended by reason would be demanded.[56]

When one reads the preface in his *Critical Remarks*, it becomes evident that Geddes is as much cut off from Anglicanism or Presbyterianism as he is from Roman Catholicism, and that he has no longer any regard for the historical creeds of Christianity. There are passages where he speaks like a radical critic and can be assessed as such; there are others far removed from the Pentateuch, which is supposed to be the subject of the *Critical Remarks*, where Geddes appears more in the guise of the founder of a new religion. Quotations from both of these kinds will illustrate what is meant and will reveal more about the state of Geddes's mind in 1800.

Firstly, we may take a passage where he confines himself to the province of criticism:

In my translation and explanatory notes[57] I have made it a rule to confine myself to the limited province of a mere interpreter; endeavouring to give a faithful version of my corrected originals, without comment or criticism. In the following remarks[58] I have taken a wider and bolder range: I have throughout acted the critic, and occasionally the commentator; although the office of the latter has always been made subservient to that of the former. In both these characters I have freely used mine own judgment (such as it is) without the smallest deference to inveterate prejudice or domineering authority. The Hebrew scriptures I have examined and appretiated, as I would any other writings of antiquity; and have bluntly and honestly delivered my sentiments of their merit or demerit, their beauties or imperfections; as becomes a free and impartial examiner.[59]

This is an affirmation that the critical appreciation of the Hebrew Bible is an activity of humanist scholarship, that it is autonomous and not subject to dogmatic restrictions. But Geddes is burdened with the thought of the consequences which will flow from his enterprise, and the challenge to the infallibility of the Bible which he is issuing. He cannot rid his mind of this theological anxiety, nor resist the temptation of putting in his oar and relating his criticism to religious belief, defined as rational belief:

I am well aware, that this freedom will, by the many, be considered as an audacious licence; and the cry of *heresy! infidelity! irreligion!* will resound from shore to shore. But my peaceful mind has been long prepared for, and indeed accustomed to, such harsh Cerberean barkings: and experience has made me (not naturally insensible) callous to every injury, that ignorance or malice may have in store for me ... I only enter my protest against downright misrepresentation and calumny. I disclaim and spurn the imputation of irreligion and infidelity. I believe as much as I find sufficient motives of credibility for believing: and without sufficient motives of credibility, there can be no rational belief. Indeed, the great mass of mankind have no rational belief. The vulgar Papist and the vulgar Protestant are here on almost equal terms: few, very few of either class ever think of seriously examining the primary foundations of their faith.[60]

The last sentence deserves special attention, because it underlines what was said earlier about Geddes's ambition to be the founder of an élitist religion. He introduces a concept of rational belief which is incompatible with institutional Christianity of any kind and which makes no accommodation for 'the great mass of mankind'.

So he is led on to a criticism of the Papist's belief in the infallibility of the Church and the Protestant's belief in the infallibility of the Bible. Both are accepted on authority and neither is supported by reason and evidence:

Both give up their reason, before they are capable of reasoning ... On the whole then, I think, it may be laid down as an axiom, that the bulk of Christians, whether Papists or Protestants, cannot be said to have a rational faith; because their motives of credibility are not rational motives; but the positive assertions of an assumed authority, which they have never discussed, or durst not question: their religion is the fruit of unenlightened credulity. A very small number of curious serious and learned men only, have thoroughly examined the motives of their religious belief in any communion: and it will be found, I presume, that the more curious and learned they were, the less they generally believed. Hence, perhaps, the old adage: *Ignorance is the mother of devotion.*[61]

Geddes has dissolved ecclesiastical authority and has confined rational religious belief to 'a very small number of curious, serious and learned men'. He confides that the result of all his searching is the conclusion that 'reason only is the ultimate and only sure motive of credibility, the only solid pillar of faith ... I cannot, then, be charged with *infidelity*, since I firmly believe all that reason tells me I ought to believe; nor can I be charged with *irreligion*, because I am conscious that Religion, genuine Religion, is both reasonable, and conducive to human happiness.'[62] In the light of this he redefines 'Catholic':

Catholic Christianity I revere wherever I find it, and in whatsoever sect it dwells: but I cannot revere the loads of hay and stubble which have been blended with its precious gems; and which still in every sect, with which I am acquainted, more or less tarnish and hide their lustre. I cannot revere metaphysical unintelligible creeds, nor blasphemous confessions of faith. I cannot revere persecution for the sake of conscience, nor tribunals that enforce orthodoxy by fire and faggot. – I cannot revere formulas of faith made the test of loyalty, nor penal laws made the hedge of church establishments.[63]

Geddes is not content to affirm that the critical study of the Hebrew Bible resembles the study of any other collection of ancient documents; that it is a function of humanist scholarship and a department of biblical science unfettered by theological restrictions. He extends the range of his criticism beyond a humanist scholarship and endeavours to create a critical or rational religion. The consequences are those described above. His rationalism is too narrow to make sense of religion, and he ends up with an intellectual élite in circumstances hardly less absurd than those attaching to any unyielding, dogmatic predestinarianism. His grasp of religious faith is, perhaps, defective, for it is questionable whether believing 'what reason tells me I ought to believe' is an assent of the same order as religious faith. The main criticism, however, must be that so few can jump the hurdle which he erects and that so many are excluded from the 'genuine religion' which is conducive to human happiness.

The nature of Geddes's biblical criticism

For the most part Geddes and Richard Simon have the same understanding of the tasks of biblical criticism, and for the one as for the other the element of higher criticism should not be given such prominence that the more fundamental critical activities which issue in the translation of the Hebrew Bible are allowed to disappear from view. In the first place, this is textual criticism directed at the text of the Hebrew Bible; it comprehends the ancient versions, especially the contribution they make to the recovery of the best text of the Hebrew Bible, but also the textual history of these versions in and for themselves. Criticism is also concerned with Hebrew lexicography and grammar, and with the aesthetic and practical questions which are raised when one gets down to the actual task of translating the Hebrew Bible from what is thought to be the best text and with all the lexicographical learning that can be mobilized.[64]

Beyond translation there is the duty to supply notes in the form of 'critical remarks' which spell out the problems that have been weighed and indicate how these have been resolved. But a distinction is drawn, not only by Geddes but also by Lowth, between this activity and a commentary which is directed towards edification. The limits of critical exegesis which are envisaged are not very different from those which obtain with Simon. Thus we find the following passage in Lowth's *Isaiah*:

The design of the Notes is to give the reasons and authorities on which the Translation is founded; to rectify or to explain the words of the text; to illustrate the ideas, the images and the allusions of the Prophet, by referring to objects, notions, and customs, which peculiarly belong to his age and his country; and to point out the beauties of particular passages. I sometimes indeed endeavour to open the design of the Prophecy, to shew the connection between its parts, and to point out the event which it foretells. But in general, I must intreat the Reader to be satisfied with my endeavours faithfully to express the Literal Sense, which is all that I undertake. If he would go deeper into the Mystical Sense, into Theological, Historical and Chronological disquisitions, there are many learned Expositors to whom he may have recourse, who have written full Commentaries on this Prophet; to which Title the present work has no pretensions. The sublime and spiritual uses to be made of this peculiarly Evangelical Prophet, must, as I have observed, be all founded on a faithful representation of the Literal Sense, which his words contain. This is what I have endeavoured closely and exactly to express. And within the limits of this humble, but necessary, province, my endeavours must be confined.[65]

Lowth does not question the appropriateness or necessity of 'sublime and spiritual uses', and there is a note of piety in his language ('this peculiarly Evangelical Prophet') which distinguishes him from the harder critical line and the unbending rational concentration of Simon and Geddes. Nevertheless, in the context of the intellectual climate of the eighteenth century he marked out for himself the area of biblical scholarship which he thought most deserving of his labours and talents and this did not include the 'Mystical Sense' to which he respectfully refers.

The key figure in relation to the expectations which had been raised for a decisive advance in the textual criticism of the Hebrew Bible was Benjamin Kennicott.[66] Lowth had made use of Kennicott's 'variations' in his work on *Isaiah* and attached great significance to them.[67] Newcome had similarly availed himself of them in his work on the *Minor Prophets*, and Blayney used them in his commentary on *Jeremiah and Lamentations*. Alluding to those who set their faces against Kennicott's great enterprise, Geddes remarks, 'Nor did it depend on them, that the greatest literary undertaking of this, or indeed of any other age, was not quashed in its very beginning, as hurtful to Christianity.'[68] Of the collations of Kennicott and J. B. De Rossi he says that they 'afford many important readings with regard to the sense; and of grammatical corrections, a number almost infinite'. Of Kennicott's work, in particular, he says, 'The prejudices at first raised against it, by ignorance or mistaken zeal, are daily dying away; and its value must rise, in the estimation of the learned, in proportion as it is known and examined.'[69]

Kennicott's major work was preceded by two dissertations on the state of the text of the Hebrew Bible, the first published in 1753 and the second in 1759. He began his mammoth task of searching for manuscripts of the Hebrew Bible and collating them in 1760. The list of subscribers was headed by the name of Dr Secker, who, like Lowth, had been Bishop of Oxford, and who, as Archbishop of Canterbury, was the first patron of Kennicott's work. The collation of manuscripts and printed editions went on between 1760 and 1770 and it is documented in the annual reports.[70] The first volume of *Vetus Testamentum Hebraicum cum Variis Lectionibus* appeared in 1776 and the second in 1780. The annual accounts show Kennicott at his best, managing a great enterprise with vigour and imagination, holding it to a timetable, and persuading his subscribers to continue their support of it.

His energy and enterprise beggar description. He has influential connections in every country in Western Europe, and while he and his 'Gentlemen' are busy in Oxford, he initiates an ambitious work of international co-operation, so that manuscripts are being collated in Rome, Florence, Turin, Milan, Paris, Berlin, Hamburg, Madrid and so on. British and Irish manuscripts, together with such as European libraries were willing to send to England, or which Kennicott acquired, either by using the resources of the subscription, or through the generosity of foreign patrons, were collated at Oxford. One foreign collator was Ladvocat, the Professor of Hebrew at the Sorbonne, who had taught Geddes and had received a handsome and affectionate tribute from him.[71] Ladvocat refused to accept payment and Kennicott quotes from his letter: 'We have no such custom in the Sorbonne; and we think ourselves extremely happy, both my young people and myself in being able to contribute to a work so useful, and even so necessary, to the study of the Sacred Scriptures.'[72]

Kennicott's collation, like that of De Rossi[73] later in the same century, was occupied only with the consonantal text. The text which Kennicott printed was one which had been published in Amsterdam in 1705, edited by E. van der Hooght, with points and Masora. In omitting points and Masora Kennicott was following C. F. Houbigant who had made the same consonantal text the basis of his four volumes published in Paris between 1747 and 1753.[74] Houbigant is one of Geddes's heroes and is saluted by him as a pioneer of critical biblical scholarship. He is said to have opened up 'a new and rational career to the Biblical critic', and Geddes sees himself as taking up Houbigant's torch and furthering the emancipation of textual criticism from Massoretic bondage:

Nothing can exceed the purity, simplicity, perspicuity and energy of his translation; and if he has not always been equally happy in his conjectural emendation of the text, it cannot be denied that he has, at least, carried away the palm from all those who preceded him in the same career. The clamors that have been raised against him are the clamors of illiberal ignorance, or of partiality to a system which he had turned into ridicule. While his mode of interpreting is approved by a Lowth, a Kennicott, a Michaelis and a Starck, the barkings of inferior critics will not much injure him.[75]

The publication of a consonantal Hebrew text, without points and Masora, by Houbigant, Kennicott and De Rossi is intended as a manifesto that the time of bondage to the Massoretic interpretation of the consonantal text has come to an end and that a new era in the textual criticism of the Hebrew Bible has been inaugurated. Advances in the fundamental criticism of the text of the Hebrew Bible are to be made by collating large numbers of mediaeval Hebrew manuscripts (Kennicott and De Rossi) and thereby purifying the consonantal text. The collating of Hebrew manuscripts will provide a scientific foundation for a critical text of the Hebrew Bible and this will replace the former reliance on Massoretic scholarship.

Geddes enters wholeheartedly upon this programme. He argues that flawed translations have issued from the bad Hebrew text which was translated, and he contrasts uncritical attitudes to the text of the Hebrew Bible with the pains which have been taken with classical texts.[76] He alleges that with the first elements of Hebrew learning 'the most ridiculous notions of the Rabbins' were propagated in the Christian schools; that most of those engaged in Bible translation for the last three hundred years 'have voluntarily put out their own eyes, and allowed themselves to be led on by the worst of guides'.[77]

S. Talmon[78] has remarked that in the eighteenth century textual criticism and theological concern are mixed up together, and that we should not expect a textual criticism which is free of theological motivation. The anti-Jewish sentiments of Geddes have already appeared and other expressions of them will be considered towards the end of this section. Similar prejudices come to the surface in Kennicott's writings, but the form of Kennicott's *Vetus Testamentum Hebraicum* leaves no room for the operation of a theological tendency. It can be criticized as a too mechanical collation, but with this defect it possesses a kind of objectivity, even if it be thought an arid objectivity. The theological convictions of Kennicott, which are evident in his *Dissertations*, do not encroach on the form of his *Vetus Testamentum Hebraicum*. His theology is a background which controls his expectations of what his work will achieve: it will refine the text of the Hebrew Bible from its imperfections and corruptions, including corruptions deliberately perpetrated by Jews; it will supply a Hebrew text superior to any formerly available on the basis of which a new English translation can be made.[79]

Kennicott's goal is to recover the 'original text'. This is associated with a kind of biblical fundamentalism which Geddes regards as a disease of Protestantism and for which he reserves sharp criticism.[80] Geddes, for his part, envisaged the outcome of Kennicott's collation in different terms from Kennicott himself. He accepted the thesis of Massoretic corruption, but he also had in mind an accidental contamination to which all ancient documents are subject and from which the Hebrew Bible was not exempt: 'That waters, which have rolled for ages through a thousand different soils and channels, should be still as pure and untainted as when they issued from their primitive source, would be far less wonderful, than that the Hebrew scriptures should have remained in their first integrity.'[81] Geddes was not disposed to a belief in miracles and he did not share Kennicott's concern that the Hebrew Bible should be recovered perfectly – as God had given it. This was a biblicism foreign to the Catholic texture of his mind and he remarks that belief in an 'immaculate original' is not yet universally exploded.[82] His tactic is rather to reassure the reader to whom the very idea of a better Hebrew text is disturbing, because his supposition had been that a perfect Hebrew text had always existed. Here Geddes introduces a kind of language which recalls Simon's explanation of what is meant by the 'authenticity' of the Vulgate. For a deed to be authentic it is not required that 'the most recent and remote copies of it should be exactly the same with the first autograph ... There could be no such thing, without a continual miracle. It is enough, that there is sufficient evidence of its being essentially the same with the original; and that the changes which it has undergone, whether from design or accident, are not such as can affect its authority, as a genuine record.'[83]

The case is different with Kennicott who sets out from a belief in the inerrancy of Holy Scripture. The scriptures which are inerrant are those which were written down by the biblical authors. The existence of variants is itself a mark of corrupt transmission and a scandal which calls for reformation. The purpose of his massive collation is, paradoxically, to destroy the credence of those variants which are the consequence of imperfect transmission, and to reinstate the text in its originality and purity by discerning which of the variants preserve that text. In this manner the text which truly constitutes the inerrant scriptures will be recovered and the 'Honour of Revelation' will be vindicated. Hence the importance which Kennicott attaches to the comparison of parallel passages of scripture. When he compares parallel passages which exhibit variants, he assumes that the original text can be recovered by such an examination, and the first part of his first *Dissertation*, in which he compares 1 Chron. xi with 2 Sam. v and xxiii,[84] is governed by these assumptions. The recovery of the original text may involve the selecting of a variant, now from one passage, now from another, and so it may require the exercise of critical judgement in these particulars. The overriding belief, however, is that the original text is present in one passage or the other, and that it can be recovered.

Although Geddes does not share Kennicott's theological presuppositions, he does, like Kennicott, assume, as a text-critical procedure, a 'more original' text in parallel passages of the Hebrew Bible which differ from each other, and also when he compares the text of the Hebrew Bible with the Hebrew *Vorlage* of the Septuagint. With parallel passages, he is not disposed to admit separate textual traditions, both of which should be respected, and, like Kennicott, discerns a critical duty to construct an eclectic original text. Where there is contradiction or inconsistency we may assume 'that one of them, at least, is corrupted'. It is 'the province of criticism to determine from circumstances, where the error and where the truth lies'.[85]

In the process of recovering the original text an important part is assigned by Kennicott to the ancient versions. When two parallel passages of the Hebrew Bible are being compared, the agreement of a variant with one or more of the ancient versions will be a strong indication that it preserves the original text. More generally, and this is a point which is also made by Lowth[86] and Newcome,[87] agreements between variants disclosed by Kennicott's collation and the ancient versions reinforce the conclusion that these variants represent a recovery of the original text. In connection with the contribution of the Septuagint to the textual criticism of the Hebrew Bible, Geddes discerns the primary need to be a new critical edition of the Septuagint, and he maintains that 'the old original version' can be recovered by a scientific collation of manuscripts. Like Simon he supposes that a principal aim of Origen was to improve the Greek text which 'had contracted many blemishes'[88] in his time. In his Hexapla, however, he was too heavily influenced by Jewish scholarship and 'emboldened by his new guides he ventured now to *slash with his desperate book* the venerable texture of the old version ... The great authority of Origen made every one, who was possessed of a Greek Bible, revise his copy by the Hexaplar standard.'[89] The confusion was deepened by the inaccurate reproduction of the text-critical symbols:

His distinguishing marks, without adulterating the Septuagint, would have indicated the then state of the Hebrew text, and put it in our power, even at this day, to appretiate both: whereas through the carelessness of ignorant transcribers, or the caprice of future correctors, disorder grew every day greater and greater; until, at length, it became irremediable.[90]

Geddes undertakes to repair the damage, if adequate financial support is forthcoming: 'The most trifling novelty draws, every season, from the purses of the good people of England, a far greater sum than would be adequate to the purpose. With five thousand pounds, I would undertake, in less than three years, to collate every valuable Greek manuscript/of the Bible [that is, the Septuagint] in Europe.'[91] In the meantime, he considers that the most valuable resource which is available is the Codex Alexandrinus in the edition of J. E. Grabe.[92]

There are indications that Geddes views the Hebrew *Vorlage* of the Septuagint as, in general, a more original Hebrew text than that of the Hebrew Bible. He notices that there are citations in Josephus which disagree with our extant Hebrew text and agree with the Septuagint. He supposes that Josephus would not have tolerated this state of affairs in his work and that these discrepancies between the Hebrew and the Greek texts did not exist in his time: 'The only fair conclusion we can draw from his disagreeing with our present Hebrew text, where he agrees with the Septuagint, is that our present Hebrew text and his Hebrew text are not the same.'[93] Where Josephus 'deposes against the present Hebrew text in favour of the Septuagint, there is great reason to suspect that the former is corrupted'.[94] Geddes is influenced by the consideration that the Hebrew text at the time when it was translated into Greek must have been nearer to the original than the extant text of the Hebrew Bible: 'It was excellently translated into Greek, at a period when the copies must have been much less imperfect than they afterwards became: this translation we have entire, though not uncorrupted.'[95]

It is an easy step from this to Geddes's criticism of Jerome's *Hebraica veritas*, and to his perception of the role of the Vulgate in the textual criticism of the Hebrew Bible. On Jerome he says, 'The greatest imperfection of St Jerome's version arises from too great a confidence in his Jewish guides, and from his being prepossest with an idea, that the Hebrew copies were then absolutely faultless. This leads him to blame the Septuagint in many places, where they are not blameable, and where they read and render better than he.'[96] But he perceives a reconciliation of Catholic and Protestant critical scholarship – extremists on both sides are yielding to a more balanced criticism – and this tends to pull his argument in a direction the reverse of that indicated by his remarks on *Hebraica veritas*:

The Catholics are ready to own that the Vulgate is not so pure a rivulet, as some of their too zealous predecessors maintained; and the Protestants as readily acknowledge that the present Hebrew text is not so untainted a source as was long believed. Thus both contribute, in different ways, towards a re-establishment of the true text. Those [the Catholics] without hesitation correct the Vulgate by the original [the extant Hebrew text], where the Vulgate is evidently faulty; and these [the Protestants] make no scruple to make use of the Vulgate in restoring the true text of the original, when the original is evidently or probably corrupted.[97]

Hence Geddes combines a perception that the Hebrew *Vorlage* of the Septuagint is often better than Jerome's *Hebraica veritas* with another, that the *Hebraica veritas*, reflected in Jerome's Vulgate, is sometimes better than our extant Hebrew text. It is in view of the latter persuasion that he can assign to the Vulgate a function in connection with the textual criticism of the Hebrew Bible.

Both Kennicott and Geddes agree with one aspect of Simon's appraisal of the Samaritan Pentateuch, that it is an independent primary witness to the Hebrew text of the Pentateuch and is not derived from the type of text which is extant in our Hebrew Bible. In Simon's terminology it is a 'copy' and not a 'version'. They differ from Simon in the preference which they express for the Samaritan Pentateuch which, according to Kennicott, should in general be given precedence and, particularly, where it has the support of one or more of the ancient versions. Geddes holds that the Samaritan Pentateuch is 'a far more faithful representative of the prototype, than any Masoretic copy, at this day extant'.[98] Simon submitted the two texts[99] to a kind of scrutiny which pointed to a conclusion different from those of Kennicott and Geddes. No doubt this was one of the results of Simon's scholarship which Geddes had in mind when he remarked that Simon 'adopted in part' Massoretic prejudices.[100]

There is an indubitable anti-Massoretic trend in Simon's work, but he is not anti-Jewish in the sense that Kennicott and Geddes are. The reasons for a growth in anti-Jewishness in eighteenth-century Christian biblical scholarship are not obvious, but they deserve some probing and suggestions can be made. In the meantime, it should be remarked that in modern times G. R. Driver has held that the Samaritan Pentateuch is a text independent of the Massoretic text, though he attaches much less significance to it for the criticism of the Hebrew Bible than Kennicott and Geddes.[101] The view which is expressed by Talmon,[102] following Gesenius, Frankel and Kohn, is that the Samaritan Pentateuch is derived from the Massoretic text and that its variants are the consequence of a revision of that text, so that it is not to be considered as an independent textual tradition.

An extreme expression of the anti-Massoretic sentiment of Geddes occurs in his statement that those engaged in Bible translation for 'these last three hundred years have voluntarily put out their own eyes, and allowed themselves to be led on by the worst of guides'[103] – a reference to the dominance of Massoretic scholarship. He continues,

The same imposing set of men, who had the audacity and art to make the Christian world believe that they had preserved the text of their Scriptures in its original integrity, by a pretended enumeration of every word and letter, found it equally easy to perswade them, that the true reading and meaning had also been preserved by the punctuation of every syllable, and the distinction of every pause. This was a second part of that wonderful MASORA, without which the Hebrew text was supposed to be a mere dead letter, a nose of wax, a body without a soul.[104]

In remarks distributed through his work there are other indications of an anti-Jewish tendency in Geddes. Jewish editors, influenced by the Massoretes, are 'text-torturers',[105] and Christian scholars have given credence to those whom in other respects they regard as 'the vilest impostors'.[106] Geddes believes that there has been a wilful corruption of the scriptures by Jews: 'For, although we should not, perhaps, easily admit that so many passages have been designedly corrupted, as a certain class of writers would have us believe; yet it cannot, I think, be well denied, that there are, in some instances, such strong marks of wilful contamination, as to leave little room for doubt.'[107] Christians have, in all ages, been more or less 'the dupes of Rabbinism'.[108] Origen and Jerome were imposed on by the Jews: Origen's knowledge of Hebrew was too scanty for him to do without them, and, unsuspecting, he adopted the first two columns of his Hexapla from them.[109] There was malice in the literalism of Aquila: a desire to deviate as much as possible from the Septuagint.[110] Geddes's view of the Targums is emphatically anti-Jewish, 'The very worst of them will be found to have its use; and, even from the dunghill of the Jerusalem Targum, a pearl may be here and there picked up.'[111] The Targums, other than Onkelos and Jonathan, 'are an obscure and anonymous herd; who seem to vie with one another, which shall advance the greatest absurdities'.[112] Lowth, for his part, remarks that earlier Christian scholars would have achieved better results if the Massoretic pointing had been regarded as something to be consulted rather than accepted as an authority: it is 'an assistant', not 'an infallible guide'.[113] He too, however, supposes that falsifications have been perpetrated by Jews, that to natural sources of error 'the Jewish Copyists have added others, by some absurd practices, which they have adopted, in transcribing'.[114]

Independent of the polemical admixture, there are questions which arise with Geddes's appraisal of the significance of the great eighteenth-century collations of the Hebrew consonantal text. The matter which neither Kennicott nor Geddes considers with sufficient clarity is to what extent a consonantal Hebrew text can be regarded as a sufficient written representation. If the correctness of the Massoretic vocalization is not to be assumed, another vocalization has to be supplied to make the written representation complete and to furnish a base for the further interpretation of the text. Simon had been aware of this and it had influenced his approach to the textual criticism of the Hebrew Bible in important respects, particularly in relation to the Septuagint. Material differences between the consonantal text of the Hebrew Bible and the reconstructed Hebrew *Vorlage* of the Septuagint entered into this consideration, but more interesting was Simon's perception that there are many instances where the Septuagint rendering indicates the same consonantal text as the Hebrew Bible, differently vocalized.

This aspect of the matter is neglected, wherever it is supposed that the text-critical problems of the Hebrew Bible can be solved by the collation of the consonantal text of a large number of mediaeval Hebrew manuscripts. Lowth has some inkling of this situation which Simon expresses so clearly, namely, that an 'interpretation', consisting of the vocalization of the consonantal Hebrew text, has to be interposed between the stage of textual criticism and that of translation. Lowth states this awkwardly when he says that the vocalization supplied by the Massoretes should be regarded 'as their Translation of the Old Testament'.[115]

Geddes has an answer to these criticisms, but his answer is wrong. He makes a point which is also found in Simon, but which he draws out much more. The advent of external Massoretic vocalization is said to have made vowel letters redundant and to have given frequent occasion to throw them out as useless, 'and that very thing, which was absurdly looked upon as the chief preservative of the sacred text from future errors, largely contributed to make it still more erroneous'.[116] Hence he supposes that a collation of the consonantal text of Hebrew manuscripts will show that *scriptio defectiva* (the absence of the vowel letters *waw*, *yodh* and *he*, representing long vowels) has resulted from scribal omissions consequent on the introduction of external vowel points, and that the way forward is the recovery of *scriptio plena* in a better consonantal Hebrew text. Thus he criticizes the Massoretes:

Even their greatest pretended utility, that of supplying a number of servile letters which are wanting in our printed Hebrew Bibles,[117] is in a great measure superseded by the collation of manuscripts; in which we luckily find those very letters, which the punctuists would have us ridiculously believe, were originally wanting in the autographs; although the want of them leaves such grammatical irregularities in the text, as no written language every acknowledged.[118]

Thus the description 'consonantal text' is not one which Geddes is willing to accept and he is arguing that the vocalization effected by vowel letters is entirely adequate. Presumably, he is not going so far as to assert that every vowel was represented by a vowel letter, but what is, at any rate, clear is that he regards the original written representation of Hebrew in the Hebrew Bible as not essentially different from the written representation of Latin and Greek.[119] When he makes this comparison, he is not comparing like with like: he is comparing a partially vocalized Hebrew text, which requires a supplementary vocalization to make it a complete written representation, with a fully vocalized representation (Latin and Greek). However, the most important thing to be said is that the orthographical evidence which we have contradicts Geddes's view that *scriptio plena* represents an earlier stage of the spelling of Hebrew than *scriptio defectiva*, and lends no support to the contention that *scriptio defectiva* is the product of the omission of vowel letters consequent on the furnishing of an external vocalization. For example, internal 'pure long' vowels are not represented by vowel letters in the late eighth-century B.C. Siloam inscription,[120] unless the 'pure long' vowel derives from a diphthong.[121]

Problems of translation

As he passes from textual criticism to the lexicography of the Hebrew Bible Geddes notices that the ascertaining of the true meaning is often as hard as the ascertaining of the true reading, and he continues,

If there are terms and phrases in Shakespeare, who wrote in our own language and touched almost on our own days, already become unintelligible to our best glossarists; how difficult must it be to decypher the words of a language, that has ceased to be a living one for two thousand years; is all contained in one not bulky volume; and of which several words and modes of expression occur but seldom, or only once?[122]

He thus directs attention to the lexicographical problems created by the antiquity of biblical Hebrew, by the smallness of the *corpus* and by the proportion of rare words and *hapax legomena* which are encountered.[123] He enlarges on the aspect of obscurity by recalling the obstacles to intelligibility created by the distance and strangeness of the larger context to which the literary deposit belongs. There are types of literature which present special difficulties, 'proverbial sayings, poetical licences, uncommonly bold metaphors, and obscure allegories'.[124] There is a need for a wide range of ancillary, extra-linguistic learning to complete the process of understanding the literature of an ancient society in which there are 'references to monuments that no more exist' and 'frequent allusions to facts that are not recorded or but barely hinted'.[125] 'The very great differences of laws, manners and local usages; which are well-known to have great influence on the language of a nation' are all impediments which have to be overcome, 'so that the route of the Bible-translator is neither smooth nor even; and ... it behoves him to walk in it with the utmost wariness'.[126]

Reflections on the smallness of the corpus of biblical Hebrew ('The whole text together makes but an ordinary volume'),[127] and on the other obstacles to lexicographical elucidation which it presents, lead to a recognition of the need to have recourse to a comparative Semitic philology, and also to a warning against too heavy a reliance on an etymological method: 'The best lexicons are yet very imperfect: the signification of many words is extremely dubious and their etymology very often equivocal. Hence he, who aspires at but a competent knowledge of it [Biblical Hebrew], must frequently have recourse to the other Oriental dialects.'[128] Comparative Semitic philology has recently been a preoccupation of lexicographers of biblical Hebrew and Geddes's words have a modern ring, but it is not clear that he is seizing on the fallacy of 'etymologizing' as it has been perceived in recent times.[129] He is perhaps saying that the resources of comparative Semitic philology may facilitate an etymological decision in an area of uncertainty and that such a resolution would enable a lexicographical advance to be made in biblical Hebrew. If this is so, he is not representing the modern insight that use may set etymology at a distance, that a lexicon of biblical Hebrew can do more than classify occurrences and lay down guide-lines, and that subtler differentiations and nuances can only be tested by a scrutiny of particular contexts.

It is the precise way in which a word is poised in a particular sense-unit which determines the 'meaning' it has and the *mot juste* to render it.

Geddes is not manifestly pushing in this direction, and some of the remarks which he makes in praise of 'uniformity' in a translation might be thought to give a reverse indication.[130] It may be agreed that he has a point in complaining about the lack of uniformity in English translations of the Hebrew Bible, in so far as he is attacking different renderings of the same Hebrew word which arise solely from a failure in overall superintendence and produce an unnecessary unevenness. This is a tiresome task of revision, but Geddes is no doubt right to say that it should not be neglected, as he alleges it was in the case of the King James Version. It arose, according to Geddes, from the 'committee' character of this translation and was not overcome by the six persons 'assembled for this purpose'. 'When we consider, that they were only nine months about this revision, we cannot well look for a rigorous examination of the fidelity of the version; much less, for a reduction of its stile to the same colour and complexion'.[131]

In so far as 'uniformity' simply demands that a Hebrew word should be translated by the same English word throughout if there is no reason for deviation, its achievement requires good organization and a meticulous thoroughness, but otherwise it is not a complex or subtle matter. When, however, the examples of lack of uniformity in Geddes' letter to Lowth are examined, it becomes evident that it is not this simple species of uniformity on which his points turn, and that, on occasions, he is pressing for a uniformity which reveals his lack of sensitivity to the constraints which context places on a translator. The discussion is interwoven with what, in principle, is a separate matter, the extent to which Hebraisms, which arise from turning a string of Hebrew words into an equivalent string of English words, are tolerable in an English translation. Geddes argues that 'lifting up the feet' (Gen. xxix 1) is not a harsher Hebraism than 'lifting up the eyes', and that if 'lifting up the eyes' is an acceptable rendering, so is 'lifting up the feet'. The acceptance of the one and avoidance of the other is an unwarrantable lack of uniformity. He contrasts 'Then Jacob went on his journey' (KJV) with the earlier English versions, 'Jacob lifted up his feet and went', and he holds that if 'lifted up his feet' had been retained, the long use and familiarity which made 'lifting up the eyes' acceptable English would have operated similarly for 'lifting up the feet': 'I am aware it will be said, that the first seems more uncouth to our ears than the last; but I am persuaded it was not more uncouth, when the last was first adopted; and that if they had also adopted the first, it would now be as familiar to us as the other.'[132]

Whatever we may think of the historical argument, the matter is essentially one of aesthetic judgement. If the translators were wrong, they were not wrong because they neglected to observe an 'identity of phrasing'[133] or because they followed the Vulgate, but because they judged that 'lifting up the eyes' for 'looking up' was tolerable English, while 'lifting up the feet' for 'departing' was intolerable. It is their literary taste which has to be challenged, but we would be inclined to confirm it from our stance in a later age.

Gen. xlvii 8, KJV 'How old *art* thou?' Gen. xlvii 9, KJV 'The days of the years of my pilgrimage *are* an hundred and thirty years': Geddes[134] complains of an unnecessary change at Gen. xlvii 9 from the renderings at Gen. xlvii 8 and 28. He fails to appreciate that it is the context which makes the change necessary. The Hebraism 'How many are the years of your life?' (xlvii 8) can easily be transformed into the English idiom 'How old are you?', but the substitution of מגורי 'my pilgrimage' for חייך 'your life' at xlvii 9 places a new demand on the translator. Although the following word-strings are almost identical with the one which occurs at xlvii 8, they are not susceptible of the same treatment. The King James Version takes refuge in a literal translation, but that there is a problem for the translator, however it is solved, can be seen from the New English Bible's rendering of xlvii 8 f.: 'Pharaoh asked Jacob his age, and he answered, "The years of my earthly sojourn are one hundred and thirty; hard years they have been and few, not equal to the years that my fathers lived in their time".' 'Age' will not do as a rendering of 'the days of the years of my life' or 'the days of the years of the life of my fathers' at xlvii 9, and Geddes misses these subtler contextual considerations when he presses his demand for uniformity.

A translator discovers that it is not so simple a matter to translate consistently a Hebrew word with the same English word as might on the surface appear. Sympathy for the context produces different English renderings for the same Hebrew word. Among the Hebrew words which Geddes supposes are allowed too great a variety of translations in English he includes כלי,[135] but the complicated entry for כלי in a lexicon of biblical Hebrew[136] will give some indication of the semantic spread of this word, and it should not be regarded as strange that a range of different renderings emerge to catch its various senses and nuances (clay-pot, bag, utensil, item of furniture, equipment, weapon and so on). Geddes's precise complaint would seem to be that different English words 'though nearly of the same import' are used in translation, and the implication is that one English word would have sufficed in all these cases. It may be suspected that here again he is insensitive to the small variations in renderings demanded by different contexts. At any rate, כלי is not an appropriate word with which to pursue his thesis.

As Simon had done, Geddes conducts a critical review of newer translations of the Hebrew Bible, beginning with Latin translations, proceeding to vernacular translations, and concentrating on the English versions, especially the King James Version. His general criticism of most of these productions is that they suffer from a wrong point of departure, a Massoretic bias, and he regards this as the 'chief and peculiar imperfection' of Protestant versions, which 'followed too implicitly the Masoretic text, and paid too little regard to the ancient versions'.[137] Of those who translated into Latin he praises especially Castalio[138] (Basle, 1551) who shook off the Massoretic bondage and 'had the courage to strike out a path for himself'.[139] He did not 'Judaically despise' the ancient versions, and his more balanced textual criticism was matched by the aesthetic virtues of his translation, even if he was too lavish with 'his oratorial graces and classical refinements' and obscured the idiomatic simplicities of the original.[140] Despite the defects, textual and aesthetic, on which Geddes seizes, he concludes that 'a more compleat, more impartial or more faithful version will not easily be found'.[141]

Geddes's criticism of Luther's translation of the Hebrew Bible into German (1535)[142] is much more generous than that of Simon. He praises its high literary quality: 'If it be considered in what turbulent times, and amid what variety of other avocations it was made, we are at a loss to comprehend how one man who had no model to follow ... could, in so short a space and with such scanty helps, accomplish so great a work.'[143] Geddes admires the elegant German which Luther has achieved and dismisses the 'idle sneer' of Simon 'that Luther seemed to have only in view to make the Holy Ghost speak good German'.[144] This, in fact, is 'a great panegyric' and the aim of Luther ought to be that of every other translator.[145] But the new chapter which was opened by Houbigant[146] has made Luther's translation archaic, though 'it retains, in a great measure, its first celebrity; and has not only triumphed over all former attempts to supersede it, but is, at this day, preferred by many Germans to their latest versions'.[147] Geddes, for his part, looks to the German version of J. D. Michaelis (Old Testament, 1769), who follows the critical path of Houbigant, and whose German translation of the Old Testament 'must appear to those, who can relish all its beauties, one of the best that ever was made'.[148]

The claim to impartiality and candour on which Geddes sets great store is well borne out by the tenor of his criticisms. He urges that a biblical critic, and especially a translator, should be entirely free of dogmatic bias or critical anxiety, and there is impressive evidence that he has achieved this state of mind as a translator. He has a list of the qualities which are needed in a translator, first, a mastery of Hebrew and of the language into which Hebrew is being translated. He derides the scholastic maxim *Quanto eris melior grammaticus, tanto pejor dialecticus et theologus*, for which he substitutes, *Quanto melior theologus, tanto pejor interpres*. Next, there is the need for aesthetic discrimination and versatility, which will enable the translator to reflect in his translation the different styles and idiomatic characteristics of different kinds of Old Testament literature.[149] 'He must prosecute his always serious, often unengaging studies, with all the warm enthusiasm of a poet or painter; and yet with all the patient drudgery of a laborious mechanic ... If writing the dictionary of a single language be, as Scaliger thought, an adequate punishment for parricide; what crime may not be atoned for by translating the Hebrew scriptures?'[150] The reference to the 'laborious mechanic' is a reminder that Geddes did not content himself with theorizing about the translation of the Hebrew Bible from a distance, but that he had first-hand experience of the problems which arise on the work-bench. The thought he had given to vexatious, practical details, to the craft of the translator as opposed to the theory, is evident in the snags which he discusses in his *Letter*, and the devices for solving or ameliorating them which he proposes.[151]

The crowning virtue of a translator is 'an honest impartiality':

Unwedded to systems of any kind, literary, physical or religious; a translator of the Bible should sit down to render his author, with the same indifference he would sit down to render Thucydides or Xenophon. He should try to forget that he belongs to any particular society of Christians; be extremely jealous of his most rational prepossessions; keep all theological consequences as far out of his sight as possible; and investigate the meaning of his original, by the rules only of a sound and sober criticism, regardless of pleasing or displeasing any party.[152]

He modestly awards the palm to others for 'learning, genius and judgment', but for 'candor, impartiality and uprightness of intention'[153] he will yield to none. His work on the English versions bears him out. On Matthew's Bible (1537) he dismisses allegations of a fundamental religious bias or of 'capital defects' in the version itself. Sectarian proclivities are to be gathered from the introductory material and the notes, but he does not find that a theological partisanship has seriously injured the linguistic honesty of the translation:

It was far from being a perfect translation, it is true, but it was the first of the kind; and few first translations will, I think, be found preferable to it. It is astonishing how little obsolete the language of it is, even at this day; and in point of perspicuity and noble simplicity, propriety of idiom and purity of stile, no English version has yet surpassed it.

Its critics (including Sir Thomas More) 'are generally too severe, often captious and sometimes evidently unjust'.[154]

Geddes discerns in Tyndale, where English synonyms are available to the translator, a tendency to choose the word which best accords with his own 'religious notions' and, where there is ambivalence in the Hebrew, to prefer 'that which seemed the least favourable to the tenets which he had renounced'. He adds in mitigation, 'This was, doubtless, a partiality which every translator ought carefully to avoid; but how few translators have always been sufficiently on their guard against its influence.'[155] He views more severely as 'an idle affectation in Tyndal' the use of *overseer*, *elder* and *congregation* for *bishop*, *priest* and *church*, since *bishop*, *priest* and *church* 'are, in reality, of the same import with those he substituted in their place; and there is no more diversity between the terms (to use an expression of Coverdale) than between *four-pence and a groat*'.[156] Other substitutions made by Tyndale, *image* for *idol*,[157] *ordinance* for *tradition*, *secret* for *mystery* or *sacrament* are described as 'unfair and, perhaps, insidious'.[158]

The translation which 'became the favourite version of the puritan party'[159] (The Geneva Bible), and which went through many editions in the reigns of Elizabeth and James, was pronounced by James, in the conference at Hampton Court, to be 'the worst of all English translations'. 'Yet', continues Geddes, 'his own translators borrowed more plentifully from it, than from any other; and, to say the truth, as a mere Masoretic version, it has considerable merit.'[160] Geddes approves of the Bishops' Bible (1568) in so far as it provides evidence of a loosening of the Massoretic yoke and a regard for the witness of the Septuagint and the Vulgate.[161]

In his *Letter* Geddes puts the following question to Lowth: 'How far ought the stile and phraseology of our last English version to be adopted or rejected, in a new translation?'[162] Although Geddes is a Catholic, he assumes without question that the King James Version is the 'English version' and that this is the translation which has to be revised. He finds no redeeming features in the Rheims New Testament (1582) or The Douai Old Testament (1609):

It is a literal and barbarous translation from the Vulgate, before its last revision;[163] and accompanied with acrimonious and injurious annotations. Their residence in a foreign country, and what they deemed a cruel exile from their own, had corrupted the translators' language, and soured their tempers; and it was, unhappily, the common custom of those lamentable times, to season every religious controversy with gall and vinegar. We do not find that Withers, Fulke and Cartwright, who drew their quills against the Douay annotators, were a bit more courteous in their retorts.[164]

Although Geddes addresses Lowth in tones of great deference, he does not, in fact, meekly surrender his own judgement, and their respective views on the King James Version do not coincide. Lowth says, 'For as to the style and language it admits but of little improvement; but, in respect of the sense and the accuracy of interpretation, the improvements of which it is capable are great and numberless.'[165] If we measure Geddes's attitude against this opinion, there is agreement, founded on common considerations (a better Hebrew text and improved lexicography), that an improvement in accuracy and faithfulness can be achieved by a new translation.[166] When Geddes is listing the virtues of a good translator, he begins on this note: a faithful translation must express 'all the meaning and no more than the meaning of the original'.[167] Two extremes are to be avoided, an excessively literal rendering and a paraphrase. Jerome, in so far as he translated larger sense units than words, is a model to be imitated. His method of translation is 'sentential', that is, his aim is to make every sentence of his translation correspond as exactly with the Hebrew as the difference of the idioms of Hebrew and Latin will permit.[168]

When it comes to a discussion of the literary qualities of the King James Version, Geddes is less enamoured of it than Lowth. In his remarks on the Geneva Bible he had already asserted that the finery of the version consisted of borrowed clothes, and when he discerns an idolatrous attachment to it, he makes this point with greater force:

The great merit of James's translators did not certainly consist in beautifying or meliorating the style of former versions, but in correcting their errors, and making a version more strictly conformable to the letter, not always the spirit, of their supposed indefectible originals. Their fidelity and accuracy deserve great commendation;

and that is almost all they have a just claim to. The style they found in their prototype; and the diction and phraseology they borrowed from their predecessors in translation; and it was well that they had such models; for their own preface evinces that their taste was none of the best. We have indeed some difficulty to believe that it could be written by the same persons.[169]

Moreover, it is clear that Geddes finds the version excessively literal and unidiomatic, and he cites an opinion of John Seldon[170] that the Hebrew is 'rather translated into English words than into English phrase'. In this respect it does not conform with his model of a 'sentential' translation, and as a consequence is 'in many places obscure and ambiguous, where a small variation in the arrangement of the words, would have made it clear and unequivocal'.[171]

There are two matters to be taken up, the first concerning 'literal translation' and the second, not unconnected with the first, the importance of word-order in a translation of the Hebrew Bible into English. Geddes rejects the concept of literal translation in principle, because it is a word for word translation rather than a 'sentential' one and amounts to under-translation or non-translation. Moreover, it is ugly, and may be obscure or ambiguous: 'It is ... absolutely impossible to translate literally from any language whatever, without being often barbarous, obscure and equivocal; and this alone is a sufficient reason for translating freely.'[172] Adequate translation requires a much greater degree of transformation than is allowed by the notion of literal translation, not the least of whose fallacies is the assumption that a one to one correspondence, which imposes on English the same word-order as is proper in Hebrew, will produce a translation. In respect of word-order the demands of English idiom are different from those of Hebrew idiom, and an important aspect of the discrimination needed by a translator is the manner in which he devises the transformations which catch the Hebrew idiom in an English word-order.

More general aesthetic considerations also focus on the achievement of an effective word-order in an English translation from the Hebrew Bible. Geddes has the perception that small variations can make a great deal of difference to the strength of word-strings, and that a translator needs an ear that can distinguish between true cadences and false ones, between phrases which wax strongly to a climax and an order of words which peters out in a miserable ending: 'It is certain that nothing contributes more to elegance than the apposite arrangement of words.'[173] Thus Anthony Purver's[174] rendering of Gen. i 1, 'God created the heaven and the earth in the beginning' is distinctly inferior to 'In the beginning God created the heaven and the earth' – which happens to be closer to the Hebrew word-order.

In his *Letter* Geddes asks: 'What are the tolerable limits of the manipulations of Hebrew word-order in an English translation, and where should the line of demarcation between an idiomatic rendering and a paraphrase be located?' Geddes perceives that a translator 'will see strong reasons for changing the order even in poetry, and still more frequently in prose. This will happen either in the arrangement of the several words of a single sentence, or of the several members of a compound sentence, or of several different sentences together.'[175] When he reaches the third of these categories, he has passed from translational problems of word-order to the entirely different matter of conjecturally rearranging pieces of Hebrew text prior to translation. In a word, he has passed from translation to textual criticism. He is not unaware of this, but it is an uncharacteristic confounding of separate questions. On the rearranging of pieces of Hebrew text he says that it is a contentious issue: 'Is it lawful', he asks Lowth, 'to transpose whole complete sentences, when their natural order seems to be inverted, and when there is reason to suspect that they have been shifted from their first place in the original?'[176] Geddes indicates that he would not embark on this kind of emendation, unless it was supported by textual evidence:

If there were found a diversity of order in the Hebrew manuscripts, or in the ancient versions, I should think myself at liberty to follow that order which should appear to me the most consistent with the context; but if all the manuscripts and versions agreed, I should be apt to look upon it as an original synchysis; and content myself with pointing out, in a note, a seemingly more natural order.[177]

Geddes notices that the use of italics in the King James Version is bound up with the fallacious idea of literal translation which he has criticized, namely, that there should be a one – one correspondence between the Hebrew words of the original and the English words of the translation. If more English words than there are Hebrew words have to be employed in order to effect the translation, this surplus is italicized. In encumbering their version 'with a load of useless Italics'[178] the translators disclose a double defect in their method of translation: they accept the erroneous assumption that every Hebrew word should be represented by an English word instead of translating 'sententially', and then they save the sense by means of patches which they italicize. The result is doubly unsatisfactory, and they are misled by a mistaken view of what constitutes a faithful translation. Either the words in italics are indispensable to the translation or they are not: if the first, they should not be italicized; if the second, 'they are generally ill assorted and clumsy ekes, that may well be spared; and which often disfigure the narration under pretence of connecting it'.[179]

Geddes takes up the subject of italics in his *Letter*, where he holds that 'ellipses' in Hebrew may be 'with propriety supplied, if the supplements be virtually contained in the elliptical phrase'.[180] This is a use of italics separable from the one discussed above and it arises from the circumstance that Hebrew forms of expression may be more economical or laconic than would be tolerable in English, and, consequently, have to be filled out. Newcome[181] had urged that such 'supplemental words' should be italicized, but Geddes praises Lowth who had not employed italics in his *Isaiah*. Arius Montanus had started the practice and he became 'a model to posterior translators; and continued to be so, until your Lordship broke the enchantment'.[182]

Geddes is occupied with the problem of balancing the need for perspicuity in a translation with the special quality of language which is required to convey the sense of religious literature. He sets his face against the cultivation of obscurity or 'mystery', but, on the other hand, he does not suppose that a Bible translator should run with linguistic fashions and he knows that 'plainness' is not enough: there is a kind of plain language which is too ordinary or trite and is not sufficiently tense or elevated to secure the effects at which he is aiming. First, on perspicuity, he says:

A translator ... who, under the pretext that his originals are obscure, affects to give an obscure translation, betrays either his idleness or his ignorance; offers an insult to his reader; and throws an oblique ridicule on the author he pretends to interpret ... That there are certain mysterious words of the originals, which should not be rendered, may be a pious, but it is not a rational notion. The Greek and Hebrew are not, of their own nature, more sacred languages than the Welch or Wallachian: and surely, to a mere English reader, *pass-over* and *praise ye the Lord*, are not less significant and far more edifying sounds than *pasch*, and *hallelujah*.[183]

The right proportions of elevation and elegance in Bible translation will be achieved only if aberrations of different kinds are avoided, among which Geddes mentions obsolete words, trite language and a too ornate style: 'It may ... happen that a word shall properly enough express the meaning of the original, and yet be inelegant and inadmissible, either, because it is altogether obsolete, or is of low and trite usage, or has some ludicrous idea annexed to it, or, in fine, savours of affectation and pedantry.'[184] An important constituent of elegance, already noted, is 'the apposite arrangement of words'[185] which makes all the difference between vigorous and melodious phrasing, and mediocre word-strings, but simplicity is also an essential ingredient of elegance: 'The elegance that suits it [The Bible] is simple and unaffected; not the elegance of a court-lady decked out for a ball or birth-day, but that of a rural beauty in her Sunday's apparel, modestly decorated with such flowers as grow in her native meads.'[186] Nevertheless, Geddes supposes that there are cases where Latinisms should be given preference, 'assemble' instead of 'gather together', 'convoke' instead of 'call together', and 'gratuitously' instead of 'freely'.[187]

There is a quaintness and an imbalance in Geddes's views about archaic language, in so far as he envisages possibilities of over-turning obsolescence by a process of revival. In his *Prospectus* he notices that the language of the King James Version was, in some respects, already old-fashioned at the beginning of the seventeenth century: 'They generally, indeed, preferred old English terms to recently imported ones; and, at this day, they may appear to have sometimes carried that preference beyond due bounds: but we should consider, that 174 years are passed since their translation was made; and that many words are now grown familiar to us which were not then at all in use; while many others, that were then of the best usage, have gradually gone into desuetude.'[188] Nevertheless, Geddes is conservative in matters of language, and while he recognizes that some of the language of the King James Version is, in his day, unintelligible or ambiguous or infected with a 'plebeian triteness',[189] he is cautious about disposing of linguistic capital and asks Lowth: 'But is the same liberty to be taken with other words and phrases, which, though obsolete in common use, are still intelligible to one acquainted with the Scripture stile, and have in reality nothing in them to debase its dignity?'[190]

Geddes would retain 'such old words as are still, though rarely used' and would even 'revive many that have gradually gone into disuse; if they be equally analogical, and at the same time more significant and harmonious than those that custom has introduced in their room'.[191] The revival of such obsolete words would express the meaning required 'with more discriminating accuracy'.[192] The example which he offers (הבדיל) does not enhance our confidence in his judgement: because Latin *distinguo* means 'to separate', he suggests 'and God distinguished light from darkness' as a rendering of ויבדל אלהים בין האור ובין החשך (Gen. I 4).

The most significant implication of all of this is that Geddes contemplates a 'Biblical English' which, in important respects, is a different language from the common tongue, which does not aim at modernity, and which revives old words or old meanings, provided they do not create unintelligibility or ambiguity and secure the effects of elevation and elegance. Hence Geddes's quest for perspicuity is part of a complex of considerations different from those which are associated with some modern attempts to render the Bible into 'plain English', in so far as these are designed to overcome any residue of apartness in the vocabulary and style of biblical English, and to make the English of the Bible the same as the English in common currency in our time. Geddes is aware of the danger of ordinariness and knows that there is a kind of plainness which a religious literature ought not to have, but there are elements of obscurantism in his idea of a special biblical English which would counteract the flow of the history of the English language by preserving or reviving archaic words.

Given the kind of linguistic resolution just described, with its archaic tendencies, it is odd that Geddes has a deficient grasp of the forces which make for liturgical conservatism, that he is insensitive to the degree of ecclesiastical disturbance produced by new translations of the Bible, and that he dismisses all opposition as nothing more than 'ill founded prejudices'[193] which are not widely influential and whose absurdity can be easily demonstrated by rational argument. His disquisitions on this topic are a mixture of right and wrong, but the blend raises deep questions whether he is describing common people who do not exist and whether the exclusiveness of his rational attitudes does not isolate him from the realities of institutional religion. He is right to insist that a translation of the Bible, like all other translations, is susceptible of continuous improvement as text-critical, lexicographical and philological science advances,[194] but he has no proper appreciation of the depth of attachment which worshippers have to familiar words, or the extent to which the music and sequences of these words have become essential to their participation in worship. It is doubtful whether he understands all that is at stake when he says, 'The people should be taught (for they are not indocil) that it is to the meaning, and not the words, of Scripture – to the sense, not the sound, that they ought to attend.'[195] It is not simply that he does not reckon with the power of prejudice against a new translation of the Bible, or the strength of a popular conservatism, but rather that he does not weigh the claims of linguistic science and accuracy against other factors, aesthetic and religious, which need sensitive treatment and which are also part of the truth.

Geddes assumes that any opposition to a new translation of the Bible can be dismissed as an activity of forces of superstition and darkness, and the enlightenment which he desires for the common people does not reckon with their forms of liturgical participation. He is convinced that the faithful in the Church are waiting for a lead and that all the noisy opposition comes from a rump of backwoodsmen. The people have a right to share in the new biblical learning 'and, knowing all this, they will not only be not averse to a new translation, but expect it with eagerness, and receive it with pleasure; with a pleasure proportioned to their zeal and devotion. For as to that class of devotees, if such there be, who believe that our present version was written with the finger of the Almighty; and that to alter a tittle of it, is to be guilty of blasphemy, it would be worse than weak to encourage their prejudices; it would be to abet a real blasphemy, for fear of incurring, in their extravagant ideas, the imputation of an imaginary one.'[196] Again:

The truth is, as far as I have been able to learn, that the people in general are sufficiently sensible of the expediency of a new version, or a thorough revisal of the old one. There are few, even of the lowest class, who have not heard of the imperfections of the public version; our preachers are constantly correcting particular passages in it ... In short, the prejudices of the people against an improved version either do not exist at all, or are such as may be easily removed, or deserve not to be regarded.[197]

If Geddes had reflected on the circumstance that the only part of Jerome's translation of the Hebrew Bible which did not establish itself in the Vulgate was his work on the Psalms, where the Gallican version survived, and that it was the liturgical centrality of the book of Psalms and the power of liturgical conservatism which contributed to that effect, he would not have misjudged differences between the Book of Common Prayer and the King James Version in the way he does. He turns the truth on its head by supposing that differences in the English versions of the Decalogue and the Psalms as between the Book of Common Prayer and the King James Version are evidence that new departures in the translation of the Hebrew Bible into English are easily tolerated: 'The words, and even the style of the Psalms, in the Book of Common Prayer are more different from those in the Bible [KJV] than they can well be in any improved translation; nay, the very Decalogue itself is expressed in different terms; and yet I never heard that any one was scandalized at this difference, or in either did not recognize the Bible. The Bible must be sadly travestied indeed, in a translation, before it cease to be recognizable.'[198] In fact, what the Prayer Book versions of the Decalogue and the Psalms[199] show is the strength of conservatism in areas which are liturgically crucial and a resistance to change in the verbal texture of the liturgy.

Criticism and theology

In many respects the range of Geddes's critical interests is comparable with that of Simon, but he is not satisfied with the objective of critical autonomy and he invades the sphere of Christian theology with his 'rational principles' in a manner foreign to Simon. It was Simon's view that the critical study of the Bible could be allowed complete independence without its constituting any threat to the Catholic Church in those areas of order and belief where her immunity to change was asserted. Far from having any ambitions as an ecclesiastical and theological innovator, Simon perceived that his hope of being granted the critical freedom which he sought lay in his ability to demonstrate that the results of biblical criticism did not impinge destructively on dogma.

Geddes does not have this awareness of walking a tight-rope. He was certainly, as a consequence, more bold than Simon, but this boldness is less closely reasoned than Simon's attempt to match his Catholic awareness of ecclesiastical order and dogmatic stability with his demand for freedom in biblical criticism. It is arguable that Simon's approach has more intrinsic interest than a biblical criticism which spills over into a rationalizing of biblical religion, and that there is a finer discrimination and a more subtle balance in his work than in that of Geddes.

Geddes's treatment of the Vulgate and its 'authenticity' will serve as an initial example of the similarities and differences of his thinking and that of Simon. The view which 'long prevailed' in the Catholic Church 'that the Scripture should not be translated into vulgar tongues' is dismissed by Geddes as incompatible 'with any principle of reason, religion, or sound policy', to be ascribed 'to the ignorance and prejudices of a barbarous age', and associated with a kind of intellectual illiberality which was characteristic of the Inquisition.[200] On the 'prejudice' that Catholics must translate from the Vulgate he says that there was a time when this limitation made sense, because 'there were few or none capable of translating from the originals',[201] but that it has been overtaken by a revival of Greek and Hebrew scholarship: 'But if this motive had unluckily influenced St Jerom, we should this day have no Vulgate: for, from the same principle, he would have been obliged to translate [the Old Testament] from the Greek; which had been much more generally received, as a public standard, than ever the Latin [Jerome's Vulgate] was.'[202]

In asserting the critical unsoundness of translating into vernacular languages from the Vulgate, Geddes is influenced by Lowth who remarked of Catholic translators, 'In general the Vulgate is their Original Text; and they give us a Translation of a Translation; by which second transfusion of the Holy Scriptures into another tongue, still more of the original sense must be lost, and more of the genuine spirit must evaporate.'[203] With this should be compared, 'In the very first transfusion, from one idiom to another, some part of the author must necessarily evaporate: how much more must he lose, on a second or third operation?'[204] The Vulgate itself (as Geddes says) cannot be properly appreciated, unless it is compared with the Hebrew and the Greek from which it was translated: 'The words of the Vulgate are Latin words, it is true; but they have sometimes so uncommon acceptations, and are so peculiarly phrased, that it requires a thorough acquaintance with the Oriental stile and knowledge of the Oriental tongues to comprehend their meaning; particularly in the poetical books.'[205] Hence 'it would be ... easy to shew that the greatest part of those, who have translated from the Vulgate, have very often mistranslated it, from not understanding or not attending to the originals'.[206] The conclusion is that 'a translator, who works on the originals, can derive but little help from versions made from the Vulgate'.[207]

When Geddes states that the decree of the Council of Trent 'did nothing more than what has been done in Protestant countries',[208] he takes no account of the different doctrine of the Church in which the Bible is located in these two contexts. An 'authorized version' in a Protestant setting, where the avowed intention is to make the Church entirely answerable to the Bible, is a different matter from the authenticity of the Vulgate in a context where new translations of the Bible might disturb ecclesiastical formulations perceived as unchanging truth. What is being expressed here is not necessarily disagreement with Geddes's critical opinions, but a sense that he fails as a Catholic to appreciate the delicacy of his own critical stance. It is not simply his views on the authenticity of the Vulgate in the setting of the Council of Trent which are in play, since his reference to Jerome as a translator[209] shows that he has a defective understanding of the shock-waves which were sent through institutional Catholicism by Jerome's new translation. He deals with this as if it were only a matter of Jerome translating the Hebrew Bible into Latin and overlooks the circumstance that the Western Church accepted his new translation and departed from the Old Latin. Thus as a Catholic Geddes has insufficient sympathy with Simon's insight that the Old Latin, derived from the Septuagint, was also authentic scripture, and that the break in the continuity of the Catholic Church caused by the adoption of Jerome's translation was more violent than it ought to have been. Geddes has even less appreciation of Simon's further thought that the Catholic Church could not have endured a second shock of similar dimensions in the sixteenth century, that, at so late an hour, no new translation could have displaced the Vulgate, as the Vulgate had earlier displaced the Old Latin.[210] Geddes, because his Catholic awareness had faded, did not understand, as Simon did, that, as a biblical critic, he was on a knife-edge.

For much of the way, however, Simon and Geddes are journeying along the same road and are describing their objectives in similar language. This is the case with respect to translation, but the agreement extends to a common view of what is involved in the critical exegesis of the Hebrew Bible which they distinguish from the *genre* of the pre-critical commentary on which both place a low value. Geddes encourages the apprentice biblical scholar with the assurance that the task which confronts him is not so Herculean as might appear: 'But let him not despair; I will venture to assure him that the quintessence of all he seeks for is to be found judiciously collected in Poole's *Synopsis*.[211] Had I always been convinced of this truth, I should have spared myself much fruitless labour, and saved a great deal of lost time.'[212]

The bad old days of biblical scholarship were dominated by polemics, between Catholics and Protestants, but also between Catholic and Catholic, and Protestant and Protestant: 'Instead of endeavouring to free the text from the adventitious rubbish, that time and blundering transcribers had heaped upon it; they applied their whole art and industry, to convert the rubbish into genuine ore; or, at least, into such mixt metal, as was current in their own communion.'[213] But Geddes has hopes that 'the age of polemical scurrility' has passed away: 'Writers of every persuasion will henceforth, we trust, reciprocally assist one another, towards discovering the genuine signification of such texts or terms as admit of ambiguity; without insidiousness or rancour.'[214]

Geddes agrees with Simon's view that the critical exegesis of the Hebrew Bible should not transgress the boundaries of plain-sense interpretation, and he grumbles at the quality of 'the huge masses of indigested matter, that issue yearly from the presses of Fleet-Street and Pater-Noster-Row'. These 'are generally better calculated to throw ridicule on the sacred text, than to explain it ... Expunge from those motly performances the unmeaning mystic jargon, the nauseous cant of enthusiasm, and the trite and tedious maxims of a common-place morality; all that is left behind of any value may be comprest into a nut-shell.'[215] In a similar vein of criticism Geddes presents the case for rational coolness and for the 'literal sense' even more explicitly:

Let profound mystics and subtle casuists be, if they will, employed in discovering *allegorical, anagogical* and *moral* meanings; let professed polemics torment the text, to make it agree with their favourite hypothesis; it is the business of the mere interpreter, much more of the translator, to give the obvious literal sense of his author; with a view to no particular system, and without regard to parties or principles.[216]

In his preface to *Psalms* he repeats his commitment to the plain sense: 'I have, throughout, strictly confined myself to the direct and literal meaning of my authors. Indirect and secondary applications, whether typical or allegorical, I leave to professed commentators. I will only say, that it is my firm belief, that every Psalm has a primary literal meaning, independent of allegorical interpretation.'[217]

When specimens of his exegetical work, whether from his *Critical Remarks* or from his *Psalms*, are examined, it is evident that he has little time for Christological interpretation of Old Testament texts, even though he is aware that such a tradition of interpretation had been attached to them within the Church.

Gen. i 2, RSV 'and the Spirit of God was moving over the face of the waters' (NEB, 'a mighty wind'): Simon argues that in the phrase רוח אלהים a superlative function is discharged by אלהים, and that אל has the same grammatical function in הררי אל 'great mountains' (Ps. xxxvi 7) and ארזי אל 'great cedars' (Ps. lxxx 11). רוח אלהים is to be translated 'mighty wind' (agreeing with NEB) not 'Spirit of God'. He continues: 'Those who have found in the רוח אלהים of Genesis the *person* of the Holy Ghost, have been very little versed in the language of the East; and paid very little attention to the construction of the Text.'[218] But one may opt for 'the spirit of God' rather than 'a mighty wind' without having any intention of identifying that spirit with the Holy Ghost of Christian theology, and Geddes's assertion that 'the spirit of God' does violence to the construction of the text is not obviously true. The assertion assumes that verse 2 throughout is describing the bleak waste of chaos, but if the second part of verse 2 is a bridge between chaos and creation, an intimation that a creative force is stirring, 'the spirit of God was brooding on the face of the waters' is an acceptable translation. Geddes knows that the lexicographical obscurity of מרחפת hinders the elucidation of the verse, and that רחף appears only here and at Deut. xxxii 11 and Jer. xxiii 9. At Deut. xxxii 11 Geddes attaches the sense 'hovereth' to מרחפת.

On Gen. i 26 Geddes remarks, 'The Christian fathers considered these words as addressed to Jesus Christ, in his pre-existing state. Some of the antient Jews thought that he [God] spoke to his surrounding angels.'[219] In his *Critical Remarks* Geddes notices the view of John Chrysostom[220] that it is Christ who is addressed by God when he says, 'Let us make man in our own image' and comments, 'It would be hard, I think, for either Jew or Arian to support their respective opinions with more ingenuity or eloquence; whatever may be the solidity of the good Father's argument.'[221] 'As a critic' Geddes observes that נעשה is not necessarily an indication of plurality, points to Cant. i 11 and viii 8, where נעשה refers to Solomon only, notices that God refers to himself in the plural in the Qur'an, although 'the Musulmans are certainly no Trinitarians', and alludes finally to the use of 'We' among the western nations 'in the mouths of the great men of the earth'.[222]

Gen. xlix 10, NEB 'until he comes to Shiloh (footnote) and the obedience of the nations is his': Geddes translates, 'till there come peaceful prosperity, and to him the nations be obedient',[223] and remarks that 'the generality of interpreters apply all this to Jesus Christ'. When he refers to his translation in his *Critical Remarks*, he asks, 'But what, then, becomes of the Messiah?', and replies, 'Become of him what will, I confess I cannot here find a vestige of him: nor did the Messiah himself, nor any of his apostles or evangelists apply this text to him; which is wonderful indeed, if they looked upon it as applicable.'[224] Geddes vocalizes שילה as 'Shiloh' and connects it with 'the peaceful enjoyment of the land of Chanaan mentioned (Jos. xi 23; xviii 1), when the land rested from war, and the tabernacle was set up at Shiloh (so denominated, probably, from that very circumstance); or to the still more peaceful reign of Solomon, when the government was fully established in the tribe of Judah, and the promises made to Abraham, Isaac and Jacob, with respect to territory, accomplished'.[225] It is only the second of these suggestions which completely matches his translation, by establishing an identification of 'him' with Solomon.

The absence of any interest in the Messianic interpretation of Old Testament texts, with a view to applying them to Jesus Christ, is just as striking in Geddes's treatment of the Psalms: Ps. ii 7, NEB 'You are my son', he said, 'this day I become your father': Geddes makes nothing of these mysterious words which Christian interpreters had supposed were spoken by God concerning Jesus Christ ('You are my son, this day I have begotten you'). Even without a Christian interpretation, the verse points to a relationship of peculiar intimacy between Yahweh and the Davidic king, but Geddes's translation ('To-day I have adopted thee') is reductionist (Hebrew, ילדתיך), and in his note on *adopted* he says, 'lit. childed: *begotten* is here an improper term'.[226] He does not explain why he thinks *begotten* is inappropriate for ילד, or in what respects *childed* has a different meaning from *begotten*, and he makes no comment on 'Thou art my son'.

In his preface to Ps. cx Geddes remarks, 'As to its general purport and particular applications, I leave all that to commentators: my aim shall be to give as fair and literal a version of my original as I can.'[227] The words of verse 1 (NEB, 'The LORD said to my lord, "You shall sit at my right hand, when I make your enemies the footstool under your feet"') lend themselves to a Christological interpretation, as being a conversation between the Father and the Son. Geddes comments on, 'To my lord Jehovah hath said': 'My lord whom? David evidently in the literal sense: whatever it be in the mystical. – The courtly bard, in consequence of the people's general wish, attempts to persuade the king not to expose his own person to the dangers of war; and introduces God himself as giving him that counsel: Be thou content to rule at home: I, Jehovah, will fight for thee: and thy people will spontaneously offer themselves for thy defence.'[228]

Geddes advertises that the question of the authorship of the Pentateuch 'will necessarily occupy a considerable place' in his projected general preface, and so he contents himself with giving 'in very few words' the results of his investigations.[229] He begins with the premiss that 'external testimony' is of little avail and that proofs must be derived from 'intrinsic evidence' only. He sets out three conclusions: the first is that the Pentateuch in its present form was not written by Moses, the second that it was composed in Canaan, and probably at Jerusalem, and the third that it is not earlier than the age of David and not later than the age of Hezekiah. He inclines towards the reign of Solomon, 'The long pacific age of Solomon (the Augustan age of Judaea) is the period to which I would refer it; yet, I confess, there are some marks of a posterior date, or at least of posterior interpolation.'[230]

The Pentateuch was 'compiled from ancient documents, some of which were coeval with Moses, and some even anterior to Moses'. Oral traditions are also to be reckoned with, since it is Geddes's view that the Hebrews did not have historiography until the time of Moses, 'and that all their history prior to that period, is derived from monumental indexes, or traditional tales'.[231] Moses had been taught all the wisdom of the Egyptians (Acts vii 22) and was, most probably, the first Hebrew writer, or, at least, the first to apply writing to a historical composition. From the journals of Moses 'a great part of the Pentateuch seems to have been compiled'. Whether or not he was the original author of the primaeval history (Gen. i – xi) and the patriarchal narratives is left open by Geddes, but he suggests that Moses 'may have drawn the whole or a part of his cosmogony and general history, both before and after the deluge, from the archives of Egypt'. 'Those original materials, collected first by Moses, may have been worked up into their present form by the compiler of the Pentateuch in the reign of Solomon. But it is also possible, and I think more probable, that the latter was the first collector; and collected from such documents as he could find, either among his own people or among the neighbouring nations.'[232] Geddes is referring here to the sources for the primaeval history and for the period prior to the age of Moses, and is expressing his preference for the view that these sources were first collected by the postulated Solomonic editor of the Pentateuch rather than by Moses.

Geddes knows of two books[233] in which a source-critical hypothesis had been formulated for the book of Genesis. This view 'that Moses composed the book of Genesis from two different written documents' does not find favour with him: 'Although I really look upon this as the work of *fancy*, and will elsewhere endeavour to prove it to be so; I am not so self-sufficient as to imagine, that I may not be in the wrong, or that they may not be in the right.'[234] On this showing Geddes cannot be regarded as having adumbrated the later, more elaborate, hypothesis that the Pentateuch is a composite narrative in which different sources are interwoven.

The exploration of Geddes's views on inspiration is difficult, because we have to be content with the crumbs which fall here and there, and he intimates in a number of places that he is postponing a more systematic treatment for inclusion in a general preface.[235] It is not seriously misleading to say that he excludes inspiration more rigorously in his treatment of Old Testament historiography than he does in respect of Mosaic law, although it is doubtful whether he ever intends to admit it in the fully-fledged theological sense in which it was used, or with the supernatural connotations which attached to it. That this is so is an impression which is reinforced by his rationalist treatment of anthropomorphisms in the Hebrew Bible and by his dismissal of the miraculous. These considerations will be taken up in what follows.

Geddes's attitude to historiography has already emerged in what has been said about his account of the composition of the Pentateuch. He gives notice to his readers that he has set aside the idea of inspiration and will consider 'the historical part of the Pentateuch as a mere human composition'.[236] History is written on the basis of direct participation in the events which are its subject-matter, or else on the foundation of oral traditions or written documents to which the historian has access and which he compiles. Old Testament historiography begins with the patriarchal narratives, but it is historiography mixed with mythology and legend which has to be sifted in order to separate the historically credible product from the rest:

Let the father of Hebrew history be tried by the same rules of criticism as the father of Greek history. Let the marvellous in both be distinguished from what is not so; the natural from the unnatural; the highly probable from the barely possible: and I believe we shall find, in both, nearly the same genuine marks of veracity on the whole; though, with respect to some particular parts, we may be a little inclined to scepticism.[237]

By modern standards his confidence in the historicity of the patriarchal narratives is robust and even uncritical:

Who, for example, that has ever read the Pentateuch, can entertain a doubt of Abraham's coming originally from Chaldaea into Chanaan, of his sojourning in Egypt and Palestine, and of his being the father of Isaac; of Isaac's being the father of Jacob; and of Jacob's being the father of Reuben, and eleven other sons? Who can doubt that Jacob went down to Egypt with his family; that his posterity were then reduced into a state of servitude, and thence escaped under the conduct of Moses? Who can doubt of their having wandered many years in the wilderness, before they reached the land of Chanaan; and of their having received, during that interval, a code of laws, which they believed to be of divine origin?[238]

When Geddes compares Hebrew historians with classical historians, he finds that they are inferior in factual accuracy and professionalism: they are not to be weighed in the same scales with Herodotus, Thucydides, Livy, Caesar and Sallust. They have a greater resemblance to 'Homer than to Herodotus, and to Herodotus than to Thucydides'. In many regards they are strikingly similar to Homer:

Like him, they are continually blending real facts with fanciful mythology, ascribing natural events to supernatural causes, and introducing a divine agency on every extraordinary occurrence. The same simplicity of narration, the same profusion of metaphors, the same garrulous tautology pervade them both: in both we meet with a *poetical history*.[239]

In the sphere of historiography Geddes's rejection of the supernatural is total. The *genre* has no room for 'acts of God', and wherever they are represented the credibility of Hebrew historians is destroyed. They must all be removed before a worthwhile historical deposit can be reached. Looking to the wider readership to which he is directing his work, Geddes says:

It is true, they will meet with an incredible number of prodigies, which they need not literally believe; and a most frequent interposition of the Deity and his agents, which it is not necessary to admit; and which a slight acquaintance with the genius of the eastern nations and their idioms will readily enable them to explain. In truth, a great number of passages in the Hebrew writings appear inexplicable, and sometimes ridiculous, only from their being ascribed to the Spirit of God.[240]

Instead of treating the supernatural and the miraculous with theological seriousness, Geddes has a programme of reductionism, conducted on rational principles, which will show that such narratives of divine invasions, while in accord with 'the genius of the eastern nations' at the time when they were written, cannot be invested with theological seriousness in the eighteenth century. Whatever offends against rational principles degrades religion and the Deity, and so biblical anthropomorphisms are marks of a primitivism which must be discarded: the ancient Hebrews were anthropomorphists, 'and to this alone, I think, we are to ascribe all those expressions concerning the Deity, that seemingly degrade the Deity. At any rate, all such expressions must be regarded as metaphorical imagery, adapted to the ideas of a stupid, carnal people; if we would support the general credit of Hebrew scripture on rational principles.'[241]

This useless supernatural baggage is entrenched in the doctrine of inspiration which is thought to guarantee the inerrancy of the Bible and to bestow theological authority on all its contents. What should be explained away as primitive relics is defended as Word of God, and absurdities are perpetrated as a consequence. It is no longer necessary to maintain that Hebrew historiographers are infallible, 'others may, possibly, be equal to such Herculean tasks; but I candidly acknowledge my disability'.[242] Geddes's criticism of the doctrine of inspiration ranges from his perception that it leads to the absurd claim that Hebrew historians are infallibly accurate, to his more fundamental debunking of the supernatural and the miraculous on which belief in the inerrancy of scripture has conferred an ultimate theological authority. He does all this on behalf of a religion which does not conflict with rational principles.

The manner in which Geddes appraises the laws of Moses shows that he approves of them because he supposes that he can reduce them to his rational principles. There can be little doubt that if he had found them in conflict with these principles, this would have weighed more heavily with him than his weak statement that they are inspired in some sense.[243] The scheme of government which Moses presents to the Israelites is 'a pure republic, in the best sense of the word'. 'The municipal laws of Moses', he remarks, 'must be allowed ... to be excellent on the whole, and almost unexceptionable in every part. Although he makes no formal declaration of the *Rights of Man*, all his decrees relative to property and personal safety are evidently founded on that principle. In the eye of the law, all Israelites are equal, and all capable of being raised to the highest civil offices in the state.'[244]

It remains, finally, to reinforce what was said about the Socinian outcome of Geddes's criticism at the end of the first section of this chapter. The objective of Simon had been to establish that the spheres of biblical criticism and of Catholic doctrine, could be separated, and that, consequently, critical freedom did not pose any threat to Catholic truth. The objective of Geddes is to achieve a criticism which is all-embracing, to accord with which a 'critical religion' emerges, a biblical religion so transformed that it does not conflict with rational principles:

In the Hebrew scriptures are many beauties, many excellent precepts, much sound morality: and they deserve the attentive perusal of every scholar, every person of curiosity and taste. All those good things I admit, and admire, and would equally admire them in the writings of Plato, Tully, or Marcus Antoninus: but there are other things, in great abundance, which I can neither admire nor admit; without renouncing common sense, and superseding reason: a sacrifice which I am not disposed to make, for any writing in the world.[245]

At the end of his *Critical Remarks* Geddes undertakes to answer a question put to him by a friend, whether or no Moses was inspired, and he encapsulates his reply in a Latin poem. In sum, he says that Moses was inspired, but not in a sense different from the inspiration of other renowned law-givers, though he, perhaps, merits a place at the top of that league. Inspiration of a unique order is to be attributed only to *Ille homo CHRISTUS*.[246] Does this mean that Geddes has set a limit to the operation of his rational principles and given priority to religious faith and devotion in the presence of Jesus Christ? The *Letter* which he wrote to the Reverend Dr Priestley in 1787, which was directed against Priestley's Unitarianism,[247] and is described as an attempt 'to prove by one prescriptive argument that the divinity of Jesus Christ was a primitive tenet of Christianity' might encourage such a conclusion. But the account which he gives of his allegiance to Jesus Christ in his *Critical Remarks* shows that his attachment to the teaching of Jesus is unqualified, only because he perceives it to be entirely in accord with reason:

The gospel of Jesus is my religious code; his doctrines are my dearest delight: his yoke (to me) is easy and his burden is light: but this yoke I would not put on; these doctrines I could not admire; that gospel I would not make my law, if Reason, pure Reason, were not my prompter and preceptress.[248]

Although Geddes's poem is remarkable for the warmth and intensity of the religious sentiment which it conveys, it does not manifestly go beyond the Christianity 'in accord with reason' which Geddes describes in his prose. It may be supposed that he is asserting the divinity of Jesus Christ in the line *Ille etenim solus, divino Numine plenus*, 'He alone is filled with divine Power'; or in the words *Ast tu, Nate Deo, qui cum PATRE omnia possis*, 'But you, Born of God, who, with the FATHER can do all things'. There is a reference to Jesus Christ as an object of trust and a source of hope (*TU mihi speratam, SPES mea!*), but the hymn sets out from a contrast between Moses and Jesus who is principally portrayed as the only perfect law-giver (a spring of pure water) and as the light of the world: 'You have promised and your words endure, "Whoever follows me will not walk in darkness".' Jesus is both the Leader and the Way, who summons his followers to climb arduous and dangerous mountain-passes, through hardship to the stars, and to whom Geddes responds:

TE Duce, callis ego metuenda pericula spernam
Angusti, et Tecum gnaviter astra petam.

CONCLUSION

A study of the Hebrew Bible in the Christian Church, conducted through a survey of selected Hebraists, began with Origen and Jerome. The concern of both these scholars to recover the Hebrew Bible may be related to a desire to be better equipped for Christian – Jewish controversy, but it transcends such apologetic considerations. Certainly in Jerome it stems from a conviction that the most original and purest form of the Old Testament is to be found in the Hebrew Bible. Yet there is a continuing reaction in the Church against this Bible, founded on the perception that its Jewishness constitutes a threat to the Christian appreciation of the Old Testament.

Jerome's success in having his Vulgate accepted within Western Christendom, and thereby robbing the Old Latin of its ecclesiastical rank, was a final victory for the Hebrew Bible at the level of translation. However suspect in text-critical respects his concept of *Hebraica veritas*, however it obscured the history of the Hebrew text and whatever injustice it did to the Septuagint and Old Latin, from then on the Hebrew Bible was established as the original text of the Old Testament. In the context of the Reformation in sixteenth-century England it constituted the first fountain and spring, and so Fulke is in complete agreement with Jerome about the source which has to be translated. The divide between Catholics and Protestants on this subject, as expressed in the conflict between Fulke and Martin, or in the position taken by Simon in the seventeenth century, is caused by different attitudes to the Vulgate.

There are two prime considerations which influence Fulke: that the advances which have been made in linguistic science pave the way for a more accurate translation of the Hebrew Bible than that achieved by Jerome, and that, in any case, the Hebrew Bible must be translated into English. The Catholic disagreement with this does not call in question that the Hebrew Bible is the original text, but it rejects the view that the Vulgate can be superseded: if vernacular translations are to be made, they should be done from the Vulgate. The nature of the victory won by the Hebrew Bible through Jerome's translation is nicely illustrated by the complexity of Simon's stance. He undermines the scientific validity of Jerome's concept of *Hebraica veritas*, but in the context of contemporary Roman Catholicism he magnifies the authority of the Vulgate and represents it as an immovable ecclesiastical pillar. Whatever he may have to say about the virtues of the Septuagint and the Old Latin, he knows that in a Western Catholic context they can never now be any more than text – critical helps for repairing deficiencies in the text of the Hebrew Bible.

The charges of deliberate falsification directed against Jewish scholarship have a special text-critical expression which is more prominent in the eighteenth-century work of Benjamin Kennicott than it is in the attitudes of William Fulke in the sixteenth century. These charges grew in proportion with an increase in Christian interest in the textual criticism of the Hebrew Bible. There is not much of this in Fulke, whereas Kennicott's great scholarly enterprise is focused on it. The Christian polemic is directed against Massoretic scholarship and the main theme is that the Massoretes have deliberately corrupted the text of the Hebrew Bible in order to obscure or destroy Christological references in it.

An important confirmation of this was thought to be elicited by a comparison of the Massoretic Pentateuch with the Samaritan Pentateuch, but the view that the Samaritan Pentateuch is textually superior, which was held by Kennicott, is one which Simon, his seventeenth-century predecessor, rejects. It was part of Kennicott's case against the Massoretes that the 'variations' which emerged from his collation of Hebrew manuscripts had significant support from the ancient versions, that they represented readings which could be converted into the same Hebrew text as that of the variations. In judging Kennicott's anti-Jewish bias regard must be had to the high expectations associated with his collation and the need to convince himself that his gigantic enterprise was a fundamental and indispensable process of textual purification. In this estimate of the text-critical significance of his Herculean labours he was mistaken.

The fear of Judaizing tendencies awakened in the Church by the Hebrew Bible and the Jewish scholarship associated with it is an important part of the story which has been told in this book. Wherever Christian scholars established relations with their Jewish counterparts, in situations where they were linguistically and exegetically inferior, it is evident that what they learned about the Hebrew Bible would have a Jewish and not a Christian content. Already Jerome, who relied on his Jewish assistants to enable him to obtain his translation from Hebrew into Latin, had to answer charges of Judaizing, but it is beyond the stage of translation in the area of exegesis that the expression of the conflict is sharpest. Andrew of St Victor conversed with Jews in French and Christological interpretations of the Old Testament are unlikely to have been included in these conversations. Andrew's interest in the literal sense of the Old Testament was all-devouring and the Jews added to the sum of his knowledge, but what particularly gave offence to his Christian brethren was the attention he lavished on Jewish interpretations of texts and passages which, according to the Church, did not have a literal interpretation that could be developed in an Israelite setting. The production of Jewish interpretations for texts which were alleged to have no other sense but a Christological one set the alarm bells sounding.

Fulke is devoted to the Christian interpretation of the Hebrew Bible and he describes the 'Rabbins' who reject it as 'froward', but he has a high regard for their Hebrew scholarship which he follows in pruning back the extravagant growth of Christian interpretations of Old Testament texts. He is consequently at loggerheads with Gregory Martin who perceives him as corrupted by Judaizing influences. For Martin the relation between Jewish and Christian scholarship is one of outright incompatibility: it is an opposition of falsehood and truth.

Andrew of St Victor's preoccupation with the literal sense and the historical frameworks which draw it out had shown that at a fundamental level of interpretation, determined by grammar and historical setting, the Hebrew Bible is not a Christian book. Given the conviction that the Old Testament is a Christian book and only serves the ends of the Church as such, it is understandable that the nature of Andrew's exegetical concentration should appear on the Christian side as a Judaizing tendency. Andrew was not a critical scholar and once the assumptions and methods of a critical scholarship, essentially humanist in conception, were applied by Christian scholars to the Hebrew Bible, the antithesis of Jewish and Christian exegesis gave way to a differently organized antithesis of historical – critical exegesis and Christian exegesis.

If it is held that the only valid method is a rigorous historical – critical interpretation of the Hebrew Bible, and that this constitutes a comprehensive biblical exegetical science, there will be no accommodation for a Christian content. Room can be found for this only in so far as it is argued that within the Old Testament itself, and in the relation of the Old Testament to the New Testament, texts and passages can be disengaged from their original historical contexts and further unfold their significance in new historical contexts. They are then carried forward from the past into the future by a historical movement which is assumed to press towards a fulfilment, rather than fixed immovably at a point in the past with a sense given to them by their one and only historical anchorage. The validity of a historical – critical method is not thereby overthrown, but its exhaustiveness is denied and the Christian sense of the Old Testament is associated with a claim that its contents are open to a future in which new historical settings extend and deepen the sense given by a primary historical – critical exegesis.

This has taken us beyond the critical initiatives associated with our selected Hebraists, and when we return to a consideration of Simon and Geddes we are at the stage of a more general antithesis of critical and Christian exegesis. With Simon this takes the form of an exegesis of the Old Testament divested of all elements of Christian interpretation. This is connected with a claim that critical exegesis should be separated from Christian theology. It should be acknowledged that at the level of critical scholarship the Old Testament is theologically obscure and that it is the task of the Catholic theologian and not of the critical exegete to elucidate and define its Christian content. With Geddes, on the other hand, there is an advance into the domain of Christian theology in the name of critical biblical scholarship. Its results are held to demand a fundamental redefinition of the content of Christian Faith in virtue of which its Trinitarianism is to be dismantled and a new Christianity more agreeable to the dictates of reason born.

We may glance finally at William Robertson Smith, a Scottish Hebraist of the second half of the nineteenth century. In him a historical – critical exegesis of the Old Testament achieves its complete expression and he holds that it lies entirely within the province of a biblical science. If properly conducted it should yield the same results for scholars of different religious persuasions or of no religious persuasion. Nevertheless, Smith did define the Old Testament theologically as 'Word of God', but it was the content given by a historical – critical exegesis, and so not a Christian content, which was so defined. The name of Robertson Smith has been introduced because he has the appearance of a Protestant counterpart to Richard Simon: the one introduces Christian theology into the Old Testament by enlisting the authority of the Catholic Church and the other does it by appealing to the authority of the Bible. The comparison is beguiling, but too much store should not be placed on it. It is true that Smith's method of making a transition from critical biblical exegesis to theology through an appeal to the authority of the Bible is a form of Protestant piety which stands in stark contrast with the boldness of his Old Testament criticism: it is the testimony of the Holy Spirit given directly to the individual Christian believer which produces an immovable certitude that the Old Testament is the Word of God.

There is, however, a further difference between Simon and Smith which is more fundamental than any parallelism between them which may be perceived. The Catholic Church in Simon's account contributes a level of Christian exegesis to the Old Testament additional to the critical one, whereas the Holy Spirit, according to Smith, adds nothing to the historical – critical exegesis of the Old Testament. Smith's theology does not impinge on exegesis. It is confined to an elucidation of the content of historical – critical exegesis as Word of God and this is done by shifting attention to the authority of the Bible. Biblical science and the exegetical truth which it yields enhance the authority of the Bible and the Holy Spirit testifies to the Christian believer so as to fill him with certitude that what is thereby disclosed is Word of God.[1]

APPENDIX 1

THE MILAN PALIMPSEST[1]

The format of the palimpsest is said by Kahle[2] to support the conclusion that there were no asterisks and obeli in the fifth column of the Hexapla and that the material assembled there received its text-critical consummation in another work by Origen. It was in this work that a Greek text corresponding quantitatively with the Hebrew text was constructed, and the fifth column of the Hexapla simply contained a text of the Septuagint. The evidence which is available in the Psalm fragments of the Milan palimpsest is not of a kind to establish this conclusion. If the Septuagint is defined as the text of the Codex Vaticanus[3] or of the Göttingen Septuagint,[4] which, for the most part, coincide in these Psalm fragments, the most important features to be noted are these:

A. Where a quantitative equivalence with the Massoretic text is achieved by additions to the Septuagint.

xxx 8 (MT xxxi 8): ἔγνωκας (without asterisk and metobelos) represents ידעת, whereas ἔσωσας (without obelos and metobelos) retains the reading of the Septuagint.[5]

xxx 22 (MT xxxi 22): MT לי is represented by ἐμοί.[6]

xxxiv 20 (MT xxxv 20): ארץ דברי is not represented by the Septuagint, whereas the Milan palimpsest (γῆς ἐλάλουν) represents ארץ דברו (cf. Aquila and Quinta, γῆς ῥήματα; Symmachus, γῆς λόγους).[7]

B. Where a plus in the Septuagint over against the Massoretic text is deleted rather than marked with obelos and metobelos.

xvii 36 (MT xviii 36): καὶ ἡ παιδεία σου αὐτή με διδάξει is not represented.[8]

xxx 20 (MT xxxi 20): κύριε is not represented.[9]

xxx 23 (MT xxxi 23): ἄρα is not represented.[10]

xlv 11: This is a complicated example, because the Hebrew text in the first column is shorter than the Massoretic text, whereas the Septuagint agrees with the longer Massoretic text. Nevertheless, it does illustrate the deletion of ὑψωθήσομαι ἐν τοῖς ἔθνεσιν which appears in the Septuagint.[11]

xlviii 12 (MT xlix 12): αὐτῶν is not represented.[12]

C. Where a plus in the Septuagint over against the Massoretic text is retained and not marked with an obelos and metobelos.

xvii 36 (MT xviii 36): εἰς τέλος.[13]

xxix 13 (MT xxx 13): ἡ δόξα μου (MT כבוד).[14]

xxx 2 (MT xxxi 2): καὶ ἐξελοῦ με.[15]

xxx 20 (MT xxxi 20): τὸ πλῆθος.[16]

xxxiv 17 (MT xxxv 17): ῥῦσαι. This does not appear in Codex Vaticanus or in Rahlfs' text, but it is noted by him as a variant.[17]

xlviii 13 (MT xlix 13): τοῖς ἀνοήτοις.[18]

D. Where the Septuagint is reproduced, when an addition is needed to achieve quantitative equivalence with the Massoretic text:

xxxi 10 (MT xxxii 10): κυκλώσει (MT יסובבנו; Aquila and Symmachus, κυκλώσι αὐτόν).[19]

xxxiv 20 (MT xxxv 20): ὅτι ἐμοὶ μὲν (MT כי לא; Aquila, ὅτι οὐ; Symmachus, οὐ γὰρ εἷς).[20]

Thus there are Hexaplaric tendencies in the Milan palimpsest, although they are not uniform. They appear to a small extent in additions to the Septuagint, unmarked by asterisks and metobeli, designed to achieve quantitative equivalence with the Hebrew. They are also evident in deletions from the Septuagint whose aim is likewise to achieve quantitative equivalence with the Hebrew. This is a practice which is directed towards the same end as enclosing surpluses in the Septuagint over the Hebrew text in obeli and metobeli, but which achieves this end less conservatively. Nor do the Septuagint surpluses over the Hebrew text which are found in the fifth column of the Milan palimpsest necessarily constitute an anti-Hexaplaric feature, because, Hexaplaric manuscripts without asterisks and obeli are a well-established phenomenon.[21] The only anti-Hexaplaric tendency which can be observed in the fragments is the reproduction of the Septuagint when an addition or alteration is needed to achieve equivalence with the Hebrew text. Hence Kahle's claim that Origen's reconstructed text was not located in the fifth column of his Hexapla but in an independent text-critical work cannot be founded on the absence of asterisks and obeli in the Milan palimpsest, nor on the composition of the Greek text in the fifth column of these Psalm fragments.

THE SEPTUAGINT TEXT USED BY ORIGEN IN HIS HOMILY ON THE BOOK OF JEREMIAH

The nature of the Greek text cited by Origen when he was preaching on the book of Jeremiah can be tested by picking out the cases where there is a difference between the text of the Septuagint, as measured by Ziegler's text[1] or that of Codex Vaticanus,[2] and the text of the Hebrew Bible, and by searching Origen's quotations for instances of these. When this is done for Jeremiah i–xxv, the results obtained may be set out as follows:

A. There are examples[3] of a quantitative equivalence between Origen's Greek text and the text of the Hebrew Bible. The additions which are made to the Septuagint to achieve this are recorded in the Hexaplaric material assembled by Field[4] and Ziegler.[5] We may conclude in these instances that Origen is using the text which he had constructed in the fifth column of his Hexapla.

B. There are two quotations[6] which have additions made under the influence of the Hebrew text, but which are not completely equalized with the Hebrew text. Again these additions can be traced in the remains of the Hexapla and are Hexaplaric.[7]

C. There are eleven examples[8] of a Greek text which coincides with the text of Ziegler or that of Codex Vaticanus and which has no Hexaplaric additions. That these additions were made to the Septuagint in the fifth column of the Hexapla, in respect of these particular passages, is shown by their existence in the Hexaplaric remains recorded by Field[9] and Ziegler.[10]

D. There are three quotations[11] in which the differences between the Septuagint and the Massoretic text are other than quantitative.

Some of these examples are of sufficient interest to merit a more detailed treatment and we may begin with two cases of a partial assimilation to the Hebrew text. At Jer. xi 4[12] κατὰ πάντα is a literal rendering of ככל (Septuagint, πάντα ὅσα), but אותם is not represented. At Jer. xv 15[13] Origen has a Greek text which represents אתה ידעת, and this is an addition over against the Septuagint, but his text agrees with the Septuagint in not representing תקחני. This is a significant difference, because μὴ εἰς μακροθυμίαν, connected with what precedes, is a plea that Yahweh should not show forbearance to Jeremiah's persecutors, whereas the Hebrew text, with a different punctuation and the addition of תקחני, is a plea that Yahweh in his forbearance may not 'remove' Jeremiah: 'Withhold your anger and do not remove me.'

In section A, iv 8[14] has the appearance of a paraphrase, but it incorporates an addition (θυμὸς ὀργῆς compared with θυμός of the Septuagint) and this produces an equivalence with חרון אף. Jer. xx 2, which is picked out by Nautin,[15] is located in section D, because it does not illustrate a quantitative difference between the Septuagint and the Hebrew, but, apparently, the use by the Seventy of a Hebrew *Vorlage* different from the Massoretic text: οἴκου ἀποτεταγμένου is perhaps a rendering of בית מני 'house of appointment' (?). Origen has βενιαμίν, agreeing with בנימין (Massoretic text). This has some affinity with the state of affairs at Jer. xv 16[16] (under D), where Origen follows the Septuagint, connecting verse 15 with verse 16, and has a sense far removed from the Massoretic text. This is brought about not only by a difference in punctuation but also, apparently, by a Hebrew text, different from the Massoretic text, which underlies the Greek translation: ὑπὸ τῶν ἀθετούντων τοὺς λόγους σου. συντέλεσον αὐτούς indicates something like מנאצי דבריך כלם instead of נמצאו דבריך ואכלם (Massoretic text).

The reason why an assured conclusion cannot be drawn from xii 3[17] (C) is that Origen cites only part of the verse, but the absence of καὶ before ἅγνισον could be taken as an indication that he had the shorter text of the Septuagint in mind, without the Hexaplaric addition[18] which produces quantitative equivalence with the Massoretic text (*ἄθροισον αὐτοὺς ὡς πρόβατα εἰς σφαγήν καὶ ✓). In another case, xvi 17[19] (A), the assured conclusion that Origen is citing the Hexaplaric text can be reached by combining the evidence in two different places: καὶ οὐκ ἐκρύβησαν ἀπὸ προσώπου μου (לא נסתרו מלפני) in one[20] and καὶ οὐκ ἐκρύβη τὰ ἀδικήματα αὐτῶν ἀπέναντι τῶν ὀφθαλμῶν μου (ולא נצפן עונם מנגד עיני) in another.[21]

JEROME'S USE OF THE SEPTUAGINT IN HIS COMMENTARY ON JEREMIAH

Jerome regularly inserts parenthetically (*sive*) in his translation from Hebrew a rendering from the Septuagint which captures the sense of the Hebrew somewhat differently, and in all these cases he is assuming that the Seventy had the same Hebrew text as he himself is translating. An example of this is Jer. xxv 34f.,[1] where he translates הילילו as *ululate* 'wail', but notices LXX *iubilate* (ἀλαλάξατε, 'shout for joy'), which he explains as *in malem partem*, an ironic or sinister use of *iubilum*. The LXX alternative for *quasi vasa pretiosa* (ככלי חמדה) is given as *quasi arietes electi* (ὥσπερ οἱ κριοὶ οἱ ἐκλεκτοί); for *asperigite vos cinere optimates gregis* (והתפלשו אדירי הצאן) the alternative rendering is *plangite arietes ovium* (κόπτεσθε οἱ κριοὶ τῶν προβάτων); and, finally, for *optimatibus*, in *ab optimatibus gregis* (מאדירי הצאן), *arietibus* (ἀπο τῶν κρίων τῶν προβάτων) is given. Hence, with reference to the Septuagint, Jerome is indicating alternative meanings for כלי ('pot'/'ram'), for התפלשו ('sprinkle with ashes'/'lament') and for אדירים ('noblest'/'rams').

At Jer. xiii 16 Jerome prefers the reading assumed by the Seventy (שָׁמָּה) which he equates with שָׁם 'there') to that which now appears in the Massoretic text, and so for ושמה לצלמות he has *et ibi umbra mortis*, 'but the shadow of death was there'. He then offers the other pointing as an alternative (שָׂמָה): *sive iuxta Hebraicum: et ponet eam in umbram mortis* 'but he turns it into the shadow of death'[2] (cf. Vulgate, *et ponet eam in umbram mortis*).

His use of the Septuagint or other Greek versions to explore problems of Hebrew lexicography or to develop his exegesis is illustrated by the following examples. At Jer. xx 3 he does not notice the non-representation of מסביב in the Septuagint, but he gathers various senses of מגור (NEB 'terror') from the Septuagint, Theodotion, Aquila and Symmachus. He renders מגור as 'fear' (*pavorem*), but the other meanings which he picks up from the Greek versions are 'migrant' – that is, 'deportee' (Septuagint, Theodotion, Aquila), 'gathered' or 'carried off' (Symmachus).[3] He translates משא (NEB 'burden') at Jer. xxiii 36, 38 as *onus* 'burden', but he notices λῆμμα in the Septuagint which he renders *assumtio* 'acceptance', that is, indicative of Yahweh's favour. He adds that λῆμμα non solum *assumtionem* sed et *donum munusque* significat, and he uses these senses of 'gift' and 'provision' in order to relate משא יהוה (λῆμμα κυρίου) to promises of unbroken safety and prosperity on which the Judaeans still rely, although they have forfeited all right to them.[4]

At Jer. xxiv 9 the New English Bible follows the shorter Greek text ('I will make them repugnant to all the kingdoms of the earth'). Jerome renders ונתתים לזועה לרעה as *et dabo eos in vexationem afflictionemque*, but he calls attention to the shorter Greek text (לרעה is not represented) which he renders as *in dispersionem* (εἰς διασκορπισμόν). The Greek translator has detected a reference to exile in לזועה, influenced by the context which refers to an exile already accomplished and issues a threat of deportation in the future. Jerome deals with this in his exegesis, but he does not mention εἰς διασκορπισμόν particularly.[5] He tackles the obscure מסגר (xxiv 1) which he renders as *inclusorem* 'a jeweller' – one who sets precious stones. He remarks that מסגר has been taken to mean *vinctos* 'vanquished' in the Septuagint ut captivitatis significarent malum ('in order to signify the evil of captivity') and that the Greek text is longer than the Hebrew (καὶ τοὺς δεσμώτας καὶ τοὺς πλουσίους, 'and the prisoners (*vinctos*) and the wealthy').[6]

Jer. xxv 20 is another case where Jerome's exegesis is influenced by the Septuagint, although he does not incorporate its nuance of הערב into his translation from the Hebrew. He renders ואת כל הערב as *et universis generaliter*, but takes account of καὶ πάντας τοὺς συμμείκτους (Septuagint) and renders τοὺς συμμείκτους as *misticios* (NEB 'rabble of followers'). The Septuagint is influential in shaping his exegesis which identifies *misticios* as non-Egyptian elements of population which had infiltrated into Egypt (vulgus non Aegyptiae regionis, sed peregrinum et adventicium).[7]

Jer. xiii 12 will serve to bring these illustrations of Jerome's use of the Septuagint and other Greek versions to a conclusion. He makes no comment on the shorter Greek text, but he notices καὶ ἐρεῖς πρὸς τὸν λαὸν τοῦτον (sive, *ad populum*), representing ואמרת אל העם הזה over against ואמרת אליהם (*Dices ergo ad eos*) of his Hebrew text. The lexicography of נֶבֶל is pursued with reference to the Septuagint and the other Greek versions. The question is whether נֶבֶל is a wine-skin or an earthenware jar (NEB, 'Wine jars should be filled with wine') and in his translation from the Hebrew Jerome indicates the latter, although he notices that the Septuagint (ἀσκός – *uter*) points to the former. He records that נֶבֶל is translated 'flask' by Aquila, 'bowl' by Symmachus and 'dish' by Theodotion. His own preference for earthenware vessel (supported by Aquila, Symmachus and Theodotion) is a reasonable one, given the pattern of the use of נֶבֶל in biblical Hebrew,[8] but it also accords with his exegetical intentions, since he connects Jer. xiii 12 with 2 Cor. iv 7 ('We have this treasure in earthen vessels').[9]

ANDREW OF ST VICTOR ON ISAIAH I 31

At Isa. i 31 the Vulgate has *Et erit fortitudo vestra ut favilla stuppae, et opus vestrum quasi scintilla* (RSV, 'And the strong shall become tow, and his work a spark'). The Vulgate has rendered החסון ('the strength') as 'your strength', has understood נערת as 'embers of flax' and has transformed 'his work' (פעלו) into 'your work'. Andrew's comment is, vel fortitudinem et opus eorum [que] comparat purgamento stuppe, ut habetur in Hebreo, et Symmachus transtulit, et scintille.[1] The information about Symmachus was available to Andrew in Jerome's commentary, where there is a rendering which agrees with the Vulgate (*Et erit fortitudo vestra ut favilla stuppae*), followed by a comment, pro favilla ἀποτίναγμα interpretatus est Symmachus.[2] Jerome explains that on this view נערת is the dust which is disengaged when the flax is combed (ἀποτίναγμα 'what is shaken off') and not 'embers' (Vulgate – *favilla*): your strength will be reduced to sweepings of flax. It is this translation for which Andrew (*purgamento stuppe*) is claiming the support of the Hebrew, and נערת, which occurs only here and at Judg. xvi 9, is usually taken to mean 'tow'. In his commentary Jerome offers a translation of the remainder of verse 31 and *et opus ejus* shows us that the text on which he was commenting differed from that of the Vulgate. Moreover, his comment on *et opus ejus*[3] is revealing in connection with the rendering on which he eventually settled in the Vulgate. We can discern how he arrived at *et opus vestrum*: the suffix of פעלו refers back to החפוך (rendered *fortitudo vestra*) and means 'its outworking', that is, the displays of your strength. If Jerome's rendering in his commentary is compared with the Septuagint, the close correspondence noted in the previous examples is seen not to obtain here. The Septuagint has interpreted החסון as 'their strength' (ἡ ἰσχὺς αὐτῶν) and has rendered the singular suffix of פעלו with a plural suffix, 'and their work' (καὶ ἐργασίαι αὐτῶν). ὡς καλάμη στιππύου ('like a fibre of flax') is nearer to the Hebrew and Symmachus than the Vulgate.

A sufficient summing-up of this example is that Jerome's *et opus ejus* is an earlier rendering than the *et opus vestrum* of the Vulgate and that Andrew's claim to reproduce the Hebrew text is largely justified. Since he is so dependent on Jerome in the other examples, we might suppose that the reference to Symmachus is taken from Jerome's commentary and that his *opus eorum* (which is not a literal rendering of פעלו) is a modification of Jerome's *opus ejus*. It should be noted, at any rate, that Jerome substitutes *opus eorum*[4] for *opus ejus* in the course of his commentary on Isa. i 31 and that this agrees with the Septuagint. But the literal rendering of החסון as *fortitudo* 'the strength' cannot be traced to Jerome's commentary or to the Septuagint, and it may be that Andrew got all his information about the Hebrew text of i 31 from his Jewish mentors, in which case there is an important difference between this and the examples discussed earlier (Isa. i 12, 14, 22). It cannot be said that the *in Hebreo* which appears in his comment on Isa. i 31 does great damage to the opinion that he knew some Hebrew, whereas the testimony of Isa. i 12, 14, 22 is especially damning.

Andrew's translation of Isa. i 31 and the exegesis which arises from it almost agree with the Septuagint (and so presumably with the Old Latin), and this is what has been said of Isa. i 12, 14, 22. The difference lies in this, that the text of the Old Latin cannot be derived from Jerome's commentary on Isaiah in the case of i 31, as it can be for i 12, 14, 22; also in this, that the texts of the Septuagint, and presumably the Old Latin, do not diverge from the Hebrew in i 31 as they do in verses 12, 14, 22. It could be an accident that Andrew has avoided serious error at i 31, but his literal rendering of החסון (*fortitudo* – 'the strength'), which he did not get from Jerome's commentary, suggests that he had independent information, in all likelihood from Jews.

WILLIAM FULKE ON ISAIAH XXVIII 11 AND 1 CORINTHIANS XIV 21

Isa. xxviii 11, NEB 'So it will be with barbarous speech and strange tongue that this people will hear God speaking.' 1 Cor. xiv 21, NEB 'I will speak to this nation through men of strange tongues, and by the lips of foreigners; and even so they will not heed me, says the Lord.'

Fulke cites Jerome:

We read in the apostle, 'In other tongues and lips will I speak to this people, and neither shall they hear me, saith the Lord', which seemeth to me to be taken out of this present chapter, according to the Hebrew.[1]

The Septuagint and the New Testament represent two different interpretations of the Hebrew text. The Septuagint follows the Hebrew in the order 'lip' and 'tongue', but this is reversed in 1 Cor. xiv 21. The Septuagint assumes that the subject who speaks a harsh and unintelligible language is an invader and that is why ידבר has been taken as a collective singular and translated as a plural (λαλήσουσιν). The same speaker is assumed at Isa. xxviii 12 and אמר אליהם is rendered as λέγοντες αὐτοῖς – again a plural. This assumption does not make good sense of verse 12 and המרגעה (NEB 'repose') is mistranslated as τὸ σύντριμμα 'destruction'.

At 1 Cor. xiv 21 it is assumed that God is the subject of ידבר, and so in a first person utterance, with God the speaker, ידבר is converted into λαλήσω. A jump is then made from the end of Isa. xxviii 11 to the end of verse 12: καὶ οὐδ' οὕτως εἰσακούσονται μου, λέγει Κύριος is a rendering of ולא אבו שמוע, 'and even so they will not heed me', with the addition of 'says the Lord'. If we read אָבוּ with the Isaiah[a] scroll and many Hebrew manuscripts (MT אָבוּא), the Septuagint (καὶ οὐκ ἠθέλησαν ἀκούειν) coincides with the Hebrew, and there is nothing in either corresponding to λέγει κύριος at 1 Cor. xiv 21.[2] The New Testament text may fairly be described as a paraphrase and abridgement of the Hebrew text, with a different understanding of ידבר from that of the Septuagint. Since the connection between verse 11 and verse 12 in the Hebrew is difficult, and since the subject of אמר (verse 12) must be God, it is understandable that God has been taken as also the grammatical subject of ידבר (so NEB at Isa. xxviii 11).

The conclusion is that 1 Cor. xiv 21 does not arise from the Septuagint, and that it is either a paraphrase and abridgement which derives immediately from the Hebrew, or else it is mediated through a Greek version other than the Septuagint which rendered ידבר with a singular verb. On Isa. xxviii 11 Jerome remarks *Symmachus, Theodotio et LXX de hoc loco diversa senserunt;*[3] that is, they differ from MT, but he does not tell us how Symmachus and Theodotion differ from the Septuagint. Origen, having cited the Greek text of 1 Cor. xiv 21, comments: εὗρον γὰρ τὰ ἰσοδυναμοῦντα τῇ λέξει ταύτῃ ἐν τῇ τοῦ ᾿Ακύλου ἑρμηνείᾳ κείμενα, 'I have found present in Aquila's translation a reading having the same force as this one.'[4] It is improbable that Aquila would convert ידבר into λαλήσω, as has been done at 1 Cor. xiv 21, and Origen's meaning is more likely to be that Aquila has translated ידבר as λαλήσει and not λαλήσουσιν (Septuagint). This would be in accord with Aquila's devotion to literal translation, and Origen may be taking it as an indication that Aquila supposed God to be the grammatical subject of both ידבר and אמר (verse 12). This is the interpretation of the New English Bible. Hence the point of departure of λαλήσω at 1 Cor. xiv 21 may be the rendering λαλήσει which was in Aquila and represented a different interpretation of ידבר in verse 11 from λαλήσουσιν of the Septuagint.

NOTES

Introduction

1. A. J. Baumgartner, *Calvin Hébraïsant et Interprete de L'Ancien Testament* (Paris, 1889), p. 24.
2. S. M. Jackson, *Selected Works of Huldreich Zwingli* (Philadelphia, 1901), pp. 49–57; cf. R. H. Bainton, 'The Bible and the Reformation', *CHB* III (Cambridge, 1963), p. 4.

1. *The foundations*

1. The Greek text of the Letter of Aristeas with an introduction by H. St J. Thackeray appears in H. B. Swete (revised by R. R. Ottley), *An Introduction to the Old Testament in Greek*, 2nd edn (Cambridge, 1914), pp. 533–606. There is an English translation in H. St J. Thackeray, *The Letter of Aristeas. Translated with an Appendix of Ancient Evidence on the Origin of the Septuagint* (London, 1917).
2. *De Vita Mosis*, ii 5–7. *Philonis Alexandrini Opera Quae Supersunt*, iv, ed. L. Cohn (Berlin, 1902), pp. 206–10. There is an English translation in Thackeray, *The Letter of Aristeas*, pp. 96–100.
3. Cf. Irenaeus, *Adv. Haer* III.21.2, *PG* 7 (Paris, 1882), 947. There is an English translation in Thackeray, *The Letter of Aristeas*, pp. 103f. For an account of Christian references to the origin of the Septuagint see Thackeray, ibid., pp. 101–16.
4. See G. W. Anderson, 'Canonical and Non-Canonical', *CHB* I (Cambridge, 1970), p. 142; cf. R. H. Charles, *The Apocrypha and Pseudepigrapha of the Old Testament*, I (Oxford, 1913), p. iv. Charles describes the Apocrypha as the excess of the Septuagint over the Hebrew Bible, but he adds: 'This volume differs from the Apocrypha proper at once in the way of excess and in the way of defect. 3 Maccabees has been added after 2 Maccabees, since it is contained in many MSS of the LXX, and 4 Ezra has been transferred to vol. 2, since it is essentially a Pseudepigraph.'
5. P. E. Kahle, *The Cairo Geniza*, 2nd edn (Oxford, 1959), pp. 209–15.
6. For different views see E. J. Bickermann, 'The Septuagint as a Translation', *Proceedings of the American Academy for Jewish Research* 28 (1959), pp. 7–11; B. H. Stricker, *De Brief van Aristaeas. De hellenistische codificaties der praehelleense godsdiensten*. Verhandelingen der Koninklijke Nederlandse Akademie van Wetenschappen, afd. Letterkunde, Nieuwe Reeks, 62, no. 4 (Amsterdam, 1956). According to Bickermann the translation was undertaken under the patronage of Ptolemy II, Philadelphos; according to Stricker it was imposed on the Jews by the same Ptolemy and its imposition was resisted by them.
7. A. C. Sundberg, *The Old Testament of the Early Church*. Harvard Theological Studies 20 (Cambridge, Mass. and London, 1964).

8. H. B. Swete. *The Old Testament in Greek According to the Septuagint*, 3rd edn (Cambridge, 1907), II, p. 644; ὁ νόμος καὶ αἱ προφητεῖαι καὶ τὰ λοιπὰ τῶν βιβλίων.

9. P. E. Kahle, 'Problems of the Septuagint', *Studia Patristica*, I, part 1, K. Aland and F. L. Cross (ed.). *Texte und Untersuchungen* V.viii (1957), pp. 335f. Ben Sira's grandson came to Egypt in the thirty-eighth year of King Euergetes I, that is, 132 B.C. Kahle argues on the basis of ἐπὶ in ἐπὶ τοῦ Εὐεργέτου Βασιλέως that the king is deceased and that the translation by Ben Sira's grandson could not have been done earlier than 116 B.C.

10. Sundberg, *Old Testament*, pp. 82–103.

11. D. Barthélemy, *Les Devanciers d'Aquila*, *SVT* (Leiden, 1963), pp. 3–30. Barthélemy relates the manner of Aquila's translation to the exegetical methods of Rabbi Akiba.

12. *Pace* Kahle, 'Problems of the Septuagint', p. 337: 'It is very likely that the tripartite Canon was known in Egypt long before it was known in Palestine.'

13. F. C. Burkitt, *Early Christianity Outside the Roman Empire* (Cambridge, 1899), pp. 1f.

14. Ibid., pp. 3f.

15. F. C. Burkitt, *The Gospel History and its Transmission* (Edinburgh, 1906), pp. 126f.; cf. K. Stendahl, *The School of St Matthew and its Use in the New Testament*. Acta Seminarii Neotestamentici Upsaliensis, 20 (Uppsala, 1954), pp. 207–17.

16. Eusebius *HE* iii,39, *PG* 20 (Paris, 1857), 300: Ματθαῖος μὲν οὖν Ἑβραΐδι διαλέκτῳ τὰ λόγια συνεγράψατο. Ἡρμήνευσε δ'αὐτὰ ὡς ἠδύνατο ἕκαστος, 'Matthew compiled the Logia in the Hebrew language, and each one interpreted them as he was able.'

17. Burkitt, *Early Christianity*, p. 5.

18. Mk v 41: Ταλιθά κούμι or Ταλιθά κούμ (see B. M. Metzger, *A Textual Commentary on the Greek New Testament* (London and New York, 1971), p. 87); Mk vii 34: Εφφαθά; Mk xiv 36 (cf. Rom. viii 15 and Gal. iv 6): Ἀββᾶ ὁ πατήρ.

19. M. Black, *An Aramaic Approach to the Gospels and Acts*, 3rd edn (Oxford, 1967). M. Wilcox, *The Semitisms of Acts* (Oxford, 1965).

20. Mk xv 34 (Mt. xxvii 46). The Hebrew text of Ps. xxii 2 is אֵלִי אֵלִי לָמָה עֲזַבְתָּנִי. Codex Sinaiticus has Aramaic throughout in both New Testament passages (Ἐλωΐ Ἐλωΐ λεμᾶ σαβαχθανί), and Codex Bezae has Hebrew throughout (Ἐλί Ἐλί λαμά ζαφθανί). The other uncials waver between Hebrew and Aramaic in respect of Ἠλί/Ἐλωΐ and λαμά/λεμῶ. See Metzger, *Textual Commentary*, pp. 70, 119f. Metzger (p. 119) describes the Hebrew of Codex Bezae as 'a scholarly correction representing the Hebrew of Ps. 22.1'. Cf. J. A. Emerton, 'Did Jesus speak Hebrew?', *JTS* N.S. 12 (1961), pp. 199f. The Aramaic original would have been אֱלָהִי אֱלָהִי לְמָה שְׁבַקְתַּנִי.

21. A. Diez Macho, *Neophytii 1: Targum Palestinense MS De La Biblioteca Vaticana. Tomo V Deuteronomio* (Madrid, 1978), p. 255 (Aramaic text); p. 554 (English translation by M. McNamara and M. Maher).

22. Cf. A. T. Hanson, *The Living Utterances of God. The New Testament Exegesis of the Old* (London, 1983), p. 37.

23. C. H. Dodd, *According to the Scriptures* (London, 1952).

24. Cf. B. Lindars, *New Testament Apologetic. The Doctrinal Significance of the Old Testament Quotations* (London, 1961). Lindars expresses broad agreement with Dodd's idea of selected passages which constitute a sub-structure of Christian theology. Lindars, however, supposes that the principal function of this sub-structure is

apologetic and so defensive, whereas Dodd is more concerned with it as a positive contribution to Christian theological understanding.

25. J. Rendell Harris, *Testimonies*, I–II (Cambridge, 1916, 1920).
26. Dodd, *According to the Scriptures*, pp. 28–110; 'Testimonies' and 'The Bible of the Early Church'.
27. Cf. Lindars, *New Testament Apologetic*, p. 30. Lindars remarks that the tendency of Dodd's study to 'tear the quotations from their contexts in the Gospels' loosens their connection with the historical Jesus.
28. See Kahle, *The Cairo Geniza*, pp. 218–28.
29. Barthélemy, *Devanciers d'Aquila*, pp. 163–272.
30. Septuaginta Vetus Testamentum Graecum Auctoritate Societatis Litterarum Gottingensis editum.
31. Barthélemy, *Devanciers d'Aquila*, p. 179; cf. S. Jellicoe, *The Septuagint and Modern Study* (Oxford, 1968), p. 93. Jellicoe holds that 'supposed Palestinian recensions antedating Aquila were importations from Alexandria, where translational and recensional activity was a continuous process and relations with Jerusalem remained constant and close up to A.D. 70'.
32. Kahle, *The Cairo Geniza*, pp. 235–47; cf. p. 236, 'How can we find an *Urtext* of two different translations!'
33. Ibid., p. 212.
34. Ibid., p. 236.
35. E. Tov, *The Text-Critical Use of the Septuagint in Biblical Research*. Jerusalem Biblical Studies (Jerusalem, 1981), p. 46.
36. This is the only sensible interpretation which can be put on Kahle's remarks (*The Cairo Geniza*, p. 236): 'The Jews soon abandoned the standard text of the Greek Bible, fixed towards the end of the second century B.C. in Alexandria. More and more they had become used to Greek texts which had been assimilated to the Hebrew original.'
37. Tov, *Use of the Septuagint*, p. 43.
38. J. Ziegler (ed.), *Ieremias, Baruch. Threni. Epistula Ieremiae*. Septuaginta Vetus Testamentum Graecum Auctoritate Societatis Litterarum Gottingensis editum, XV (Göttingen, 1957, 1976²).
39. E. Tov, *The Septuagint Translation of Jeremiah and Baruch. A Discussion of an Early Revision of Jeremiah 29–52 and Baruch 1:1–3:8*. Harvard Semitic Monographs 8 (Missoula, 1976); 'L'incidence de la critique textuelle sur la critique littéraire dans le livre de Jérémie', *Revue Biblique* 79 (1972), pp. 189–99; 'Exegetical Notes on the Hebrew *Vorlage* of the LXX of Jeremiah 27 (34)', *Zeitschrift für die alttestamentliche Wissenschaft* 91 (1979), pp. 73–93; 'Some Aspects of the Textual and Literary History of the Book of Jeremiah', *Bibliotheca Ephemeridum Theologicarum Lovaniensium* 54 (1981), pp. 145–67.
40. Ziegler, *Ieremias*, p. 373; *Beiträge zur Ieremias-Septuaginta*. Nachrichten der Akademie der Wissenschaften in Göttingen. Philologisch-Historische Klasse (1958), pp. 52f.
41. Ziegler, *Ieremias*, p. 232; *Beiträge*, p. 43.
42. Ziegler, *Ieremias*, p. 202; *Beiträge*, p. 42.
43. This is seen in the title of his book cited above (n. 37) and also in the title of an earlier article, 'The Nature of the Hebrew Text underlying the LXX', *Journal for the Study of the Old Testament* 7 (1978), pp. 53–68. This is, understandably, the way in which a commentator on the Hebrew Bible approaches the Septuagint. See W. McKane, *A Critical and Exegetical Commentary on Jeremiah*. International Critical Commentary (Edinburgh, 1986), pp. xvi–xxvii.

44. W. Kappler, 'Ziele und Aufgaben des Göttinger Septuaginta-Unternehmens', *Göttingische Gelehrte Anzeigen* 202 (1940), pp. 117f., 122.
45. Tov, *Use of the Septuagint*, pp. 47–95, especially p. 80; 'On "Pseudo Variants" reflected in the Septuagint', *Journal of Semitic Studies* 20 (1975), pp. 165–77.
46. Barthélemy, *Devanciers d'Aquila*, pp. 156, 246, 271f.
47. Ibid., pp. 213–17.
48. Ibid., p. 148.
49. Ibid., p. 148.
50. Kahle, *The Cairo Geniza*, p. 227.
51. See n. 36. Cf. Barthélemy, *Devanciers d'Aquila*, p. 151: 'Inquiets de voir les juifs hellénphones s'appuyer sur des textes qui divergeaient souvent fortement de ceux qu'utilisaient les hébréophones, ils ont voulu modeler avec plus d'exactitude la traduction grecque sur la forme autorisée du texte hébraïque qu'ils s'efforçaient par ailleurs d'imposer. Ainsi espéraient-ils protéger leurs frères de la diaspora contre les propagandistes hérétiques.'
52. Ibid., p. 148.
53. Sundberg, *Old Testament*, p. 92: 'Since Greek was known by many Palestinian Jews and since the Septuagint circulated among them, it is evident that the Christian church was not restricted for a source of the Greek scriptures to Alexandrian and diaspora Judaism. Palestine, also, is now seen as a possible source locale.'
54. J. N. Sevenster, *Do you know Greek? How much Greek could the first Jewish Christians have known?* Supplements to Novum Testamentum, 19 (Leiden, 1968).
55. Ibid., p. 190.
56. C. F. D. Moule, 'Once more, who were the Hellenists?' *ET* 70 (1959), pp. 100–2.
57. Sevenster, *Do you know Greek?*, pp. 23–8.
58. M. Hengel, 'Zwischen Jesus und Paulus', *ZThK* 72 (1975), pp. 151–206. English translation, *Between Jesus and Paul* (London, 1983), pp. 1–29.
59. Moule, 'Who were the Hellenists?', pp. 100f.
60. Ibid., p. 100; Sevenster, *Do you know Greek?*, pp. 31f.; Hengel, *Between Jesus and Paul*, pp. 1–11.
61. Agreeing with M. Hengel, 'Die Ursprünge der Christlichen Mission', *NTS* 18 (1971), pp. 15–38. English translation, *Between Jesus and Paul*, pp. 48–64, especially 54–8.
62. Burkitt, *Early Christianity*, p. 1.
63. Ibid., p. 5.
64. *De Vita Mosis*, ii, 7; Cohn, *Philonis Alexandrini opera*, IV, p. 209; Thackeray, *The Letter of Aristeas*, p. 99. Cf. Irenaeus who represents the translators of the Septuagint as inspired and inerrant: Unus enim et idem Spiritus Dei, qui in prophetis quidem praeconavit, quis et qualis esset adventus Domini, in senioribus autem interpretatus est bene quae bene prophetata fuerant (*Adv. Haer.* III.21.4, *PG* 7, p. 950; Thackeray, *The Letter of Aristeas*, pp. 103f.).
65. C. H. Dodd, *The Bible and the Greeks* (London, 1935, 1954), pp. xif.
66. W. McKane, *Proverbs: A New Approach*. Old Testament Library (London, 1970), pp. 43–7.
67. W. McKane, *A Critical and Exegetical Commentary on Jeremiah*, i, chapters i–xxv. International Critical Commentary (Edinburgh, 1986).
68. Dodd, *According to the Scriptures*, p. 132.
69. C. K. Barrett, 'The Interpretation of the Old Testament in the New', *CHB* I (Cambridge, 1970), pp. 377–411.

70. Ibid., pp. 402f., 411; C. F. D. Moule, *The Birth of the New Testament*, 2nd edn (London, 1966), p. 85.
71. Dodd, *According to the Scriptures*, p. 132.
72. Ibid., p. 133; cf. Lindars, *New Testament Apologetic*, pp. 16f. Lindars reinforces Dodd's view that when a text is given a Christian interpretation, the original context in which it occurs is not neglected.
73. Dodd, *According to the Scriptures*, p. 133: The interpretation of Old Testament passages in the New Testament 'is not only consistent and intelligent in itself, but also founded upon a genuinely historical understanding of the process of the religious – I should prefer to say the prophetic – history of Israel as a whole'.
74. For further biographical detail see E. de Faye, *Origène, sa vie, son oeuvre, sa pensée*, I (Paris, 1923), pp. 1 – 50; J. Daniélou, *Origène* (Paris, 1948), translated into English by W. Mitchell, *Origen* (London and New York, 1955), pp. 3 – 22.
75. *HE* vi.16, *PG* 20 (Paris, 1857), 557f.: ἰδίως τὴν Ἀκύλου καὶ Συμμάχου καὶ θεοδοτίωνος ἔκδοσιν ἅμα τῇ τῶν Ἑβδομήκοντα ἐν τοῖς Τετραπλοῖς ἐπικατασκευάσας. 'He made a further separate arrangement of the edition of Aquila and Symmachus and Theodotion together with that of the Seventy in the Tetrapla' (J. E. L. Oulton, *Eusebius The Ecclesiastical History* II. The Loeb Classical Library (London and New York, 1932), pp. 52f.
76. J. Card. Mercati (ed.), *Psalterii Hexapli Reliquiae* (Rome, 1958).
77. *HE* vi.16, *PG* 20, 555f. Oulton, *Eusebius*, pp. 52f.: 'In the Hexapla of the Psalms, after the four well-known editions, he placed beside them not only a fifth but also a sixth and a seventh translation; and in the case of one of these he has indicated again that it was found at Jericho in a jar in the time of Antoninus, the son of Severus.' Eusebius mentions (*HE* vi.16), that one of these additional Greek translations was found at Nicopolis near Actium (ἐν τῇ πρὸς Ἀκτίοις Νικοπόλει) and notes of Origen which have survived state that the Quinta was found at Nicopolis and the Sexta in a jar near Jericho (Kahle, *The Cairo Geniza*, pp. 241f.). The Greek text of these notes appears in Mercati, *Psalterii Hexapli*, p. xxxi.
78. See above, p. 17.
79. Barthélemy, *Devanciers d'Aquila*, p. 260.
80. P. E. Kahle, 'The Greek Bible Manuscripts used by Origen', *JBL* LXXIX (1960), p. 115; also E. Würthwein, *Der Text des Alten Testaments*, 4th edn (Stuttgart, 1973). There is an English translation by E. F. Rhodes, *The Text of the Old Testament* (London, 1980), p. 56.
81. See above, p. 12.
82. I. Soisalon-Soininen, *Der Charakter der asterisierten Zusätze in der Septuaginta*. Annales Academiae Scientiarum Fennicae, ser. B, 114 (Helsinki, 1959), pp. 159f., 197.
83. See Appendix 1.
84. Comm. in Matt. xv, 14: θεοῦ διδόντος, εὕρομεν ἰάσασθαι, *PG* 13 (Paris, 1862), 1293.
85. Two examples of how Origen's textual criticism operated may make matters clearer. In the first of these (Jer. i 10) the Hebrew text is longer than Origen's Septuagint text, and he indicates the addition which is needed to make the Greek quantitatively equivalent with the Hebrew. The Hebrew Bible reads, 'to uproot and to pull down and to destroy and to demolish, to build and to plant'. The addition which is needed to make the Greek almost identical with the Hebrew is 'and to demolish', and Origen marks this by putting an asterisk before it and a metobelos after it (∗ καὶ κατασπᾶν ✓). See F. Field (ed.) *Origenis Hexaplorum*

quae supersunt, II (Oxford, 1875), p. 573; Ziegler, *Ieremias*, pp. 150f. In the second example, at Gen. i 6, the Hebrew Bible reads, 'Let there be a firmament between the waters to separate water from water.' Origen's Greek text reads, 'Let there be a firmament between the waters to separate water from water. And it was so.' The subtraction which has to be indicated to achieve Origen's objective is 'And it was so', and this is marked by putting an obelos before it and a metobelos after it (÷ καὶ ἐγένετο οὕτως ✓)). Field, *Origenis Hexaplorum*, I, p. 8.

86. See above, p. 17.

87. Barthélemy, *Devanciers d'Aquila*, pp. 138f.; Cf. Soisalon-Soininen, *Charakter der asterisierten Zusätze*, p. 195, who states that Origen's text of the Septuagint is best preserved in the remains of the fifth column of the Hexapla, and who supposes that the Origenic text promoted by Pamphilus and Eusebius was this Hexaplaric text (so also Würthwein, *Text des Alten Testaments*, p. 57).

88. Soisalon-Soininen, *Charakter der asterisierten Zusätze*, pp. 12f., 193.

89. Ibid., p. 197; cf. Jerome, see below, p. 34.

90. See above, pp. 14–17.

91. Barthélemy, *Devanciers d'Aquila*, p. 139.

92. Kahle, 'The Greek Bible Manuscripts used by Origen', pp. 116f.; cf. Jerome, *PL* 28 (Paris, 1865), 594f.: Et nomen Domini tetragrammaton in quibusdam Graecis voluminibus, usque hodie antiquis expressum litteris invenimus.

93. Soisalon-Soininen, *Charakter der asterisierten Zusätze*, pp. 158, 197.

94. *HE* vi, 16: 'And so accurate was the examination that Origen brought to bear upon the divine books, that he even made a thorough study of the Hebrew tongue and got into his own possession the original writings in the actual Hebrew characters, which were extant among the Jews' (Oulton, *Eusebius*, pp. 52f.; *PG* 20, 553f.).

95. Kahle, 'The Greek Bible Manuscripts used by Origen', pp. 114f.

96. See above n. 77; cf. Kahle, *The Cairo Geniza*, pp. 241–5.

97. Cf. J. A. Emerton, 'Were Greek Transcriptions used by Jews before the Time of Origen?', *JTS* N.S. 21 (1970), pp. 17–31. Emerton concludes that the use by Jews of Greek transcriptions of the Hebrew Bible prior to the time of Origen is not substantiated by the evidence to which appeal has been made.

98. Kahle, 'The Greek Bible Manuscripts used by Origen', p. 114; ἡ μὲν γραφὴ τῆς Ἑβραϊκῆς ἐξόδου ἀνέγνωσται καὶ τὰ Ῥήματα τοῦ μυστηρίου διασεσάφηται πῶς τὸ πρόβατον θύεται καὶ πῶς ὁ λαὸς σώζεται.

99. *The Chester Beatty Biblical Papyri*, Fasc. VIII, *Enoch and Melito* (London, 1941), p. 10 n. 1.

100. The editor of the Greek text does not even entertain this idea. He makes two suggestions, the first of which he favours: (a) The reference is to the public reading of the passage in Greek, followed by a paraphrase of it. (b) The reference is simply to a reading of the passage and καὶ τὰ Ῥήματα τοῦ μυστηρίου διασεσάφηται is a stylistic reinforcement (*parallelismus membrorum*). See Campbell Bonner, *The Homily on the Passion. By Melito Bishop of Sardis*. Studies and Documents XII (London, 1940), pp. 30–6, 86f.

101. Kahle, 'The Greek Bible Manuscripts used by Origen', p. 114.

102. Ibid., pp. 114f.

103. Cf. J. A. Emerton, 'The Purpose of the Second Column of the Hexapla', *JTS* N.S., 7 (1956), pp. 83–6. Emerton holds that the transliteration provided vocalization for Origen and lesser Christian scholars. It was used in conjunction with the Hebrew consonantal text in column one and was a guide as to how that text should be read.

104. M. F. Wiles, 'Origen as Biblical Scholar', *CHB* I, p. 457. According to Eusebius (see above, n. 94) he 'even made a thorough study of the Hebrew tongue' (ὡς καὶ τὴν Ἑβραΐδα γλῶτταν ἐκμαθεῖν); cf. R. P. C. Hanson, *Allegory and Event* (London, 1959), pp. 171f.

105. P. Nautin, *Origène Homélies sur Jérémie*, Sources Chretiennes 232 (Paris, 1976), I, pp. 117f.

106. Kahle, *The Cairo Geniza*, p. 240.

107. Soisalon-Soininen, *Charakter der asterisierten Zusätze*, p. 195.

108. Nautin, *Origène*, p. 116, *car il ne savait pas lui-même l'hébreu*; cf. Homily xvi, 10, ibid., II, pp. 154f, δῆλον ὅτι κειμένην ἐν τῷ Ἑβραϊκῷ which Nautin renders, *évidemment parce qu'elle figure dans l'hébreu*, that is, as an admission by Origen that he does not have access to the Hebrew.

109. See above, n. 97.

110. S. P. Brock, 'Origen's aims as a Textual Critic of the Old Testament', *Studia Patristica* 10 (Berlin, 1970), pp. 215–18. Collected in *Studies in the Septuagint: Origins, Recensions and Interpretations*, ed. by S. Jellicoe (New York, 1974), pp. 343–6.

111. Ibid., p. 217.

112. Ibid., p. 216.

113. *Ep. ad Afric.* 5, *PG* 11 (Paris, 1857), 59–62. The translation is that of Wiles, *Origen*, p. 456.

114. *Ep. ad Afric.* 4, *PG* 11, 57–60; Wiles, *Origen*, p. 456.

115. *Comm. in Matt.* xv, 14, *PG* 13 (Paris, 1862), 1293f. The translation is that in Kahle, *The Cairo Geniza*, p. 240, with small modifications. The Greek text for *Ep. ad Afric.* 4–5 and *Comm. in Matt.* xv, 14 is given by Soisalon-Soininen, *Charakter der asterisierten Zusätze*, pp. 10f.

116. Cf. Wiles, *Origen*, pp. 456f.: 'But Origen was not only acting from a sense of cautious realism. He was not only, not even primarily, a critical scholar. He too was a child of the Church. If the Septuagint was the Church's Old Testament, it must on theological grounds be an inspired text, its divergences from the earlier Hebrew notwithstanding. A proper recognition and authority had to be given to both.'

117. Cf. Kahle, *The Cairo Geniza*, p. 240: 'He [Origen] could not, however, speak frankly about these problems. He had to be cautious. The "Septuagint" was regarded as the canonical text inspired by God. So we only occasionally find in his works a remark on these problems.'

118. See below, p. 40.

119. See above, pp. 27f.

120. 'And also may be able to make positive use of what is found there, even when it is not to be found in our scriptures', *Ep. ad Afric.* 5, *PG* 11, 61f. (καὶ ἵνα συγχρησώμεθα τοῖς φερομένοις παρ᾽ ἐκείνοις, εἰ καὶ ἐν τοῖς ἡμετέροις οὐ κεῖται βιβλίοις).

121. *Ep. ad Afric.* 4, *PG* 11, 55f. (πολλὰ δὲ τοιαῦτα καὶ ἐν τῷ Ἰερεμίᾳ κατενοήσαμεν, ἐν ᾧ καὶ πολλὴν μετάθεσιν καὶ ἐναλλαγὴν τῆς λέξεως τῶν προφητευομένων εὕρομεν).

122. Nautin, *Origène*, I, pp. 115f.

123. See Appendix 2.

124. Nautin, *Origène*, II, p. 68; cf. I, p. 117.

125. Δεῖ οὖν καὶ τὸ καθημαξευμένον καὶ φερόμενον ἐν ταῖς ἐκκλησίαις διηγήσασθαι καὶ τὸ ἀπὸ τῶν Ἑβραϊκῶν γραφῶν ἀδιήγητον μὴ καταλιπεῖν.

126. Nautin, *Origène*, II, pp. 154–9.
127. Ibid., II, p. 154: 'Αμαρτία Ἰούδα γέγραπται ἐν γραφείῳ σιδηρῷ ἐν ὄνυχι ἀδαμαντίνῳ ἐγκεκολαμμένη ἐπὶ τοῦ στήθους τῆς καρδίας αὐτῶν.
128. Ibid., pp. 156–9.
129. *Praef. in Job, PL* 28 (Paris, 1865), 1142.
130. *Ep.* 66,14. J. Labourt, *Saint Jérôme Lettres*. Collection des Universités de France, III (Paris, 1953), p. 180: a reference to family property. *Ep.* 3,5, I (Paris, 1949), p. 15: a reference to domestic servants. Cf. J. N. D. Kelly, *Jerome. His Life Writings and Controversies* (London, 1975), pp. 6f.
131. *Ep.* 84,3, Labourt, *Saint Jérôme Lettres*, IV (Paris, 1954), p. 126: Dum essem iuvenis, miro discendi ferebar ardore.
132. *Praef. in Job, PL* 28, 1141.
133. *Comm. in Hab.* ad iii 14, *PL* 25 (Paris, 1965), 1393. When the death of the Emperor Julian brought to a sudden end the persecution of Christians in A.D. 362, he was a boy at school, presumably in Stridon.
134. *Chron. Euseb., PL* 27 (Paris, 1866), 501f., under A.D. 359: Donatus grammaticus praeceptor meus.
135. Rufinus, *Apol.* ii, 9, *PL* 21 (Paris, 1849), 590f. For Rufinus Tyrannius, also called Rufinus of Aquileia, see *New Catholic Encyclopaedia* XII (New York and London, 1967), pp. 702–4.
136. *Apol.* iii, 6. Pierre Lardet. *Saint Jérôme Apologie contra Rufin*. Sources Chrétiennes 303 (Paris, 1983), p. 228: Ego philosophus, rhetor, grammaticus, dialecticus, hebraeus, graecus, latinus, trilinguis?
137. H. F. D. Sparks, 'Jerome as a Biblical Scholar', *CHB* I (Cambridge, 1970), p. 517.
138. *Ep.* 125,12, Labourt, *Saint Jérôme Lettres*, VII (Paris, 1961), pp. 124f.
139. *Ep.* 84,3, ibid., IV, pp. 126f.
140. *Ep.* 18, ibid., I (Paris, 1949), pp. 53–78.
141. *Ep.* 15,1, ibid., I, p. 46; 16,2, ibid., I, p. 50.
142. *Ep.* 3,3, ibid., I, p. 12.
143. *Ep.* 22,30, ibid., I, pp. 144f.
144. Rufinus, *Apol.*, II, 7, 8, *PL* 21, 588f.
145. *Ep.* 22,30. Labourt, *Saint Jérôme Lettres*, I, p. 144.
146. *Praef. in Esa., PL* 28, 828.
147. *Praef. in Dan., PL* 28, 1358f.; *Comm. in Gal.*, iii (Prol.), *PL* 26 (Paris, 1866), 427: Sed omnem sermonis elegantiam, et Latini eloquii venustatem, stridor lectionis Hebraicae sordidavit; *Ep.* 30, Labourt, *Saint Jérôme Lettres*, II (Paris, 1951), pp. 31f.: quia propter barbariem linguae memoria elabitur; cf. J. Barr, 'St. Jerome's Appreciation of Hebrew', *Bulletin of the John Rylands Library*, XLIX (1967), pp. 287f., 301.
148. *Ep.* 125, 12. Labourt, *Saint Jérôme Lettres*, VII, pp. 124f.
149. *Ep.* 16,2, ibid., I, p. 50: Si quis cathedrae Petri iungitur, meus est.
150. Sparks, 'Jerome', *CHB* I, p. 502.
151. *Ep.* 127,7, Labourt, Saint Jérôme Lettres, VII, p. 142.
152. Ibid., p. 142: Et quia alicuius tunc nominis aestimabar super studio scripturarum.
153. *Ep.* 45,3, ibid., II (Paris, 1951), p. 97. What he said Damasus proclaimed (Damasi os meus sermo erat) and the view that he would be a worthy occupant of the Chair of St Peter was widely held (Omnium paene iudicio dignus summo sacerdotio decernebar).

154. *Apol.* ii,20. Lardet, *Saint Jérôme Apologie*, p. 158.

155. *Praef. in Quat. Evang.*, *PL* 29 (Paris, 1865), 558f.

156. See above, n. 140.

157. *Preface to the 'Gallican' Psalter*, *PL* 29, 121–3.

158. *Ep.* 32,1. Labourt, *Saint Jérôme Lettres*, II, p. 38.

159. *Ep.* 39,6, ibid., p. 82: Quousque genus detestabile monachorum non urbe pellitur, non lapidibus obruitur, non praecipitatur in fluctus?

160. *Ep.* 22,30, ibid., I, p. 144.

161. *Ep.* 108,14, ibid., V (Paris, 1955), p. 176.

162. *Comm. in Esa.* VI, ad xvi, 14, *PL* 24 (Paris, 1865), 246: ut Vulgata editio habet.

163. *Ep.* 106,2. Labourt, *Saint Jérôme Lettres*, V, p. 105: The Old Latin (Vulgata) is a translation of the corrupt Greek 'common edition' (κοίνη).

164. ἐγώ εἰμι ὁ θεὸς ὁ ὀφθείς σοι ἐν τόπῳ θεοῦ (ego sum deus quem vidisti in loco dei). B. Fischer, *Vetus Latina. Die Reste der altlateinischen Bibel. Genesis* (Freiburg, 1951–4), p. 330.

165. ἐν ὅλῳ τῷ οἴκῳ (in tota domo eius). Ibid., p. 336.

166. καὶ ἀπώλεσεν αὐτά (et perdidit ea); ἕως τῆς σήερον ἡμέρας (usque in hodiernum diem). Ibid., p. 368.

167. *Praef. in Pent.*, *PL* 28, 182f.; *Praef. in Jos.*, ibid., 505; *Praef. in Job* (Vulg.), ibid., 1137f.; *Quaest. in Gen.*, *PL* 23 (Paris, 1865), 985.

168. *Preface to the 'Gallican' Psalter*, *PL* 29, 123f.; *Praef. in Job*, ibid., 64; *Praef. in Paralip.*, ibid., 426; *Praef. in Libros Salomonis*, ibid., 425–8; cf. *Ep.* 57,11, Labourt, *Saint Jérôme Lettres*, III (Paris, 1953), pp. 70f.; *Ep.* 112,19, ibid., VI, pp. 38f.

169. *PL* 29, 123–420 (side by side with the 'Roman' Psalter).

170. Ibid., 63–118.

171. *Comm. in Tit.* ad iii 9, *PL* 26, 630.

172. *Praef. in Pent.*, *PL* 28, 179; *Praef. in Job* (Vulg.), ibid., 1139; *Praef in Paralip.* (Vulg.), ibid., 1393.

173. *Preface to the 'Gallican' Psalter*, *PL* 29, 124: qui simplicitate sermonis a Septuaginta Interpretibus non discordat.

174. *Praef. in Paralip.* (Vulg.), *PL* 28, 1391f.; *Praef. in Libros Salomonis* (Sept.), *PL* 29, 426f.; *Ep.* 106,2, Labourt, *Saint Jérôme Lettres*, V, p. 105. Jerome describes his 'Hexaplaric' Latin translation as a correction of the Old Latin version: Curiosissima veritate correxi (*Praef. in Libros Salomonis*).

175. *Praef. in Pent.*, *PL* 28, 182f.

176. *Praef. in Paralip.* (Sept.), *PL* 29, 426.

177. For Christian references to this belief see Thackeray, *The Letter of Aristeas*, pp. 101–16.

178. *Praef. in Pent.*, *PL* 28, 182: sed in una basilica congregatos, contulisse scribant, non prophetasse. Aliud est enim vatem, aliud esse interpretem. Ibi Spiritus ventura praedicit: hic eruditio et verborum copia, ea quae intelligit, transfert.

179. *Ep.* 106,2, Labourt, *Saint Jérôme Lettres*, V, pp. 105f. Jerome describes the Hexaplaric text which he translated into Latin: Ipsa est quae in eruditorum libris incorrupta et immaculata Septuaginta interpretum translatio reservatur.

180. *Ep.* 106,2, ibid., p. 106: Quicquid ergo ab hac [Origen's Hexaplaric text] discrepat, nulli dubium est, quin ita et ab Hebraeorum auctoritate discordet.

181. *Praef. in Job* (Vulg.), *PL* 28, 1142: Utraque editio, et Septuaginta juxta Graecos, et mea juxta Hebraeos, in Latinum meo labore translata est. Eligat unusquisque quod vult, et studiosum me magis, quam malevolum probet.

182. *Praef. in Jos.*, *PL* 28, 505.

183. *Praef. in Ezram*, *PL* 28, 1473f.

184. *Praef. in Job* (Vulg.), ibid., 1139.

185. *Praef. in Job* (Vulg.), ibid., 1141f.

186. *Praef. in Sam. et Malachim.*, ibid., 603f.; *Preface to the Hebrew Psalter*, ibid., 1185f.

187. Rufinus, *Apol.* ii, 12, *PL* 21, 595: a deliberate corruption of Baranina (see below, n. 212): Ille vero de Synagoga Barabbas tuus pro Christo electus (cf. Jn. xviii 40, *Non hunc sed Barabbam*).

188. *Ep.* 32,1 (A.D. 384), Labourt, *Saint Jérôme Lettres*, II, pp. 37f.

189. *Praef. in Esa.*, *PL* 28, 828.

190. *Preface to the Hebrew Psalter*, *PL* 28, 1184f.; *Ep.* 57,11, Labourt, *Saint Jérôme Lettres*, III, pp. 70f.

191. *Apol.* iii, 25. Lardet, *Saint Jérôme Apologie*, pp. 282f.

192. *Ep.* 27,1, ibid., II, p. 17.

193. *Praef. in Job*, *PL* 28, 1139.

194. *Praef. in Jos.*, ibid., 505.

195. *Preface to the Hebrew Psalter*, ibid., 1185f.

196. *Praef. in Sam. et Malachim*, *PL* 28, 603: Lege ergo primum, Samuel, et Malachim meum: meum, inquam, meum. Cf. W. H. Semple 'St Jerome as a Biblical Translator', *Bulletin of the John Rylands Library*, XLVIII (1966), p. 233.

197. *Ep.* 32,1, Labourt, *Saint Jérôme Lettres*, II, p. 38.

198. *Ep.* 134,2, ibid., VIII (Paris, 1963), p. 70.

199. *Ep.* 57,11, ibid., III, p. 71: σὺν τὸν οὐρανὸν καὶ σὺν τὴν γῆν/ את השמים ואת הארץ (Gen. i, 1).

200. *Ep.* 57,5, ibid., pp. 59f.: In quibus non pro verbo verbum necesse habui reddere, sed genus omnium verborum vimque servavi (p. 60); non verbum e verbo sed sensum exprimere de sensu (p. 59). *Praef. in Chron. Euseb.*, ii,1, *PL* 27 (Paris, 1866), 223f.

201. *Ep.* 57,5, Labourt, *Saint Jérôme Lettres*, III, p. 59: absque scripturis sanctis, ubi et verborum ordo mysterium est.

202. *Ep.* 112,19, ibid., VI, p. 39: sensuum potius veritatem, quam verborum interdum ordinem conservantes; cf. *Ep.* 106,29, ibid., V, pp. 116f. on Ps.xlviii 15 (Heb. xlix 15): et non debemus sic verbum de verbo exprimere, ut dum syllabam sequimur, perdamus intellegentiam.

203. *Ep.* 48(49), 4, ibid., II, p. 118: Porro eloquentiam quam pro Christo in Cicerone contemnis in parvulis ne requiras. Ecclesiastica interpretatio, etiam si habet eloquii venustatem, dissimulare eam debet et fugere, ut non otiosis philosophorum scholis paucisque discipulis, sed universo loquatur hominum generi.

204. אגילה באלהי ישעי / χαρήσομαι ἐπὶ τῷ θεῷ τῷ σωτῆρι μου / *exsultabo in Deo Iesu meo.*

205. See below, p. 54.

206. *Praef. in Paralip.* (Sept.), *PL* 29, p. 423: de Tiberiade legis quondam doctorem, qui apud Hebraeos admirationi habebatur, assumpsi.

207. *Ep.* 84,3, Labourt, *Saint Jérôme Lettres*, IV, p. 127.

208. *Praef. in Job* (Vulg.), *PL* 28, 1140.

209. *Ep.* 48(49),4, Labourt, *Saint Jérôme Lettres*, II, p. 118: Libros sedecim prophetarum, quos in Latinum de Hebraeo sermone verti. The sixteen books of the Prophets presumably consist of the 'Latter Prophets' in the Hebrew canon with the addition of the book of Daniel.

210. Preface to the *'Gallican' Psalter*, *PL* 29, 121-3.
211. See above n. 169.
212. *PL* 28, 1189-1306.
213. Cf. E. F. Sutcliffe, 'Jerome', *CHB* II (Cambridge, 1969), p. 99: 'The "textus vulgatus" spoken of in the thirteenth century was a particular recension drawn up in the University of Paris and received with wide favour.'
214. *Ep.* 27,1, Labourt, *Saint Jérôme Lettres*, II, p. 17: Quibus si displicet fontis unda purissimi, caenosos rivulos bibant.
215. *Praef. in Quat. Evang.*, *PL* 29, 558f.
216. *Praef. in Job* (Vulg.), *PL* 28, 1141.
217. *Ep.* 71,5, Labourt, *Saint Jérôme Lettres*, IV, p. 13: Ut enim veterum librorum fides de hebraeis voluminibus examinanda est, ita novorum graeci sermonis normam desiderat.
218. *Praef. in Quat. Evang.*, *PL* 29, 559.
219. *Ep.* 28,2, *PL* 33 (Paris, 1861), 112.
220. *De Civ. Dei*, xviii, 43, *PL* 41 (Paris, 1864), 603f.
221. *Ep.* 71,4, *PL* 33, 242.
222. *Ep.* 82,35, ibid., 291: perturbemus plebes Christi. For a consideration of the correspondence between Augustine and Jerome see W. H. Semple, 'Some Letters of St Augustine', Bulletin of the John Rylands Library, XXXIII (1951), pp. 111-30.
223. *Ep.* 71,5, ibid., 242.
224. Cf. Jerome, *Ep.* 112, 21,22, Labourt, *Saint Jérôme Lettres*, VI, p. 42. Jerome says that *cucurbita* is wrong and that he avoided a falsification; a mere transcription of קיקיון would have been unilluminating, and so, in agreement with others he has rendered קיקיון as *hedera*.
225. *Etymol.* vi, 4, *PL* 82 (Paris, 1878), 236.
226. Reproduced by H. B. Swete, in *The Old Testament in Greek According to the Septuagint*.
227. J. Ziegler, Septuaginta Vetus Testamentum Graecum Auctoritate Societatis Litterarum Gottingensis editum (Göttingen, 1957, 1976²).
228. W. McKane, *A Critical and Exegetical Commentary on Jeremiah*, i, chs. i-xxv. International Critical Commentary (Edinburgh, 1986), pp. xvi-xxi.
229. S. Reiter, *Sancti Eusebii Hieronymi in Hieremiam Prophetam*, Corpus Scriptorum Ecclesiasticorum Latinorum, LIX (Vienna and Leipzig, 1913): ii 17 (p. 25); xxi 12 (p. 251); xxii 25 (p. 266); xxiii 7-8 (p. 275); xxiii 28 (p. 292); xxiv 9 (p. 296); xxv 20 (p. 308); xxv 24 (p. 309); xxv 25 (p. 310); xxv 26 (p. 311).
230. See Appendix 3.
231. *Apol.* ii,24, Lardet. *Saint Jérôme Apologie*, p. 170. Sparks interprets this passage differently and supposes that Jerome is referring to his 'Hexaplaric' Latin translation throughout 'Jerome as a Biblical Scholar' (*CHB* i, p. 515; cf. Sutcliffe, 'Jerome' *CHB* ii, p. 95).

2. Andrew of St Victor

1. For this biographical section of the chapter I am entirely dependent on B. Smalley, 'Andrew of St Victor, Abbot of Wigmore: a Twelfth-Century Hebraist', *Recherches de Théologie Ancienne et Mediévale*, X (1938), pp. 358-73. For the Boston of Bury entry on Andrew see p. 363 n. 19: Andreas canonicus S. Victoris et Auditor Magistri Hugonis floruit A.D. - et scripsit multa. There follows a list of Andrew's commentaries.

2. Ibid., p. 363 n. 20, sed Anglus natione.

3. Ibid., p. 363 n. 21, in Anglia parentibus Anglis natus.

4. Ibid., p. 364 n. 22: Alii novem ex actis domus S. Victorinae fuere ... Andreas ...; quos inter *eminet* Andreas cuius in Isaiam aliosque plures Sanctae Scripture libros commentaria manuscripta commendantur.

5. Ibid., p. 364, n. 23.

6. In *Monasticum Anglicanum* VI (London, 1846), ed. W. Dugdale, pp. 344–8. Smalley uses photographs of the manuscript which was at Berkeley Castle when it was read by Dugdale and which is now at the University Library, Chicago, No. 334 (Smalley, 'Andrew of St Victor', p. 364).

7. Smalley, p. 369. The John Rylands Library MS is Lat. 215.

8. Ibid., p. 365.

9. Ibid., p. 366.

10. Ibid., p. 365.

11. Ibid., p. 367.

12. *The Letters and Charters of Gilbert Foliot*, ed. Z. N. Brooke, Dom A. Morey and C. N. L. Brooke (Cambridge, 1967), p. 181. Foliot urges the abbot of St Victor to provide a superior for the house at Wigmore. The editors accept Smalley's view that *Wigoriensis* (Worcester) in Foliot's letter is a lapse for *Wygem* (Wigmore), and Foliot's reference to a daughter-house of St Victor in his letter points to this (cf. Smalley, 'Andrew of St Victor', p. 367).

13. Smalley, p. 369.

14. Ibid., p. 369.

15. Ibid., p. 369 (*Annals*): *fundata est abbatia de Wygem* is an inaccuracy, but the reference must be to the foundation of the abbey church.

16. Ibid., p. 369 (*Annals*).

17. Ibid., p. 369 (*Annals*).

18. Samuel and Kings or I, II, III and IV Kings are counted as one book (cf. G. W. Anderson, 'Canonical and Non-Canonical', *CHB* I (1970), pp. 137f.). See also n. 20.

19. Smalley, p. 371 n. 46, MS Pembroke Cambridge 45, fo. 17[c]: Quid sit Phiton in nostra super Samuelem expositiuncula prout potuimus aperuimus.

20. Ibid., p. 371 n. 51, MS Mazarine Paris 175, fo. 93[b]: Proposui, sicut olim super Pentateuchum et Iosue et Iudicum et Malachim, ita et nunc, magis ope divina quam viribus fretus, aliquam explanatiunculam super obscura prophetarum scripta cudere.

21. Ibid., p. 371 n. 50, MS Corpus Christi Cambridge 30, fo. 87[d]: Ad opuscula Salomonis iuxta littere superficiem explananda multis amicorum precibus compulsi ...

22. Ibid., p. 371, MS Mazarine Paris 175, fo. 93[b]: ... mee paupertati que non potest semper pre manibus vel commentarios vel libros habere glosatos consulo, que in predictis sparsim diffuseque dicta sunt libris, ad historicum quidem spectantia sensum summatim colligens, et quasi in unum corpus succincte compingens. This is reproduced in B. Smalley, *The Study of the Bible in the Middle Ages* (Oxford, 1983[3]), p. 377 and is translated on p. 123.

23. Smalley, 'Andrew of St Victor', p. 358.

24. R. Bacon, *Compendium Studii Philosophae*. Rerum Britannicorum Medii Aevi Scriptores 15, ed. J. S. Brewer (Rolls Series, London, 1859), pp. 480–2.

25. Smalley, 'Andrew of St Victor', p. 361.

26. Smalley, *The Study of the Bible*, pp. 169 f.
27. See below, pp. 97 f.
28. Hugh is commenting on *At vero Melchisedech proferens panem et vinum* and he remarks: Quod inter gentiles signum est pacis, sicut et oliva solebat esse. He does, however, add non purus cibus, sed sacrificium (*Adnot. Eluc. in Pent.*, *PL* 175 (Paris, 1879), 51). Cf. Smalley, 'Andrew of St Victor', p. 360.
29. *De Emmanuele*, *PL* 196 (Paris, 1880), 601 f.: Super illum autem locum, *Ecce virgo concipiet, et pariet filium*, Judaeorum objectiones vel quaestiones ponit, nec solvit, et videtur velut eis palmam dedisse, dum eas veluti insolubiles relinquit.
30. Ibid., 638: Nolite dicere magistri mei, sed Judaeorum. Nam ponit eam sane, non quasi suam, sed quasi illorum.
31. Ibid., 638 f.: Et hoc ipsum quaeratur ex ipsa, utrumnam sua sit, an aliena.
32. Ibid., 639: quando suam, et veram, quando Judaeorum, et falsam, posuisset.
33. Bacon, *Compendium*, p. 482.
34. Smalley, *The Study of the Bible*, p. 383 (trans. p. 134). MS Bibl. Nat. Lat. 356 Paris, fo. 11ª.
35. Cf. Smalley, ibid., pp. 132–4.
36. Ibid., p. 134 (slightly modified).
37. Ibid., p. 384 (trans. p. 135). MS Bibl. Nat. Lat. 356, fo. 11ᶜ
38. Ibid., fo. 11ᶜ⁻ᵈ: In recapitulationibus tamen quedem frequenter adduntur, sed que supradicta non destruant. Cum supradictum sit Deum omnia in sex diebus diversis fecisse, in recapitulatione dicere eum omnia simul fecisse, hoc non est supradictis aliquid addere, sed omnia supradicta penitus destruere. (The translation is Smalley's, p. 135.)
39. Ibid., pp. 112–85.
40. G. A. C. Hadfield, *Andrew of St Victor, a twelfth century Hebraist; an investigation of his works and sources* (unpublished D.Phil. thesis, Oxford, Bodleian Library, 1971).
41. Bacon, *Compendium*, p. 482: Sed omnino utitur litera Latina, secundum quod construitur Hebraeum ad literam, ut superius dixi, et non est nostra translatio [the Vulgate]. Propter quod nescio de quo intromittit se de hac expositione, quia literam nostram deberet exponere, et non aliam, quae etiam nullius translationis est, sed solius literalis constructionis Hebraei.
42. Ibid., p. 482: Haec ideo dixi propter multas qui dant auctoritatem Andreae, cum nec hic nec alibi sit ei danda; eo quod post Bedam non fuit aliquis cui ecclesia dederit auctoritatem in expositione Scripturae, sicut patet in decretis, et constat Andream ibi non esse nominatum.
43. Ibid., p. 483: Pauci enim cogitarent de vera expositione istius passus et aliorum multorum nisi Andream respicerent in hac parte. (The translation is Smalley's, *The Study of the Bible*, p. 175.)
44. Bacon, *Compendium*, p. 482: Quamvis igitur fuerat literatus homo, et probabiliter sciverit Hebraeum ...
45. Hadfield, *Andrew of St Victor*, p. 84; cf. p. 18.
46. Cf. Hadfield, ibid., p. 19. For example Andrew does this at the beginning of his comments on Isa. vii 14, after having made a Christological affirmation about the verse: Insurgentes in nos Iudei, veritatis inimici, cavillationis ariete firmissimum fidei nostre murum labefactare conantur. Hadfield, ibid., p. 142 (MS Pembroke Cambridge 45, fo. 15ª). Andrew thereafter pays close attention to the Jewish exegesis of the passage.
47. At Isa. vii 14 (see n. 46): Hanc de conceptione et nativitate nostri salvatoris et

integritate et virginitate matris eius semper virginis apertissimam prophetiam (ibid., fo. 15[a]); also at Isa. xi 2 (fo. 20[c–d]), on *spiritus Domini*: Secundum nos, qui ista de Domino exponimus, spiritus Domini, Spiritus Sanctus, tertia videlicet in Trinitate persona, accipitur. Secundum Hebreos vero, qui ista de eo quem adhuc expectant Messia exponunt, spiritus Domini speciale donum divinitus inspiratum accipi potest (Hadfield, p. 165); also at Isa. li 5 (ibid., fo. 70[b]) on *Prope est iustus meus*: vel Cyrum, vel secundum nos Dominum et Salvatorem nostrum, vel secundum Hebreos suum Messiam, intellige (Hadfield, p. 235).

48. Smalley, *The Study of the Bible*, p. 169: 'He [Andrew] has no idea of laying down new principles. He would shun such a thing; for Andrew, clear and intelligent about details, is a positive addle-pate about theories.'

49. Hadfield, *Andrew of St Victor*, p. 160. But Hadfield attributes too much deliberation and calculation to Andrew when she holds that he was 'someone who had trained himself in separating his scholarly activities from his duties as a churchman' (cf. pp. 161 n. 1, 215, 258, 263).

50. Smalley, *The Study of the Bible*, p. 376; MS Mazarine 175, fo. 93[a]: Nemo nos ea vanitate captos existimet ut vel novorum auctores librorum vel aliorum doctores haberi desideremus. Absit ut usque adeo desipuerimus quatinus nosmetipsos non metientes et ad que attingere non possumus extendentes propriarum metas virium excedamus, cum potius sit solide subsistere in se quam inaniter rapi supra se. Bene nobiscum nostrique similibus agitur si quos legimus et audimus totos in nos transfudimus. Smalley translates (p. 122): 'Let no one conclude us to be so besotted with vanity as to set ourselves up as an author or as a teacher. God forbid that we should be so foolish as to stretch out self-confidently for what we cannot reach, exceeding our measure. It is better to stay safely on one's own level than to rise vainly above it. Enough for us, and those like us, if we thoroughly take in what we are taught.'

51. See above, n. 22.

52. Hadfield, *Andrew of St Victor*, p. 112; also p. 267: Andrew would have argued 'that the Jews found the significance of the prophecies on the level of the literal interpretation, while for the Christians the spiritual sense disclosed their deepest meaning'.

53. Smalley, *The Study of the Bible*, p. 138. MS Pembroke 45, fo. 20[c].

54. MS Pembroke 45, fo. 20[c]–21[b] (cf. Hadfield, *Andrew of St Victor*, pp. 163–73. On xi 1 Andrew comments that the verse refers to deliverance from the immediate peril constituted by the Assyrian attack on Jerusalem, but that it awakens hope for the ten tribes in exile (the former Northern Kingdom). In the more distant future a reign of peace and prosperity, when enemies will be reconciled, is envisaged: quanta Domini misericordia super Israel et Iudam in eos, in unum a quatuor plagis terre convocandos et conciliandos, in diebus illius qui de Iesse nasciturus est futura, paucis explicat.

55. See above, n. 22; cf. Smalley, *The Study of the Bible*, pp. 123, 169.

56. Cf. Smalley, ibid., p. 156, 'Andrew's most interesting and original contributions to exegesis … are not ascribed to his *Hebraei* and seem to be of his own invention.'

57. Hadfield, *Andrew of St Victor*, p. 19.

58. Secundum Hebreos; Hebrei dicunt; Hebrei tradunt; Hebreus meus dicit; consuetudo Hebreorum.

59. Cf. Hadfield, p. 84 n. 1. Hadfield notices an example of Hebrew script and

translation copied from Hugh (*PL* 175, 1879, 72): Pro *doctrina et veritate* in Hebraeo habetur *urim* ורים *tumim* תמים .

60. Hadfield, ibid., pp. 69–71. MS Bibl. Nat. Lat. 356, fo. 65ᶜ.

61. *PL* 175, 71: Quidam hoc altare nec tectum desuper nec fundum deorsum habuisse dicunt, sed parietes tantum positos terra repleri. Secundum quod dicit (Hugh then cites Exod. xx 4).

62. ומזבח אדמה הוא מזבח הנחשת שהוא ממלאין חללו אדמה במקום חנייתן

63. Hadfield, *Andrew of St Victor*, pp. 79f.; MS Bibl. Nat. Lat. 356, fo. 51ᵈ–52ᵃ.

64. In Hebreo, ut aiunt, habet emisti.

65. Ibid., fo. 52ᵃ⁻ᵇ.

66. The near identity of the two word-strings, עם זו גאלת (verse 13) and עם זו קנית (verse 16) suggests that one verb can be substituted for the other.

67. See above, p. 51.

68. Hadfield, *Andrew of St Victor*, p. 78; MS Bibl. Nat. Lat. 356, fo. 44ᶜ.

69. Ibid., p. 185; MS Pembroke 45 Cambridge, fo. 22ᵈ.

70. אטום שפתים – noted by Hadfield.

71. ליבשה כדי יעברו בו גליות ישראל ממצרים.

72. Ibid., p. 81, fo. 56ᵇ.

73. Ibid., p. 133; MS Pembroke 45, fo. 4ᵈ. Cf. p. 106.

74. Ibid., p. 82; MS Bibl. Nat. Lat. 356, fo. 60ᶜ.

75. Ibid., pp. 249f.; MS Pembroke 45, fo. 71ᵇ⁻ᶜ.

76. *PL* 24, 524: Pro *sitienti*, Aquila interpretatus est, *invia*, ut virginitatis privilegium demonstraret, quod absque ullo humano semine de terra prius invia sit creatus.

77. See above, n. 76.

78. Smalley, *The Study of the Bible*, p. 168; MS Corpus Christi Cambridge 30, fo. 42ᵇ: In Hebreo et in translatione Origenis habet: *cuius revelatus est oculus*, que littera convenientiam habet cum circumstantia, cum nostra translatio qua utimur multum adversari eidem circumstantie inveniatur; sed in exponenda falsa littera laborare non modo est otiosi sed etiam furiosi. Cum cetera omnia in commendatione sui dicat quomodo in hoc solo se culparet? Preterea cum statim post dicat quod apertos habet oculos quomodo hic dicit se habere obscuratos cum hec tam contraria sint?

79. *Numeri*, ed. J. W. Wevers (Göttingen, 1982), p. 288. Otherwise the later Greek versions (οἱ λοιποί) have ἐμπεφραγμένοι οἱ ὀφθαλμοὶ αὐτοῦ at verse 4.

80. Thus Procopius Gazaeus, *Commentarii in Numeros PG* 87, (Paris, 1875), 868: ἐμπεφραγμένοι ὡς ἐν ὕπνῳ δηλονότι κεκλεισμένοι ὅπερ οὐκ αἰσθητήν, προφητικὴν δὲ σημαίνει τὴν ὅρασιν. Cf. F. Field, *Origenis Hexaplorum quae supersunt*, I (Oxford, 1875), p. 255 n. 3.

81. Smalley, *The Study of the Bible*, p. 162; MS Pembroke 45, fo. 7ᵇ: Potest etiam secundum Hebreos qui, pro *excelso*, *in quo* legunt (verbum enim Hebraicum equivoce et *excelsum* et *in quo* significat) sic legi: Vos qui in die ultionis Domini preliante contra nos rege Babylonis Nabugodonosor fiduciam in Pharaonem regem et brachium vestram carnalem i.e. Egyptum qui est homo non Deus posituri estis, quiescite ab illo, i.e. cessate frustra spem in illo ponere, quia in quo reputatus est ipse vel a Deo vel ab hominibus? Quasi diceret: nichil est et nullius momenti, etiam se ipsi adesse insufficiens. Baculus enim arundineus est Pharao omnibus in ipsum sperantibus.

82. Andrew observes that according to the Vulgate (*excelsus*) the verse aperta est de Christo prophetia. Jerome (*PL* 24, 55–58) comments on the absence of the verse

from the Septuagint (Non possum invenire rationem quare LXX tam perspicuam de Christo prophetiam in Graecum noluerint vertere), rejects the *in quo* rendering of במה and founds a Christological exegesis on *excelsus*: Moneo atque praecipio, ut quiescatis ab eo qui secundum carnem quidem homo est, et habet animam, et ita spirat, et naribus halitum trahit, ut nos homines spiramus et vivimus; sed secundum divinam majestatem *excelsus* et est, et reputatur, et creditur.

83. See above, pp. 46f.
84. Hadfield, *Andrew of St Victor*, p. 77; MS Bibl. Nat. Lat. 356, fo. 43ᶜ.
85. Ibid., p. 76, fo. 43ᵇ.
86. Ibid., p. 76.
87. Verbum Hebraicum pro quo nos in hoc loco et in Iosue *petram* habemus, *aciem* proprie significat. Andrew is wrong about Josh. v 2, where צור is rendered by the Vulgate as *cultros lapideos*.
88. Ibid., pp. 211f.; MS Pembroke 45, fo. 63ᵃ⁻ᵇ.
89. Ibid., pp. 133–7.
90. Ibid., p. 133; MS Pembroke 45, fo. 4ᵈ.
91. *PL* 24, 34.
92. Hadfield, *Andrew of St Victor*, p. 133.
93. Ibid., p. 135; MS Pembroke 45, fo. 5ᵃ.
94. *PL* 24, 35.
95. Hadfield, *Andrew of St Victor*, pp. 136f.; MS Pembroke 45, fo. 6ᵃ.
96. *BDB*, p. 554.
97. *PL* 24, 38f.
98. משקים שלכם מעורבים במים .
99. See Appendix 4 on Isa. i 31.
100. So Smalley, 'Andrew of St Victor, Abbot of Wigmore: a Twelfth-Century Hebraist'; and Hadfield, *Andrew of St Victor, a twelfth century Hebraist*.
101. Smalley, 'Andrew of St Victor', p. 361; *The Study of the Bible*, p. 185.
102. Hadfield, *Andrew of St Victor*, p. 126; MS Pembroke 45, fo. 4ᵇ: scilicet, *devoraturos*, verbum enim presentis pro verbo futuri temporis ex nimia certitudine posuit.
103. Ibid., p. 131; fo. 4ᶜ.
104. Frequenter tamen tam apud nos quam apud Hebreos huiusmodi superfluitates reperiri solent.
105. At Ps. cv 26 (אהרן אשר בחר בו), where אשר ... בו yields 'whom', the Vulgate has copied the Hebrew slavishly and included an unnecessary *ipsum*, while at Ps. cxxii 3 *in idipsum* is a similar copying of לה, but there are greater defects in this translation (*cuius participatio eius in idipsum*) which makes little sense of the Hebrew: כעיר שחברה לה יחדו 'like a city which is well put together'.
106. Hadfield, *Andrew of St Victor*, p. 250, fo. 71ᶜ: Suspiravimus et doluimus eum esse despectum et abiectissimum hominum. Quia suspiria desiderium elicit, *desideravimus* et pro *suspiravimus* non absurde legi potest.
107. Smalley, *The Study of the Bible*, p. 164.
108. Ibid., pp. 116f.
109. MS Pembroke 45, fo. 124ᵈ: Ab otiosis enim et in tempore otii et non a discurrentibus et perturbationis tempore sapientia discitur.
110. See W. McKane, *Proverbs: A New Approach* (London, 1970), pp. 407f.
111. Smalley, *The Study of the Bible*, p. 116; MS Corpus Christi Cambridge 30, fo. 106ᵃ: ... pudeat ergo religionem professos tot et tanta superflua querentes, immo a dispensatoribus suis extorquentes.

112. Ibid., p. 116.
113. Ibid., p. 117. G. Calandra, *De historica Andreae victorini expositione in Ecclesiasten* (Palermo, 1948), p. 12: Inquisitionem et investigationem de omnibus, *pessimam* appellat *occupationem*, quia multum in ea laboratur et parum proficitur. *Dedit Deus filiis hominum*. Divinitus data hominibus haec occupatio esse dicitur *ut occupentur in ea* (Vulgate, *occuparentur*) propter animam a Deo datam, cui insitum et naturale est inquirere et investigare de omnibus, ut quasi fugientem et latentem veritatem – latet enim omne verum – quibus potest pedibus, consequatur et comprehendat.
114. Smalley, *The Study of the Bible*, pp. 121 f., 375; MS Mazarine 175, fo. 93[a]: Tenetur quodammodo mentis acies et quasi quibusdam tenebris obducitur, ne fructiferas sapientie salutaris irrigationes in obscuris prophetarum verbis perspicere valeat ... Quando et per quos placuerit, his quoque nonnullam lucis portiunculam tenebris infundere cecutientesque cordis oculos, immissis intelligentie radiis, illustrare et in perspicacitatem revocare.
115. Ibid., pp. 124, 378; MS Mazarine 175, fo. 40[b]: Novit certe, novit vir eruditus ... quam alte subsederit, quam procul a mortalium oculis se in profundum demerserit, quam paucissimos admiserit, quanto labore ad eam penetratur, a quam paucis vel potius nullis ad eam pervenitur, quam difficiliter et minutatim eruitur. Sic se tamen obstitit et occultavit ut non penitus lateat. Sic a diligenter querentibus invenitur, ut item si diligenter quesita fuerit inveniatur. Nemini tota contingit; particulatim, et ut ita dictum sit, frustratim eruitur.
116. Ibid., pp. 140–3, 385–7; MS Pembroke 45, fo. 76[c]–77[b].
117. *PL* 24, 708 f.
118. MS Pembroke 45, fo. 77[a]: In puerilibus adhuc annis constitutum, Dominus ad prophetandum ferocissimis prophetam gentibus et in manibus populi missurus, fiduciam et securitatem, ex collatis iam misericorditer beneficiis, ut in tempus omne futurum, prestat.
119. Smalley, *The Study of the Bible*, p. 143.
120. Ibid., pp. 142, 387; MS Pembroke 45, fo. 77[b]: Et approbationis mee et dilectionis dignatione, etiam cum adhuc intra materni vulvam uteri detinereris, tantam tibi contuli sanctitatem ut et nascentium portam egresso nichil nisi sanctum et mundum placere potuisset.
121. With this should be compared Jerome's Christological exegesis of the verse and especially: Iste enim vere priusquam in utero virginali formaretur, et antequam exiret de vulva matris, sanctificatus in utero est (*PL* 24, 709).
122. Smalley, *The Study of the Bible*, p. 160; MS Laud Lat. 105, fo. 96[d]: Nos vero qui litteram exponere non distorquere vel destruere studemus, hanc litteram sic exponimus ... tolles VII masculos et tolles VII feminas.
123. Ibid., pp. 165, 391; Hadfield, *Andrew of St Victor*, pp. 252 f.; MS Pembroke 45, fo. 71[c]: Propheta se illis connumerat, qui populum in captivitatem iturum propter peccata sua captivandum et tanquam leprosum a populo Domini separandum, exigentibus peccatis suis, a Domino percutiendum et humiliandum fore putaverunt.
124. Smalley, *The Study of the Bible*, pp. 165, 392; MS Pembroke 45, fo. 71[d]: Hoc non potest nisi de illis dici qui voluntariam prophetarum consilio, unde ut Ieconias et qui cum eo Babyloniis se tradiderunt, transmigrationem subierunt.
125. Ibid., pp. 120 f.
126. Cf. Smalley, ibid., p. 131: 'The author of the Pentateuch and his purpose claim us

instantly.' Also, 'Andrew concentrates on Moses and his Jewish audience.' What
is involved in recovering the intention of an Old Testament author, so far as
Andrew is concerned, will be considered in a subsequent section of this chapter.

127. Ibid., p. 121; MS Bibl. Nat. Lat. 356, fo. 1^d: Nos quoque quid alii in hac operis
parte de angelis dicendum esse senserint, quid etiam ipsi nos, si quid inde
sentiamus, ex industria pretermisimus.

128. Ibid., p. 145.

129. Ibid., p. 150.

130. Ibid., p. 171.

131. Ibid., pp. 152 f.

132. Ibid., p. 171,

133. Ibid., p. 152.

134. Ibid., p. 153.

135. Ibid., p. 153.

136. Ibid., pp. 144,388 f., MS Bibl. Nat. Lat. 14432, fo. 38^a: Si quis contendere
voluerit apertos fuisse celos, ut per eos radius oculorum prophete directus Deum
et que in superioribus fiunt videret, nos nichil impedimus quin in suo sensu
habundaret; ipse tamen viderit an ratio rerumque natura fieri sinat quod asserere
contendit. Sin autem ad hoc confugerit ut dicat non per naturam sed per divinam
potentiam factum ut in terris homo positus ultra celos celorum aciem dirigat,
scientes Deo nichil esse impossibile, nichil resistimus. Verumtamen in scripturarum expositione cum secundum naturam res de qua agitur nullatenus fieri
potest tunc demum ad miracula confugienda noverit.

137. *De Genesi ad Litteram*, Book XII, chs. 23–4 (*PL* 34 (Paris, 1861), 473–5).

138. Smalley, *The Study of the Bible*, pp. 143, 388: Non divisione firmamenti, sed
fide credentis, cui revelata sunt secreta coelestia, 'Not by the division of
the firmament, but by the faith of the believer, to whom celestial secrets are
revealed.'

139. On the singular *visionem* Andrew comments: Huic sententie Hebraica veritas
consonare videtur (Smalley, ibid., p. 388; MS Bibl. Nat. Lat. 1443², fo. 38^a).
The Massoretic text has the plural (מראות אלהים) and there is no evidence
from Hebrew manuscripts to support מראה. It is, however, a Hexaplaric
reading: οἱ λοιποί ὄπτασιν ἤ ὄρασιν (*Ezekiel* (Göttingen 1952), ed. J. Ziegler,
p. 91).

140. Smalley, *The Study of the Bible*, pp. 144,388, fo. 38^a: Sensus est: quod visi
visionem, et intellexi quid vobis et his qui in terra remanserunt et urbi super-
venturum est, non a me sed a Deo est. Quibus verbis et suam non ingrati
humilitatem munus acceptum profitentis, et illos et iis que dicturus est tamquam
divinitus inspiratis adquiescere debere patenter aperit. Secundum hanc
sententiam apertio celorum quid aliud innuit nisi quod hoc celitus munus illi
collatum fuit?

141. Ibid., pp. 148,389; MS Pembroke 45, fo. 5^c: Nec fedior, sive in veste sive in
vase, quam rubea crurosis macula, que plus etiam ceteris apparere solet, inveniri
potest, nec pullutorum mundatio melius apparet quam si in candorem versa
fuerint, ad exprimendam peccati feditatem, coccinum et vermiculum, ad
significandam candorem, nivem et lanam ponit.

142. Ibid., pp. 148,389; MS Pembroke 45, fo. 5^d: Peccata coccino vermiculoque
in ruboremque sanguini assimilari voluit, quia illa ruborem intensius exprimunt.

143. Ibid., p. 148.

144. Hadfield, *Andrew of St Victor*, p. 63, fo. 51^b: Quem ideo spiritum Dei vocat, quia ab eo immissus erat et eius voluntatem explebat.
145. Ibid., p. 183; MS Pembroke 45, fo. 22^d.
146. Ibid., p. 183, fo. 22^d.
147. Ibid., p. 213, fo. 63^b: Hic inter cetera Iudeorum simplicitas, vel potius fatuitas sibi promittit, quando de cunctis locis in quibus dispersi sunt dispersos Israel Dominus congregabit, quod, sicut dictum est *vox clamantis* audietur, et valles implebuntur, et omnis mons et collis humiliabitur, et erunt prava in directa, et aspera in vias planas.
148. Ibid., p. 188.
149. Ibid., pp. 188f.
150. Ibid., p. 254; cf. p. 258; also p. 210, 'He (Andrew) illumines the words spoken by the prophet in their historical situation.'
151. Ibid., p. 192, 'According to Ibn Ezra it is impossible that even a divinely inspired prophet can anticipate the exact history of the days to come.'
152. M. Friedländer, *The Commentary of Ibn Ezra on Isaiah* (London), I (1873, English translation) and II (1877, Hebrew text); I–II in one vol. (New York, 1972). I am citing from the 1972 edition.
153. Ibid., I, p. 170; II, p. 64.
154. Cf. Hadfield, *Andrew of St Victor*, p. 191: 'According to Ibn Ezra, the prophecies concerning the return from Babylon are not real prophecies; they have an illustrative purpose and value only.'
155. Friedländer, *Commentary*, I, p. 170; II, p. 64.
156. See L. Jacobs, *Jewish Biblical Exegesis* (New York, 1973), pp. 20f.
157. Smalley, *The Study of the Bible*, pp. 136,379; MS Mazarine 175, fo. 40^{b-c}.
158. Hadfield, *Andrew of St Victor*, p. 234; MS Pembroke 45, fo. 70^a.
159. Ibid., pp. 234f.; fo. 70^a.
160. Ibid., pp. 243f.; fo. 71^{a-b}.
161. Smalley, *The Study of the Bible*, pp. 165,392; MS Pembroke 45, fo. 71^d: Quidam etiam Hebreorum totam hanc pericopam super Isaia interpretantur, 'But some of the Jews interpret the whole passage as referring to Isaiah.' Cf. Hadfield, *Andrew of St Victor*, p. 261.
162. Smalley, *The Study of the Bible*, p. 165.
163. Cf. Hadfield, *Andrew of St Victor*, 211–61.
164. Smalley, *The Study of the Bible*, pp. 165f.
165. Ibid., pp. 165,391; MS Pembroke 45, fo. 71^c: de populo agens tamquam de uno homine loquitur, quem vocat *virum dolorum*. Such a collective interpretation was known to Origen: 'I remember that once in a discussion with some whom the Jews regard as learned I used these prophecies [Isa. lii 13–liii 8]. At this the Jew said that these prophecies referred to the whole people as though of a single individual, since they were scattered in the dispersion and smitten, that as a result of the scattering of the Jews among the other nations many might become proselytes' (H. Chadwick, *Origen Contra Celsum* (Cambridge, 1965), p. 50). The Greek text is in *Origène Contra Celse*, Sources Chrétiennes 132, edited and translated by M. Borret, I (Paris, 1967), p. 224.
166. Smalley, *The Study of the Bible*, pp. 165,391: His verbis innuit propheta quod populus qui in captivitate Babylonica affligendus erat, non solum sua sed et maiorum luiturus erat peccata. Vere ille vir dolorum languores et dolores, quos ob nostra ferre debuimus peccata, portabit.

167. Hadfield, *Andrew of St Victor*, p. 167; MS Pembroke 45, fo. 20ᵈ–21ᵃ.
168. Ibid., p. 168, fo. 21ᵃ,22ᵃ.
169. Ibid., p. 169, fo. 21ᵃ⁻ᵇ.
170. Ibid., pp. 173 f., fo. 21ᵇ, 22ᵇ⁻ᶜ.
171. Ibid., p. 238, fo. 70ᵈ.
172. Ibid., p. 236, fo. 70ᵇ⁻ᶜ.
173. See above, pp. 66f.
174. Hadfield, *Andrew of St Victor*, pp. 193, 258, 267.
175. See above, pp. 67f.
176. Ibid., p. 170; MS Pembroke 45, fo. 22ᵃ⁻ᵇ.
177. Ibid., pp. 175 f., fo. 22ᶜ⁻ᵈ.
178. Ibid., pp. 161 n. 1, 171.
179. See above, pp. 48–50.
180. Cf. Smalley, *The Study of the Bible*, p. 171, 'Andrew learnt from St Augustine that each text had a literal meaning. He deduces, incorrectly but excusably, that the literal meaning of a text must necessarily be what the Jews say about it. If you want to know the literal sense, go to the Jews.' Also, 'For Andrew the "literal sense" is the Jewish explanation' (p. 163).
181. Ibid., p. 171.
182. Hadfield, *Andrew of St Victor*, p. 240, has some awareness of this when she remarks that Andrew may have excluded Christological exegesis from his definition of the 'literal sense'. 'In any case', she continues, 'he does not take such interpretations as being included in the original meaning of the prophet himself, as Langton will do after him.'
183. See above, pp. 45 f.
184. *PL* 24, 110.
185. *PL* 196, 608; *Becula* (*sic*) in Hebraeo idem sonat quod apud nos *virgo*. Sed in Hebraeo hoc loco non legitur *becula*, sed *alma*, quod interpretatur *juvencula*, vel *abscondita*. Moreover, Richard reproduces *verbatim* Jerome's comments on עלמה (604–6).
186. Cf. *BDB*, pp. 761 f. and KB³, pp. 789 f.: I עלם 'to conceal' and II עלם 'to be sexually mature'. These are homographs, because in Hebrew *ayin* has to serve for two phonemes which are distinguished in Arabic and Ugaritic.
187. Exod. ii 8 (νεᾶνις; *puella*); Ps. lxviii 26 (ἐν μέσῳ νεανίδων; *in medio iuvencularum*); Prov. xxx 19 (ἐν νεότητι; *in adolescentia*); Cant. i 3 (νεάνιδες; *adolescentulae*); Cant. vi 7 (νεάνιδες; *adolescentularum*).
188. Ps. ix 1 (ὑπὲρ τῶν κρυφίων; *pro occultis*) and xlv 1 (ὑπὲρ τῶν κρυφίων; *pro arcanis*). At 1 Chron. xv 20 the Septuagint transliterates (ἐπὶ ἀλαιμώθ), while the Vulgate has the translation *arcana*.
189. *PL* 24, 110–12.
190. Hadfield, *Andrew of St Victor*, pp. 142–5.
191. MS Pembroke 45, fo. 15ᵃ⁻ᵈ.
192. *PL* 24, 110: Sin autem juvencula vel puella, ut Judaei volunt, et non virgo pariat, quale signum poterit appellari, cum hoc nomen aetatis sit, non integritatis? Richard is also much occupied with this in his *De Immanuele*, *PL* 196, 615–34.
193. Hadfield, *Andrew of St Victor*, p. 143; MS Pembroke 45, fo. 15ᵃ: A quibus cum opponentes querimus quomodo future liberationis signum esse possit quod iunioris etatis femina vel abscondita et secreta concipiat et pariat, cum hoc frequentissime fieri videamus, respondent dicentes in hoc signum erat, quod

ea que nondum conceperat in prima ad eam viri accessione conceptura erat et masculum paritura, qui ab ipso populo vel matre Emmanuel nominaretur.

194. Ibid., pp. 157 f.: 'Others, according to him [Rashi], look for a sign in the fact that the woman was a virgin and was not able to have children.'

195. I. Epstein (ed.), *The Babylonian Talmud, Seder Ṭohoroth, Niddah*, translated into English with notes, glossary and indices by J. W. Slotki (London, 1948), p. 454. For the Hebrew text see M. Auerbach, *Mischnajot. Die sechs Ordnungen der Mischna*, Teil VI (Basel, 1968³), p. 550.

196. *Niddah*, 60a.

197. Hadfield, *Andrew of St Victor*, pp. 144 f.; MS Pembroke 45, fo. 15^d: Nos itaque nostris viribus emensis fortiora fortioribus liquentes, ceptam literalis sensus explanationem exequamur.

198. Ibid., fo. 15^d: On *Emmanuel* Andrew comments, Ideo tali nomine vel domo Iuda vel matre vocante puer nominabitur, quia Deum propitium et adiutorem sibi futurum intelligent, cum puerum quem sibi in signum se daturum promisit, iam natum perspexerint. Vel quia in diebus nativitatis eius iam illis Dominus benefacere ceperat.

199. Ibid., p. 234, fo. 70^a. On *Dominus dedit mihi linguam eruditam* Andrew remarks: Ad vos veniens Dominus, inquit propheta, nec viriliter agentes, nec sibi obedientes invenit. Me autem, cui ipse linguam tam eruditam dedit ut sciam etiam reum in causa defendere, et fortiter contra adversa agentem et sibi in omnibus obedientem ⟨invenit⟩.

200. *PL* 24, 496: Hoc illi dixerint, qui omni ratione conantur de Christo evertere prophetias, et ad perversam intelligentiam prava interpretatione torquere.

201. Hadfield, *Andrew of St Victor*, p. 234; MS Pembroke 45, fo. 70^a: On *Corpus meum dedi percutientibus* Andrew comments, Contumelias et illusiones quas hic enumerat forsitan in diebus Manasse, qui Ierusalem a porta usque ad portam prophetarum sanguine replevit, propter verbum Domini propheta sustinuit.

202. Salvatorem autem nostrum, excepta barbe et generum vulsione, quod tamen etsi scriptum non sit – neque enim omnia scripta sunt – forsitan pertulit, hec omnia pertulisse evangelio docente didiscimus.

203. See above, p. 54.

204. *PL* 24, 428: Quae nos super persona Christi et vocatione gentium et praedicatione Evangelii atque idolorum condemnatione interpretati sumus, quidam ad Cyrum regem Persarum referunt.

205. Hadfield, *Andrew of St Victor*, p. 216; MS Pembroke 45, fo. 64^c : *Dabit* et cetera futuri temporis verba que apud nos sunt potius Cyro convenire possunt.

206. Thus the defence which Hadfield constructs for Andrew (pp. 161 f.) does not effectively defend him: 'Andrew was not a great dialectical thinker who pondered deeply over the consequences of inserting in his commentaries Jewish explanations of texts normally regarded as referring to Christ. He realized that they presented a problem ... but he did not consider one explanation to be exclusive of the other. What he wanted to show was that the Jewish interpretation often seemed more in accordance with the letter of the text, and therefore more acceptable in a literal explanation of the Old Testament, without, in so doing, necessarily denying its references to Christ.'

207. See above, p. 49.

208. See above, pp. 49f.

3. *William Fulke and Gregory Martin*

1. C. W. Boase (ed.), *Register of the University of Oxford*, vol. I (1449–63; 1505–71). Printed for the Oxford Historical Society at the Clarendon Press (Oxford, 1885), p. 244.

2. *The New Testament of Iesus Christ, translated faithfully into English, out of the authentical Latin* (Rhemes, 1582).

3. *The Holie Bible faithfully translated into English, out of the authentical Latin* (Doway; I, 1609; II, 1610).

4. A. Wood (ed.), *Athenae Oxonienses*, a new edition with additions and a continuation by Philip Bliss (London, 1813), p. 487.

5. *Dictionarium quatuor linguarum, Hebraicae, Graecae, Latinae et Anglicae*. Given on p. 489 of *Athenae Oxonienses*, without further particulars. The item does not appear in the list of Martin's works in the *British Museum General Catalogue of Printed Books*, vol. 153 (London, 1962), 972–3.

6. *A Discoverie of the Manifold Corruptions of the Holy Scriptures by the Heretikes of our daies, specially the English Sectaries, and of their foule dealing herein, by partial and false translations to the advantage of their heresies, in their English Bibles used and authorised since the time of Schisme* (Rhemes, 1582), abbreviated as *A Discoverie*.

7. *Athenae Oxonienses*, p. 489 (with the spelling modernized).

8. *DNB* XX (London, 1889), pp. 305–8; C. H. and T. Cooper (eds.), *Athenae Cantabrigienses*, vol. II (Cambridge, 1861), pp. 57–61.

9. *DNB* IX (London, 1887), pp. 226–30.

10. J. Strype, *Annals of the Reformation and Establishment of Religion*, vol. I, part 2 (Oxford, 1824), p. 156; cf. J. Strype, *The Life and Acts of Matthew Parker*, vol. I (Oxford, 1821), p. 393.

11. *DNB* XLIII (London, 1895), p. 258; cf. Strype, *The Life and Acts of Matthew Parker*, vol. I, p. 313.

12. *DNB* XX, p. 305; cf. Strype, *Annals*, vol. I, part 2, p. 154.

13. *Athenae Cantabrigienses*, p. 57.

14. Ibid., p. 57.

15. *A Defense of the sincere and true Translations of the holie Scriptures into the English tong, against the manifolde cavils, frivolous quarels, and impudent slaunders of Gregorie Martin, one of the readers of Popish divinitie in the trayterous Seminarie of Rhemes* (London, 1583). The citations are from the Parker Society edition (Cambridge, 1843), abbreviated as *A Defence*.

16. G. Burnet, *The History of the Reformation of the Church of England*, revised by N. Pocock, vol. I (Oxford, 1865), p. 498.

17. *DNB* XX, p. 422.

18. Cf. the preface to the Rheims New Testament (1582 – unpaginated). One of the three heads set out on the first page is: Of the causes why this New Testament is translated according to the auncient vulgar Latin text.

19. *The Holie Bible*, preface, p. vii.

20. *A Defence*, pp. 589f.

21. Ibid., p. 66.

22. Ibid., p. 571.

23. I.e., the Rheims New Testament.

24. *A Defence*, p. 69 (*A Discoverie*, preface, para. 35, unpaginated).

25. For the details see the Parker Society edition of *A Defence*, p. vi. See also T. Hornberger (ed.), *A Goodely Gallerye. William Fulke's Book of Meteors (1563)*. Memoirs of the American Philosophical Society, 130 (Philadelphia, 1979).
26. *A Defence*, p. 78; cf. p. 100.
27. Ibid., p. 13.
28. Ibid., p. 117 (*A Discoverie*, p. 8); cf. the preface to *The Holie Bible*, pp. vii f.
29. *A Defence*, p. 75; cf. p. 58: 'You shall never be able to prove by any translation of ours (though perhaps in some we may err), that we have any purpose either to falsify the truth, or to change the text, though it were possible for us. In translating we have dealt with a good conscience, albeit not always peradventure we have attained to the full truth, which in translating out of one tongue into another is a very hard point throughly to observe.'
30. Ibid., p. 60.
31. G. Lloyd Jones, *The Discovery of Hebrew in Tudor England: A Third Language* (Manchester, 1983), p. 40.
32. *CHB* III, p. 92.
33. G. Lloyd Jones, *The Discovery of Hebrew*, pp. 43 f.
34. *A Defence*, p. 527 (*A Discoverie*, p. 275).
35. *Vulgata editio Veteris et Novi Testamenti, quorum alterum ad Hebraicam, alterum ad Graecam veritatem emendatum est quam diligentissime, ut nova editio non facile desideretur, et vetus tamen hic agnoscatur* (Venice, 1542, 1557, 1564).
36. *A Defence*, pp. 62 f.
37. See above, p. 39.
38. E. F. Sutcliffe, 'The Council of Trent on the "Authentica" of the Vulgate', *JTS* XLIX (1948), p. 36.
39. F. J. Crehan, 'The Bible in the Roman Catholic Church from Trent to the Present Day', *CHB* III, p. 204.
40. *Encyclopaedia Judaica*, 8 (Jerusalem, 1971), 17.
41. See the first page of the preface to the Rheims New Testament. The translation into English is made, 'upon special consideration of the present time, state, and condition of our countrie, unto which divers things are either necessarie, or profitable and medicinable now, that otherwise in the peace of the Church were neither much requisite, nor perchance wholly tolerable'. Similar views are expressed by Cardinal William Allen in a letter to Dr. Vendevile (T. J. Knox, *The First and Second Diaries of the English College Douay and an Appendix of Unpublished Documents* (London, 1878), pp. xl f.
42. *A Defence*, pp. 28–33.
43. Ibid., p. 33.
44. Ibid., p. 33.
45. Ibid., p. 20.
46. Ibid., pp. 24 f.
47. Ibid., p. 20.
48. Ibid., p. 222.
49. Ibid., pp. 237 f.
50. Ibid., p. 255.
51. Ibid., p. 255.
52. Ibid., pp. 266 f.
53. *De Doctr. Chr.* ii, 14; *PL* 34 (Paris, 1861), 45 f.
54. *A Defence*, pp. 9 f.

55. Ibid., p. 37.
56. Ibid., p. 77.
57. Ibid., p. 65.
58. Ibid., p. 10.
59. Ibid., p. 13.
60. Ibid., p. 13.
61. Ibid., p. 47. Cf. Jerome, above, p. 39.
62. Ibid., p. 78, 'We acknowledge the text of the Old Testament in Hebrew and Chaldee (for in the Chaldee tongue were some parts of it written), as it is now printed with vowels, to be the only fountain, out of which we must draw the pure truth of the scriptures for the Old Testament.'
63. Ibid., p. 25.
64. Ibid., p. 100.
65. Ibid., p. 146 (*A Discoverie*, p. 18).
66. Ibid., p. 147.
67. Ibid., p. 80 (*A Discoverie*, preface, para. 45).
68. See above, p. 14.
69. *De Doctr. Chr.* ii, 15 (*PL* 34, 46); *De Civ. Dei* xviii, 43; *PL* 41 (Paris, 1864), 603 f.
70. *A Defence*, p. 53, 'But this doth St Jerome utterly deny, and derideth the ground of this imagination, those seventy-two cells at Alexandria, as a fable and a lie.' *Praef. in Pent.*, *PL* 28 (Paris, 1865), 181–4.
71. *A Defence*, p. 521; cf. p. 373, 'Although it were no hard thing to prove that the Greek text of the Psalms, which now we have, is none of the Seventy translation, as even Lindanus might teach you.'
72. Ibid., p. 521.
73. Ibid., p. 80 (*A Discoverie*, preface, para. 45).
74. Ibid., p. 25.
75. Ibid., p. 72 (*A Discoverie*, preface, para. 37).
76. Ibid., pp. 311 f. (*A Discoverie*, pp. 119 f.).
77. Ibid., p. 312.
78. A. Montanus, *Royal Antwerp Polyglot*, p. 26; cf. *A Defence*, pp. 55 f., 78.
79. *A Defence*, p. 11 (*A Discoverie*, preface, para. 4).
80. Ibid., p. 41, 'Thus you see, how the mouse of Geneva (as I told you before of Marcion the mouse of Pontus) nibbleth and gnaweth about it, though he cannot bite it off altogether' (*A Discoverie*, preface, para. 16).
81. Ibid., p. 41.
82. Ibid., p. 42 (*A Discoverie*, preface, para. 17).
83. Ibid., pp. 42 f.
84. Ibid., p. 43.
85. Ibid., p. 43.
86. Agreeing with B. Metzger, *A Textual Commentary on the Greek New Testament*, (London/New York, 1971), p. 73: the phrase 'in Isaiah the prophet' is found in 'the earliest representative witnesses of the Alexandrian, the Western and the Caesarean types of text'.
87. Lloyd Jones, *The Discovery of Hebrew*, pp. 151–6.
88. *A Defence*, p. 37.
89. Ibid., p. 312.
90. Ibid., p. 573.
91. Ibid., p. 313.

92. Ibid., p. 575. See the quotation on p. 103.
93. Ibid., p. 45 (*A Discoverie*, preface, para. 119).
94. Ibid., p. 46.
95. Ibid., p. 79.
96. The second Rabbinic Bible of Jacob ben Chayyim, printed by Daniel Bomberg at Venice in 1524/25; cf. E. Würthwein, *Der Text des Alten Testaments*, 4th edn (Stuttgart, 1973), translated by E. F. Rhodes, *The Text of the Old Testament: an Introduction to Biblia Hebraica* (London, 1980), p. 37.
97. היך כאיה נכתין is explained by Fulke as a conflate text: נכתין for כארו and היך כאריה for כארי. He is aware of a different text in the Antwerp Polyglot where כארו is represented by נכתין (*A Defence*, p. 80). It is not obvious that נכתין 'wound' is a rendering of כארו 'dug'. It may be a periphrastic addition whose aim is to make sense in combination with the otherwise unintelligible כארי .
98. *Fixerunt*, PL, 28 (Paris, 1865), 1204.
99. *A Defence*, p. 318 (*A Discoverie*, p. 125).
100. Ibid., p. 129; cf. p. 158, and especially Martin's irony (p. 83), 'But for "hell" we will say "grave" in all such places of scripture as might infer *limbus patrum*, if we should translate "hell"' (*A Discoverie*, preface, para. 47).
101. Ibid., p. 319.
102. Ibid., p. 301.
103. Ibid., p. 300.
104. Ibid., p. 299 (*A Discoverie*, p. 112).
105. See PL 34 (Paris, 1861), 730, on Num. xvi 32, 33; and PL 37 (Paris, 1865), 1093–95, on Ps. lxxxvi 13 (Vulgate, lxxxv 13).
106. *A Defence*, p. 307.
107. W. McKane, *Proverbs: A New Approach* (London, 1970), pp. 479 ff.
108. *A Defence*, p. 301.
109. Coverdale (1535); Geneva (1560); Bishops' Bible (1572); KJV (1611).
110. See above, p. 80ff.
111. See above, n. 69.
112. See above, n. 70.
113. *A Defence*, p. 53.
114. *Hexam.* iii, 5; PL 14 (Paris, 1845), 164: Multa enim non otiose a Septuaginta viris Hebraicae lectioni addita et adjuncta comperimus.
115. *A Defence*, p. 53. But Ambrose is almost certainly affirming the prophetic freedom of the Seventy to make additions to the Hebrew text which they were translating. Cf. Augustine, above, p. 40.
116. Ibid., p. 69; cf. pp. 46 f. (*A Discoverie*, preface, paras. 65, 20).
117. *De Doctr. Chr.* ii, 11, 12 (*PL* 34, 42–44).
118. *A Defence*, pp. 47 f.
119. Ibid., p. 48; *De Doctr. Chr.* ii, 11 (*PL* 34, 42): Et Latinae quidem linguae homines, quos nunc instruendos suscepimus, duabus aliis ad Scripturarum divinarum cognitionem opus habent, Hebraea scilicet et Graeca; ut ad exemplaria praecedentia recurratur, si quam dubitationem attulerit Latinorum interpretum infinita varietas.
120. *A Defence*, p. 70.
121. Ibid. p. 70.
122. Ibid., p. 70.

123. Ibid., pp. 147 f.; cf. *The Holie Bible*, preface, p. viii; cf. *A Discoverie*, pp. 18 f.
124. *A Defence*, p. 148.
125. *Ad Evang.*, *PL* 22 (Paris, 1877), 680 (with *Abram* for *Abraham* and *ejus* for *ipsius*[2]).
126. *A Defence*, p. 148.
127. *Ep.* lxiii, *Et Melchisedech, rex Salem, protulit panem et vinum*. Fuit autem, sacerdos Dei summi, et benedixit Abraham. *PL* 4 (Paris, 1844), 376.
128. *De Mysteriis* viii, 45: tunc illi occurrit Melchisedech et protulit ea quae Abraham veneratus accepit. Non Abraham protulit, sed Melchisedech. *PL* 16 (Paris, 1882), 404.
129. *Enarr. in Ps.*, Ps. xxxiii: Et tantus erat Melchisedec, a quo benediceretur Abraham. Protulit panem et vinum, et benedixit Abraham, et dedit ei decimas Abraham. *PL* 36 (Paris, 1865), 303.
130. *A Defence*, p. 68.
131. Ibid., p. 74 (*A Discoverie*, preface, para. 39).
132. Ibid., p. 75.
133. Ibid., p. 95 (*A Discoverie*, p. 2).
134. Ibid., p. 97.
135. Ibid., p. 98. Another view is that the reference is to the Great Bible (1539). See J. F. Mozley, *Coverdale and his Bibles* (London, 1953), pp. 112–15; F. F. Bruce, *The English Bible. A History of Translations* (London, 1961), p. 56 n. 1.
136. *A Defence*, p. 48: *De Doctr. Chr.* ii, 11–12, Quae quidem res plus adjuvit intelligentiam, quam impedivit, si modo legentes non sint negligentes. Nam nonnullas obscuriores sententias plurium codicum saepe manifestavit inspectio (*PL* 34, 43).
137. *A Defence*, p. 60; see above, pp. 82ff.
138. See above, pp. 78–80.
139. Cf. M. F. Wiles, 'Origen as Biblical Scholar', *CHB* I (Cambridge, 1970), p. 472.
140. *A Defence*, p. 571 (*A Discoverie*, pp. 306 f.).
141. Ibid., p. 571 (*A Discoverie*, p. 307).
142. Ibid., p. 572.
143. Ibid., p. 573.
144. Ibid., p. 471 (*A Discoverie*, p. 230).
145. כי שפתי כהן ישמרו דעת ותורה יבקשו מפיהו
146. Ibid., p. 481.
147. Cf. Fulke, ibid., pp. 482 f.
148. See above, p. 82.
149. *A Defence*, p. 97.
150. Ibid., p. 100 (*A Discoverie*, p. 3).
151. Ibid., pp. 179 f. (*A Discoverie*, p. 33).
152. Ibid., p. 180.
153. Ibid., p. 207 (*A Discoverie*, p. 52).
154. Wiles, 'Origen', *CHB* I, p. 503.
155. *A Defence*, p. 9 (*A Discoverie*, preface, para. 3).
156. Ibid., pp. 313, 573.
157. Ibid., p. 313.
158. Ibid., p. 575.
159. See above, pp. 71–75.
160. See above, p. 94.
161. KB[3], p. 473.

162. *A Defence*, p. 78, 'an evident prophecy of Christ's nailing to the cross' (*A Discoverie*, preface, para. 44).
163. Ibid., p. 74.
164. Ibid., pp. 81–4, 158, 280f. (*A Discoverie*, preface, para. 47; pp. 22f., 101).
165. See above, p. 100.
166. Ibid., p. 524 (*A Discoverie*, p. 273).
167. Ibid. pp. 523f.
168. Ibid., p. 525.
169. Ibid., p. 522 (*A Discoverie*, p. 271).
170. I have not succeeded in tracking down this reference to Jerome.
171. *De Civ. Dei*, xvii, 20 (*PL* 41, 555).
172. *Ep.* lxiii. *PL* 4 (Paris, 1844), 377f.
173. *A Defence*, p. 522.
174. Ibid., pp. 524f.
175. Ibid., p. 43 (*A Discoverie*, preface, para. 18).
176. Ibid., pp. 77f. (*A Discoverie*, preface, para. 43).
177. Ibid., p. 43.
178. Cf. Metzger, *A Textual Commentary*, pp. 66f.
179. *A Defence*, p. 50.
180. Ibid., p. 50.
181. Ibid., p. 50 (*A Discoverie*, preface, para. 21).
182. *De Civ. Dei* xviii, 43 (*PL* 41, 604): Quidquid est in Hebraeis codicibus, et non est apud interpretes Septuaginta, noluit ea per istos, sed per illos prophetas Dei Spiritus dicere. Quidquid vero est apud Septuaginta, in Hebraeis autem codicibus non est, per istos ea maluit, quam per illos, idem Spiritus dicere, sic ostendens utrosque fuisse prophetas.
183. *A Defence*, p. 51. See above, p. 40.
184. Ibid., pp. 49f.
185. Cf. *BDB*, p. 950.
186. *A Defence*, p. 45.
187. Ibid., p. 45.
188. Ibid., p. 46.
189. Ibid., pp. 81f.
190. Ibid., p. 81 (*A Discoverie*, preface, para. 46).
191. Ibid., p. 83 (*A Discoverie*, preface, para. 47).
192. Ibid., p. 83.
193. Ibid., p. 82.
194. Ibid., p. 281.
195. Ibid., p. 280.
196. H. G. Liddell and R. Scott, *A Greek-English Lexicon*, 9th edn (Oxford, 1940), 2026.
197. For a more complicated example see Appendix 5.

4 Richard Simon

1. It already extended to Hebrew, Syriac and Arabic by the end of his novitiate. See A. Bernus, *Richard Simon et son Histoire Critique du Vieux Testament. La Critique Biblique au Siècle de Louis XIV* (Lausanne, 1869), p. 17.
2. P. Auvray, *Richard Simon 1638–1712. Étude bio-bibliographique avec des textes inédits* (Paris, 1974), pp. 22–7.

3. Cf. Bernus, *Richard Simon et son Histoire Critique*, p. 10.

4. Auvray, *Richard Simon*, p. 140.

5. J. Steinmann, *Richard Simon et les origines de l'Exégèse Biblique* (Paris, 1960), p. 327.

6. *Le Nouveau Testament de nôtre Seigneur Jésus-Christ traduit sur l'ancienne édition latine, avec des remarques litérales et critiques sur les principales difficultez*, I (Trévoux, 1702), preface (unpaginated): the words quoted appear on the fourth page of the preface.

7. So Auvray, *Richard Simon*, p. 79.

8. Cf. Auvray, ibid., p. 85.

9. Cf. Auvray, ibid., p. 183.

10. *Religio Laici*, 252–69, in J. Kinsley, *The Poems of John Dryden*, vol. I (Oxford, 1958), pp. 317f.; cf. *CHB* III, p. 195.

11. Simon, Richard, *Histoire Critique Du Vieux Testament* (Rotterdam, 1685), abbreviated as *HCVT*, p. 8.

12. *HCVT*, p. 1.

13. *HCVT*, p. 8, cf. pp. 13f.

14. *HCVT*, pp. 15ff.; cf. *CHB* III, p. 194; Auvray, *Richard Simon*, p. 173.

15. *HCVT*, p. 45.

16. Cf. L. Jacobs, *Jewish Biblical Exegesis* (New York, 1973), pp. 20f.

17. Steinmann, *Richard Simon*, pp. 100f.

18. *HCVT*, pp. 15ff.

19. Cf. W. McKane, *Studies in the Patriarchal Narratives* (Edinburgh, 1979), pp. 17–66.

20. *HCVT*, pp. 30f.

21. *HCVT*, p. 21.

22. *HCVT*, p. 19: 1. The Book of the History of Solomon (1 Kgs xi 41) 2. The Book of the History of the Kings of Israel (1 Kgs xiv 19 and elsewhere). 3. The Book of the History of the Kings of Judah (2 Kgs xxiv 5 and elsewhere).

23. *HCVT*, pp. 2–6.

24. *HCVT*, pp. 30f.

25. *HCVT*, p. 92.

26. *HCVT*, p. 117.

27. *HCVT*, p. 117.

28. *HCVT*, pp. 94f.

29. For example, שלהבת for להבת at Ezek. xxi 3; Job xv 30; Cant. viii 6; זרענים at Dan. i 16; מלכין at Prov. xxxi 3 and מלין at Job iv 2.

30. *HCVT*, pp. 170f.

31. *HCVT*, pp. 15ff.

32. Auvray, *Richard Simon*, p. 175 n. 2.

33. *HCVT*, p. 1.

34. See above, pp. 94, 103.

35. *HCVT*, pp. 225f.

36. *HCVT*, p. 102.

37. *HCVT*, p. 103.

38. *C. Tryphon*, 43, 84, *PG* 6, 569f.; 67, 11, *PG* 6, 629f.

39. *HCVT*, pp. 104f.

40. *HCVT*, p. 104.

41. *HCVT*, p. 106.

42. *HCVT*, p. 106.

43. *Contra Celsum*, i, 34–35, *PG* 11, 726f.

44. *Epist. ad Afric.*, 55–62, *PG* 11, 60f.

45. *Quaest. in Gen.*, *PL* 23, 986.
46. See, however, above, p. 29.
47. *Quia interdum coguntur loqui, non quod sentiunt, sed quod necesse est dicunt.* According to Simon this comes from *Apol. adv. Ruf.*, but I have not succeeded in finding it.
48. *HCVT*, pp. 108 f.
49. See note 47.
50. *HCVT*, p. 109.
51. *HCVT*, p. 109.
52. J. Morin, *Exercitationes Biblicae*, pars prior, (Paris, 1633), p. 48.
53. *HCVT*, p. 109.
54. *Apol.* ii 24, *PL* 23, 468. *Tam stultus eram, ut quod in pueritia didici, senex oblivisci vellem?*
55. *De Doctr. Chr.*, ii, 15, *PL* 34, 46. See above, p. 40; p. 229 n. 115.
56. *HCVT*, p. 109.
57. *HCVT*, p. 109, cf. p. 353.
58. See above, pp. 93 f.
59. See above, p. 92.
60. *HCVT*, p. 111, cf. pp. 183, 194.
61. *HCVT*, p. 203.
62. *HCVT*, p. 111.
63. *HCVT*, p. 128.
64. Agreeing with GK 145n and L. H. Brockington, *The Hebrew Text of the Old Testament. The Readings adopted by the Translators of the New English Bible* (Oxford and Cambridge, 1973), p. 75.
65. *HCVT*, p. 129.
66. *HCVT*, p. 141.
67. *PL* 24, 171.
68. *HCVT*, pp. 142, cf. pp. 353 f.
69. *HCVT*, pp. 141 f.
70. *HCVT*, p. 142.
71. *HCVT*, p. 146.
72. L. Cappell, *Arcanum punctationis revelatum* (Leiden, 1624).
73. *HCVT*, pp. 146 f.; p. 203.
74. *HCVT*, pp. 149–53.
75. *HCVT*, pp. 147 f.
76. *HCVT*, p. 65.
77. J. Morin, *Exercitationes ecclesiasticae in utrumque Samaritanorum Pentateuchum* (Paris, 1631), pp. 309–14.
78. *HCVT*, p. 230, cf. p. 418.
79. *HCVT*, pp. 67–70.
80. See below, p. 170.
81. *HCVT*, pp. 67 f.
82. *HCVT*, pp. 71 f.
83. *PL* 23, 934.
84. *HCVT*, p. 72.
85. *HCVT*, p. 72.
86. Cf. the Septuagint οἱ δύο and the Peshiṭta *tryhwn*. NEB reads the Massoretic text but translates, 'and the two become one flesh'.
87. *HCVT*, pp. 74 f.
88. *HCVT*, p. 73.

89. *HCVT*, p. 70.
90. *HCVT*, p. 92.
91. Cf. Richard Simon, *Critical Enquiries into Various Editions of the Bible* (London, 1684), pp. 194f. Abbreviated as *CE*.
92. *HCVT*, pp. 95f.
93. KJV 'desolation'; NEB חָרָב 'bustard' (Brockington, *Hebrew Text*, p. 263).
94. *HCVT*, p. 96.
95. *HCVT*, pp. 167 – 76.
96. *HCVT*, p. 203.
97. *HCVT*, pp. 210f.
98. *HCVT*, p. 201.
99. Cf. *HCVT*, pp. 180ff.
100. *HCVT*, p. 222.
101. *HCVT*, p. 191.
102. *HCVT*, p. 232.
103. See above, pp. 26f.
104. Published at Alcala, 1521 – 2.
105. *HCVT*, p. 193; cf. *CHB* III, pp. 56f.
106. *HCVT*, p. 186.
107. *HCVT*, p. 196.
108. *HCVT*, p. 186.
109. *HCVT*, pp. 187f.
110. *HCVT*, p. 190.
111. *HCVT*, pp. 186f., 246.
112. *HCVT*, p. 194.
113. *HCVT*, p. 203.
114. *HCVT*, p. 182.
115. J. Cardinal Mercati, *Psalterii Hexapli Reliquiae* (Rome, 1958).
116. *HCVT*, pp. 293f.
117. *HCVT*, p. 235. See above, p. 38.
118. *HCVT*, pp. 106, 194, 195.
119. See above, pp. 27 – 29.
120. *HCVT*, p. 196.
121. In the preface to his translation of the Psalms from Hebrew, dedicated to Sophronius, *PL* 28, 1183 – 88.
122. See above, p. 29.
123. *HCVT*, pp. 193f.; *CE*, pp. 176f.
124. Ep. 106, 2 *Ad Sunniam et Fretelam*, *PL* 22, 838f.
125. *HCVT*, pp. 238f. Cf. Barthélemy, above, p. 25.
126. Ep. 112, 19, *PL* 22, 928. Jerome says no more than that what is marked by asterisks has been added from Theodotion.
127. *HCVT*, p. 199.
128. *HCVT*, p. 198.
129. *HCVT*, p. 198; cf. p. 195.
130. *HCVT*, pp. 238f.
131. *HCVT*, p. 198. Agreeing with Jerome, above, p. 34.
132. *HCVT*, p. 199.
133. P. E. Kahle, 'The Greek Bible Manuscripts used by Origen', *JBL* 79 (1960), p. 116.

134. See Appendix 1, pp. 195f.
135. *HCVT*, pp. 214–30.
136. *HCVT*, pp. 213, 228.
137. *HCVT*, p. 214.
138. *HCVT*, p. 220.
139. Brockington, *Hebrew Text*, p. 8.
140. *HCVT*, p. 218.
141. J. Barr, *Comparative Philology and the Text of the Old Testament* (Oxford, 1968), pp. 57, 270, 330; cf. J. A. Emerton, 'Some Difficult Words in Genesis 49', *Words and Meanings*, D. Winton Thomas Festschrift, ed. P. R. Ackroyd and B. Lindars (Cambridge, 1968), pp. 81–3.
142. *HCVT*, p. 224.
143. See Brockington, *Hebrew Text*, p. 125: גָּל = גְּלָל.
144. *HCVT*, p. 226.
145. Brockington, *Hebrew Text*, p. 125, לבבם.
146. *HCVT*, p. 227.
147. Brockington, *Hebrew Text*, p. 125, ונפשי לו חיה.
148. *HCVT*, pp. 216f.
149. 'Planks treated with bitumen', *PL* 23, 998.
150. *HCVT*, pp. 252f.
151. *HCVT*, p. 222.
152. *HCVT*, p. 218.
153. *HCVT*, pp. 223f.
154. *HCVT*, p. 216.
155. BDB, p. 192.
156. *HCVT*, p. 216.
157. *PL* 23, 996f.
158. Cf. A. E. Speiser, 'YDWN, Gen. 6.3', *JBL* 75 (1956), pp. 126–9. Speiser proposes a derivation of יְדֹן (יִדּוֹן = יְדֹן) from דנן, Accadian *danānu* 'to shield', 'to protect'. He suggests tentatively that נדן may be a variant root on the basis of Hebrew נָדָן (1 Chron. xxi 27) and Biblical Aramaic נְדַן (Da. vii 15), 'sheath'.
159. *HCVT*, p. 218.
160. *HCVT*, p. 224.
161. *PL* 28, 1203.
162. *HCVT*, pp. 246f.
163. *Apol.* ii, 33–36, *PL* 21, 612–15; cf. Jerome, *Apol.* i, 13, *PL* 23, 425f. See above, pp. 36, 38.
164. *HCVT*, p. 191.
165. *HCVT*, p. 246.
166. *HCVT*, p. 247.
167. *Apol.* i, 13, *PL* 23, 425f.; ii, 34, *PL* 23, 476f.
168. *HCVT*, p. 245.
169. *HCVT*, p. 248.
170. *HCVT*, p. 259.
171. *HCVT*, pp. 259f.
172. *HCVT*, p. 245.
173. See above, pp. 125–33.
174. *HCVT*, p. 250.
175. *PL* 23, 988f.

176. *HCVT*, pp. 258 f.
177. *HCVT*, p. 256.
178. *PL* 23, 1026.
179. *HCVT*, p. 259.
180. The phonemes should be רצות and רציון in Hebrew (cf. Hebrew רצון with biblical Aramaic רעו at Ezra v 17 and vii 18).
181. Cf. *BDB* (p. 946) and KB^2 (p. 900).
182. *HCVT*, p. 250.
183. *HCVT*, p. 252.
184. *HCVT*, p. 255.
185. *PL* 23, 992 f.
186. *HCVT*, p. 255.
187. J. W. Wevers (ed.), *Genesis* (Göttingen, 1974), p. 170.
188. *HCVT*, p. 255.
189. *HCVT*, pp. 256 f.
190. *HCVT*, pp. 250 f.
191. *HCVT*, p. 255.
192. See above, p. 135.
193. *HCVT*, p. 252.
194. *PL* 23, 989.
195. *HCVT*, pp. 249 f.
196. *HCVT*, p. 255.
197. Cf. the Old Latin: *Egressus est Lot et locutus est ad generos suos qui acceperant filias ejus.*
198. *PL* 23, 1016.
199. *HCVT*, p. 257.
200. *PL* 23, 993.
201. *HCVT*, p. 251.
202. *HCVT*, p. 358.
203. *HCVT*, p. 259.
204. *HCVT*, p. 258.
205. *HCVT*, p. 259.
206. *HCVT*, p. 394.
207. *HCVT*, p. 415.
208. *HCVT*, p. 417.
209. *HCVT*, p. 436.
210. *HCVT*, p. 435.
211. *HCVT*, p. 439.
212. *HCVT*, p. 439.
213. G. Lloyd Jones, *The Discovery of Hebrew in Tudor England: A Third Language* (Manchester, 1983), p. 203.
214. *HCVT*, p. 443.
215. See *Biographie Nationale de Belgique*, VI (Brussels, 1878), pp. 66 – 8.
216. *HCVT*, p. 440.
217. *CHB* III, pp. 77, 178.
218. *HCVT*, pp. 443 f.
219. *HCVT*, p. 444.
220. Cf. *CHB* III, p. 92.
221. *HCVT*, p. 444.
222. See 'Edward Lively: Cambridge Hebraist', Essays and Studies Presented to

Stanley Arthur Cook, ed. D. Winton Thomas, Cambridge Oriental Series No. 2 (London, 1950), pp. 95–112. *DNB* 33 (1893), pp. 378f. Lively was appointed Regius Professor of Hebrew at Cambridge in 1575 and was one of the fifty-four learned men appointed by King James in 1604 to make the 'authorised' version of the Bible. The work to which Simon refers is *Annotationes in quinq. priores ex Minoribus Prophetis eum Latina interpretatione ... ad normam Hebraicae veritatis diligenter examinata* (London, 1587).

223. *HCVT*, p. 445.
224. *HCVT*, p. 380.
225. B. Walton, *Biblia Sacra Polyglotta* (London, 1657), Prolegomenon I, 3–5.
226. *HCVT*, p. 483.
227. *HCVT*, p. 484.
228. *HCVT*, p. 487.
229. *HCVT*, pp. 360f.
230. *CHB* III, pp. 71f., 120.
231. *HCVT*, pp. 185f., 361.
232. See above, p. 83.
233. *HCVT*, p. 185.
234. See above, p. 83.
235. *HCVT*, p. 185.
236. *CHB* III, p. 71; Jones, *Discovery of Hebrew*, pp. 48–52.
237. *HCVT*, pp. 185f.
238. *HCVT*, p. 361.
239. See above, p. 134.
240. *HCVT*, p. 407.
241. *HCVT*, p. 363.
242. *HCVT*, p. 363.
243. *HCVT*, p. 352.
244. Cf. his criticism of Protestant vernacular versions of the Bible; *HCVT*, p. 184.
245. *HCVT*, pp. 352–6.
246. *HCVT*, pp. 357, 370f.
247. E. Ullendorff, 'Is Biblical Hebrew a Language?', *BSOAS* 34 (1971), p. 243.
248. Ibid., p. 252.
249. Abraham Ibn Ezra, David Kimchi and Elias Levita. For the last mentioned see *CHB* III, pp. 45f. and Jones, *Discovery of Hebrew*, pp. 254f.
250. *HCVT*, pp. 440f.
251. *HCVT*, pp. 373–5.
252. Jacobs, *Jewish Biblical Exegesis*, p. 11.
253. Ibid., p. 18.
254. *HCVT*, p. 357.
255. *HCVT*, pp. 358, 389, 427f., 434f.
256. *CHB* III, p. 239.
257. *HCVT*, p. 454.
258. Cf. *HCVT*, pp. 448–54.
259. *HCVT*, p. 386.
260. *HCVT*, p. 429.
261. *HCVT*, p. 386.
262. *HCVT*, p. 376.
263. *HCVT*, pp. 218f.

264. *HCVT*, pp. 225 f.
265. *HCVT*, p. 98.
266. Cf. Emerton, 'Difficult Words in Genesis 49', pp. 83 f.
267. *HCVT*, pp. 390 f.
268. *HCVT*, p. 225.
269. See above, p. 94.
270. See above, pp. 71–73.
271. *HCVT*, p. 103.
272. *HCVT*, pp. 250 f.
273. See above, pp. 103 f.
274. *Religio Laici*, 305–10, in Kinsley, *Poems of John Dryden*, p. 319; cf. *CHB* III, p. 197.
275. See above, pp. 144f.
276. *HCVT*, p. 386.
277. *HCVT*, p. 493.
278. See above, p. 113.
279. *HCVT*, p. 492.
280. *HCVT*, p. 453.
281. *HCVT*, p. 386.
282. *HCVT*, p. 389.
283. *HCVT*, p. 400.
284. *HCVT*, p. 392.
285. *HCVT*, pp. 404 f.
286. *HCVT*, p. 407.
287. *HCVT*, p. 405.
288. *HCVT*, p. 405.
289. *HCVT*, p. 405.
290. Cf. *CHB* III, pp. 91 f.
291. *HCVT*, p. 419.
292. This is said to come from *Praef. in Pentat.* I have not had access to it, but Cardinal Thomas De Vio (Cajetan) commented on the Pentateuch which was the first volume of his *Opera omnia quotquot in Sacrae Scripturae expositionem reperiuntur* (Lyon, 1639).
293. *HCVT*, p. 420.
294. Cf. *CHB* III, p. 239.
295. *HCVT*, pp. 361 f.
296. Cf. Auvray, *Richard Simon*, pp. 93–100; Steinmann, *Richard Simon*, pp. 91–6.
297. *HCVT*, p. 420.

5 *Alexander Geddes*

1. *Dr Geddes's General Answer to the Queries, Counsils and Criticisms that have been communicated to him since the publication of his Proposals for printing a New Translation of the Bible* (London, 1790), p. 2.
2. *P*, pp. 120 f. See below, p. 251, for the key to the abbreviations of Geddes's works.
3. R. C. Fuller, *Alexander Geddes, 1737–1802: Pioneer of Biblical Criticism*, Historic Texts and Interpreters in Biblical Scholarship, 3, ed. J. W. Rogerson (Sheffield, 1984), p. 159.
4. Ibid., p. 24.
5. Ibid., p. 23.

6. *DNB*, XXI (London, 1890), p. 98.
7. Ibid., p. 98.
8. Fuller, *Alexander Geddes*, p. 25.
9. *Select Satires of Horace* (London, 1779).
10. *DNB* XXI, p. 99.
11. *A New Translation of the Book of Psalms from the Original Hebrew, with various readings and notes* (London, 1807), preface, p. 3. Geddes's work consists of Ps. i – cxviii 11 and cl.
12. Ibid., p. 7.
13. *P*, p. 110.
14. *DNB*, XXI, p. 99.
15. *P*, p. 111.
16. *DNB*, XXII (1890), p. 228.
17. *P*, p. 95.
18. *L*, pp. 2, 41, 76 f.
19. *P*, p. 110.
20. *P*, p. 107.
21. *P*, p. 144.
22. *Psalms*, preface, p. 8.
23. *DNB*, XV (1888), pp. 98 – 100.
24. *DNB* VIII (1836), pp. 45 – 7. For the historical context of the conflict between 'the episcopal party' and 'the Cisalpines' in which Geddes has to be placed, see E. Duffy, 'Ecclesiastical Democracy Detected', *Recusant History* 10 (1969 – 70), pp. 193 – 209; 309 – 31; 13 (1975 – 6), pp. 123 – 48.
25. *P*, p. 37.
26. *P*, p. 38.
27. *P*, p. 38.
28. *P*, pp. 99 f.
29. Newcome, *An Attempt towards an Improved Version. A Metrical Arrangement and an Explanation of the Twelve Minor Prophets* (London, 1785).
30. Blayney, *Jeremiah and Lamentations: A New Translation with notes, critical, philological and explanatory* (Oxford, 1784).
31. *L*, pp. 64 – 7.
32. *P*, pp. 99 f., 125; *L*, pp. 34, 54.
33. *L*, pp. 72 f.
34. *Psalms*, preface, p. 4.
35. *P*, pp. 143 f.
36. *L*, p. 55.
37. *P*, p. 100.
38. R. Lowth, *De Sacra Poesi Hebraeorum* (Oxford, 1753); 2nd edn (Oxford, 1763). The second edition is translated into English by G. Gregory, *Sacred Poetry of the Hebrews*, I – II (London, 1787).
39. Gregory, *Sacred Poetry*, II, p. 4.
40. R. Lowth, *Isaiah: A New Translation with a Preliminary Dissertation and Notes, Critical, Philological, and Explanatory* (London, 1778).
41. Newcome, *Minor Prophets*, p. xiii.
42. Lowth, *Isaiah*, pp. xxxiv – lii.
43. Ibid., p. xxxiv.
44. *L*, p. 41.

45. *L*, p. 42.
46. *L*, p. 43.
47. *L*, p. 45.
48. *L*, p. 77.
49. *P*, p. 145.
50. Cf. Fuller, *Alexander Geddes*, pp. 160–2.
51. *P*, p. 145.
52. *HB* II, p. iv.
53. He quotes Erasmus in a note: *Doctrinam meam non contendam, ut approbem omnibus: aequis ac bonis confido me approbaturum.*
54. *HB* II, p. iv.
55. *DNB*, XXI, p. 100.
56. Cf. Duffy, 'Ecclesiastical Democracy Detected', pp. 205 f., 307.
57. I.e., attached to *HB* I.
58. I.e., his critical remarks on the Hebrew text of the Pentateuch (*CR*).
59. *CR*, p. iv.
60. *CR*, p. v.
61. *CR*, p. v.
62. *CR*, p. vi.
63. *CR*, p. vi.
64. Cf. Lowth, *Isaiah*, p. liii.
65. Ibid., pp. lxxiii f.
66. See W. McKane, 'Benjamin Kennicott. An Eighteenth Century Researcher', *JTS* NS 28 (1977), pp. 445–64.
67. Lowth, *Isaiah*, pp. lxx–lxxiii.
68. *P*, p. 9.
69. *P*, p. 20.
70. B. Kennicott, *The Ten Annual Accounts of the Collation of Hebrew MSS of the Old Testament.* Begun in 1760 and compleated in 1769 (Oxford, 1770).
71. *P*, pp. 120 f.
72. Kennicott, *The Ten Annual Accounts*, pp. 65 f.
73. J. B. De Rossi, *Variae Lectiones Veteris Testamenti*, I–IV (Parma, 1784–8).
74. C. F. Houbigant, *Biblia Hebraica cum Notis Criticis et Versione Latina* (Paris, 1747–53).
75. *P*, p. 81.
76. *P*, p. 2.
77. *P*, pp. 6, 63.
78. S. Talmon, 'The Old Testament Text', *CHB* I (Cambridge, 1970), p. 171.
79. Kennicott, *The Ten Annual Accounts*, p. 176. The disappointing outcome of the collations of Kennicott and De Rossi is summed up by Samuel Davidson, *Lectures in Biblical Criticism* (Edinburgh, 1839), p. 226; cf. p. 224.
80. *P*, p. 6.
81. *P*, p. 15.
82. *P*, p. 123.
83. *P*, p. 16.
84. B. Kennicott, *The State of the Printed Hebrew Text of the Old Testament Considered: A Dissertation in Two Parts* (Oxford, 1753), pp. 19–259.
85. *P*, p. 21.
86. Lowth, *Isaiah*, pp. lxiii–lxix.
87. Newcome, *Minor Prophets*, p. ix.

88. *P*, p. 30.
89. *P*, p. 32.
90. *P*, pp. 32 f.
91. *P*, p. 34.
92. *P*, p. 38. Grabe's edition is *Vetus Testamentum juxta Septuaginta interpretum. Ex MS Alexandrino descriptum*, I – IV (Oxford, 1707 – 20). See above, p. 155.
93. *P*, pp. 54 f.
94. *P*, p. 55.
95. *HB* I, p. xx.
96. *P*, p. 48.
97. *P*, p. 52.
98. *P*, p. 19; *HB* I, p. xx.
99. See above, pp. 121 – 3.
100. *P*, p. 6.
101. *The New English Bible: The Old Testament* (Oxford and Cambridge, 1970), p. xi; cf. Kennicott's first *Dissertation*, p. 337.
102. *CHB* I, pp. 172 f.
103. *P*, p. 63.
104. *P*, p. 63: *nasum cereum, corpus expers animae* is a quotation from the preface of P. Guarin, *Grammatica Hebraica et Chaldaica*, 2 vols. (Paris, 1724 – 6).
105. *P*, p. 4.
106. *P*, p. 5.
107. *P*, p. 14.
108. *P*, p. 25.
109. *P*, pp. 31 f. See above, pp. 26 f.
110. *P*, p. 27. Cf. Jerome, above, p. 36.
111. *P*, p. 42.
112. *P*, p. 42.
113. Lowth, *Isaiah*, p. lv.
114. Ibid., p. lviii.
115. Ibid., p. liv.
116. *P*, p. 15.
117. This is presumably a reference to Qere – Ketib.
118. *P*, p. 70.
119. *P*, p. 71.
120. J. C. L. Gibson, *Textbook of Syrian Semitic Inscriptions*, I: *Hebrew and Moabite Inscriptions* (Oxford, 1971), p. 22: lines 1, 4 החצבים; l. 2 אש אל רעו; l. 2 אש; l. 3 בצר ובים, l. 4 אש; קל אש.
121. Ibid.: l. 1 בעוד; l. 2 ובעוד; l. 5 מוצא.
122. *P*, pp. 61 f.
123. Cf. Lowth, *Isaiah*, p. liv.
124. *P*, p. 62.
125. *P*, p. 62.
126. *P*, p. 62.
127. *P*, p. 72.
128. *P*, p. 139.
129. Cf. J. Barr, *The Semantics of Biblical Language* (Oxford, 1961), pp. 107 – 60.
130. *L*, pp. 5 – 14.
131. *P*, p. 94.

132. *L*, pp. 9 f.
133. *L*, p. 9.
134. *L*, p. 12.
135. *L*, p. 7.
136. BDB, pp. 479 f.
137. *P*, p. 101.
138. Sebastian Castellio (*CHB* III, pp. 71 f.).
139. *P*, p. 76.
140. *P*, pp. 76 f.; cf. Simon, *HCVT*, pp. 185, 361 f.
141. *P*, p. 77.
142. Cf. *CHB* III, p. 98.
143. *P*, p. 83.
144. *P*, p. 129.
145. *P*, p. 129.
146. *P*, pp. 80 f.
147. *P*, pp. 83 f.
148. *P*, p. 84.
149. *P*, pp. 137 – 40.
150. *P*, p. 141.
151. *L*, pp. 30 – 3, 46 – 50.
152. *P*, pp. 141 f.; cf. Newcome, *Minor Prophets*, p. xxxvii.
153. *P*, p. 142.
154. *P*, p. 89.
155. *P*, p. 89.
156. *P*, p. 89.
157. See above, pp. 101 f.
158. *P*, p. 89.
159. *P*, p. 90.
160. *P*, p. 91.
161. *P*, p. 91.
162. *L*, p. 2.
163. Bishop Challoner's revision (1750).
164. *P*, p. 110.
165. Lowth, *Isaiah*, p. lxxiii.
166. *L*, pp. 78 f.
167. *P*, p. 126.
168. *P*, p. 127.
169. *L*, pp. 76 f.
170. *DNB* LI (London, 1897), pp. 212 – 24.
171. *P*, p. 93.
172. *P*, pp. 127 f.
173. *P*, p. 134.
174. A. Purver, *A New and Literal Translation of all the Books of the Old and New Testament, with notes, critical and explanatory* (London, 1764).
175. *L*, p. 36.
176. *L*, pp. 37 f.
177. *L*, p. 38.
178. *P*, p. 95.
179. *P*, p. 95.

180. *L*, p. 33.
181. Newcome, *Minor Prophets*, p. xl.
182. *L*, p. 34.
183. *P*, pp. 128f.
184. *P*, p. 131.
185. *P*, p. 134.
186. *P*, pp. 135f.
187. *L*, p. 59.
188. *P*, p. 134.
189. *L*, p. 2.
190. *L*, p. 2. ·
191. *L*, p. 2.
192. *L*, p. 57.
193. *L*, p. 78.
194. *L*, pp. 78f.
195. *L*, p. 78.
196. *L*, p. 79.
197. *L*, p. 79.
198. *L*, p. 80.
199. Cf. *CHB* III, p. 161. S. L. Greenslade says of editions of the Bishops' Bible subsequent to 1572: 'Then, as now, the Prayer-Book Psalter, Coverdale's version, was too deeply loved to be abandoned, and in subsequent editions (except 1585) this alone was printed'. Cf. *CHB* III, p. 164. John Reynold's reason for specifying older corrupt versions in proposing a new translation (KJV) was 'their use in the Book of Common Prayer'.
200. *P*, pp. 101f.; cf. p. 87.
201. *P*, p. 103.
202. *P*, p. 105.
203. Lowth, *Isaiah*, p. lvi.
204. *P*, p. 106.
205. *P*, pp. 106f.
206. *P*, p. 106.
207. *P*, p. 107.
208. *P*, p. 104.
209. *P*, p. 105, quoted above, p. 182.
210. Cf. *L*, p. 76, 'In fact the lapse of thirteen centuries has given no more real value to the Vulgate, than it had when it first appeared.'
211. Matthew Poole, *Synopsis criticorum aliorumque Sacrae Scripturae interpretum*, I – IV (London, 1669 – 76).
212. *P*, p. 118.
213. *P*, p. 117.
214. *P*, p. 117.
215. *P*, p. 124.
216. *P*, pp. 124f.
217. *Psalms*, preface, p. 12.
218. *CR*, p. 13.
219. *HB* I, p. 3.
220. *Hom. viii in Gen.*, *PG* 53 (Paris, 1862), 71.
221. *CR*, p. 21.

222. *CR*, pp. 21 f.
223. *HB* I, p. 93.
224. *CR*, p. 148.
225. *HB* I, p. 93.
226. *Psalms*, p. 3.
227. *Psalms*, p. 210.
228. *Psalms*, p. 211.
229. *HB* I, p. xviii.
230. *HB* I, p. xviii.
231. *HB* I, p. xix.
232. *HB* I, p. xix.
233. J. D'Astruc, *Conjectures sur les Mémoires Originaux dont il paroit que Moise s'est servi pour composer la Genèse* (Brussels, 1753); J. G. Eichhorn, *Einleitung ins Alte Testament*, II (Leipzig, 1787).
234. *HB* I, p. xix.
235. *HB* I, pp. ii, xii; II, p. xiv.
236. *HB* I, p. xi.
237. *HB* I, p. xi.
238. *HB* I, p. xii.
239. *HB* II, p. xii.
240. *HB* II, p. xiii.
241. *HB* I, p. xii.
242. *HB* II, p. xii.
243. *HB* II, pp. iv, xii.
244. *HB* I, pp. xiv f.
245. *CR*, p. vi.
246. *CR*, p. 475.
247. *CHB* III, p. 251.
248. *CR*, p. vi.

Conclusion

1. Cf. W. Robertson Smith, *The Old Testament in the Jewish Church*, 2nd edn (London, 1895). The statement that 'the whole business of scholarly exegesis lies with this human side' (p. 13) should be compared with: 'It is only the Spirit of God that can make the Word a living Word in our hearts, as it was a living word to him who first received it. This is the truth which the Westminster Confession expresses when it teaches, in harmony with all the Reformed Symbols, that our full persuasion and assurance of the infallible truth and divine authority of Scripture is from the inward work of the Holy Spirit, bearing witness by and with the word in our hearts' (pp. 13 f.).

Appendix 1. *The Milan palimpsest*

1. J. Card. Mercati (ed.), *Psalterii Hexapli Reliquiae* (Rome, 1958).
2. P. E. Kahle, 'The Greek Bible Manuscripts used by Origen', *JBL* LXXIX (1960), p. 116.
3. H. B. Swete (ed.), *The Old Testament in Greek according to the Septuagint*, 3rd edn, II (Cambridge, 1907).

4. A. Rahlfs (ed.), *Psalmi cum Odis*. Septuaginta Societatis Scientiarum Gottingensis Auctoritate, X (Göttingen, 1931).
5. *Psalterii*, p. 33.
6. Ibid., p. 35.
7. Ibid., p. 57.
8. Ibid., p. 5.
9. Ibid., p. 35.
10. Ibid., p. 35.
11. Ibid., p. 79.
12. Ibid., p. 89.
13. Ibid., p. 5.
14. Ibid., p. 25.
15. Ibid., p. 31.
16. Ibid., p. 35.
17. Ibid., p. 55; cf. Rahlfs, *Psalmi cum Odis*, p. 133.
18. Mercati, *Psalterii*, p. 89.
19. Ibid., p. 45.
20. Ibid., p. 57.
21. Cf. Soisalon-Soininen, *Charakter der asterisierten Zusätze*, p. 14.

Appendix 2. The Septuagint text used by Origen

1. J. Ziegler (ed.), *Ieremias, Baruch, Threni, Epistulae Ieremiae*. Septuaginta Vetus Testamentum Graecum Auctoritate Societatis Litterarum Gottingensis editum, XV (Göttingen, 1957).
2. H. B. Swete (ed.), *The Old Testament in Greek according to the Septuagint*, 4th edn, III (Cambridge, 1912).
3. Jer. iv 8 (Nautin, *Origène*, I, pp. 326f.): v 19 (Nautin, I, pp. 346f.); xiii 12 (Nautin, II, pp. 10f.); xvi 17 (Nautin, II, pp. 142f.); xvii 1 (Nautin, II, pp. 154–9); xvii 12 (Nautin, II, pp. 166f.); xviii 4 (Nautin, II, pp. 184f.); xviii 8 (Nautin, II, pp. 188f.); xviii 11 (Nautin, II, pp. 204f.); xx 3 (Nautin, II, 218f.; cf. II, pp. 230f.).
4. F. Field (ed.), *Origenis Hexaplorum quae supersunt*, II (Oxford, 1875).
5. Ziegler, *Ieremias*.
6. Jer. xi 4 (Nautin, I, pp. 384f.).
7. Field, *Origenis Hexaplorum*, pp. 600, 613; cf. Ziegler, *Ieremias*, p. 226.
8. Jer. iii 9 (Nautin, I, pp. 258f.); xi 21 (Nautin, I, pp. 402f.); xi 22 (Nautin, I, pp. 402f.); xii 3 (Nautin, I, pp. 408f.); xiii 4 (Nautin, I, pp. 424f.); xiii 17 (Nautin, II, pp. 30f.); xvii 16 (Nautin, II, pp. 170f.); xx 3 (Nautin, II, pp. 218f.); xx 5 (Nautin, II, pp. 220f.); xx 6 (Nautin, II, pp. 220f.); xxii 28 (Nautin, II, pp. 322f.).
9. Field, *Origenis Hexaplorum*, II, pp. 579, 603, 606, 607, 617, 618, 623, 624, 630.
10. Ziegler, *Ieremias*, pp. 162, 208, 209f., 213, 216, 234, 236, 249, 249f., 261f.
11. Jer. xv 10 (Nautin, II, pp. 68f.; cf. I, p. 117); xv 16 (Nautin, II, pp. 94–7); xx 2 (Nautin, II, pp. 218f.).
12. Nautin, *Origène*, I, p. 384.
13. Ibid., II, p. 94.
14. Ibid., I, p. 326.
15. Ibid., I, p. 116; cf. II, p. 218.
16. Ibid., II, pp. 94, 96.

17. Ibid., I, p. 408.
18. Field, *Origenis Hexaplorum*, II, p. 603; Ziegler, *Ieremias*, pp. 209f.
19. Nautin, *Origène*, II, p. 142.
20. Ibid., p. 142 (Hom. xvi. 4. 44).
21. Ibid., p. 142 (Hom. xvi. 5. 6f.).

Appendix 3. Jerome's use of the Septuagint

1. Reiter, *Sancti Eusebii*, p. 318.
2. Ibid., p. 165;
3. Ibid., p. 239f.
4. Ibid., p. 293.
5. Ibid., p. 296.
6. Ibid., p. 297.
7. Ibid., p. 308.
8. W. McKane, 'Jeremiah 13:12–14. A Problematic Proverb'; *Israelite Wisdom: Theological and Literary Essays in Honor of Samuel Terrien* (Missoula, 1978), pp. 107–120.
9. Reiter, *Sancti Eusebii*, pp. 162f.

Appendix 4. Andrew of St Victor on Isaiah i 31

1. Hadfield, *Andrew of St Victor*, p. 137; MS Pembroke 45, fo. 6[c–d].
2. *PL* 24, 42.
3. Id est, fortitudinis vestrae sive idololatriae, in qua erraveratis, parvula scintilla consumet.
4. Commenting on *Et succedetur utrumque simul: et non erit qui exstinguat* he remarks: quod et magistri et discipuli pariter pareant, et omne opus eorum ignis pabulum sit.

Appendix 5. William Fulke on Isaiah xxviii 11 and 1 Corinthians xiv 21

1. *A Defence*, p. 54: Jerome, *Comm. in Esa.* at xxviii 11 (*PL* 24, 331). Jerome is citing 1 Cor. xiv 21: Legimus in Apostolo: *In aliis linguis, et labiis aliis loquar populo huic, et nec sic exaudient me, dicit Dominus*.
2. It might be supposed that λέγει Κύριος derives from a corruption of אמר אליהם (אָמַר אֱלֹהִים) at the beginning of Isa. xxviii 12, but Κύριος is an improbable rendering of the postulated אֱלֹהִים.
3. *Comm. in Esa.* at xxviii 11, *PL* 24, 331.
4. J. A. Robinson, *The Philocalia of Origen: the text revised with a critical introduction and indices* (Cambridge, 1893), p. 55.

SELECT BIBLIOGRAPHY

1 The foundations

Anderson G. W., 'Canonical and Non-Canonical', *CHB* I (Cambridge, 1970), pp. 113–59.

Barr J., 'St Jerome's Appreciation of Hebrew', *Bulletin of the John Rylands Library (BJRL)*, XLIX (1967), pp. 281–302.

Barrett C. K., 'The Interpretation of the Old Testament in the New', *CHB* I (Cambridge, 1970), pp. 377–411.

Barthélemy D., *Les Devanciers d'Aquila, SVT* X (Leiden, 1963).

Black M., *An Aramaic Approach to the Gospels and Acts*, 3rd edn (Oxford, 1967).

Burkitt F. C., *Early Christianity outside the Roman Empire* (Cambridge, 1899).

The Gospel History and its Transmission (Edinburgh, 1906).

Charles R. H., *The Apocrypha and Pseudepigrapha of the Old Testament*, I (Oxford, 1913).

Cohn L., *Philonis Alexandrini Opera Quae Supersunt*, IV (Berlin, 1902).

Daniélou J., *Origène* (Paris, 1948). English translation by Mitchell W., *Origen* (London and New York, 1955), pp. 3–22, 131–99.

Dodd C. H., *The Bible and the Greeks* (London, 1935, 1954).

According to the Scriptures (London, 1952).

Emerton J. A., 'The Purpose of the Second Column of the Hexapla', *JTS* N.S., VII (1956), pp. 83–6.

'Did Jesus speak Hebrew?', *JTS* N.S., XII (1961), pp. 189–202.

'Were Greek Transcriptions of the Hebrew Old Testament used by Jews before the Time of Origen?', *JTS* N.S. 21 (1970), pp. 17–31.

de Faye E., *Origène, sa vie, son oeuvre, sa pensée*, I (Paris, 1923), pp. 1–50, 66–95, 104–37.

Field F., *Origenis Hexaplorum quae supersunt*, I–II (Oxford, 1875).

Hanson A. T., *The Living Utterances of God. The New Testament Exegesis of the Old* (London, 1983).

Hanson R. P. C., *Allegory and Event* (London, 1959), pp. 133–231, 359–74.

Harris J. Rendell, *Testimonies*, I–II (Cambridge, 1916, 1920).

Hengel M., *Between Jesus and Paul* (London, 1983).

Jellicoe S., *The Septuagint and Modern Study* (Oxford, 1968).

Kahle P. E., 'Problems of the Septuagint', *Studia Patristica* I, part 1, Aland K. and Cross F. L. (ed.). *Texte und Untersuchungen* V.viii (1957), pp. 328–38.

'The Greek Bible Manuscripts used by Origen', *JBL* lxxix (1960), pp. 111–18.

Kelly J. N. D., *Jerome. His Life, Writings and Controversies* (London, 1975), especially pp. 141–67.

Labourt J., *Saint Jérôme Lettres*. Collection des Universités de France, I–VIII (1949–63). Latin text with a French translation.

De Langhe N. R. M., *Origen and the Jews. Studies in Jewish – Christian Relations in Third Century Palestine* (Cambridge, 1976).

Lardet P., *Saint Jérôme Apologie contra Rufin*. Sources Chrétiennes 303 (Paris, 1983). Latin text with a French translation.

Lindars B., *New Testament Apologetic. The Doctrinal Significance of the Old Testament Quotations* (London, 1961).

Mercati J. Card. (ed.), *Psalterii Hexapli Reliquiae* (Rome, 1958, 1965).

Metzger B. M., *A Textual Commentary on the Greek New Testament* (London and New York, 1971).

Moule C. F. C., *The Birth of the New Testament*, 2nd edn (London, 1966).
'Once more, who were the Hellenists?', *Expository Times* 70 (1959), pp. 100 – 2.

Nautin P., *Origène Homélies sur Jérémie*, I – II, Sources Chrétiennes 232 (Paris, 1976 – 77), Greek text with a French translation.

Oulton J. E. L., *Eusebius The Ecclesiastical History* I – II. Loeb Classical Library (London and New York, 1932). Greek text with an English translation.

Reiter S., *Sancti Eusebii Hieronymi in Hieremiam Prophetam*, Corpus Scriptorum Ecclesiasticorum Latinorum, LIX (Vienna and Leipzig, 1913).

Semple, W. H., 'Some Letters of St Augustine', *Bulletin of the John Rylands Library (BJRL)*, XXXIII (1951), pp. 111 – 30.
'St Jerome as a Biblical Translator', *BJRL* XLVIII (1966), pp. 227 – 43.

Sevenster J. N., *Do you know Greek? How much Greek could the first Jewish Christians have known?* Supplements to Novum Testamentum, 19 (Leiden, 1968).

Soisalon-Soininen I., *Der Charakter der asterisierten Zusätze in der Septuaginta*. Annales Academiae Scientiarum Fennicae, Ser. B, 114 (Helsinki, 1959).

Sparks H. F. D., 'Jerome as a Biblical Scholar', *CHB* I (Cambridge, 1970), pp. 510 – 41.

Stendahl K., *The School of St Matthew and its Use in the New Testament*. Acta Seminarii Neotestamentici Upsaliensis, 20 (Uppsala, 1954).

Sundberg A. C., *The Old Testament of the Early Church*. Harvard Theological Studies, 20 (Cambridge, Mass. and London, 1964).

Sutcliffe E. F., 'Jerome', *CHB* II (Cambridge, 1969), pp. 80 – 101.

Swete H. B. (revised by Ottley R. R.), *An Introduction to the Old Testament in Greek*, 2nd edn (Cambridge, 1914), containing the Greek text of the Letter of Aristeas.

Thackeray H. St J., *The Letter of Aristeas* (London, 1917).

Tov E., *The Text-Critical Use of the Septuagint in Biblical Research*. Jerusalem Biblical Studies (Jerusalem, 1981).

Wiles M. F., 'Origen as Biblical Scholar', *CHB* I (Cambridge, 1970), pp. 454 – 89.

Wright F. A., *Select Letters of Jerome*. Loeb Classical Library (London and New York, 1933). Latin text with an English translation.

Würthwein E., *Der Text des Alten Testaments*, 4th edn (Stuttgart, 1973). English translation by Rhodes E. F., *The Text of the Old Testament: an Introduction to Biblia Hebraica* (London, 1980).

2 *Andrew of St Victor*

For access to the manuscripts which contain Andrew's Old Testament commentaries I am principally dependent on Beryl Smalley and G. A. C. Hadfield.

Bacon R., Compendium Studii Philosophae, ed. Brewer J. S., Rerum Britannicorum Medii Aevi Scriptores 15 (Rolls Series, London, 1859).

Brown F., Driver S. R., Briggs C. A., *A Hebrew and English Lexicon of the Old Testament* (Oxford, 1907; reprinted with corrections, 1966); abbreviated as *BDB*.

Calandra G., *De historica Andreae victorini expositione in Ecclesiasten* (Palermo, 1948).

Chazan R., *Medieval Jewry in Northern France* (Baltimore, 1973).

Dugdale W. (ed.), *Monasticum Anglicanum* VI (London, 1846).

Friedländer M., *The Commentary of Ibn Ezra on Isaiah* (London), I (1873, English translation) and II (1877, Hebrew text); I – II in one volume (New York, 1972).

Hadfield G. A. C., *Andrew of St Victor, a twelfth century Hebraist: an investigation of his works and sources* (unpublished D.Phil. Thesis, Oxford, Bodleian Library, 1971).

Jacobs L., *Jewish Biblical Exegesis* (New York, 1973).

Koehler L. and Baumgartner W., *Hebräisches und Aramäisches Lexikon zum Alten Testament* (Leiden, 3rd edn, 1967, 1974, 1983); abbreviated as KB[3].

Loewe R., 'The Mediaeval Christian Hebraists of England', *Transactions of the Jewish Historical Society of England*, XVII (1951 – 2), pp. 245 – 9.

'Herbert of Bosham's Commentary on Jerome's Hebrew Psalter. A Preliminary Investigation into its Sources', *Biblica* XXXIV (1953), pp. 44 – 7, 159 – 92, 275 – 98.

Migne J. P. (ed.), *Patrologiae Latinae* (Paris); abbreviated as *PL*.

Rashi (Rabbi Shelomo ben Yiṣḥaq) is cited from *Miqrā'ôth Gᵉdôlôth*.

Rosenthal E. I. J., 'Medieval Jewish Exegesis: its character and significance', *Journal of Semitic Studies*, IX (1964), pp. 265 – 81.

'The Study of the Bible in Medieval Judaism', *CHB* II (1969), pp. 252 – 79.

Smalley B., 'Andrew of St Victor, Abbot of Wigmore: a Twelfth-Century Hebraist', *Recherches de Théologie Ancienne et Mediévale*, X (1938), pp. 358 – 73.

'The School of Andrew of St Victor', *Recherches de Théologie Ancienne et Mediévale*, XI (1939), pp. 145 – 67.

'A Commentary on the *Hebraica* by Herbert of Bosham', *Recherches de Théologie Ancienne et Mediévale*, XVIII (1951), pp. 29 – 65.

The Study of the Bible in the Middle Ages (Oxford, 1953); 3rd edn (Oxford, 1983).

'The Bible in the Medieval Schools', *CHB* II (1969), pp. 197 – 220.

3 *William Fulke and Gregory Martin*

(a) *Works by William Fulke which are cited*

Antiprognosticon (London, 1560), translated into English by W. Painter, *Antiprognosticon, that is to saye, an Invective agaynst the vaine and unprofitable predictions of the astrologians, as Nostrodame etc.* (London, 1561).

A goodly gallerye with a most pleasaunt prospect into the garden of naturall contemplation to beholde the naturall causes of all kinds of meteors (London, 1563). See T. Hornberger (ed.), *A Goodly Gallerye, William Fulke's Book of Meteors.* Memoirs of the American Philosophical Society, 130 (Philadelphia, 1979).

A Defense of the sincere and true Translations of the holie Scriptures into the English tong, against the manifolde cavils, frivolous quarels, and impudent slaunders of Gregorie Martin, one of the readers of Popish divinitie in the trayterous Seminarie of Rhemes (London, 1583). The quotations are from the Parker Society edition (Cambridge, 1843), abbreviated as *A Defence*.

The text of the New Testament of Jesus Christ translated out of the Vulgar Latine by the Papists of the traiterous Seminarie at Rhemes (London, 1589).

A complete list of Fulke's works is given in the Parker Society edition of *A Defence* (pp. v – xi).

(b) Works by Gregory Martin which are cited

A Discoverie of the Manifold Corruptions of the Holy Scriptures by the Heretikes of our daies, specially the English Sectaries, and of their foule dealing herein, by partial and false translations to the advantage of their heresies, in their English Bibles used and authorised since the time of Schisme (Rhemes, 1582), abbreviated as *A Discoverie*.

A Treatyse of Christian Peregrinatione; written by M. Gregory Martin, Licentiate, and late Reader of Divinitie, at Remes. Whereunto is adioyned certen Epistles written by him to Sundrye his frendes; the copies whereof were since his decease founde amonge his writings. Nowe especially published for the benefite of those that either erre in religione of simplicitie, or folow the worlde of frailty (London, 1583).

Dictionarium quatuor linguarum, Hebraicae, Graecae, Latinae et Anglicae, et vocabulorum ac phrasium secundum cujusque linguae proprietatem (see Chapter 3, n. 5).

(c) Other sixteenth- and seventeenth-century works relating to Fulke and Martin

The New Testament of Iesus Christ, translated faithfully into English, out of the authentical Latin (Rhemes, 1582).

The Holie Bible faithfully translated into English, out of the authentical Latin (Doway, 1609–10).

Cartwright T., *A Confutation of the Rhemists translation, glosses, and annotations of the New Testament, so farre as they containe manifest impieties, heresies etc.* (Leyden, 1618).

Wither G., *A view of the marginal notes of the Popish Testament, translated into English by the English fugitive Papists resiant at Rhemes in France* (London, 1588).

(d) Other works relating to Fulke and Martin

Athenae Oxonienses, ed. A. Wood; a new edition with additions by Philip Bliss (London, 1813).

Athenae Cantabrigienses, ed. C. H. and T. Cooper, vol. II (Cambridge, 1861).

Bruce F. F., *The English Bible. A History of Translations* (London, 1961).

Carleton J. G., *The Part of Rheims in the Making of the English Bible* (Oxford, 1902).

Dictionary of National Biography, vol. IX (London, 1887); vol. XX (London, 1889); vol. XXXVI (London, 1893); vol. XLII (London, 1885).

Hammond G., *The Making of the English Bible* (Manchester, 1982).

Jones G. Lloyd, *The Discovery of Hebrew in Tudor England: A Third Language* (Manchester, 1983).

Knox T. F., *The First and Second Diaries of the English College Douay and an Appendix of Unpublished Documents* (London, 1878).

Mozley J. F., *Coverdale and His Bibles* (London, 1953).

Pollard A. W. (ed.), *Records of the English Bible. The Documents Relating to the Translation and Publication of the Bible in English 1525–1611* (Oxford, 1911).

Register of the University of Oxford, ed. C. W. Boase, vol. I (1449–63; 1505–71). Printed for the Oxford Historical Society at the Clarendon Press (Oxford, 1885).

Westcott B. F., *A General View of the History of the English Bible*, 3rd edn, revised by W. A. Wright (London, 1905).

4 Richard Simon

(a) Works by Richard Simon which are cited

Critrical Enquiries into Various Editions of the Bible (London, 1684). Abbreviated as *CE*.

Histoire Critique du Vieux Testament (Rotterdam, 1685). Abbreviated as *HCVT*.

Le Nouveau Testament de nôtre Seigneur Jésus-Christ traduit sur l'ancienne édition latine, avec des remarques litérales et critiques sur les principales difficultez, I (Trévoux, 1702).

(b) Seventeenth-century books mentioned by Simon which are cited
Cappell L., *Arcanum punctationis revelatum* (Leiden, 1624).
Mariana J., *Tractatus VII*, containing *Pro Editione Vulgata* (Cologne, 1609).
Exercitationes ecclesiasticae in utrumque Samaritanorum Pentateuchum (Paris, 1631).
Morin J., *Exercitationes Biblicae*, pars prior (Paris, 1633).
De Vio (Cajetan) T. (Cardinal), *Opera omnia quotquot in Sacrae Scripturae expositionem reperiuntur* (Lyon, 1639).
Walton B., *Biblia Sacra Polyglotta*, I (London, 1657).

(c) Other works on Simon
Auvray P., *Richard Simon 1638–1712. Étude bio-bibliographique avec des textes inédits* (Paris, 1974). This contains Simon's *Notice autobiographique*, first published in 1863.
Batterel L., *Mémoires domestiques pour servir à l'histoire de la congregation de l'Oratoire*, I – V (1902 – 11). The *mémoire* on Simon is in IV, pp. 233 – 95.
Bernus A., *Richard Simon et Son Histoire Critique du Vieux Testament. La Critique Biblique au Siècle de Louis XIV* (Lausanne, 1869).
Bruzen de la Martinière A., *Éloge historique de Richard Simon, prêtre*, in *Lettres choisies de M. Simon*, I (Amsterdam, 1730).
Fahey M. A., 'Richard Simon, Biblical Exegete', *Irish Ecclesiastical Review* 49 (1963), pp. 236 – 47.
Graf K. H., 'Richard Simon', *Beiträge zu den theologischen Wissenschaften von den Mitgliedern der theologischen Gesellschaft zu Strassburg* (Jena, 1847), pp. 158 – 242.
Monod A., *La Controverse de Bossuet et de Richard Simon au sujet de la Version de Trévoux*, *Cahiers de la revue d'histoire et de philosophie religieuse* (Strasbourg, 1922).
Steinmann J., *Richard Simon et les Origines de l'Exégèse Biblique* (Paris, 1960).
Stummer Fr., *Die Bedeutung Richard Simons für die Pentateuchkritik*, Alttestamentliche Abhandlungen III, 4 (Münster, 1912).
Yardini M., 'La Vision des Juifs et du judaïsme dans l'oeuvre de Richard Simon', *Revue des Etudes juives*, CXXIX (1970), pp. 179 – 203.

5 *Alexander Geddes*

(a) Abbreviations of works by Alexander Geddes which are cited
P *Prospectus of a New Translation of the Holy Bible from corrected Texts of the Originals, compared with the Ancient Versions, with Various Readings, Explanatory Notes and Critical Observations* (London, 1786).
L *A Letter to the Right Reverend the Lord Bishop of London, containing Queries, Doubts and Difficulties, relative to a Vernacular Version of the Holy Scriptures* (London, 1787).
HB I and II *The Holy Bible; or the Books accounted sacred by Jews and Christians; otherwise called the Books of the Old and New Covenants: faithfully translated from corrected texts of the originals, with various readings, explanatory notes and critical remarks*, I (London, 1792); II (London, 1797).
CR *Critical Remarks on the Hebrew Scriptures corresponding with A New Translation of the Bible. Volume I containing Remarks on the Pentateuch* (London, 1800).

(b) Other works by Geddes which are cited
Idea of a New English Edition of the Holy Bible for the Use of the Roman Catholics of Great Britain and Ireland (London, 1782).

A Letter to the Rev Dr Priestley in which the Author attempts to prove by one prescriptive argument that the divinity of Jesus Christ was a primitive tenet of Christianity (London, 1787).

Dr Geddes's General Answer to the Queries, Counsils and Criticisms that have been communicated to him since the publication of his Proposals for printing a New Translation of the Bible (London, 1790).

A New Translation of the Book of Psalms from the Original Hebrew, with various readings and notes (London, 1807). Psalms I–cxviii 11 and cl are the work of Geddes.

A complete bibliography will be found in R. C. Fuller, *Alexander Geddes, 1737–1802: Pioneer of Biblical Criticism* (Sheffield, 1984), pp. 156–9.

(c) Eighteenth and nineteenth-century works relevant to Geddes which are cited

Blayney B., *Jeremiah and Lamentations: A New Translation with notes, critical, philological and explanatory* (Oxford, 1784).

Davidson S., *Lectures in Biblical Criticism* (Edinburgh, 1839).

The Hebrew Text of the Old Testament revised from critical sources: being an attempt to present a purer and more correct text than the received one of Van der Hooght (London, 1856).

Kennicott B., *The State of the Printed Hebrew Text of the Old Testament Considered: A Dissertation in Two Parts* (Oxford, 1753).

Dissertation The Second (Oxford, 1759).

The Ten Annual Accounts of the Collation of Hebrew MSS of the Old Testament. Begun in 1760 and compleated in 1769 (Oxford, 1770).

Vetus Testamentum Hebraicum cum Variis Lectionibus, I–II (Oxford, 1776 and 1780).

Lowth R., *De Sacra Poesi Hebraeorum* (Oxford, 1753); 2nd edn (Oxford, 1763). Translated into English by G. Gregory, *Sacred Poetry of the Hebrews*, I–II (London, 1787).

Isaiah: A New Translation with a Preliminary Dissertation and Notes, Critical, Philological, and Explanatory (London, 1778).

Newcome W., *An Attempt towards an Improved Version. A Metrical Arrangement and an Explanation of the Twelve Minor Prophets* (London, 1785).

De Rossi J. B., *Variae Lectiones Veteris Testamenti*, I–IV (Parma, 1784–8).

(d) Other works on or related to Geddes

Bullough S., 'Dr. Alexander Geddes, 1737–1802', *Scripture* XVII/37 (1965), pp. 14–22.

Chadwick H., *Lessing's Theological Writings*. A Library of Modern Religious Thought (London, 1956), pp. 9–49.

Cheyne T. K., *Founders of Old Testament Criticism. Biographical, Descriptive and Critical Studies* (London, 1893), pp. 1–12.

Duffy, E., 'Ecclesiastical Democracy Detected', *Recusant History* 10 (1969–70), pp. 193–209, 309–31; 13 (1975–6), pp. 123–48.

Fuller R. C., *Alexander Geddes 1737–1802: Pioneer of Biblical Criticism*. Historic Texts and Interpreters in Biblical Scholarship, 3, ed. J. W. Rogerson (Sheffield, 1984).

Good J. M., *Memoirs of the life and writings of the Rev. A. Geddes* (London, 1803).

McKane W. 'Benjamin Kennicott: An Eighteenth Century Researcher', *JTS* N.S. 28 (1977), pp. 445–64.

Pope H., 'Alexander Geddes: Unhappy Biblical Scholar', *Irish Ecclesiastical Record*, 56 (1940), pp. 321–42.

Rogerson John, *Old Testament Criticism in the Nineteenth Century: England and Germany* (London, 1984), pp. 154–7.

Symington J. L., 'Alexander Geddes: An Early Scots Higher Critic', *Records of the Scottish Church History Society*, 9 (1947), pp. 19–36.

GENERAL INDEX

INDEX OF MODERN AUTHORS

SCRIPTURE REFERENCES

INDEX OF EARLY CHRISTIAN LITERATURE